Special Sermons

SPECIAL SERMONS

GEORGE SWEETING

MOODY PRESS

CHICAGO

The use of selected references from various versions of the Bible in this
publication does not necessarily imply publisher endorsement of the versions in their entirety.

The titles compiled in this volume have been published separately as:
> *Special Sermons for Special Days*
> *Special Sermons on Special Issues*
> *Special Sermons on the Family*
> *Special Sermons on Major Bible Doctrines*
> *Special Sermons for Evangelism*

Library of Congress Cataloging-in-Publication Data
Sweeting, George, 1924-
  Special Sermons.

  A compilation of the author's five previously
published Special sermon volumes.
  1. Sermons, American. I. Title.
BV4253.S833   1985   252   85-21782
ISBN 0-8024-8211-2 (pbk.)

1 2 3 4 5 Printing/LC/Year 89 88 87 86 85

Printed in the United States of America

*Dedicated
to that very select company
of pastors who attend
the flock of God.*

Contents

Book 3 Special Sermons on the Family

Book 4 Special Sermons on Major Bible Doctrines

Book 5 Special Sermons for Evangelism

Book 1

SPECIAL
SERMONS
FOR SPECIAL DAYS

With warm appreciation to Wayne Christianson, Mark Sweeney, and Judy Paney, who have assisted me in research and script writing.

ONE

THE NEW YEAR
AND FEAR

Stepping through the door into a new year should be an exciting experience. Yet for millions of people, the adventure of entering the New Year is overshadowed by fear.

The cold breath of fear knows all ages and every walk of life. Some people are afraid to go to the supermarket or corner store even in broad daylight. Others are afraid they may not find a job. Parents are afraid that the next ring of the phone might bring bad news about their children. Sick people are afraid of what the doctor may say the next time they go to see him. And thousands are afraid of the future. Fear, without a doubt, is one of the great enemies of successful living.

Not long ago, a group of distinguished scholars met in Chicago. They listened as a noted scientist gave a very gloomy picture of the next twenty-five years. He reported that a person born today may well live to be a hundred years old. During that time, he will possibly see the world run out of oil and natural gas. He may also see a massive drought across America, worldwide famine, and a major American city leveled by an earthquake. That's a very dark and gloomy forecast.

Despite the many reports like this, the future does have great possibilities. There are many exciting prospects for the years ahead. Yet fear itself is destructive. Like a drop of ink in a glass of water, a little is enough to color everything.

Fear does not depend on how good or bad conditions are. It depends on our response to them. Fear can tie us in knots. It can paralyze our thinking and our actions. It can make our lives a living hell.

What is fear? The dictionary defines it as a "painful emotion marked by alarm or dread or disquiet." It is response to what we think may be unpleasant.

Fear is as old as sin. It began in the Garden of Eden the day that Adam and Eve disobeyed God. In Genesis 3:8, we find Adam and Eve hiding fearfully from God "amongst the trees of the garden."

Ever since that tragic day, fear has followed every member of the human race. We fear as babies. We have fears in our childhood and great and growing fears in our youth. More fears hound us through adulthood and even in old age.

But then, not all fear is bad. The fear that keeps a small child from stepping into a busy street may save his life. As adults, we need the kind of fear that keeps us from touching a high-voltage wire or driving through a stoplight. Yes, there are some fears that are helpful.

Above all else, we need the fear of God: a reverential respect and awe for the God who made us. Repeatedly the Bible tells us that it is the fear of the Lord which is the beginning of wisdom.

Do you have this kind of fear—a reverential respect and awe for God? Only those who do can expect to know Him and enjoy His blessings.

Three times in Psalm 103—that wonderful poem of thankfulness—David reminds us that God's blessings are only for "them that fear him." This kind of fear is the kind that blesses, that builds, that strengthens.

The kind of fear that burdens is something else. It is an anxious fear, a fear that chills and freezes and kills. God is against this fear. Again and again, when God has spoken to men, His first words have been, "Fear not." Don't be afraid.

The key to overcoming fear is faith: faith in God. He loves us, and He holds the future. If we fear the future, we do not have faith. If we have faith, we cannot live in fear.

The Bible says that anxious fear is sin. In fact, Revelation 21 puts fear first in a list of sins that will keep men out of heaven. Notice how verse 8 begins: "But the fearful, and unbelieving, and the abominable, and murderers, and whoremongers, and sorcerers, and idolaters, and all liars, shall have their part in . . . the second death." You see, God wants us to walk in faith, not fear.

For years, God's servant David was hounded by King Saul. But he found help. "I sought the LORD," he writes in Psalm 34: 4, "and he heard me, and delivered me from all my fears." David looked to the Lord and found relief. In the same psalm, he adds, "The angel of the LORD encampeth round about them that fear him, and delivereth them" (v. 7).

My friend, this is the promise of God in His Word.

Put God first in your life. Respect and reverence Him, and He will deliver you from fear. Consider some of the promises of Scripture:

Psalm 23:4, "Yea, though I walk through the valley of the shadow of death, I will fear no evil."

Psalm 27:1, "The LORD is my light and my salvation: whom shall I fear? the LORD is the strength of my life; of whom shall I be afraid?"

Psalm 32:7, "Thou art my hiding place; thou shalt preserve me from trouble; thou shalt compass me about with songs of deliverance."

Psalm 34:9, "O fear the LORD, ye his saints: for there is no want to them that fear him."

Psalm 56:3, "What time I am afraid, I will trust in thee."

Psalm 91:2, "I will say of the LORD, He is my refuge and my fortress: my God; in him will I trust."

Psalm 112:1, 7, "Blessed is the man that feareth the LORD. . . . He shall not be afraid of evil tidings: his heart is fixed, trusting in the LORD."

As you face the year ahead, what fears threaten your peace of mind? Psychologists tell us there are four basic fears that plague people. But the comforting truth is that God, in His Word, provides the solution to each one of them.

BASIC FEARS

1. THE FEAR OF WANT

You may be haunted by the fear of want. "What if I lose my job?" you say. "What if I take a cut in salary or I'm sick and cannot work? What if my family is sick or if the bills outstrip my income?" Are these legitimate fears? The Bible says they are not. Why? Because God is the great Provider.

In His great Sermon on the Mount in Matthew 6, Jesus puts the issue plainly. "Wherefore, if God so clothe the grass of the field, which to day is, and to morrow is cast into the oven, shall he not much more clothe you, O ye of little faith?" And then He adds, "Therefore take no thought, saying, What shall we eat? or, What shall we drink? or, Wherewithal shall we be clothed? . . . for your heavenly Father knoweth that ye have need of all these things" (vv. 30-32).

Is Jesus Christ sufficient to supply your needs? Is He faithful? Can you count on His love? The issue is fear or faith. Which will it be? In Psalm 37:25, David says, "I have been young, and now am old; yet have I not seen the righteous forsaken, nor his seed begging bread."

2. THE FEAR OF SUFFERING

Are you facing the fear of suffering? This is the pain of body or of spirit. People can hurt us deeply. We fear sickness or sorrow, loneliness or grief. But can God help you here? Yes, He can and He will! God will not shield you from all suffering, for this is part of life. But He will limit and control it. And He will use it for your good.

Not many years ago, a woman was critically injured in a highway accident. She spent pain-filled months recovering. But in those months, her Christian faith grew and deepened more than in all her previous Christian life. Today she looks back on this experience as the most valuable time of her life.

Suffering may be for the glory of God. It may be for the accomplishing of His purposes. It may be used to refine our character. Whatever the reason, we can trust the God who permits it, rest on His gracious provision, and leave the outcome in His hands.

Often suffering provides an opportunity to know the presence and upholding power of Christ in a way we otherwise would never know it. This was the experience of the apostle Paul. In his second epistle to the Corinthian church, he states that three times he asked God to remove his affliction, and God said, No. Paul goes on to say, "And he said unto me, My grace is sufficient for thee: for my strength is made perfect in weakness. Most gladly therefore will I rather glory in my infirmities, that the power of Christ may rest upon me" (12:9).

We need not fear suffering! God is in control of every circumstance. When He permits it, He will use it for His glory and our good. And He will be with us.

3. THE FEAR OF FAILURE

A very common kind of fear is the fear of failure. Many people are afraid of falling short in school, on the job, in social situations, or in various types of competition. We want to do well. We want to rise to the top. We want to achieve.

This, in fact, is the key to our problem. We fear failure because we rely on ourselves and not the Lord. We want our desires and not His.

God is concerned with faithfulness, obedience, and uprightness of character. If we set our sights on doing God's will, He will help us to succeed. The whole roster of the heroes of faith in Hebrews 11 is made up of men and women who made it the business of their lives not only to believe God, but to do His will.

The opening chapter of the book of Joshua gives us three good rules for success: go forward, trust God, be guided by the Word of God. And God promises, "I will not fail thee, nor forsake thee" (v. 5). We need not fear failure when God is with us.

4. THE FEAR OF DEATH

The greatest fear of all is the fear of death. First Corinthians 15:26 tells us that "the last enemy that shall be destroyed is death." The good news of the Gospel is that Christ has won victory over death, and no man or woman who trusts in Jesus Christ needs to be afraid of death. Jesus says, "Because I live, ye shall live also" (John 14:19).

My friend, do you know that Christ came to deliver you and your loved ones from the fear of death? How? By dying in your place, that you and I might never have to know real death.

We celebrate at Christmas because God became man and was born in a lowly stable. But why did Jesus come? In order to become one of us, to deliver us from death.

The writer of Hebrews tells us that Jesus "took part of the same; that through death he might destroy him that had the power of death, that is, the devil; and deliver them who through fear of death were all their lifetime subject to bondage" (2:14-15).

God has delivered from the fear of death those who trust His Son. That's why David could say, in Psalm 34, "I sought the LORD, and he heard me, and delivered me from all my fears" (v. 4).

CONCLUSION

God delivers us, in a fear-filled world, from all our fears, but only as we believe Him. Will it be fear or faith for you, as you face another year? Will you receive His Son as your Saviour and your Lord?

Fear or faith. You have a choice. God invites you to trust Jesus Christ and be free—free from the power of fear.

TWO

HOW TO HAVE
A HAPPY NEW YEAR

Introduction

The apostle Paul was an amazing, God-controlled man! He was perhaps the most dynamic Christian to be found in the entire Bible. But successful people, like champions, are generally made, not born. Paul did not become the man he was by accident. He did not, all of a sudden, become a brilliant spokesman for God. At least three words characterize his life, and these same three words will help you discover "how to have a happy new year," as well as a triumphant life.

The three life-changing words that I want to share are *purpose, attitude,* and *motivation.* They are words that describe the writing of Paul in his epistle to the Philippians (Phil 3:10-14).

1. Purpose

Whether the apostle Paul was mending tents or writing a letter to an infant church or preaching to a crowd in the marketplace, he was driven by one all-consuming, all-controlling, dynamic purpose, and that was "to know God." Paul expressed this purpose in Philippians 3:10, "That I may know him, and the power of his resurrection, and the fellowship of his sufferings, being made conformable unto his death."

In season and out of season, awake or asleep, consciously and subconsciously, Paul relentlessly pursued this dynamic purpose. He possessed a deep desire not merely to know about Jesus Christ but to know Him intimately in all of His glory and humiliation.

Paul's purpose was very much like David of the Old Testament, who prayed, "My soul followeth hard after thee, O God" (Psalm 42:1).

Most of us are familiar with the background of Paul's conversion experience. Acts 7 and 8 relate how Paul, whose pre-Christian name was Saul, persecuted the followers of Jesus. In fact, Paul was responsible for the attack against the church in Jerusalem. In Acts 9, we find him "breathing out threatenings and slaughter" (v. 1) against the disciples of Jesus. In his hands were letters authorizing the arrest of the believers in Damascus. His plan was to bring them bound to Jerusalem.

But as he journeyed to that city, the Lord God of Israel appeared to him. There was a brilliant light and a voice from heaven. Paul knew this was beyond the natural: it was supernatural. In his amazement, he called out, "Who art thou, Lord?" And the Lord said, "I am Jesus whom thou persecutest" (v. 5).

When Paul heard these staggering words, he immediately recognized, for the first time, that Jesus of Nazareth was the Lord God of Israel. Instantly he submitted, calling out, "What wilt thou have me to do?" (v. 6). Paul, the arrester, was arrested by God Almighty. From that very moment on, throughout life, his purpose was "to know God."

Benjamin Disraeli, the former prime minister of Great Britain, said, "The secret of success is *constancy of purpose.*" His emphasis was on the phrase "constancy of purpose." Too often our purpose in life keeps changing from year to year. There is nothing dynamic about it at all. Not so with Paul. His life was a torrent of spiritual desire. His single-mindedness is again expressed in the phrase, "this one thing I do" (Phil 3:13). All his God-given gifts were focused on this one purpose: "that I may know him."

To all those who major in minor concerns, the words of Owen Meredith apply:

> He who seeks all things, wherever he goes
> Only reaps from the hopes which around him he sows
> A harvest of barren regrets.

As a child, I recall having a very interesting jackknife. It had two blades, a gimlet, a corkscrew, a scissors, a can opener, and even a nail file. The whole thing cost a dollar, and it wasn't worth a quarter. The problem was, it was too versatile.

On my desk is a simple reminder: Keep off the detours. I think the apostle Paul felt this way. Humanly speaking, nothing is so powerful in life as single-mindedness.

The apostle James underscored this truth when he warned, "A double minded man is unstable in all his ways" (1:8). It is interesting to realize that the word for worry in the Greek language is *merimino,* which simply means "a divided mind."

Matthew 6:22 states, "If therefore thine eye be single, thy whole body shall be full of light." Jesus was really saying, "Be a one-eyed man."

The picture we are given in Philippians 3 is that of a runner. His eyes are fixed on the goal. As a disciplined athlete, Paul reminds us, "I keep under my body" (1 Cor 9:27). In other words, all the strings of his personality were pulled together in one holy, concerted drive to lay hold of his full potential for the glory of God. My friend, what is the all-consuming, dynamic purpose in your life?

2. ATTITUDE

Attitudes are extremely important. Why? Because attitudes determine actions. They conquer who believe they can. The context of Philippians 3 expresses something of the believing attitude of the apostle Paul. Just notice a few of the powerful, uplifting phrases we find in this passage.

"That I may win Christ" (v. 8).

"That I may know him" (v. 10).

"I follow after" (v. 12).

"Forgetting those things which are behind" (v. 13).

"Reaching forth unto those things which are before" (v. 13).

"I press toward the mark" (v. 14).

Can you feel something of the heartbeat of this aggressive servant of God?

But, you ask, how is it possible, in a chaotic world like ours, to have a believing attitude? How can anyone be that optimistic? I must confess that when I look within at my own heart, I become discouraged. When I look without at our confused world, I am equally overwhelmed. But, when I look up to Jesus Christ, I find a reason for hope and optimism.

The specific word for man in the Greek language is *anthropos,* which is literally, "the up-looking one." The cattle of the field look down. Horses look down. Dogs look down. But men and women who have been born from above are created *to look up,* to fix their eyes on the One who is the source of all hope and strength, the One who is in control of this universe.

The Bible teaches that this kind of attitude begins when one is born anew. This is where it all starts. Salvation is foundational. After we receive Christ, we look up to Him for our every need. First, we're born from above. Then, when we need wisdom, we look up and ask of God (James 1:5).

We are also taught that "every good gift and every perfect gift is from above, and cometh down" (James 1:17). The exhortation of Scripture is "looking unto Jesus."

But you ask, "In a world like ours, how can anyone have a believing attitude?" The answer is found first of all in our new position in Jesus Christ. Romans 5:17 teaches that we can "reign in life" right now, by Jesus Christ. On this particular occasion, the apostle Paul was in a Roman prison awaiting death. Yet enthusiastically he wrote, "Rejoice in the Lord alway: and again I say, Rejoice" (Phil 4:4), and on another occasion, "What shall we then say to these things? If God be for us, who can be against us?" (Rom 8:31). The key to this kind of attitude of faith and victory is in realizing and assuming your position *in* Jesus Christ. Paul's attitude is expressed in that beautiful phrase, "forgetting those things which are behind."

There have been a number of books written in recent years telling how to have a good memory. And I would agree that a good memory is a worthwhile goal. I also firmly believe that it is important to have a good "forgettery." All of us know of people who are defeated in their Christian experience simply because they've never learned how to forget.

A. WE NEED TO FORGET OUR PAST SIN

It is very likely that Paul was guilty of murder. At least he was an accomplice in the death of Stephen. Yet Paul totally repented. After thoroughly dealing with his sin and claiming God's complete forgiveness, he moved on. He forgot those things that were in the past and pressed on in his diligent service for Christ.

B. WE ALSO NEED TO FORGET OUR PAST FAILURES

Why let the blunders of yesterday palsy the hand of today? Perhaps some of you have tried to guide a person to Christ without success, and you have said, "That's not for me." Or you've tried to teach a Sunday school class, and the children were just about impossible, and you said, "That's not for me." Or maybe you tried to pray in public, and the words failed to come, and you said, "That's not for me." But, my friend, it is for me and you. Seek God's cleansing now, and He will enable you.

C. WE NEED TO FORGET OUR PAST SORROWS

All of us, at some time or other, have had our hearts broken. Tears are the common crush of humanity. What are we to do with the sorrowful experiences of life? We must bring them to Jesus. That's what the disciples of John the Baptist did in Matthew 14:12: "And his disciples came, and took up the body, and buried it, and went and told Jesus."

Some of us permit the shattering experiences of life to destroy our usefulness. But that kind of spirit is self-destroying. Let us not say with Naomi, "The Almighty hath dealt very bitterly with me" (Ruth 1:20), but rather, with the hymn writer Johnson Oatman, "Count your many blessings, name them one by one,/ And it will surprise you what the Lord hath done." Always remember that the chisel of the sculptor cuts, but it is to make the image more attractive. The fingers of the potter press in upon the clay, but it is only to make the vessel more beautiful. Let us always remember that every sorrow is the shadow of God's hand and, also, "Whom the Lord loveth he chasteneth" (Heb 12:6).

3. MOTIVATION

In Philippians 3:14 we read, "I press toward the mark for the prize of the high calling of God in Christ Jesus."

Consider the phrase "I press."

The Christian life is not a picnic; it requires discipline plus determination. The words "I press" are strenuous. The picture is that of a runner, straining every muscle, every fiber, every tissue in his forward movement toward the mark.

The Christian life involves work. It is true that we are saved by grace, but let us also remember that "we are his workmanship, created in Christ Jesus unto good works" (Eph 2:10).

True Christianity *demands* discipline plus determination. Just as the runner who is not disciplined will lose the contest, so the believer who is not disciplined will not enjoy success.

The Old Testament tells how flesh hooks were used to adjust the sacrificial offering to the center of the altar. So we also need to take the flesh hooks of discipline and determination and center our lives on the altar of God's will.

When Napoleon became emperor of France, he selected the bee as the emblem of the new France, because it symbolized work and industry. Napoleon wrote, "I love to work. Even when I sleep, I dream about work." He had an insatiable appetite for work. And the program of Christ also demands work. Jesus said, "My Father worketh hitherto, and I work" (John 5:17). "The night cometh, when no man can work" (John 9:4).

But what was Paul's motivation in this particular passage? It is found in Philippians 3:14: "I press toward the mark for the prize of the high calling of God in Christ Jesus." Some scholars believe that the phrase "high calling" refers to the day when believers will be caught away to be with Jesus Christ. They translate the phrase "high calling" as "upward calling."

The context of Philippians 3 also underscores that Paul lived in the light of this grand future event. Paul continues, "For our conversation is in heaven; from whence also we look for the Saviour, the Lord Jesus Christ: who shall change our vile body, that it may be fashioned like unto his glorious body" (Phil 3: 20-21). Paul looked for the coming of the Saviour. This was one of the great motivations of his life. He literally lived in the glow and excitement of the return of Jesus Christ.

CONCLUSION

Some years ago, former president Dwight Eisenhower was in the city of Denver, Colorado. After attending morning worship in his wife's home church, he visited the home of a little boy who was stricken with terminal cancer. The president came unannounced, went up to the little white frame home, and knocked at the door.

The boy's father came to the door and, of course, was overwhelmed by whom he found there. He had been working around the house, and his hair was uncombed and his face unshaven. He was wearing an old T-shirt and torn blue jeans, and there stood President Eisenhower and his assistants.

Well, the presidential party was ushered into the humble home, and a little gift was given to the boy. The president picked him up in his arms and took him out to look at the limousine. In fifteen minutes' time the presidential party was gone. Everyone was excited, and the whole neighborhood was buzzing. That is, everyone was excited except the father; all he could think of was his uncombed hair, bearded face, dirty T-shirt, and torn blue jeans. What a way to meet the president of the United States of America!

One of these days Jesus Christ will come. Are you living in

the excitement of the "upward calling"? The apostle Paul lived in the glow of Christ's return.

One day, according to tradition, the apostle Paul knelt in a Roman arena. In a moment, the sword of Nero crashed on his neck and his head rolled into the dust, and the prize of the high calling of God in Christ was his. Paul was true to his purpose.

For a happy New Year, let me encourage you to resolve to develop a dynamic purpose, a believing attitude, and a heavenly motivation.

THREE

HAVE YOU SEEN
THE KING?

INTRODUCTION

Most people love a parade. Some people will literally wait for hours, just to see some famous person: the president or a royal visitor or even an astronaut. Most processions are soon forgotten.

A few stand out and are remembered because of the occasion and their drama and color. I personally watched the coronation of Queen Elizabeth II, in 1953. Eight perfectly matched horses pulled the royal coach in which Queen Elizabeth II rode from the Tower of London to Westminster Abbey. What an unforgettable procession that was!

A far more humble procession, however, has been remembered for nearly twenty centuries. It is remembered on the day we call Palm Sunday.

Have you ever wondered why this brief and seemingly incidental happening should be recalled each year at Easter? Is it because it opened the events of Passion Week? Or could it be because this event marked a high point in the recognition given Jesus? Let's see what the Bible has to say on this subject.

As we study the Bible, we find that all four gospel writers describe the triumphal entry. John speaks of it briefly in chapter 12, verses 12 to 19. Matthew gives a more full account in chapter 21. In Mark, it is found in chapter 11; in Luke, chapter 19.

You remember what took place. Jesus was about to enter Jerusalem for His final visit. On nearing the city, He sent two disciples with instructions to go to a specific place, where they would find an ass tied with her colt. They were to bring the animal on which no one yet had ridden.

When they brought the colt, they placed their coats upon its back. Then, the record says, "They set Jesus thereon" (Luke 19:

35), and spreading their clothes as a red carpet for Jesus, they moved off toward the city of Jerusalem.

Luke 19:37 and 38 describe what happened next. "And when he was come nigh, even now at the descent of the mount of Olives, the whole multitude of the disciples began to rejoice and praise God with a loud voice for all the mighty works that they had seen; saying, Blessed be the King that cometh in the name of the Lord: peace in heaven, and glory in the highest."

But the acclaim given to Jesus didn't last long. The crowd soon faded, never to rally around Jesus like that again.

Before that happened, however, Luke tells us that there were Pharisees who thought the whole procession was highly improper. "Rebuke your disciples," they urged Him. But Jesus answered, "I tell you that, if these should hold their peace, the stones would immediately cry out" (Luke 19:40).

What was Jesus saying? A careful look at Scripture makes it clear. God's plan for the world is bound up in His promise of a King, a King who can solve the problems of our sick and confused world. That brief recognition two thousand years ago declared that God had kept His promise.

God's King had come. He would not rule right then, for He had a greater purpose. But His eternal Kingdom has been established.

The events of Palm Sunday, then, point to three amazing facts that affect every person born. They are very important and very relevant to you this Palm Sunday. Let me summarize them briefly: (1) God's King *has come* to earth; (2) God's King *will come* to earth again; and (3) God's King *has already begun to reign.*

Each of these facts is true. One does not contradict the other. They are three links in God's eternal purpose. Let me explain.

1. GOD'S KING HAS COME TO EARTH

God's plan for the ages revolves around His King. He was promised to the Jews while the twelve tribes were on the way from Egypt. One of the clearest statements of this promise is in Numbers 24:17 and 19, "There shall come a Star out of Jacob, and a Sceptre shall rise out of Israel. . . . Out of Jacob shall come he that shall have dominion." This prophecy speaks clearly of a scepter and of power.

During the centuries, the promise was repeated and enlarged. The great King to come would have an everlasting Kingdom. He would rule not only over the Jews but also over the Gentiles. He would bring peace and blessing for which the world has longed since its beginning.

Who was the coming King? The answer is, The One who rode into Jersualem that spring day in what we now describe as the triumphal entry. That procession itself became another proof that Jesus of Nazareth was the long-awaited King.

Five centuries before His birth, the prophet Zechariah had described the entry in minute detail. You'll find the prophecy in Zechariah 9:9: "Rejoice greatly, O daughter of Zion; shout, O daughter of Jerusalem: behold, thy King cometh unto thee: he is just, and having salvation; lowly, and riding upon an ass, and upon a colt the foal of an ass."

Zechariah's statement, of course, was but one of many reminders that Jesus is God's great King, as well as His great Prophet and Priest.

A. He was born a king

True, His birthplace was a stable. But you remember that the wise men who came to find Him asked, "Where is he that is born King of the Jews?" (Matt 2:2).

B. He lived with the affairs of a kingdom on his mind

Oh, yes, His way of life was humble, but He had much to say about His Kingdom. Along with John the Baptist, He preached that the Kingdom of heaven was at hand. He warned Nicodemus that, "Except a man be born again, he cannot see the kingdom of God" (John 3:3). He spoke often to His disciples and others, as well, about that Kingdom.

C. HE DIED AS A KING

True, He was crucified, but as a King. The Roman governor, Pilate, asked Him at His trial, "Are you King of the Jews?" And Jesus' answer was yes (Luke 23:3).

Pilate understood! Do you? At the governor's orders, His cross bore this inscription, in there languages, for all to read: "THIS IS JESUS THE KING OF THE JEWS" (Matt 27:37).

Can you take in what this means? This divided, warring, groping world has had a visit from its King. His time of glory and honor are in the future, but He came.

A week before His death, the little Palm Sunday crowd had seemed to sense it briefly. But he turned aside from reigning then in order to become the Saviour. Have you turned aside from the interests which fill your life to receive His great salvation?

2. GOD'S KING IS COMING AGAIN

If it seems incredible, in a day when we hear much of credibility gaps, that God's King is coming again, probably it is only because nothing like it has ever happened before. But may I remind you that nothing like His first coming had ever happened either. Nor did anyone before Jesus overcome death and the grave.

Jesus did die. He was buried, and He rose the third day, leaving an empty tomb! These facts are among the best attested in all history.

Because these things had really taken place and were known to that very generation, the apostle Paul, a few years later, could speak of them boldly on Mars' Hill in Athens. And speak of them he did.

Standing in the intellectual forum of that day, he promised the King's return to judge the earth, as we read in Acts 17. "God . . . commandeth all men every where to repent," he said, "because he hath appointed a day, in the which he will judge the world in righteousness by that man whom he hath ordained."

Then note the final statement: "Whereof he hath given assurance unto all men, in that he hath raised him from the dead" (Acts 17:30-31). The resurrection of Jesus Christ, Paul says, is God's affirmation of a climactic purpose. That purpose is to place His Son on earth to judge and rule.

Again and again the Bible speaks of the King's return. It is the subject of Psalm 2. The King's return is promised by the angels in Acts, chapter 1. Christ Himself spoke of His return in John 14 and in other passages of Scripture. The New Testament contains more than three hundred references to this second coming.

Have you thought of what this means? One of these days you are going to meet eternity's King! You are going to stand before Him. Will He be your Saviour and your King, or will He be your Judge? The Bible warns us plainly that every knee shall bow and "every tongue . . . confess that Jesus Christ is Lord, to the glory of God the Father" (Phil 2:10-11).

3. GOD'S KING HAS ALREADY BEGUN TO REIGN

The Lord Jesus, and others after Him, spoke of the Kingdom more than 125 times in the New Testament. Many of the references are to the glory Kingdom which is to come. But by no means all. Several refer to an unseen Kingdom already in existence.

In Luke 17:20 and 21, the Lord told the Pharisees, "The kingdom of God cometh not with observation . . . for, behold, the kingdom of God is within you," or, "in the midst of you."

What did Jesus mean by that? He was saying that His Kingdom had already begun. Unseen, but very, very real. It is operative in those who discern His lordship and respond to His will.

In the centuries since Christ's ascension, His Kingdom has grown until it circles the globe. Everyone receiving Him as Lord is a citizen of this Kingdom. Thus Colossians 1:13 reminds us that every believer has been delivered from "the power of darkness, and . . . translated . . . into the kingdom of his dear Son."

What does it mean to be in Christ's invisible, yet mighty, Kingdom today? It means all the things that Christians have known and rejoiced in since the day of Pentecost.

It means forgiveness of sins and newfound peace with God.

It means assurance of a home in heaven.

It means being born again and receiving a new heart and mind and will.

It means strength so we can say with Paul, "I can do all things through Christ which strengtheneth me" (Phil 4:13).

It means a special calling to be an ambassador for Christ and for His Gospel.

It means comfort and peace of mind. If you are in Christ's Kingdom, you can know that nothing or no one can separate you from the love of God.

CONCLUSION

Yes, the King is coming. But He has already come, and He is reigning now in the hearts of those who are His own. Have you let Christ place you in His eternal, certain Kingdom? There is no other Kingdom like it. The Word of God says that "of the increase of his government and peace there shall be no end." It will be a kingdom "with judgment and with justice from henceforth even for ever. The zeal of the LORD of hosts will perform this" (Isa 9:7).

There were many that first Palm Sunday in Jerusalem who did not see the King. Have you seen Him now in our day?

FOUR

THE CROSS
OF JESUS CHRIST

INTRODUCTION

Often we divide humanity into many classes: rich and poor, black and white, educated and uneducated. But Jesus drew a line through all these distinctions and divided humanity into just two classes: the unconverted and the converted.

No other division really matters. This is the division that divides! It divides between time and eternity, and Christ and His cross make the difference.

In Matthew 27 we are supplied with some of the details of the crucifixion of Jesus Christ.

1. THE PATH OF THE CROSS

"Then released he Barabbas unto them: and when he had scourged Jesus, he delivered him to be crucified" (Matt 27:26).

Jacob Behemen said, "Man is sometimes like a wolf, cruel and merciless, thirsty for blood; sometimes man is like a dog, snappish, malicious, envious, and grudging as a dog is with a bone; sometimes like a fox, cunning and sly; sometimes like a bear, cruel and ugly; sometimes like a leopard, slippery and fast; sometimes like a snake, sly and fast as zig zag lightning."

We see these very characteristics in the people surrounding the cross. One of the reasons for which Christ came into the world was to give us a new nature in place of our sinful nature. Mankind needs to be changed!

The days prior to the crucifixion portrayed the beastly nature of mankind. The pathway of Jesus grew increasingly dark. The victims of this type of torture were usually chained to a pillar. Rude, barbarous men would surround the prisoner with their whips. The clothing was torn from the body; and the face, pressed hard against the pillar. After firmly tying the one condemned, the soldiers' shameful work began. The scene was dark and ugly. The lashing continued until the arms of the scourgers grew weary, then new recruits took their place, until the entire back of the victim appeared as one big gaping wound. The whips in those days were made of rawhide with slivers of sheep bone and huckle bone inserted.

The physical agony of our Lord's crucifixion was sad enough, but the mental agony was even more profound. The antagonists hurled their words against His kingly position. A threadbare robe was thrown over His beaten back. Then the branches broken from a thorn tree were woven into a crown of thorns and pressed hard upon His head. To complete the image of a mock king, they put in His hands a stick to resemble a kingly scepter. Then they bowed down in mock worship and jeered Him, saying, "Hail, King."

Some slapped Him about the head while others had the arrogance to spit into His face. Still others snatched the reed and beat Him about the head until the thorns dug deep into His forehead.

The gospel reads, "And they stripped him, and put on him a scarlet robe. And when they had platted a crown of thorns, they put it upon his head, and a reed in his right hand: and they bowed the knee before him, and mocked him, saying, Hail, King of the Jews! And they spit upon him, and took the reed, and smote him on the head" (Matt 27:28-30).

These were some of the experiences of Jesus on the path to the cross.

2. THE PLACE OF THE CROSS

"And when they were come unto a place called Golgotha, that is to say, a place of a skull . . . they crucified him" (Matt 27:33-35).

Golgotha. What a frightful name! When interpreted, it

44

means "the place of a skull." The word *Calvary* comes from the Latin, also meaning "a skull." The place of the crucifixion was skull hill.

This hill was located outside the city of Jerusalem. Foreshadowed in the Old Testament sin offering, Jesus was led outside the city wall, and there He became the final and eternal offering for sin.

Golgotha was the death place. It was also a playground for the vultures, jackals, and hyenas. Yet it was from this hill that there came the hope of the world. From this dark spot flows life, light, and liberty. Around this hill, those of every color, clime, and country clasp hands in the name of Jesus.

"And they crucified him."

You are familiar with the method used. Christ's hands and feet were nailed to the tree. Here was love incarnate, rejected, tortured, and now crucified. The darkest sin of earth was Golgotha. The foulest spot of humanity was Golgotha. The blackest page of history was Golgotha. The place of the crucifixion was "Golgotha."

3. THE PERSON OF THE CROSS

But who was this One so horribly treated? Who was this One who stood the scourging with lamblike patience? Who was this Lamb among wolves? Who was this Dove in the claws of vultures? Who was this One? Who was this One who was to die a criminal's death? My friend, this was none other than the perfect Son of God. This was heaven's "bright and morning star" (Rev 22:16). God Himself said, "This is my beloved Son, in whom I am well pleased" (Matt 3:17).

Rousseau said to Voltaire, "Socrates died like a man, but Jesus died like God." Other men, when crucified, would curse and spit upon the ones who drove in the nails, but Jesus said, "Father, forgive them; for they know not what they do" (Luke 23:34).

Here was heaven's Sun in eclipse, heaven's Lily spotted, heaven's Rose of Sharon dying.

45

The first Adam was created to be a king. He was given dominion over Eden. God dressed him in a garment of glory. But he sinned. His glory changed to shame and nakedness. His crown degenerated into thorns. He became a slave to sweat, toil, and sin.

The last Adam, Jesus Christ, gathered up the thorns and wove a crown for His head; He wrapped Himself in the robe of mockery and died to restore lost mankind. The God who clothed the valleys and the hills, who hears the raven when it calls, forsook His Son and answered not His cry.

No wonder the earth rocked and reeled in protest. No wonder all the people there on that ugly hill, beholding the things which were done, smote their breasts and returned. No wonder the rocks broke and the earth quaked in view of such divine love. This was Jesus, God's only Son, dying for you and for me.

4. THE PURPOSE OF THE CROSS

The cross shows God pointing His finger at sin and saying, "I hate sin." Sin is a transgression of God's Law. It must be dealt with.

The Bible clearly states that "the wages of sin is death" (Rom 6:23). It also tells us, "The soul that sinneth, it shall die" (Ezek 18:20). Sin is not a minor discord, but a major offense. It is so major that God gave His Son to die for you and me because of it.

What was the purpose of the cross? Matthew records the mockery of the crowd: "He saved others; himself he cannot save" (Matt 27:42). The sarcasm is true! Absolutely true! Jesus died on the cross to redeem others.

God is just. He will never demand two payments for one debt. While on the cross, Jesus said, "It is finished" (John 19:30). What was finished? Throughout His ministry, Jesus told how He would die for the sins of the world, and now that work and purpose was finished.

All the Old Testament offerings found fulfillment in the crucifixion. No more lambs needed to be offered; no more bullocks needed to be bound. Redemption was fulfilled. Redemption was complete as atonement was made through His blood shed on the cross.

American history records the building of a great transcontinental railroad that joined the United States by rail from the Atlantic Ocean to the Pacific Ocean. During its construction, financial failure overtook the promoters, and only with difficulty did they secure the funds to finish the railroad.

There was great enthusiasm when the work was resumed. The day came when the last rail was to be laid on the border between New Mexico and Colorado. It was planned to be a great event. A special order was sent to California for a laurel wood tie, and two silver spikes were ordered, one for Colorado and one for New Mexico. The governor of each state was invited. They were to drive the two silver spikes into the laurel wood tie, thus completing the construction and making a way of transportation from ocean to ocean. As the governors drove the two silver spikes into the laurel tie, the great crowd applauded and a telegraph wire bore the news with a flash to the entire world. It was a great accomplishment!

But there was an infinitely greater day when four spikes were driven, not into a laurel tie, but into the hands and feet of Jesus. They were not spikes of silver, but of iron and steel, and they were driven while heaven, earth, and hell looked on. When the last spike was driven, a shout went up from all creation—the news flashed to the ends of the world—for a way of salvation from earth to heaven had been completed. And Jesus cried, "It is finished."

The way is now open from earth to heaven for you!

Isaiah said, "He hath borne our griefs, and carried our sorrows. . . . He was wounded for our transgressions, he was bruised for our iniquities" (Isa 53:4-5). Peter said, "Who his own self bare our sins in his own body on the tree" (1 Pet 2:24).

CONCLUSION

My friend, our sins nailed Christ to the cross. It is true that Judas betrayed Jesus to Caiaphas. Caiaphas gave Jesus to Pilate. Pilate condemned Him to the cross. But behind Judas, behind Caiaphas, and behind Pilate, were our sins. Our sins crucified Jesus.

Friend, will you see yourself guilty before a holy God? Can you hear the invitation of the crucified, risen, interceding Saviour? At this special season of the year, will you place your trust in the Christ of the cross?

FIVE

THREE ATTITUDES
TOWARD
THE RESURRECTION

INTRODUCTION

A broken man sat in the ruins of his own household. His family had been snatched away by tragedy; his earthly possessions, destroyed. As he viewed the remains of what was once a happy home, he asked this question: "If a man die, shall he live again?" (Job 14:14).

Job's question has been asked repeatedly down through the centuries. Whenever man is faced with death, his thoughts go naturally to the subject of life after death. Death is inescapable. Death comes to us from our streets and highways, and even from our own neighborhoods. Someone has said that in today's society, death has become the most real fact of life. Like it or not, welcome it or dread it, sooner or later we all must die. The Bible states, "It is appointed unto men once to die" (Heb 9:27). No one can avoid death.

For the child of God, death is not the end. It is not a reason for sorrow or despair. Jesus comforted His fearful disciples by saying, "Because I live, ye shall live also" (John 14:19). Only the Christian can look to the future with certainty and a spirit of optimism. Easter speaks of the resurrection of Jesus Christ, and this is our hope.

In Acts 17, we find the apostle Paul waiting for his fellow workers in the godless city of Athens. "Now while Paul waited for them at Athens, his spirit was stirred in him, when he saw the city wholly given to idolatry. Therefore disputed he in the synagogue with the Jews, and with the devout persons, and in the market daily with them that met with him" (vv. 16-17).

As Paul looked around that great city, he was disturbed by the idolatry he encountered. It seemed as if every street corner had an image, and every chariot had an idol. Paul spoke out against this in the synagogues and in the marketplace.

Verse 18 tells us that "certain philosophers of the Epicureans, and of the Stoics, encountered him." They wanted to hear more of this doctrine, "because he preached unto them Jesus, and the resurrection." These very learned men took Paul to the Areopagus on Mars' Hill and said, "Tell us more."

The apostle began by speaking about one God. He continued by telling them that this one God would some day judge the world, and the proof of this judgment to come was the resurrection of Jesus Christ. "Because he hath appointed a day," preached Paul, "in the which he will judge the world in righteousness by that man whom he hath ordained; whereof he hath given assurance unto all men, in that he hath raised him from the dead" (v. 31).

Luke tells us that when Paul spoke about the resurrection, there was a threefold reaction. These three attitudes toward Christ's resurrection are found in verses 32-34: "And when they heard of the resurrection of the dead, some mocked: and others said, We will hear thee again of this matter. So Paul departed from among them. Howbeit certain men clave unto him, and believed."

1. SOME MOCKED

"And when they heard of the resurrection of the dead, some mocked" (Acts 17:32).

The first attitude toward the message of Paul concerning Christ's death, burial, and resurrection was one of mockery. The Scripture simply says that "when they heard of the resurrection . . . some mocked." The Epicureans didn't believe in life after death, and therefore they mocked. The Stoics believed in immortality, but they didn't believe in the literal resurrection of a physical body, and so they mocked.

I used to get very upset when people would mock God. I

don't get upset anymore, and I believe this is because I understand the Bible better. I've found that in every age there have been people who mocked God. I think back to the book of Genesis, where society was on an immoral binge. The Lord looked down and recognized that sin had to be dealt with. In Genesis 6:3, the Lord said, "My spirit shall not always strive with man." Society needed to be washed clean. I think it was one of the leaders of the Woodstock Rock Festival who said the whole world needs a big wash, a big scrubdown. I'm sure he was absolutely right.

In the days of Noah, God determined to give the world a big wash by means of a flood. He dealt in judgment and permitted the flood to come. But some people mocked: "Why, Noah, it's never rained. Why waste your time with such foolishness?" However, God had said judgment would come, and it did. And the mockers perished.

Genesis 18 and 19 relate God's judgment upon the wicked city of Sodom. Sodom was so polluted that God cut it off and blotted it out to save the human race from total degeneracy. But when Lot warned his daughters and their families that they must flee, the Scripture says that his sons-in-law mocked him. They looked at their father-in-law and laughed. They thought the old man was out of his mind. Lot's life was so compromising that they couldn't believe he could be that concerned about anyone.

The same was true with Lot's wife. She couldn't make up her mind. She wanted Sodom, and she wanted salvation. She wanted deliverance, and yet she wanted the pleasures that Sodom afforded. God looked at Lot's wife as she delayed, took her hesitation to be no, and rained judgment upon her. She was transformed into a pillar of salt. Yes, the mockers and the delayers described in the Bible met the justice of God. And only those who believed and made a decision were delivered.

Some have always mocked. What about when our Lord was crucified? Instead of a regal throne there was a wooden cross;

instead of a kingly diadem, a thorny crown; instead of a regal robe, a tattered shawl; instead of a royal scepter, a stick; instead of a kingdom, the shrunken, narrow dimensions of a borrowed tomb.

Matthew 27 tells a little about that mockery: "Then the soldiers of the governor took Jesus into the common hall, and gathered unto him the whole band of soldiers. And they stripped him, and put on him a scarlet robe. And when they had platted a crown of thorns, they put it upon his head, and a reed in his right hand: and they bowed the knee before him, and mocked him, saying Hail, King of the Jews! And they spit upon him, and took the reed, and smote him on the head" (vv. 27-30).

Yes, they mocked our Lord. You see, the mockers have always been around. I think of what Paul wrote to the Galatian believers: "Be not deceived; God is not mocked: for whatsoever a man soweth, that shall he also reap" (Gal 6:7). Paul is simply saying that you can't mock God and get away with it.

In London, you can take a dog onto a city bus for half fare. One lady, who didn't feel like paying any fare at all, carried her dog in a little cardboard box with air holes in it. She got on and paid her fare, but none for the dog. In essence, she deceived the bus driver, mocked the laws of the transit authority, and thought she was getting away with it.

About three blocks down the road a man got on with a big Airedale dog that he couldn't hide. He paid his fare and the fare for his dog. Because dogs have a way of knowing when other dogs are around, there began a little sniffing and scratching and growling and barking, and soon her secret was out—and so was she. They put her off at the next stop.

When I heard this story, I thought about how people try to deceive, try to get away with things, try to mock the established laws. But God says, "Don't be fooled." He refuses to be mocked. Whatever a person sows, that is exactly what he will reap.

Genesis 37 describes how the sons of Jacob tried to mock him. Jealous of Joseph's dreams, his brothers sold him to a caravan of Ishmaelites. They then took his coat of many colors, dipped it in the blood of slain beasts, brought it to their father, and said, "This have we found: know now whether it be thy son's coat or no" (Gen 37:32). It was nothing more than a deceitful lie that they used to mock their father.

Everything seemed as though they had been quite successful. The years went by, and their sin did not find them out. But as the famine came to the sons of Jacob, they went down to the land of Egypt and came before Joseph. They, of course, didn't recognize their brother; but Joseph, who had risen to a position of authority and power, recognized them. "Joseph said unto his brethren, I am Joseph; doth my father yet live? And his brethren could not answer him; for they were troubled [literally, they were terrified] at his presence" (Gen 45:3). They had mocked their father; they had deceived Jacob; and they thought they had gotten away with it. Time seemed to have covered their sin. But time never covers sin. No one can mock God and get by with it. God will not be mocked; whatever a man sows, that is exactly what he will ultimately reap.

People try to mock God today. Some of the opponents of Christianity say that the resurrection is a deliberate invention of the Church. They say that the resurrection of Jesus is a lie. This of course, is not valid in view of the great number of witnesses to it. Why, in A.D. 56, Paul says there were 500 original witnesses of the resurrected Lord. We also must remember that the early Scripture record went out to the known world with the collective authority of the whole Church. These witnesses were men of exceptional character. They gave to the world the highest moral and ethical teaching ever known. They lived what they taught, and their opponents knew it. And how do you explain the fantastic change which occurred in these men? Could a deliberate lie produce such transforming results?

Yes, there are some who mock today. They mock by saying that the resurrection of Christ was a spiritual resurrection. But a spirit is intangible. Whoever heard of a spirit rising?

55

Some mock by saying that the disciples stole the body of Jesus. They say that Matthew, Mark, Luke, John, Peter, and Paul lied; they invented a fabrication. But those men thought it was wrong to lie. Can you believe that they would concoct a story and then have the gall to circulate the lie? If so, what did they do with the body of Jesus? And why were they willing to suffer martyrdom? For what? For a lie?

Someone might say, "The disciples didn't steal the body. The local authorities did." Well, then, why didn't they produce it when Peter stood and preached about the resurrection of Christ? When thousands were believing and the Church was multiplying greatly, why didn't the authorities produce His body then?

Some modern writers mock by saying that Jesus never died at all. The author of *The Passover Plot,* a recent best-seller, suggests that Jesus really didn't die, but fainted or swooned, and was then revived as He lay in the cold tomb. But tell me, how could He, in that wounded condition, roll away the stone? And tell me, what happened to the soldiers who guarded that sepulcher? Why didn't they stop Him? How far could He walk on wounded feet? Where did He go from there? Even some skeptics agree that this is absolutely absurd.

Peter tells us that in the last days there will be mockers who will say, "Where is the promise of his coming?" (2 Pet 3:4). As Paul stood on Mars' Hill and spoke about Christ's resurrection, they looked and laughed. Some mocked the message of the resurrection.

2. SOME DELAYED

"And others said, We will hear thee again of this matter" (Acts 17:32).

The second attitude toward the resurrection is that of delay. I don't think there are many who would mock God or who would mock Christ's death, burial, and resurrection. But I am positive that there are many who would and do take this second attitude.

I think of the delay of Pharaoh. Moses went to the king and

said, "Let my people go." Pharaoh said, "Look, I don't know your Jehovah. I know Ra, but I don't know Jehovah. I will not let Israel go." So God sent judgment.

In the midst of each judgment, Pharaoh said, "Moses, ask your God to take this plague away." And each time Moses would say, "Tell me, Pharaoh, when will you let Israel go?" Each time Pharaoh answered, "I'll let Israel go tomorrow" (Exod 8:10, author's paraphrase). At first his neck was hard, then his heart was hard, and, finally, when he pursued the children of Israel across the Red Sea, God smote him with sudden death because he hardened his will and his heart against the warnings of God. He kept delaying until "tomorrow."

Tomorrow looks so innocent; it sounds so innocent; but it isn't innocent. The men of Athens listened to Paul and said, "Not now. We'll hear more about this matter later." They delayed.

Oh, how tragic it is to say *tomorrow* when God says *today*. Proverbs 27:1 declares, "Boast not thyself of to morrow; for thou knowest not what a day may bring forth." I have found that people who intend to repent at twelve, often die at eleven. Don't count on tomorrow!

James 4:13-14 declares, "Go to now, ye that say, To day or to morrow we will go into such a city, and continue there a year, and buy and sell, and get gain: whereas ye know not what shall be on the morrow. For what is your life? It is even a vapor, that appeareth for a little time, and then vanisheth away."

Waiting for tomorrow is a mistake, because life is like a vapor. It's like an arrow speeding for a target, like an eagle chasing its prey, like a leaf falling to the ground, like a weaver's shuttle that moves so fast the eye cannot distinguish movement. The life of an individual is so brief that the wood of the cradle rubs against the marble of the tomb. It is presumptuous to say we'll wait for tomorrow. God says the only time we can count on is right now.

I think of a couple who were attending meetings a few years ago. Night after night an elderly, godly man lovingly, tenderly, tactfully, tried to persuade them to receive Christ. Each night the husband would say, "Not tonight, but tomorrow." He left the meetings without Christ, characterized by indecision and delay. One day, before he went to work, he said to his wife, "Honey, never since that meeting have I had the slightest urge, the slightest tendency to repent and get right with God." They determined that they would make time to think about their souls' salvation. But that day at work an explosion snuffed out that young man's life. He said "tomorrow" when God said "today."

Edgar Guest penned these words:

> He was going to be all that a mortal should be
>   Tomorrow.
> No one should be kinder or braver than he
>   Tomorrow. . . .
> Each morning he stacked up the letters he'd write
>   Tomorrow. . . .
> The greatest of workers this man would have been
>   Tomorrow.
> The world would have known him, had he ever seen
>   Tomorrow.
> But the fact is he died and he faded from view,
> And all that he left here when living was through
> Was a mountain of things he intended to do
>   Tomorrow.[1]

I have found that the road marked tomorrow leads to the town called never. Tomorrow is the door that's been bolted, barred, boarded; it shuts people out from the mercy and grace of God. Tomorrow is not God's time; it is Satan's time. I would suggest you write that letter today, or make that phone call today. I would suggest that if you're not right with a fellow believer, you get right today. I suggest that you make restitution today. I would suggest that if a step of obedience is needed, you take that step. I would suggest that if you have never repented and received Christ, you receive Christ while it is yet day. He-

1. Reprinted from *Collected Verse of Edgar A. Guest* by Edgar A. Guest, copyright 1934 by the Reilly and Lee Company, a division of the Henry Regnery Company, Chicago. Used by permission.

brews 2:3 asks, "How shall we escape, if we neglect so great salvation?"

Several years ago our family visited Niagara Falls. It was spring, and ice was rushing down the river. As I viewed the large blocks of ice flowing toward the falls, I could see that there were carcasses of fish imbedded in the ice. Gulls by the score were riding down the river feeding on the fish. As they came to the brink of the falls, their wings would go out, and they would escape from the falls.

I watched one gull which seemed to delay and wondered when it would leave. It was engrossed in the carcass of a fish, and when it finally came to the brink of the falls, out went its powerful wings. The bird flapped and flapped and even lifted the ice out of the water, and I thought it would escape. But it had delayed too long so that its claws had frozen in the ice. The weight of the ice was too great, and the gull plunged into the abyss. Oh the danger of delay.

No one has ever drifted to God. You don't drift to heaven. You must make an intelligent, active decision to move in the direction of heaven. You can drift from faith to reason and from reason to the senses and from the senses to animalism, but no one ever drifts toward God. Paul was drifting into a life of violence until one day, on the Damascus road, Christ arrested him and gave him the power he needed to go a new direction.

You say you don't have the power to stick by a decision. You don't have the power to live the life. You're afraid you can't last if you make a decision. Christ who saves is the One who empowers, and He will give you what you are lacking.

Matthew 25 speaks about the wise and foolish virgins. The five foolish ones were not anti-God; they were not antibridegroom. They just neglected to get oil. They were unprepared. In Matthew 25:10 we read, "And while they went to buy, the bridegroom came; and they that were ready went in with him to the marriage: and the door was shut."

The five foolish virgins were not God-rejecters. They were delayers. They were procrastinators. They failed to make a decision. Clocks that are not wound eventually refuse to tell time; white fences that are not cared for become black fences; water that is undisturbed develops a green color and a foul odor. Neglect alone will do it. Neglect will damn you.

The Bible asks the question, How do you imagine you will escape if you neglect so great salvation offered by a loving, holy God?

3. SOME BELIEVED

"Howbeit certain men clave unto him, and believed" (Acts 17:34).

The third atttiude is expressed in verse 34: "Howbeit certain men clave unto him, and believed." What is it to believe? First of all, it is to confess your sins. The word *confess* means to agree. It's to come to the Lord and say, "Lord, You're right and I am wrong." If you're a Christian out of fellowship, it's to say, "Lord, I'm out of fellowship." If you've never received Jesus Christ, it's to say, "Lord, I'm sinful, I'm dead spiritually, and I admit my need of forgiveness. I'm incomplete. I've come short of the glory of God." To believe is to acknowledge your need and to acknowledge Jesus Christ as the only One to meet that need.

Luke says that those who believed were "Dionysius the Areopagite, and a woman named Damaris, and others with them" (v. 34). Some mocked, some delayed, and some believed.

In Athens, to be a believer was to be in the definite minority. Yet these went up to Paul and held on to him and said, "Paul, we're with you. We believe, and we're not ashamed. We believe, and we'll openly acknowledge Jesus Christ. In spite of all this heathen worship, we believe. You can count on us." They held on to Paul; they clave unto him. Theirs was a public profession of faith in Christ.

Just suppose that after having discovered the final phase of the polio vaccine, Dr. Jonas Salk had said, "I'm not going to let anyone use this new discovery. I'll not share my remedy." You

60

say, "That's inhuman." I say that it is equally inhuman to receive, to believe, to accept God's gift of salvation and to keep it to yourself. The Bible says, "Whosoever therefore shall confess me before men, him will I confess also before my Father which is in heaven" (Matt 10:32).

When Nicodemus and Joseph of Arimathea saw Jesus die, their hearts were moved, and they openly begged His body and gave Him a proper burial. It took His death to turn them from secret believers to open believers. Then they identified themselves with the followers of Jesus Christ. Have you believed? Have you publicly professed your faith?

CONCLUSION

The football game was over. Four fellows piled into their car and started home. As they drove, they drank. They drove along the road ignoring all of the highway warnings. They passed signs that said, "Five miles ahead—Bridge Out"; "Four miles ahead—Bridge Out"; "Three miles ahead—Bridge Out." "One mile ahead—Bridge Out"; "500 yards ahead—Bridge Out." They drank and drove. They came to a black and white barricade with flashing lights, but in their drunkenness they drove through the barricade and into the icy water of the river. All four perished that Saturday afternoon.

Along the road of your life, God has placed many warnings. The church, a praying neighbor, a teacher, a book, a conference, some pastor or teacher or evangelist you've heard on TV. All along the road of your life there has been warning after warning after warning after warning. Finally, at the end of your life, there's a barricade, the barricade of the cross. If you perish, it's because you've neglected every kindness of God. It's because you have walked over every mercy of God. If you go out of this life without Christ, eventually you take the barricade of the cross and trample it underfoot. In spite of all that God has done, you neglect so great salvation.

Some mocked. Some delayed. But some believed.

SIX

THE GOOD NEWS OF EASTER

INTRODUCTION

Around the globe, on hundreds of fronts, medicine is waging a war on sickness and death. In 1967, in Cape Town, Africa, Dr. Christian Barnard completed the world's first heart transplant. The patient, a victim of advanced heart disease, lived only eighteen days. A second transplant attempt was unsuccessful, but a third man was operated on again in Cape Town and lived for nineteen months before succumbing to pneumonia. Since then, hundreds of heart transplants have been performed. Other remarkable advances are being made in diagnosis, medicine, and techniques of surgery.

In London, England, Dr. Alexander Comfort, director of Research for the Aging at University College, says, "We hope to find a technique for interfering with human aging within the next four or five years—not for stopping the process but for slowing it down."

Yes, science has made much progress, but death is still our greatest enemy. In a very real sense, we begin to die the moment we are born. Death is, for everyone, an inescapable fact of life.

But there is hope! Nearly two thousand years ago, a body lay in a tomb and was raised to life. And because Jesus Christ rose, you, too, can know the certainty of resurrection. This is the good news of Easter and the basic message of the Gospel, as Paul writes in 1 Corinthians 15:3-4: "For I delivered unto you first of all that which I also received." This is assurance, this is certainty, passed to us through the Word of God. Paul continues, "How that Christ died for our sins according to the scriptures; and that he was buried, and that he rose again the third day."

These are facts. Not suppositions. Though Jesus Christ rose

nearly two thousand years ago, the details of this great event are among the best attested in all history. True, we are far removed in time and distance, but we have much reliable evidence from a number of witnesses. Matthew, Mark, Luke, John, the two followers who met Jesus on the Emmaus road, Thomas, the other disciples, and many others, all tell us Jesus died and rose again!

The enemies of Jesus would have given their very lives for one single piece of evidence to show that a resurrection had not taken place. But they found none, absolutely none.

On the other hand, proofs of the resurrection are overwhelming. A recent book, *Evidence That Demands a Verdict,* by Josh McDowell, devotes no fewer than eighty-eight pages to this important subject. Proof after proof is cited confirming the fact that Christ arose and left an empty tomb.

Have you ever faced this fact and what it means to you? Let me set before you three phases of the evidence, just three of many, which no thinking person can ignore.

1. THE FACTS OF JESUS' DEATH

First, there is the fact that Jesus really died. That was the purpose of crucifixion, and the Roman soldiers were efficient.

After a night of exhaustion and abuse, He was scourged: lashed with a whip to which were fastened long pieces of bone and metal. An early Church historian says that in such scourgings, the sufferer's veins were laid bare and that "the very muscles, sinews and bowels were open to exposure." Hebrew law limited the number of strokes to forty, but the Romans had no such limitation.

Christ's sufferings on the cross are beyond our understanding. After six hours of indescribable agony, the gospels tell us, He died. At the end of the day, when Roman soldiers came to break the victims' legs, they found Him already dead. When a Roman soldier pierced His side with a spear, there flowed out blood and water. This suggests not only death by crucifixion, but rupture of the heart. Some have tried to argue that Jesus only fainted, but remember, He was certified as dead before His body was released for burial.

Our Lord's body was then wrapped in spices—John says about one hundred pounds—and left in the grave. The tomb was closed with a huge stone. It would take several men to move it. It was sealed with the Roman seal so that any person removing it would have been guilty of crime against the Roman government. As if all this were not enough, the tomb was guarded, not by one, but by several professional soldiers.

But by Easter morning the stone had been rolled away. Only the body windings were left, collapsed and empty, inside the tomb.

All Jerusalem knew these facts, but the only answer offered was a weak and absurd rumor that the soldiers had been asleep and the disciples had stolen Jesus' body.

2. THE FACT THAT JESUS WAS SEEN ALIVE BY MANY DIFFERENT PEOPLE

There is also the fact that Jesus was seen alive by different people. The list is long: Mary Magdalene, the two Marys together, Simon Peter, and two believers on the road to Emmaus. He also appeared to the disciples in the upper room when Thomas was absent and again when he was present. He met the disciples by the Sea of Tiberias. Think of this a moment. Could all these people have been deceived?

There were other meetings, too. Matthew tells of one with the disciples in Galilee, and Paul, in 1 Corinthians 15, records His appearing to more than five hundred believers at once (v. 6), and later to James (v. 7). Finally, He appeared to the disciples on the day that He went back to heaven.

Jesus talked with them. He ate food. He let them see and touch His hands and feet and side. In each case, the impression was the same. The Jesus who had been dead was now alive.

The facts themselves prove that Christ rose from the dead. The testimony of those who saw Him prove it, but there is another important proof. The believers who saw the risen Christ were changed.

3. THE FACT THAT THE BELIEVERS WHO SAW THE RISEN CHRIST WERE CHANGED

They were convinced of Jesus' resurrection. These were the very men who were on the scene. Days earlier they were crushed, defeated, discouraged, and afraid. Then, a total change came over them! In the face of opposition and almost certain death, they went out with boldness to preach a living Christ everywhere. Why? Because they knew He was alive!

CONCLUSION

Yes, Jesus Christ lives! Jesus Christ rose from the grave and lives today. You can anchor your faith to this tremendous fact. But the Good News of Easter is also something more. It is the assurance that every Christian who dies will be raised up one day, even as Christ Himself was raised.

That wonderful resurrection chapter, 1 Corinthians 15, makes this very clear. Listen to these words of assurance. "But now is Christ risen from the dead, and become the firstfruits of them that slept" (v. 20).

What are the firstfruits? The Jews knew the answer well because of their yearly feast. The firstfruits are the first sheaves of grain, the first clusters of grapes or ears of corn, in the season's harvest. They are the first visible tokens of the harvest yet to come.

The risen Christ is the first of thousands upon thousands whom God will raise from the dead because Jesus Christ was raised for us. "Because I live," Jesus told His disciples in John 14:19, "ye shall live also."

Year after year, thousands of visitors go to Forest Lawn Memorial Park in Glendale, California, to see two huge paintings. One pictures the crucifixion. The other shows the artist's concept of the outcome of Christ's resurrection. A figure in white, emerging from a tomb, depicts the risen Saviour. Behind Him is a great procession which fades into the misty distance. This is the throng of believers through the ages whose bodies will be raised like His because they have trusted Jesus.

What really happens, then, when a Christian dies? First, the spirit goes at once to be with Christ. The Bible tells us plainly that "to be absent from the body" is "to be present with the Lord" (2 Cor 5:8). Paul reminds us that this will be "far better" (Phil 1:23) than our present life.

But our bodies will not remain in the grave. At the great resurrection morning, we will respond, like Lazarus, to the voice of Christ. This is the promise of 1 Thessalonians 4:16-17: "For the Lord himself shall descend from heaven with a shout, with the voice of the archangel, and with the trump of God: and the dead in Christ shall rise first: then we which are alive and remain [those living at the time of the rapture] shall be caught up together with them in the clouds, to meet the Lord in the air: and so shall we ever be with the Lord."

Think of it! If you pass through the door of death as a true believer, Jesus Christ will one day raise your body.

We see a picture of resurrection each time we watch a seedling sprout and grow. The seed died first, time passed, and then God created life anew in the form and image of the seed that died.

If a loved one trusted Christ, we need not fear as we lay that body in the grave. The loved one will be raised in a glorious resurrection body—raised in the likeness we have known so well.

My friend, are you in bondage to the fear of death today? Jesus died and rose again to set you free. The Good News of Easter Sunday is not only that Jesus arose from the dead, not only that every Christian can experience this same mighty resurrection. It is that you have a choice to make! Christ invites you to share the promise and the reality of resurrection. In John 6:40, He says, "And this is the will of him that sent me, that every one which seeth the Son, and believeth on him, may have everlasting life." And then He adds, "And I will raise him up at the last day."

Friend, you must have Christ! No power within you can hope to overcome the bonds of death. But Jesus can, and He promises to do so. Will you put your trust in Him?

Every day, nearly half a million Americans travel by air across this country. No one has ever personally learned to overcome the hard, cold law of gravity. But they have learned a better way. One by one, they commit themselves to airliners that are made to fly. And they're carried safely to their destinations.

The Bible says that those who trust Christ are "in" Him. Trust the One who died for your sins, who rose again to give you hope and certainty of life, and He will forgive your sins. He will give you eternal life and clothe you with a resurrection body. Receive Him now and you, too, will know the Good News of Easter.

SEVEN

A SUCCESSFUL MOTHER

We are living in a changing world! Motherhood, the American flag, and apple pie are three things known for their stability and national appeal. Today, however, the price of apples is inflated, the flag is at times mistreated, and even motherhood is abused.

Napoleon once said, "Let France have good mothers and she will have good sons." Today, more than ever, we need mothers of character, mothers who will nurture their children in the ways of God. The successful mother is the key to a successful home and nation.

Several years ago, a nationwide survey was conducted by the University of Michigan. Thousands of girls between the ages of eleven and eighteen were questioned regarding their personal and social interests. When asked what they would like to do when they grew up, 80 percent of the girls expressed a desire to someday be just like their mother.

It has been said that no other force in the life of a child is as strong an influence as is his mother. This year, as each year, a special day has been officially designated as Mother's Day, the day we honor America's fifty million mothers.

Down through the centuries, the mother has been a stabilizing factor in the shaping of history. "The future destiny of the child," said Napoleon, "is always the work of the mother."

Theodore Roosevelt put it this way: "The mother is the one supreme asset of the national life. She is more important, by far, than the successful statesman, businessman, artist or scientist."

Many famous men have been greatly influenced by their

71

mothers. George Washington's mother was a patriotic and religious woman. Her son became the father of his country. Lord Bacon's mother was a woman of superior intelligence and deep piety. The mother of Patrick Henry was known for her remarkable conversational ability. Sir Walter Scott's mother was a great lover of poetry and literature.

In contrast, Byron's mother was proud, contentious, and violent. And Nero's mother was greedy, lustful, and a murderess. Without a doubt, a mother influences her children for either good or evil.

Susannah Wesley was a great Christian mother. Despite the fact that she had nineteen children, she found time to give each child an hour's religious instruction each week. She taught her children to love God and to honor the Bible. One of her sons, John Wesley, became the founder of Methodism.

In each of these examples, some of the prominent traits of the mother were passed on to the child.

After becoming president, Abraham Lincoln generously said, "All that I am, or can become, I owe to my angel mother." That's a great tribute!

An older mother once tried to explain to me why her son's marriage had failed and he had committed suicide. "Pastor," she said, "our home was a broken home, and the old saying is true, 'There are few unbroken eggs in a broken nest.'"

If ever there was a need for godly mothers, it is today.

In 1 Samuel 1, we see a beautiful portrait of a woman who honored God. Hannah of Ephraim lived in a day when the nation of Israel was in a deplorable state. The condition of that time closely resembles the corrupt society of today. The nation's leaders had failed. Gideon and Samson were nothing more than memories. Patriotism had vanished, and ideals were low. The heroes were all dead, and the prophets were unborn. The nation was in a cowardly condition. A spiritual revival was desperately needed.

The Scriptures tell us that Hannah came from a little town

called Ramathiam-zophim. It was just a wide spot in the road. The biggest thing about it was its name. And yet in this obscure little village, God had a mother, and He would eventually have His prophet.

The conditions were much the same in the year 1483. Who would have dreamed, in the little town of Eisleben, that the hope of the Reformation would be born in a miner's hut, and that God was waiting for a husky boy named Martin Luther to grow up and steer the world back to the Word of God.

God often uses the little people of this world to bring about His divine purpose. So it was with Hannah of Ramathiam-zophim.

1. HANNAH'S PRAYER

Hannah, the wife of Elkanah, was a woman with great sorrow. She had been denied that which was the crowning glory of every Hebrew woman: the privilege of motherhood.

For years Hannah had prayed for a son. She had longed to take him with her to Shiloh on the yearly pilgrimage of worship. And now, still with no child, her disappointment seemed more than she could bear.

The Scriptures tell us that she was deeply disturbed. "She was in bitterness of soul, and prayed unto the LORD, and wept sore" (1 Sam 1:10). As God listened to that prayer, He seemed to say, "I have found a concerned mother, and now I shall have a dedicated servant."

Hannah prayed to the Lord, and the Lord heard her prayer! She was just a simple woman; she was not educated; her clothing was very plain; and yet God heard her prayers.

Hannah's name would not be found among the wealthy or elite. She would not have made the society pages, but somehow she made the V.I.P. list of heaven.

2. HANNAH'S ANSWER

Hannah was a praying mother! And the Bible tells us that

the Lord heard her prayer. "It came to pass . . . that she bare a son, and called his name Samuel" (v. 20).

May I encourage you, dear mother, to be a praying mother. Your prayer life is the foundation of a godly home. Hannah was a praying mother. She prayed for a son, and God heard her. She promised God that if He would bless her with a child, she would give him back to God. She would train him in the way of the Lord.

The greatest sermon our children will ever hear is our lives. We are examples. "Apples do not fall far from the trees." What is your attitude? Is it small or big, stingy or generous? Are you negative or positive, critical or complimentary, godly or ungodly? Hannah had an attitude of praise! She taught her child to love and honor God.

The Jewish Talmud asks the question, "Who is best taught?" It then answers, "He that is taught of his mother."

Moses said, concerning the Scriptures, "Thou shalt teach them diligently unto thy children, and shalt talk of them when thou sittest in thine house, and when thou walkest by the way, and when thou liest down, and when thou risest up" (Deut 6:7). Morning, noon, or night, Moses said, "Teach God's Word." When you are sitting, walking, going to bed, getting up, whatever you are doing, stress God's Word.

A visiting friend found a young mother sitting with her baby on her lap and holding her Bible in her hand. She asked, "Are you reading the Bible to your baby?" The mother replied, "Yes." The visitor said, "Surely you do not think he understands it?" "No," said the mother, "he does not understand it now, but I want his earliest memory to be that of seeing and hearing God's Word."

The Sunday school will train the child; the church will provide Christian nurture; but nothing can take the place of the home in providing spiritual leadership.

3. HANNAH'S COMMITMENT

Hannah had made a vow to the Lord. Within a few short years, the time came for her to give Samuel back to God. She would travel to Shiloh and leave Samuel at the tabernacle. He would become a servant of Jehovah.

Hannah was made of the material of which martyrs are made. I can see her gathering her clothing, assembling all the provisions for the journey. Her heart was very heavy. She occasionally glanced at Samuel and listened to his childish words. She would miss him dearly.

At last they made the journey. Arriving at the house of the Lord, an attendant greeted them and took little Samuel and his bundle of clothes. The inevitable moment had arrived. Hannah gave her boy one last hug and turned to walk the lonely road homeward.

In 1 Samuel 1:28, Hannah's words were: "Therefore also I have lent him to the LORD; as long as he liveth he shall be lent to the LORD." What a beautiful picture of a mother dedicated to God! Hannah gave her boy to the Lord. Not to business, not to society, not even to her country. She gave him to God!

CONCLUSION

Many great men and women of God are serving Christ today not because of their great talent or ability but because they had a mother who gave them to God. Augustine, the great Church Father and theologian, had a mother who devoted her life to his Christian upbringing and his conversion to Christ. In his early years, it would have appeared that her earnest efforts were all for nought. Augustine lived in sin and immorality; he flaunted all moral restraint and actively rebelled against God. But one day he was brought to his senses; he remembered his praying mother; and he repented of his sins. He was gloriously saved and became a champion of the Christian faith.

There once was a young lady who ignored the claims of Jesus Christ. She laughed at her mother's prayers and turned her back upon her mother's God. She seemingly was headed in the wrong direction. There came a day, however, when she was moved to pen these words:

> I grieved my Lord from day to day,
> I scorned His love so full and free.
> And though I wandered far away,
> My mother's prayers have followed me.
>
> I'm coming home, I'm coming home,
> To live my wasted life anew,
> For mother's prayers have followed me,
> Have followed me the whole world through.[1]

Perhaps you had a Christian mother who prayed for you. She prayed for many years, but as yet you have not surrendered. You have refused to yield your life to Jesus Christ. Perhaps your mother has gone on to heaven. She is there waiting for you right now. Won't you receive Christ today? Jesus says, "Behold, I stand at the door, and knock: if any man hear my voice, and open the door, I will come in" (Rev 3:20).

1. Lizzie DeArmond, "Mother's Prayers Have Followed Me," copyright 1912 by B. D. Ackley. © Ren. 1940 The Rodeheaver Co., owner. Used by permission.

EIGHT

MARY, THE MOTHER OF JESUS

Have you ever wondered why God chose Mary to be the mother of Jesus? Mary was a very unique person, the only one among millions of women to be selected as God's instrument for bringing His Son into the world. She is truly unique!

But why was Mary blessed of God? Why was she so highly favored? Notice five important reasons.

1. MARY WAS PURE

The village of Nazareth, where Mary lived and grew up, lay in the path of caravans going from Capernaum to the seaports. As in every generation, there were women in that town who became involved with the traveling men. But not so with Mary! Mary was pure!

Of course, there could not have been any unfaithfulness in Mary. Otherwise God could not have chosen her. The words that came to her from Gabriel that day echoed God's full approval: "And the angel said unto her, Fear not, Mary: for thou hast found favour with God. And, behold, thou shalt conceive in thy womb, and bring forth a son, and shalt call his name JESUS. He shall be great, and shall be called the Son of the Highest: and the Lord God shall give unto him the throne of his father David: and he shall reign over the house of Jacob for ever; and of his kingdom there shall be no end" (Luke 1:30-33).

Some of the great masterpieces of art picture the angel announcing this message to Mary and presenting her with a branch of lily. The lily is a symbol of Mary's purity.

There are those today who reject that Mary was a virgin.

79

They attempt to do away with the supernatural reality of Christ's birth by suggesting Jesus was born of a natural, human union. But to deny the virgin birth of Jesus is to plainly call God a liar.

Centuries before the angel appeared to Mary, God's prophet Isaiah wrote these words: "Therefore the Lord himself shall give you a sign; Behold, a virgin shall conceive, and bear a son, and shall call his name Immanuel" (Isa 7:14).

God, through His Word, required that Mary be a virgin, pure and holy.

What is more, to reject the virgin birth is to label Mary as immoral. The Bible clearly points out that she and Joseph, to whom she was betrothed, had not yet come together. Either Mary was pure, or else she was a woman with few morals at all.

Without the virgin birth, we have an impure Mary. Without the virgin birth, we have a human Jesus and a faulty Bible. But with the virgin birth, we have Jesus Christ, Immanuel, God with us!

When Mary received the angel's announcement, she was overwhelmed. "How shall this be, seeing I know not a man?" she exclaimed (Luke 1:34). But the angel reassured her, "The Holy Ghost shall come upon thee, and the power of the Highest shall overshadow thee: therefore also that holy thing which shall be born of thee shall be called the Son of God" (Luke 1:35).

Then the angel gave more proof to Mary that her child would really be without a human father. What was this proof? "And, behold, thy cousin Elisabeth, she hath also conceived a son in her old age; and this is the sixth month with her, who was called barren. For with God nothing shall be impossible" (Luke 1:36-37).

If God could do this for Elisabeth, then He could do anything. Mary went to visit her cousin. When Mary and Elisabeth met, Elisabeth knew immediately that Mary was the woman of God's own choosing. She greeted her as the mother of her Lord, with great happiness.

Yes, Mary was pure. As God's chosen instrument, she is to be recognized for the special role she played in the coming of the Messiah.

2. MARY WAS SUBMISSIVE

When the angel finished his startling announcement that Mary was to be the mother of the Messiah, Mary beautifully responded, "Behold the handmaid of the Lord; be it unto me according to thy word" (Luke 1:38).

"Lord, I'm Your servant. Whatever You want, I want. May it happen to me according to Your word." What submission! Mary could have hesitated or even rebelled. She could have said, "I'm so unworthy. I can never be the one." Or she could have reasoned, "We have no royal home for the Son of the Highest. He should have angelic nurses to care for Him. Please don't count on me."

But she didn't. In fact, Mary was willing even to lose her beloved Joseph in order to fulfill God's plan. I'm sure in Mary's mind there were many questions: "What will I tell people since I have no husband? And what will I tell Joseph, the man I'm engaged to, the man I'm planning to marry?" How overwhelmed and confused she must have been.

But also think of what Joseph must have felt. When he heard about Mary, I'm sure he was disturbed by doubt. Yes, disturbed and heartsick. Mary had not told him how she had come to be in this condition. From Matthew's account, we learn that Joseph was understandably upset.

"Then Joseph . . . being a just man, and not willing to make her [Mary] a publick example, was minded to put her away privily. But while he thought on these things, behold, the angel of the Lord appeared unto him in a dream, saying, Joseph, thou son of David, fear not to take unto thee Mary thy wife: for that which is conceived in her is of the Holy Ghost" (Matt 1:19-20).

Mary had been willing to suffer all the shame and reproach that would result from her condition. Why? Because she totally believed God and knew that it was His supernatural hand at work within her. And the Lord rewarded Mary's submissiveness by sending an angel to Joseph.

Yes, let's recognize Mary for her purity and for her spirit of submissiveness.

3. MARY KNEW HER BIBLE

She loved the Word of God. Although she was very young, possibly still in her teens, Mary was a devout person. She knew the Scriptures well. She had studied the Law and the prophets.

Her song, or what we often call "The Magnificat," refers to portions of Scripture taken from 1 Samuel, the Psalms, Isaiah, Micah, and Exodus. It is a very beautiful passage. Part of it is found in Luke 1:46-49:

"And Mary said, My soul doth magnify the Lord, and my spirit hath rejoiced in God my Saviour. For he hath regarded the low estate of his handmaiden: for, behold, from henceforth all generations shall call me blessed. For he that is mighty hath done to me great things; and holy is his name."

It is true that Mary could have uttered these words under divine inspiration, possibly without any forethought on her part, but usually God uses the talent He has already bestowed.

Mary was familiar with the Word of God. And what she had studied and pondered in her heart broke out in glorious praise to her Lord. Mary saturated her life with the Scriptures.

4. MARY WAS INDUSTRIOUS

"Who can find a virtuous woman?" asks the writer of Proverbs, "for her price is far above rubies" (31:10). She then is described as one who "worketh willingly with her hands" (v. 13).

"She is like the merchants' ships; she bringeth her food from afar" (v. 14).

"She riseth also while it is yet night, and giveth meat to her household, and a portion to her maidens" (v. 15).

"She layeth her hands to the spindle" (v. 19).

"She stretcheth out her hand to the poor; yea, she reacheth forth her hands to the needy" (v. 20).

"Strength and honour are her clothing; and she shall rejoice in time to come" (v. 25).

These words could well describe young Mary. Apparently neither she nor Joseph came from a wealthy home. There was always much hard work to be done. Mary knew what it was to toil in the field, to grind corn, to wash her laundry at the well, and to carry water.

The usual pictures we see of Mary are probably quite different from the hardworking homemaker she really was. Mary was pure, submissive, Scripture-filled, and industrious.

5. Mary Could Keep a Secret

But more, we should honor Mary because of her willingness to ponder all the things God was doing. Mary had the ability to keep things to herself, a talent rarely found today. A. T. Robertson shares some interesting insights.

> Could Mary tell her mother the words of the angel? Was her mother living? We are told nothing, though one infers that both father and mother are dead. We do not know the names of her father and mother, though legend gives them as Joachim of Nazareth and Anna of Bethlehem. It is probable that Mary belonged to the tribe of Judah and the lineage of David as Joseph did (Luke 1:32, 69; 2:[4]). The Syriac Sinaitic manuscript for Luke 2:[4] has, "because they were both of the house of David." Mary was a kinswoman of Elisabeth (Luke 1:36) who belonged to the tribe of Levi, but that fact does not prove that Mary herself was of the tribe of Levi, for intermarriage between the tribes did occur. The family of Mary was probably a humble one as she was betrothed to Joseph the carpenter. That does not mean poverty, for the one or at least the chief carpenter of the town would naturally be a man of solid and substantial standing. Mary was already living at Nazareth when the angel Gabriel appeared to her.
>
> Mary could not and did not speak to Joseph about her wonderful secret. It was too sudden and too soon. There was only one

person in the world to whom she could go, and she had to open her heart to someone. That person was Elisabeth down in the hill country of Judea. To her she quickly made her way and found a surprising welcome, for Elizabeth knew at once that Mary was the woman of God's choice and sang her hymn of praise to Mary (Luke 1:42-45).[1]

Luke tells us that Mary pondered or, literally, considered all the things that were happening to her. She kept them in her heart (Luke 2:19).

After the angelic announcement, she pondered the message of the angel. After meeting Elisabeth, she pondered all the implications of being selected as God's chosen instrument. When the shepherds came to visit the Christ Child, she pondered the wonder of it all.

She didn't boast to the neighbors or share the news throughout the community. She pondered all these things in her heart. This pondering displays a devout, modest, worshipful, believing woman!

Mary believed in Jesus because she had pondered much about Jesus. She watched Him grow and mature. She knew that He was no ordinary son. She observed Him develop into manhood and begin His earthly ministry, and she pondered all that God was doing.

Mary was there when the crowd called out, "Crucify him! Crucify him!" She watched the soldiers nail Him to the cross, yet she did not intercede for Him, for she knew His true purpose. Mary knew that Jesus was indeed the Son of God, the Redeemer of mankind, the Saviour of the world.

CONCLUSION

May God give us mothers today like Mary!

And yet, let us remember that Mary, too, was a person with needs. Mary was a woman worthy of recognition, yet she was

1. A. T. Robertson, *The Mother of Jesus, Her Problems and Her Glory* (New York: Doran, 1925), pp. 17-18.

also a woman in need of a Saviour. Mary will be in heaven not because Jesus was her child but because Jesus was her Saviour, Lord, and Redeemer.

We honor Mary for her purity, her submissive spirit, her knowledge of the Bible, her industry, and for her willingness to ponder all the things that God had done. May each mother seek these same qualities that Mary possessed so that we, too, can bring glory to His Son, Jesus Christ the Saviour!

NINE

WHAT'S HAPPENING
TO THE FAMILY?

INTRODUCTION

What is happening to the family? Is marriage on the way out? These questions are being asked more and more as divorce rates soar and broken homes multiply. Although the American family today enjoys its highest standard of living ever, there are signs that the home is in critical condition. What are the reasons for this crisis? Several reasons have been suggested.

1. BROKEN FAMILIES

First, the family is fragmented. In other words, it does not hold together any longer than circumstances compel it to.

Thirty years ago, Harvard's sociologist Pitirim Sorokin predicted, "Divorces and separations will increase until any profound difference between socially sanctioned marriages and illicit sex-relationship disappears. . . . The main sociocultural functions of the family will further decrease until the family becomes a mere incidental cohabitation of male and female, while the home will be an overnight parking place."[1] What a horrible prediction. While this gloomy forecast has not yet been realized, there are many signs that indicate Dr. Sorokin's prediction contains much truth.

Shocking predictions are being voiced today by professional people throughout the world concerning the very institution of marriage. The *London Observer* printed a headline some time ago that asked, "Are we the last married generation?" A member of England's Official Marriage Guidance Council has predicted that engagements and weddings will soon be something of the past.

In a *Newsweek* cover story, general editor Richard Boeth sug-

1. Pitirim Sorokin, "Marriage," *Ladies Home Journal* 8 (September 1971):192.

gested that it is futile to believe there can be any reversal of this trend. "It is novel and bizarre of us latter-day Westernoids to imagine that we can make something tolerable of marriage. It doesn't seem to have occurred to any earlier era that this was even possible. The Greeks railed against marriage [while] the Romans mocked and perverted it."[2]

It is no secret that mankind has, throughout the centuries, perverted God's plan for family living. But despite the past record of sinful man, statistics tell us that today's marriage picture is the darkest ever. Divorce is bulldozing our society to ruin. In 1912, the census revealed that one in every twelve marriages ended in divorce. In 1932, one in every six marriages failed. Today there are two divorces for every three marriages performed.

Professional psychologist Dr. Lacey Hall says, "The Christian needs to realize what is happening to the family if he is to understand the forces shaping his own home, his own children, the families in his church and the homes in his neighborhood."[3]

2. ROOTLESS FAMILIES

A second reason for this crisis of the family is that the average family is rootless. Since the end of World War II, America has been on the move. Twenty percent of the population change their place of residence annually. Industry is demanding people who *will* move. One-third of all families with husbands under thirty-five years of age move each year.

In an article in *Moody Monthly,* Dr. Lacey Hall suggests that this mobility is changing the roots of the home.

> When the family moves, it has to adjust to new housing, new schools, and new friends. . . . And this often leads to insecurity and instability.
>
> A recent best-seller on the white collar class compares these conditions to the nursery that advertised, "We move our trees every

2. Richard Boeth, "Connubial Blitz: It Was Ever Thus," *Newsweek* 81 (March 12, 1973) :56.
3. Lacey Hall, "What's Happening to the American Family?" *Moody Monthly* 67 (July-August 1967) :26-28.

year so they won't grow deep roots." In other words, the nursery deliberately kept the root systems on its trees shallow so they could be transplanted easily. But they did not warn that such trees, without deep top roots, would not withstand the storms.[4]

And many of our families today are facing this same danger.

3. LONELY FAMILIES

Third, there is a lack of communication between family members today. The result of this development is a loss of oneness and togetherness. In many homes the husband, wife, and children all come and go as they please, often failing even to check in. Even though together, they are virtually alone. In an atmosphere such as this, real communication is impossible, and the family structure breaks down.

Yes, the family is in trouble. And let us remember that although the Christian home should be different, it is not exempt from these same problems.

Some time ago a mother shared with me concerning her married son who had just committed suicide. "Apples do not fall far from the trees," she said, as she spoke of the problems her son had experienced. She told me how her boy had capped a whirlwind romance by entering a hasty marriage. His wife had really never gotten to know him. All his weaknesses were brushed over until after the honeymoon.

Soon his wife discovered that he was a heavy drinker, emotionally immature, and totally lacking in responsibility. He was no more reliable than a cracked barometer. He was a poor marriage risk. Shortly after the birth of their first child, he deserted the family, and the marriage ended in divorce. Five years later he was dead, a victim of his own hand.

"He was just like his father," said the mother. "All of his faults he learned from my husband. Apples do not fall far from the trees."

Throughout the Scriptures, we are told that we reap exactly

4. Ibid.

what we sow. "Be sure your sin will find you out" (Num 32: 23).

4. SINFUL FAMILIES

The book of Exodus tells us about the children of Israel as they traveled through the wilderness. There, as they pitched their tents around Mount Sinai, God gave them His immutable Law. In explaining the first commandment, Exodus 20:5 states, "I the LORD thy God am a jealous God, visiting the iniquity of the fathers upon the children unto the third and fourth generation of them that hate me."

This verse is speaking about the sins of the parents. Moses was so impressed by this statement that he repeated it again in Exodus 34:7. And years later, when the children of Israel wavered between fervor and fear, Moses recalled these exact words in Deuteronomy 5:9. They were unforgettable to him. He saw God write them upon the tables of stone, and they were written upon the tablet of his mind. These words were terrifying then, and they are terrifying now. Our children reap the result of our sins to the third and fourth generation.

Every second, a baby is born somewhere in our world. For the most part, aside from the fact that we all are born with sinful natures, those children are emotionally, physically, and morally capable of developing into happy, adjusted adults. Yet many grow up to be just the opposite: miserable, unhappy, and frustrated. Why? Largely because of the sins of their parents.

In a study of the broken home, *Newsweek* magazine quoted one wife and mother who realized the effect her divorce had upon her eldest son: "We are very concerned with him," said the mother. "Lance has suffered psychic damage from all of this. . . . I laugh at a lot of things Lance does when I really should cry."[5] That boy suffered as a result of his parents' sin.

A Chinese proverb states, "In a broken nest there are few whole eggs." Sad to say, today there are literally thousands of

5. Boeth, p. 49.

emotionally disturbed children, products of shattered marriages. It behooves every parent to do everything possible to avoid a broken home.

Out of one thousand girls in an eastern Pennsylvania reform school, only eighty-seven came from homes in which there was a normal husband-wife relationship. More than nine hundred were from broken homes.

The late J. Edgar Hoover attributed our exploding crime rate to the sins of the parents. He felt that scandal in our nation is frequently due to broken homes, an attitude that God is not necessary in our way of life, and the idea that morality is old-fashioned.

It is not surprising to me that our nation's crime rate continues to climb. We have become a secularized society. We are living in an age when children are told God is dead, the church is irrelevant, and the former moral codes are outdated. We live in a world that is saturated by sex and given over to greed. The apostle Paul wrote to the church at Galatia, "Be not deceived; God is not mocked: for whatsoever a man soweth, that shall he also reap. For he that soweth to his flesh shall of the flesh reap corruption; but he that soweth to the Spirit shall of the Spirit reap life everlasting" (Gal 6:7-8).

"Apples do not fall far from the trees."

Lord Byron, the poet, was handsome, witty, and gifted, yet his life was a tragedy. At age thirty-six he wrote:

> The flower and fruit of love are gone.
> I've nothing left but the worm, the canker, and the grief.
> Neither glacier, mountain, torrent, forest or cloud
>   can lighten the weight upon my heart,
>   or enable me to lose my wretched identity.

Byron's ancestors, as far back as they can be traced, were violent, passionate, and unrestrained in morals. Byron lived as his parents lived. He openly violated all standards of morality and righteousness. He, indeed, bore the sins of his parents. Although

91

he left imperishable poetry, Lord Byron also left an imperishable example of what happens to children who are neglected by careless parents.

5. SUCCESSFUL FAMILIES

There is no secret of a happy home. There is no magic formula to follow. But God's Word is perfectly clear when it instructs parents to bring up their children in "the nurture and admonition of the Lord" (Eph 6:4).

A. SUCCESSFUL FAMILIES ARE BUILT ON THE WORD OF GOD

God instructed the Israelites to devote themselves to the Scriptures and to teach and instruct their children in the precepts of Jehovah. "And thou shalt teach them diligently unto thy children, and shalt talk of them when thou sittest in thine house, and when thou walkest by the way, and when thou liest down, and when thou risest up" (Deut 6:7).

This is the way it should be in every family. The careful reading of the Word of God and family prayer are essentials in building a successful family.

B. SUCCESSFUL FAMILIES RESULT FROM GODLY PARENTS

The Bible says, "Train up a child in the way he should go: and when he is old, he will not depart from it" (Prov 22:6).

The Old Testament tells us about Absalom, the third son of David. This young man had every opportunity to be something, but he was petted and fondled by overindulgent parents. He became thoughtless and reckless. Law meant nothing to him. Self-gratification was the rule of his life.

On one occasion, Absalom decided to kill his half brother for ravishing his sister. Then he conspired to overthrow his father, David. As David's soldiers went out after him, David called, "Deal gently for my sake with the young man" (2 Sam 18:5).

Absalom followed in the footsteps of his father; he was a victim of the sins of his parents.

It is a colossal sin to neglect one's family. A man's wife and children should not be forced to compete with the newspaper or television for attention. Rather, a father should give himself to the members of his family.

"And, ye fathers," writes Paul, "bring them up in the nurture and admonition of the Lord" (Eph 6:4). To bring into this world an immortal soul is probably the greatest responsibility of life. The Christian father must be an example to his family. He must be what he expects his children to become.

Two boys were compelled by their father to go to church. When they became teenagers, they stopped. The father sternly reprimanded his sons and asked the reason. The older boy said, "Dad, we figure that if church isn't good enough for you, it isn't good enough for us."

All of us are examples for good or evil. Each one of us is a blueprint by which children build their lives.

C. SUCCESSFUL FAMILIES ARE CHURCH RELATED

The Church is important because it is the organization of God, built upon the foundation of Jesus Christ. And it will never pass away. Someone has said, "Though the church has many critics, it has no rivals." Despite the turmoil and tribulation it may go through, despite the neglect it may receive, the Church will remain. It will survive every onslaught and every attack, because it is God's institution.

Once a person has received Jesus Christ as Saviour, he needs to be built up in the faith. He needs to receive spiritual instruction and to share with other believers. He needs to have opportunity for Christian fellowship. The Church, through its ministries, is an instrument of training and provides an atmosphere for spiritual growth.

I cannot overemphasize the importance of the local church in the formation of solid, spiritual, successful families. The familiar saying is true, "Families that pray together stay together." If you have church in the home, you will always have your home in church.

CONCLUSION

What is your family like? Is it anchored to the rock of God's Word, or is it drifting on the sea of uncertainty? Are you as a parent setting an example for your children to follow? Are you teaching them the Scriptures? Are you leading them into spiritual maturity? Have you guided them into a church that will encourage them in the things of God?

"Be not deceived; God is not mocked: for whatsoever a man soweth, that shall he also reap" (Gal 6:7).

TEN

THREE GREAT MEMORIALS

INTRODUCTION

What does Memorial Day mean to you? For some, it's just a holiday approaching summer, a day away from work, when budding trees and shrubs assure us that the time for outdoor enjoyment is but a breath away.

For others, Memorial Day brings memories from the past: flags, parades, flowers for a grave of some loved one who once marched off to war.

Each year during the month of March, a small group of people meets in a Chicago park. They gather to honor Clarence Darrow, the famous criminal lawyer, Braving the cold March winds, and often snow and sleet, the group conducts a brief memorial service at the bridge from which the lawyer's ashes were scattered in 1938.

That is a memorial for one man—the man who, fifty years ago, faced the famous orator William Jennings Bryan in the historic evolution trial at Dayton, Tennessee. But this Memorial Day, an entire nation will honor more than one million Americans who gave their lives in wartime for our country.

Decoration Day, as many call it, has been observed for more than a hundred years. It was first officially proclaimed in 1868, shortly after the War Between the States.

Is Memorial Day still meaningful? Or is it just another holiday? There was a day in the memory of many when each town and city turned out in full force. Men for whom military life was but a memory struggled into too-tight uniforms to march down Main Street to the cemetery. Drill squads fired salutes, and citizens returned to their homes with the notes of taps still echoing in their minds and memories. And that was good, for we need a time to pause and look back on the way we have come. We need to remember that, with all our imperfections, America is a great place to live and rear a family. It is a place of many freedoms, a nation where, in the long run, people outweigh their government.

What America is and offers has not just happened. God has moved mightily in our two hundred years of history. With Kipling we say:

> Lord God of Hosts, be with us yet,
> Lest we forget—lest we forget!

What is a memorial? The dictionary says it is something which serves to preserve remembrance, which brings to mind. It is something which helps us to remember.

A memorial can be a special day, a bridge, a building, or a musical composition. The list is almost endless. Such memorials focus on men and women from the human viewpoint. But there are also memorials which point us to the work and will of God.

One is the rainbow. Have you ever thought of the rainbow as a memorial? Genesis 9 tells us that it is God's memorial, assuring us that He will never again judge the earth by flood.

Then, too, Jacob set up a memorial at Bethel. It was the stone on which he had pillowed his head before his dream of the ladder reaching down from heaven. Through the rest of his life, it was his reminder that God had appeared and spoken to him.

Jewish men wore memorials on their garments. They were tassels with cords of blue. God commanded they wear the tassels to remind them of His commandments.

When God parted the Jordan River to let Israel cross over to the promised land, He told each tribe to carry a stone out of the riverbed. That pile of stones on the riverbank became a memorial of His great miracle in their behalf.

These were memory aids, reminders to the Jewish people that they belonged to God, that He had done great things for them, and that He had a great purpose for their lives. But God also has memorials for the whole human race. I have mentioned one, the rainbow. But there are others.

1. The Weekly Day of Rest

The Bible tells us that God created the earth in six successive days and that He rested on the seventh. In Genesis 2, we read, "And God blessed the seventh day, and sanctified it: because that in it he had rested from all his work" (v. 3).

This became the pattern for men: six days for work, one day for rest. Much later it became an important part of God's covenant with the Jews. It was also included in the Ten Commandments.

Every day of rest should be a memorial of God's creation. We should never forget, as Psalm 100 says, "It is he that hath made us, and not we ourselves; we are his people, and the sheep of his pasture" (v. 3).

The Bible tells us that our memorial day of rest also speaks of Christ's saving work on our behalf and the rest He has in heaven for those who trust in Him.

One of the great hymns of John Newton voices this important truth:

> Safely through another week
> God has brought us on our way.

A later line goes on to say,

> Day of all the week the best,
> Emblem of eternal rest.

Since apostolic times, New Testament Christians have worshiped on the first day of the week, the day on which Christ rose from the dead. Thus our Lord's Day is also a great memorial of Christ's resurrection.

I wonder, my friend, are you keeping God's memorial day of Christ's resurrection? What a meaningful memorial day it really is!

2. THE FEAST OF PASSOVER

The feast of the Passover is a special observance which has been celebrated for centuries by the Jews during the first month of the Jewish year. It recalls a wonderful but terrible night in Egypt—the night when God delivered His people from four hundred years of harsh slavery.

The Passover was God's provision for Israel's safety during the last of ten great plagues which God had brought upon Egypt. In a final, climactic blow, the God of life and death brought death to the eldest son of each family in the land. Even first-born animals died. But He spared the Jews on a very special basis.

You remember what He did. The Jews were told to kill a lamb and to place a splash of blood above and at either side of the door. You can read the record in Exodus 12: "And when I see the blood, I will pass over you, and the plague shall not be upon you to destroy you" (v. 13).

Do you get the picture? No one was to leave his blood-marked house. God simply said, "This is what I'm going to do. This is how you can be safe." And God did what He had promised. Death came that night to Egypt, from Pharaoh's palace to the humblest beggar's hovel. The Bible says, "There was a great cry in Egypt; for there was not a house where there was not one dead" (Exod 12:30).

Because of that unforgettable night, the Passover feast was a great memorial for every Jew. But it also looked ahead. In the fullness of time, there would come a day when God would say to the peoples of the world, "Here is My Passover Lamb, My only Son. I've sent Him to earth to die on a cross for you. Put His blood on the door of your life, and I will spare you for His sake."

Think about this for a moment. Suppose there had been Jews in Egypt that first Passover night who failed to get the point? Suppose they had said, "This doesn't make much sense to me. I don't need a lamb. I'll mark my house some other way." If some had done this, what would have happened in their homes?

The picture is too plain to miss. God has extended His Passover to all the world, because He loves the world. I wonder, have you marked the doorway of your life with the blood of Jesus Christ?

The feast of Passover was for God's chosen people, but it is rich with meaning for us all. Have you let its memorial message speak to you?

First we noticed God's day of rest, and then, His Passover. But there is a third memorial of God's love that we must also note. Though linked with the Passover feast, it is quite different from it.

3. THE LORD'S SUPPER

The Lord's Supper is the one memorial our Lord Himself commanded. Jesus and His disciples were in an upper room on the night of His betrayal. They were seated for the Passover meal. As they sat together at the table, Jesus passed a broken loaf of bread and a cup to each in turn.

These, He said, were to remind them of His body that would be broken and His blood that would be poured out so the gift of salvation could be free to all. "Do this," He said, "in remembrance of me." "When you do it," He added, "you will picture my death for sinners till I come again" (1 Cor 11:25-26, author's paraphrase).

Communion is God's great memorial of love for us. It reminds us that He gave Himself for us as individuals. Just as each Christian must partake of the bread and the cup individually, so he must personally receive Christ's forgiveness and new life.

The Lord's Supper is also the memorial of Christ, the person who loves us. "Do this," He said, "in remembrance of me." Communion should remind us not merely of Christ's work for us, but of our Saviour and Lord whom we will someday see.

101

ELEVEN

A TIME
TO REMEMBER

Memorial Day reminds us of the importance of "remember-ing."

Locked away, down deep inside your heart, is a treasure house that only you can open. Inside are memories and visions from the past that time can never erase.

Not all of these memories are pleasant. There are some sad recollections. Some memories are even tinged with tears. But there are happy memories, too, recollections you would not exchange for any sum of money in the world.

Memory! What a wonderful gift! Our memories neatly store away many good things from the past. Memory also helps to carry us through the present. Without the power to remember, we would stumble through a world of terror and confusion, unable to profit from anything we had learned before. We wouldn't even know that we could quench our thirst at a drinking fountain, or that a red traffic light means "stop," or that a mailbox is a place to mail a letter.

Memory is a strange and mysterious gift. Psychologists tell us that it is not really a storehouse or a file which we fill and empty at will. Rather, it is a process by which we rehearse past experiences and call up old associations. And yet, we do forget! Even important things gradually fade away. That's one reason why we have days set aside like Memorial Day. They are memory aids. Even with their help, we find ourselves forgetting things we had hoped we would remember.

Perhaps already at your house someone has been hard pressed to answer a childish question, "What is Memorial Day?" or, "Why do we have Decoration Day?"

Decoration Day emerged from the shadows of the War Between the States. It was first observed in the South. Before the close of the war, a group of women decorated the graves of those who had died in that war. A few years later, in 1868, May 30 was set aside as a day for placing flowers on the graves of soldiers throughout the United States of America. They decorated the graves.

Soon Decoration Day was observed each year across the country. Since World War I, this day in May has been used to honor the fallen dead of all our wars. We ought to honor these heroes of the past. We should remember the price they have paid for all that we enjoy today. Parents, perhaps this Memorial Day you should take your children to some cemetery. Be sure they understand that others gave their lives in sacrifice. This great heritage of ours has cost far more than they will understand.

How quickly we forget. We forget how much we owe to our country. But even more tragic, we forget how much we owe to our God. Each Lord's Day should really be a memorial day, to remind us of God's mercies. A forgetful heart soon becomes a foolish heart. An ungrateful attitude soon becomes a highway to ungodly living.

The person or nation that forgets God is as foolish and trouble-bound as the one who forgets that a red light means "stop" or that he can quench his thirst at a drinking fountain.

As we consider Memorial Day, let me remind you of four mighty truths our nation should remember.

1. REMEMBER THE GREATNESS AND GLORY OF GOD

We should remember the greatness and glory of God. First John 1 tells us that "God is light, and in him is no darkness at all" (v. 5). What is John saying? Simply that the man or woman who knows God and looks to Him will never be disappointed with God's character nor ever find Him limited. He is all light and no darkness.

You see, God is holy. This means, among other things, that His character and personality are in perfect balance. You and I may have too much temper or too little courage, or we may be too strict or too indulgent. Not so with God. He is just, yet He is gracious. He is patient, and yet exacting. He is impartial, but loving.

Oh, yes, you can make up your own concept of God, and many people do. They see Him as a God who can be fooled or deceived, a God who can be pushed around, persuaded, or put off. Others imagine Him as a God who created the world but has let it get completely out of hand. Some have even imagined a God who is no longer living.

But such concepts do not change God as He really is. He is the unchanging God, and we will one day meet Him as He really is, regardless of our concept.

For centuries God has permitted men to make their idols. Some idols are of wood or stone, while some are intellectual concepts. But God Himself remains the same. Every person will one day stand before Him as He is, not as he has imagined Him to be. What is God really like? The only way to know is through written revelation, the Bible.

We have heard much of a generation gap, a credibility gap, and other kinds of gaps. But I would remind you of a Creator gap. There is an infinite gap between man and his Creator because of sin. We were made in His image and likeness, that's true, but we are creatures subject to limitations of time and space. He is the great Creator, the Giver of life. He is infinite and eternal.

The point is that if you know God as He is, you will be compelled to reverence and honor Him, to set Him above all others and all else. That, in essence, is what the apostle Peter is saying in 1 Peter 3:15, "But sanctify [or set apart] the Lord God in your hearts."

God is to be set apart in our love, set apart in our lives, set apart in our thinking. He is to be revered, served, depended on and trusted in, obeyed, and made the rejoicing of our hearts. He should be the joy and the center of our lives.

Yes, we need to remember the greatness and glory of our God.

2. REMEMBER THE RIGHTS OF GOD

We also should remember the rights of God.

Ours is a day when many voices are raised in defense of human rights—the rights of those accused of criminal acts, the rights of men and women to use or misuse their bodies as they wish, the rights of individuals to pollute the public mind in order to make money.

We hear about the right of women to cut off the lives of infants they have helped conceive. We hear about the rights of those who deny the existence of the God who gives them breath.

But what about God's rights? What about His first rights as Creator, His rights as our Redeemer? Does He have a prior claim to obedience, to trust, and to worship?

You men who are mechanics, what would you do with a machine which could not be controlled? What would you cooks do with a dessert that quickly spoiled or that no one could enjoy?

Does not God have rights over His creation? Yet, by and large, men and women ignore these rights, neglect His Word, and choose their own prerogatives.

Revelation 4:11 reveals a scene in heaven. The elders around the throne of God are saying, "Thou art worthy, O Lord, to receive glory and honour and power: for thou hast created all things, and for thy pleasure they are and were created."

Today we hear about "the forgotten man." But the forgotten One of our day and generation is Almighty God.

Yes, we need a memorial day for remembering the greatness and the glory of God and for remembering the rights of our great God.

3. REMEMBER THE JUDGMENTS OF GOD

Judgments is an unpopular word today. It speaks of getting things right, of correction and punishment.

Does God really punish sin? Yes, He does! The entire Bible, from Genesis to Revelation, tells us that God is mighty in His judgments.

The ungodly seem to think otherwise. As the psalmist says of the wicked man in Psalm 10, verse 5, "Thy judgments are far above out of his sight."

Another passage, 1 Timothy 5:24, reminds us. "Some men's sins are open beforehand, going before to judgment; and some men they follow after." In other words, some sins bring immediate and open judgment, and, in other cases, judgment waits until after death. The apostle Paul speaks of this second kind of judgment in Romans 2:5 and 6: "But after thy hardness and impenitent heart treasurest up unto thyself wrath against the day of wrath and revelation of the righteous judgment of God; who will render to every man according to his deeds."

Does God let man get by with sin? Think of the terrible and far-reaching judgment when man sinned in Eden. The whole human race is still under that judgment.

Think of the judgment of the Flood. God waited in patience while the ark was being built. Each day brought opportunity for repentance. But the day came when God closed the door. Opportunities were past. The floods came, and a whole world perished.

And what of the nation Israel? For centuries God pleaded with them to turn from idolatry and other sins. When they kept saying no, He brought their nation down to dust.

Oh, my friends, God so hates sin that He poured out wrath and judgment on His Son. Never forget, the cross of Jesus Christ is final proof that God is a God of holiness and justice.

Revelation, chapter 6, speaks of a coming day when kings and the great and the rich and the mighty and the slaves and the free will hide themselves in caves, calling to the mountains and rocks, "Fall on us, and hide us from the face of him that sitteth on the throne, and from the wrath of the Lamb: for the great day of his wrath is come; and who shall be able to stand?" (Rev 6:16-17).

Yes, we need to remember these solemn things: the greatness and glory of God, the sovereign rights of God, the great judgments of God. But we need to remember one thing more.

4. REMEMBER THE LOVE AND GRACE OF GOD

God is holy, but He reaches down to us in pure love and grace. As Psalm 103 reminds us, "He hath not dealt with us after our sins, nor rewarded us according to our iniquities" (v. 10).

Isaiah, chapter 1, pleads, "Though your sins be as scarlet, they shall be as white as snow; though they be red like crimson, they shall be as wool" (v. 18).

The great good news of the Gospel is that God became flesh in the person of Jesus Christ. He bore our sins on the cross. He suffered and died and was buried and raised again, that we might have forgiveness.

CONCLUSION

My friend, is Jesus Christ your personal Saviour? Are you trusting and serving Him? You cannot receive His gift of forgiveness and everlasting life unless you receive Him as your own Saviour.

There are so many who have never settled their account with God. There are so many who do not have assurance of salvation. Yet God wants you to be sure. There are so many who have given their life to Christ, but who have tried to take it back again. They want it for themselves.

Life is not just food and drink. It is not merely a job and a car and a vacation once or twice a year. It is not even the "good things" of life. Before this time next year, thousands of us alive now will have passed from this life forever. Make this a real Memorial Day, a day of remembering. Remember God's greatness, His rights, His judgments, and His marvelous grace, and live by faith in Christ with eternity in view.

TWELVE

WHICH WAY, AMERICA?

Introduction

The United States of America is actually a very young nation. In fact, our entire two hundred years of history have been spanned by the lives of just four presidents. When Thomas Jefferson died, Abraham Lincoln was a young man of seventeen. Lincoln's life was short, but when he died, Woodrow Wilson was a boy of eight. By the time the nation mourned for President Wilson, Gerald Ford had reached the age of ten.

Yes, the United States has risen rapidly. But could our fall be just as quick? Let's look the future full in the face and ask, "Which way, America?"

Beginning September 1, 1976, a ban on fireworks went into effect across the United States. From now on, July 4 should be a great deal quieter than ever before. Actually, fireworks, for safety reasons, have been in full retreat for many years. But another kind of quietness is far less reassuring. For many people, there is a lack of enthusiasm in celebrating our birthday. The big bang has been quite subdued. Some have little taste for a lighthearted celebration. In fact, instead of a birthday party atmosphere, there's a serious mood across the nation.

This is the feeling coming from many directions. *Time* magazine said, "The belief that America . . . has created a kind of heaven on earth, has been badly damaged."[1] People are disillusioned and confused about their lives and the future of this country. A recent Harris survey placed Congress at the bottom of the list of United States institutions in which the public has

1. Henry Grunwald, "The Morning After the Fourth: Have We Kept Our Promise?" *Time* 106 (July 14, 1975):19.

some degree of confidence. Only 9 percent of the American people express a great deal of confidence in our congressmen. The executive branch rates only slightly higher with a confidence rating of 11 percent.

Public confidence in nongovernmental groups and individuals is little better. Only 16 percent show confidence in people running major businesses. Only 24 percent have confidence in those leading organized religion. Twenty-three percent have confidence in military leaders, and only 20 percent have confidence in the nation's press. Voters are disappointed and apathetic. We are not experiencing a material crisis, despite high prices and joblessness, but a spiritual and psychological depression. People are not happy. Many ordinary people have felt these things for some time. The United States, in spite of our incredible past, is facing some serious problems.

As Archibald MacLeish has said, the founding of America was more than a political event. It was a promise, a promise to the colonists and to the world at large, that people could govern themselves, that they could live in freedom and equality. The assumption was that they would act in accord with reason and with equity, and out of this came what we often call "the American dream."

This was the hope and dream that we and our children could reach a level of well-being and opportunity such as other nations have never known. But now many people wonder whether or not our American dream has vanished, not so much because of enemies without but because of our weaknesses within.

What is this condition which many sense as very real, yet still undefined and still untreated? Before trying to answer, let me mention some of the more obvious symptoms of our national condition.

The first is *disillusionment and cynicism.* Some have lost their enthusiasm and optimism about the future. There is a lack of old-fashioned trust and confidence in one another.

The second is a *loss of national integrity and character.* Every-

112

one knows crime is increasing. Violence throws a shadow over the security of our citizens. Stealing is epidemic. Divorce is shattering marriages at an astounding rate.

The third is *preoccupation with unworthy things* such as materialism, sex, pleasure, satisfaction here and now without regard for others. We have lost much of the will to sacrifice for the good of others and for the national good.

The fourth is—and I am persuaded that this is basic—we have *lost our fear of God* and our awareness of His sovereignty.

As a nation, how far can we go before we reach the point of no return? Some believe we have already passed that point, and that even now we lack the will and the determination to change. No nation has ever known just when it has arrived at that place until it was too late!

When I speak of turning back, I do not mean mere reform or self-correction. I personally believe that it is too late for that. I am talking about a sincere turning back to God for divine help and intervention.

Can a nation cry out to God for help when the essence of its problem lies in its lack of will to follow God? The answer is yes. God hears the weakest cry, and He responds to need. Listen to the cry of the prophet Jeremiah in Lamentations 5:21: "Turn thou us unto thee, O LORD, and we shall be turned; renew our days as of old."

This is America's need as she celebrates her birthday!

This same prayer is found in Psalm 80. Fervently and earnestly, the psalmist prays, "Turn us again, O God, and cause thy face to shine; and we shall be saved" (v. 3). This Old Testament verse tells us three vital things.

1. WE NEED TO BE TURNED

We need to be turned; we need God's help. We cannot turn ourselves by laws or legislation or education or by any kind of rational choice. Our beloved America needs a change of heart.

113

Our problems are the problems of the inner life of sinful wills and sinful ways.

The bitter truth is that though America once knew God, at least to fear Him, in two hundred years we have largely turned away. This is not to say that ours has ever been a wholly Christian nation. But we have known the moral and spiritual strength that comes from the fear of God, awareness of the Bible, and overruling faith in Jesus Christ.

In two hundred years we have moved a long way toward pride and trust in men. We have not feared to push aside the Word of God. We have magnified the rights of men and minimized the rights of God. Worst of all, we have heard the Gospel of Jesus Christ, but as a nation we have esteemed it lightly.

Romans 1:18 states, "For the wrath of God is revealed from heaven against all ungodliness and unrighteousness of men, who hold the truth in unrighteousness." America's deepest sin is its lack of esteem for the Word of God. Although we have known the Gospel, we have held the truth carelessly, and now the night is closing in.

Not only does America need to be turned.

2. WE NEED GOD'S TURNING

We need God's turning. Psalm 80 says, "Turn us again, O God of hosts" (v. 7). Only God can meet our need. He is the God of the hosts of heaven, and yet He knows the human heart.

And only God can change the heart. Knowledge cannot do it. Experience will not do it. Law cannot do it. We can try to profit from past mistakes. We can even make good resolutions. We can bind ourselves with restraints. But without the mighty Gospel of the cross, nothing will save us.

There is really only one doorway to eternal life. That door is Jesus Christ. Jesus said in John 10:9, "I am the door: by me if any man enter in, he shall be saved."

Jesus Christ did not die for nations but for people, who constitute the nations. No nation can rise above the faith and character of its individual citizens.

America has a choice to make! Either we must turn back to God by faith in Jesus Christ, or we will join the fate of other long-forgotten nations.

The Word of God warns plainly in Psalm 9:17, "The wicked shall be turned into hell, and all the nations that forget God." Let me repeat, "All the nations that forget God."

But there is hope. The prayer of Psalm 80 promises that if a nation cries out to God, we shall be saved.

3. WE SHALL BE SAVED

Yes, God can meet our nation's need. If we sincerely call out to God to "turn us again" and cause His face to shine upon us, "we shall be saved." That was the experience of Israel. Seven times in the period recorded in the book of Judges, Israel fell away from God. Seven times she knew the bitterness of bondage. Seven times, in tears, Israel turned to God. And God delivered her every time.

Yes, God responds to nations. Hear what He says in Jeremiah 18:8: "If that nation, against whom I have pronounced, turn from their evil, I will repent of the evil that I thought to do unto them." Much more is involved than just a withholding of judgment. Jeremiah 24:7 says, "And I will give them an heart to know me, that I am the LORD: and they shall be my people, and I will be their God: for they shall return unto me with their whole heart." My friend, this is what America needs: a change of heart. And only God can give that.

Historian Arnold Toynbee pointed out that nineteen major civilizations have existed since the beginning of time. Only five remain today, of which our Western civilization is one.

But you say, "We cannot turn the tide of unbelief." No, but God can ! I think of Nineveh, the capital of the great Assyrian Empire. Like modern New York, it was a complex of cities with walls nearly eight miles in circumference. Who doesn't know the story of Jonah, the reluctant prophet, who sailed the other way and refused to go preach repentance to that great city? We know all about the great fish which swallowed Jonah, only to cast him upon the shore.

But what happened next? It was to Nineveh that God sent Jonah when he was finally ready to obey. His message from God was plain and to the point. "Yet forty days, and Nineveh shall be overthrown" (3:4). The Bible tells us the whole city repented, from the greatest to the least. And God, in grace and mercy, spared the city for more than another century.

CONCLUSION

We do not need a prophet like Jonah. We have had hundreds of godly prophets. We have had the open Word of God. But we need to hear God's voice and turn to Him before it is too late. The future of our beloved United States of America may lie in the hands of our present generation. Before the next generation takes its place, America may be past the point of no return. How will you cast your vote?

Can we be trusted with the future of "the American dream"? Even more important, do American Christians have the vision and the faith to intercede and urge our nation to turn back to her rightful God and Sovereign? May we pray with the psalmist, "Turn us again, O God, and cause thy face to shine; and we shall be saved" (Psalm 80:3).

The Saviour is waiting. When the prodigal son, in the gospel of Luke, started for home, the father *ran* to meet him. If we individually turn in repentance, God's blessing *will* be upon us "and we shall be saved." As one person, will you make your decision to obey God's will? And as thousands of individuals turn to Jesus Christ, America will turn.

THIRTEEN

THE LABORER

INTRODUCTION

Each year, on the first Monday in September, America celebrates Labor Day. It's a day of parades, picnics, and political
speeches. It is a time when we pay special recognition to the
millions of Americans who are a part of this nation's mighty
working force.

Edwin Markham, in his poem "The Man with the Hoe," paints
a picture of the laborer.

> Bowed by the weight of centuries he leans
> Upon his hoe and gazes on the ground,
> The emptiness of ages in his face,
> And on his back the burden of the world.

1. WHY DO WE LABOR?

Throughout history, labor has been man's chief activity.
Thomas Carlyle put it simply: "Labor is life."

According to Webster, labor always involves either physical
or mental exertion. As a result of man's sin in the Garden of
Eden, God told Adam that he would earn his bread by the sweat
of his face (Gen 3:19). The ground would bring forth thorns
and thistles, and man would be required to labor in the field.
Gone were the ideal conditions of Eden. Instead of Adam's original occupation of "dressing" the garden, he and his descendants
would now engage in burdensome toil.

This burdensome toil was and is the result of the curse God
measured out in Genesis 3: "Cursed is the ground for thy sake; in
sorrow shalt thou eat of it all the days of thy life" (v. 17). Sorrow is inevitable; it is a reality in each and every life. It is as inescapable as the toil in which each one must engage.

God told Adam that all his life would be filled with labor. He
would toil until the day he returned to the dust of the earth from

119

which he was taken. It is interesting, yet ironic, to realize that that which we honor this week—labor—is a direct result of the judgment God passed upon man in the Garden of Eden. It is the result of sin!

The apostle Paul reminds us that all of creation groans under the blight of sin. In Romans 8:22, he writes, "For we know that the whole creation groaneth and travaileth in pain together until now." The Scripture plainly indicates that God intended for people to toil and work. The Bible sets forth the principle of labor.

Throughout the history of our country, the importance of labor has always been recognized. From its inception, this nation has been dedicated to the principle of hard work. As of Labor Day, 1976, the civilian labor force of the United States totaled close to 100 million persons. Each year our nation requires thousands of new engineers, nurses, mechanics, and sales personnel to fill the job openings developed by an expanding economy.

It is the labor of untold millions of men and women which has brought unequaled prosperity to this great land of ours. And only as we remember the value of true, hard work can we remain a strong and determined people.

Unfortunately, some people today have little respect for an honest day's work. There is a sign at the entrance of a great manufacturing plant that reads, "If you are like a wheelbarrow, going no farther than you are pushed, you need not apply for work here." Many people, it seems, need to be pushed in order to accomplish anything worthwhile.

Someone has said there are three kinds of people: those who make things happen; those who watch things happen; and those who have no idea what has happened. Today we need less watchers and more doers. It was the wise king Solomon who said, "Whatsoever thy hand findeth to do, do it with thy might" (Eccles 9:10). God's principle for man is work. God intended for us to work.

Labor Day is the day which is set aside to honor the millions of this nation's working men and women. In many cities and towns, there will be parades and special observances. But for most people, the day is dedicated to rest and recreation. It is an extra day of escape from the hectic work week.

To many, however, rest and relaxation will not come. For millions, the burdens of life will not be lifted simply because of another holiday. For despite the gigantic strides made by and for the working people of this country, despite the shorter work weeks and the greater salaries, men and women everywhere are burdened down with cares.

2. GOD'S CALL TO THE LABORER

It was to this kind of person that the invitation of Jesus was directed in Matthew 11: "Come unto me, all ye that labour and are heavy laden, and I will give you rest. Take my yoke upon you, and learn of me; for I am meek and lowly in heart: and ye shall find rest unto your souls. For my yoke is easy, and my burden is light" (vv. 28-30).

Who are the heavy ladened? On this occasion, Jesus was speaking of those who were not familiar with the grace of God. Isaiah referred to the people of his day as, "a people laden with iniquity" (Isa 1:4).

This Labor Day finds many people trapped in the web of sin and neglect of God.

Robert Burns, at a time when he was overcome by alcoholism, wrote, "O Life! thou art a galling load,/ Along a rough, a weary road,/ To wretches such as I." Robert Burns was obviously a man who was "heavy laden."

In his sarcastic description of life, William Shakespeare wrote, "Life's but a walking shadow, a poor player,/ That struts and frets his hour upon the stage,/ And then is heard no more; it is a tale/ Told by an idiot, full of sound and fury."

Atlas with the world on his shoulders had a light load compared to those away from God.

121

My friend, there are many today who "labor and are heavy laden." Many today are burdened by a lack of purpose. For them, life has no meaning and the future offers nothing but futility.

But, you ask, why is this so? Why are people heavy ladened and out of step with God? The answer is that God made man in *His* image, with rational and moral faculties. Man is a unique creation of God, different from all other creatures. And a man who fails to recognize God, a man who refuses to acknowledge God for who He is, cannot live with himself. Because of this, there can be no rest until we are reconciled or united with God through the person of Jesus Christ.

In the very beginning, God and man were friends. They walked and talked together. The Garden of Eden was a beautiful portrait of unity and friendship. Adam and God walked and talked together; they were partners.

But then rebellion entered the picture. Adam said, "I'll do things my way, I'll do what *I* want to do." As a result, men and women are weary, frustrated, and bored. They are "heavy laden" because of the rebellion and sin in their lives. Apart from Jesus Christ, life is a burden; it is a "galling load" filled with bitterness and disappointment.

3. THE GOSPEL AND THE DIGNITY OF LABOR

Labor Day is a special day on which we recognize the dignity of work and the rights of the worker. Jesus believed in the dignity of labor. He was concerned about the worker and his work. In Luke 10:7, he said, "The labourer is worthy of his hire."

Today, millions of people around the world belong to labor unions. Many of you reading this book are union members. Did you realize that the trade unions as we know them were originally an outgrowth of the spiritual revivals of John and Charles Wesley? In the early 1700s, working conditions in Britain were seemingly hopeless. Men worked sixteen or more hours a day six days a week. Little children as young as ten years of age worked long hours deep in mines and in the factories. Women worked. Many died from accidents or simply from exhaustion. The working person, man, woman, or child, was little more than a slave to be exploited. Drunkenness, immorality, and hopelessness abounded.

History tells us that social liberty in England began as a result of a great return to God under the preaching of John Wesley. Men such as Bishop William Wilberforce and Lord Shaftesbury began to force legislation which brought relief to the working classes. Whenever and wherever the Gospel of Jesus Christ is truly preached, then as now, it results in earthly as well as heavenly changes.

4. LABOR AND THE WARNING OF GOD'S WORD

As we study the Word of God, we find that the Bible speaks to both the employer and the employee. Each has his responsibilities to fulfill. In James 5, wealthy employers are warned of God's judgment upon their evil deeds. They had spent their lives on earth having fun and satisfying their every whim at the expense of their employees. To these evil men, James declares, "Behold, the hire of the labourers who have reaped down your fields, which is of you kept back by fraud, crieth: and the cries of them which have reaped are entered into the ears of the Lord of sabaoth" (James 5:4).

James is simply saying that God hears the cry of the laborer who is cheated. God is aware of injustice, and He will be the final Judge.

In the book of Exodus, God's people Israel were being exploited by the Egyptians. In chapter 3, the Lord said, "I have surely seen the affliction of my people which are in Egypt, and have heard their cry by reason of their taskmasters; for I know their sorrows" (Exod 3:7). God sees, He hears, and He knows when a worker is treated unfairly. God cares about you, my friend.

At the same time, God also sees the laborer. The worker who

loafs on the job is guilty of stealing. The employee who pads his expense account or does outside business on company time, God sees. Failure to put in a good day's work is dishonest, and God knows.

No matter what your position this Labor Day weekend, Christ's invitation is still extended today. To employer and employee alike, Jesus says, "Come . . . and I will give you rest" (Matt 11:28). To the tired farmer coming from his fields, Jesus says, "Come." To the merchant with his wares, the fisherman with his nets, the laborer with his heavy load, to all these He says, "Come unto me . . . and I will give you rest." No matter how others have treated you, I will give you rest.

To those who labor, Jesus offers rest. Not simply physical comfort and refreshment, but eternal rest for their souls.

5. How to enter God's rest

As a young man, Augustine was literally exhausted from his pursuit of sinful lusts. After he had repented of his sin and turned to Jesus Christ, he said, "Our hearts were made for Thee, O Lord, and they are restless until they rest in Thee."

My friend, are you restless? Is there something missing in your life? Do you know anything about God's rest? Are you burdened down by a load of guilt and despair? Jesus offers the same invitation to you today that He offered two thousand years ago. "Come unto me, all ye that labour and are heavy laden, and I will give you rest." Won't you come to Him today? No matter who you are, no matter what you have done, Jesus waits to receive you today.

You can enter into God's rest by acknowledging your sinful condition and by acknowledging Jesus Christ as God's provision for your sin. Accept the rest that comes from being at one with God.

6. How to enjoy God's rest

Matthew 11:29 also states our future privilege and responsi-

124

bility: "Take my yoke upon you, and learn of me . . . and ye shall find rest unto your souls." After receiving the Saviour, as partners with God, we are to *take* and *learn*. "Take my yoke" and "learn of me."

Our Lord Jesus was always submissive to God the Father. He said, "I do always those things that please him" (John 8:29). My meat is to do the will of him that sent me, and to finish his work" (John 4:34).

Our yoke is to do the will of God. When we do this wholeheartedly, we find that His yoke is easy and His burden is light.

FOURTEEN

THANKFULNESS: THE ROAD BACK TO GOD

INTRODUCTION

Three and a half centuries ago, a little band of men and women joined their hands and hearts in America's first Thanksgiving. With Indian guests, they gathered around a table for the New World's first Thanksgiving dinner. Measured by our standards, they did not have too much. Harvest was in, and they were grateful to God. But their needs were great, and there were no supermarkets down the street. Cold, hunger, and sickness threatened their very lives.

How far, in some ways, we have come since that first day of thanks in 1621. Today more than two hundred million people populate our land. We produce more food, more fuel, more finished products than any nation in the world. Measured by dollars and cents, our gross national product exceeds one trillion dollars and is climbing every year. Science and industry do our bidding. We can even send men to the moon.

But like the Pilgrims, we have great needs. We are concerned for energy and a growing number of critical materials. The richest nation in the world is perplexed and troubled by crucial shortages. Inflation is pushing up the cost of nearly everything the average family wants and needs. We have higher wages and more dollars, but they are buying less and less all the time. More serious still, our nation appears to stand at a crossroad of its history. The winds of moral and spiritual pollution threaten our future.

At such a time as this, real thankfulness may be just the turning point we need. For thankfulness to God can be a long and

127

important step back toward things we have forgotten. Why should we be thankful to God?

1. BECAUSE WE OWE IT TO HIM

In Revelation, chapters 4 and 5, we catch two glimpses of praise around the throne of heaven. In Revelation 4:11, we hear the song, "Thou art worthy, O Lord, to receive glory and honour and power: for thou hast created all things, and for thy pleasure they are and were created."

Have you ever considered this truth? God is worthy of our thanks because He is our Maker. "Know ye that the LORD he is God," says Psalm 100, "it is he that hath made us, and not we ourselves" (v. 3).

All that we are and have is from God's hand. The strength we have, the food and shelter that maintain our lives, the blood and breath within our bodies, the very time we have, here and in eternity to come, are a gift of our Creator. He is our Provider and Sustainer. Every necessity of life comes from His hand.

But God is more! In Revelation 5:12, we hear all heaven sing another song: "Worthy is the Lamb that was slain to receive power, and riches, and wisdom, and strength, and honor, and glory, and blessing." How thankful we should be that our Creator God is also our Redeemer. He was slain for our sins.

But there is another reason why we should give thanks to God.

2. BECAUSE TO ACKNOWLEDGE HIS GOODNESS IS TO SEE HIM AS HE IS

When you are thankful, you see God's love and goodness. Your eyes are wide open to His judgments. You are receptive to His will. Unthankfulness, by contrast, blinds the eyes. An unthankful person may not even know that God is in the picture.

An unthankful nation is no better. An unthankful nation is an unthinking nation, and its people are in mortal danger.

America's deepest problems come from blindness to the goodness and power of God. These are the products of unthankfulness.

What should we be thankful for? For the fulfilling of the needs of life, for food to feed our families, and for the means to help the hungry.

Do you give thanks before eating? Jesus did. Again and again, we read that He lifted His eyes toward heaven and offered thanks before beginning the simplest meal. We should be thankful every day, not simply now and then. We should be thankful for clothing to keep our families warm and houses to give them shelter, for life's privileges and freedoms. We should be thankful for God Himself. But are we?

Some months ago, a college student was deeply troubled. He was doing well in school. He had no special money problems. But he was depressed and even fearful. Life had no meaning and no purpose.

Then something happened. While reading a book on prophecy, the things he had learned about God, the Bible, and Jesus Christ began to fit together. A new light came into his life as he realized that the Gospel is all true. He began to understand God's love in that Christ died for him to give him a place in His eternal plan. That very night he confessed Christ as his Saviour and began a new and vital relationship, a new life!

This young man came alive when he saw that God was in the picture. It happens every day when people come to Jesus Christ. "The people which sat in darkness saw great light," we read in Matthew's gospel, "and to them which sat in the region and shadow of death light is sprung up" (Matt 4:16).

Has this light come into your life? If it has, be thankful every day you live.

We should be thankful for many other reasons, but let me mention just one more.

3. BECAUSE ALL THE CIRCUMSTANCES OF LIFE ARE IN GOD'S HANDS

First Thessalonians 5:18 commands, "In every thing give thanks." This means in every circumstance, in every situation. Only the child of God can really do this. But if you belong to Christ, this is your privilege. God will make all things work together for good. Nothing He does is unplanned or capricious.

Times of tears will come, but as we trust and thank Him in "all things," He will fill our lives to overflowing. We need to be thankful in all things, to recognize the hand of God in sorrow as well as joy.

In contrast, how careful we should be about unthankfulness. To become unthankful is to become nearsighted, even blind. The unthankful person no longer sees God's goodness to him. In time, he may forget that he needs God or that God even exists. And when men give up God, God will, in time, give up with men.

What happens in this tragic situation? The description of Romans 1:21 is terribly graphic. "Because that, when they knew God, they glorified him not as God, *neither were thankful;* but became vain [empty, or foolish] in their imaginations, and their foolish heart was darkened" (italics added).

Verse 26 continues, "For this cause God gave them up unto vile affections." And in verse 28, we find this added statement: "And even as they did not like to retain God in their knowledge, God gave them over to a reprobate mind"—a mind incapable of good.

My friend, the price of unthankfulness is high. You cannot ignore God's rights, God's sovereignty, God's loving-kindness, without losing touch with the One on whom your very life depends.

Can a nation slip off into darkness because it is unthankful? It can! It can! America's deepest troubles can be traced to unthankfulness and the folly of forgetting God.

130

Perhaps we have drifted farther than we know in the past three hundred and fifty years. In all their poverty, the Pilgrims were rich because they saw God clearly. Their faith was in Him. They looked to Him for help and sustenance, and He helped them.

Not so with America today. We have lost much of our basic trust in God. No longer do we clearly see His wisdom, power, and love. We have put our trust in men and they are failing. We have laid aside the Bible, not only in our schools, but in our homes and in our public life as well. Small wonder we have lost our concept of sin, our condemnation of wrongdoing. Bloodshed and violence fill our land. Again and again, we have affirmed the rights of men at the cost of God's rights. We have sold our godly birthright for humanism's pottage.

If God were to speak to America through a prophet, He could say to us as He did of Israel through Jeremiah, "For my people have committed two evils; they have forsaken me the fountain of living waters, and hewed them out cisterns, broken cisterns, that can hold no water" (Jer 2:13).

Where have we missed the way? We have made the fatal error of thinking we can be wise and good without God's help, that we can be great and happy and still reject salvation on God's terms. We must turn back. There is no better place to begin than to look up in gratitude this Thanksgiving and renew our faith in God.

CONCLUSION

Apart from the national issue, there is a personal question here. How is it with you this Thanksgiving season? Are you thankful? Can you look up and thank God every day, even sometimes through tears?

It's not a question of how much we have. Some of the most joyous and thankful people that I know live in very modest surroundings. They eat simply. They seldom take a trip. Some of them know infirmity. Why are they thankful? Because they live in the sunshine of God's love.

Are you one of God's thankful people? If not, you should be. God loves you. He made you and redeemed you. He wants to make your eternal soul "shine as the brightness of the firmament; and . . . as the stars for ever and ever" (Dan 12:3).

Jesus Christ came to separate us from our sins. He died on the cross so that you and I might know true forgiveness. Have you let Jesus Christ do what He came to do? In thankfulness receive God's "unspeakable gift."

FIFTEEN

THE FIRST CHRISTMAS

Christmas is probably the happiest day of the year!

Around the world for millions of young and old alike, this special day will again bring joy and happiness. Christmas Day is a special day. There is gladness and singing; there are decorations and presents. And, of course, there will be that special meal and a visit from all the relatives. These are some of the things that make Christmas a day to remember.

For the Christian, Christmas means a lot more than gifts and decorations. Christmas is a great day of joy, victory, and deliverance for the true believer. Dr. Robert Lee has said, "Christmas is the joyous celebration of eternity's intersection with time: 'When the fulness of the time was come, God sent forth his Son, made of a woman' (Gal 4:4)."[1]

Yes, the first Christmas celebration ever held was because of the birth of Jesus Christ. Any other reason for celebrating Christmas is false, foolish, and even sacrilegious!

Let's go back in our minds to the night when Jesus was born. On that first Christmas, there were all the elements of a magnificent worship service. What do we know about the first Christmas service? Look with me for a few moments at what the gospel writer, Luke, has to say about the most important night in history.

1. THE AUDIENCE

First, we read about the audience on that first Christmas. Who were they? "There were in the same country *shepherds* abiding in the field, keeping watch over their flock by night" (Luke

1. Walter B. Knight, *Knight's Illustrations for Today* (Chicago: Moody, 1970), p. 46.

2:8, italics added). That's remarkable! The greatest news story of all ages came to common, hardworking shepherds!

The life of a shepherd was not an easy one. Their work demanded long hours. It meant cold nights and separation from their families. They earned their living watching sheep in a rough, rugged land, a land inhabited by wild animals. Authorities tell us that these shepherds probably did not even own the sheep they tended. Rather, they were lowly, ill-clad hired hands of the religious leaders who raised animals for sacrifice in the Temple.

The greatest news story of history came not to the pious Levites, or to the scholarly religious leaders, or to the Roman governor, or even to King Herod. No, it came to the shepherds of the hills.

But why did God announce such great news to these humble laborers? Were they the only people awake at that important hour? I think He announced it to them because God delights to reveal His Good News to the lowly. The great commoner Abraham Lincoln once said, "God must love the plain people because He made so many of them."

The apostle Paul wrote, "For ye see your calling, brethren, how that not many wise men after the flesh, not many mighty, not many noble, are called: but God hath chosen the foolish things of the world to confound the wise; and God hath chosen the weak things of the world to confound the things which are mighty; and base things which are not, to bring to nought things that are: that no flesh should glory in his presence" (1 Cor 1:26-29).

That is often the way God works. Why? That no flesh should glory. That no mortal man might boast. Can you imagine how a public relations firm might have handled this event? It certainly would have been the opposite of God's approach.

When God chose a leader for Israel, He found Moses on the back side of the desert. When He chose a king, it was the youngest son of the smallest tribe—David. When Jesus chose His twelve disciples, He chose fishermen and tax collectors. Often, He chose the humble and the lowly.

Could it be that the shepherds of the first Christmas were chosen to receive the angel's message because they were humble men of simple origin? Yes, I believe so. There is something rugged and real about the common man. There is an honesty which can respond to God's revelation in a genuine way.

But more, to choose the shepherds on that first Christmas was also fitting because Jesus often pictured Himself as the Good Shepherd. Jesus says, in John's gospel, "I am the good shepherd, and know my sheep, and am known of mine" (John 10:14). Peter wrote, "When the chief Shepherd shall appear, ye shall receive a crown of glory that fadeth not away" (1 Pet 5:4). In Luke 15, it was the shepherd who went to seek and save the lost.

Incredible as it may seem, the first audience at that first Christmas service was made up of rough, rugged, lowly shepherds.

2. THE PREACHER

Second, notice the preacher at that first Christmas service: the angel of the Lord. In Luke's gospel we read, "And, lo, the angel of the Lord came upon them, and the glory of the Lord shone round about them: and they were sore afraid" (Luke 2:9).

What a contrasting sight that must have been—the lowly shepherds confronted by the angel of the Lord. And when the angel came upon them, the shepherds sensed that they were in the presence of God, for that is what "the glory of the Lord" shining around them signified. You see, to any Jew, the presence of God was thought of as a great light known as the Shekinah glory. This symbolic light began back in the days of the tabernacle in the wilderness. Man could not see God Himself, but he could see the light of God's presence.

At that first Christmas service, the angel of the Lord appeared to the shepherds, and they were suddenly surrounded by the glory of the Lord. Oh, that we today might be aware of God's

137

glory. God *has* revealed Himself. He has intervened in time and space.

The shepherds saw the revelation of God's presence and they were terrified. They were overcome with fear because their sinfulness was so obvious in the pure light of God's glory.

Of course they were terrified. The holy presence of God always strikes conviction in sinful man. Job experienced that fear when he said, "I have heard of thee by the hearing of the ear: but now mine eye seeth thee. Wherefore I abhor myself, and repent in dust and ashes" (Job 42:5-6). Isaiah, too, when he saw the glory of God filling the Temple, could only say, "Woe is me! for I am undone" (Isa 6:5).

The holiness of God and the sinfulness of man present such a contrast that man must shrink away in awe. The shepherds were afraid as "the glory of the Lord shone round about them."

3. The message

Third, notice the message that the angel of the Lord delivered at that first Christmas service. Luke relates that "the angel said unto them, Fear not: for, behold, I bring you good tidings of great joy, which shall be to all people. For unto you is born this day in the city of David a Saviour, which is Christ the Lord" (Luke 2:10-11).

At the very moment of the shepherds' fear came the joyous message of Christmas: "Fear not. . . . For unto you is born . . . a Saviour, which is Christ the Lord." The Gospel of Jesus Christ is the cure for fear.

A certain degree of fear is a normal reaction in life. In fact, it often protects us from wrong. Abnormal fear, on the other hand, tangles the mind. It destroys peace and drains our energies. More people commit suicide than die from the five most communicable diseases. Why? Because of abnormal fear! One-half of the hospital beds in the United States are occupied by mental patients who suffer from abnormal fears. A well-known doctor told me recently that 60 percent of his patients could cure *themselves* if they could get rid of fear.

What is the medicine for fear? It is the message of Christmas, that a Saviour is born. A Saviour who can forgive you of sin. A Saviour who can give you new life. A Saviour who can strengthen you, guide you, and bring order and purpose into your life.

Paul wrote, "For God hath not given us the spirit of fear; but of power, and of love, and of a sound mind" (2 Tim 1:7). The angel's message at that first Christmas service was, "Fear not!" And in this day of fear—fear of death, fear of war, fear of one another—that message is more relevant than it has ever been before.

But after stressing the negative, "Fear not," the angel accented the positive words of the Christmas message: "I bring you good tidings of great joy." That first Christmas message was one of great joy. Why? Because Jesus came to provide a way out of our dilemma. Jesus Christ came to provide forgiveness and life everlasting.

My friend, Christianity overflows with joy. God's people are to be the happiest people you will find. Whatever your capacity is today, God can fill you with Himself. David wrote, "Be glad . . . rejoice . . . and shout for joy, all ye that are upright in heart" (Psalm 32:11). To the defeated and discouraged, Jesus spoke words of joy: "In the world ye shall have tribulation: but be of good cheer; I have overcome the world" (John 16:33).

Do you know victory today? Have you experienced the joy of that first Christmas message? The New Testament begins with the angels singing a message of comfort and closes with God's children singing joyously around God's throne. True Christianity abounds with joy! Do you know this contagious, irrepressible, holy joy?

4. THE RESPONSE

I believe there is an aspect of the Christmas story which is neglected. It has to do with the fact that those common shepherds had to act upon what they heard on that night long ago. There was a response to that first Christmas service. It was a great thing to hear the news concerning the birth of the Saviour, but mere knowledge was not enough. Could those shepherds have gone back to their "business as usual" after hearing the announcement of the angel? Of course not! They could never, never be the same.

They made an immediate decision. The Bible tells us that they "came with haste" (Luke 2:16). They didn't ask questions. They were fully persuaded, and they acted upon the message which had been given to them. It meant, of course, that they had to leave the sheep, but obviously they knew that what they were about to do was far more important than their flocks.

Perhaps you today have heard this Christmas message; you have realized your need; but you have never made a decision to follow Jesus Christ. You may be reluctant to act on the Good News of Jesus Christ because of your job. Perhaps family ties are standing in the way. Maybe you consider the cost of following Christ too great. My friend, leave the sheep behind and come with haste to Christ today.

The Bible tells us that the shepherds hurried to the village of Bethlehem "and found Mary, and Joseph, and the babe lying in a manger" (Luke 2:16). God rewarded them with the realization of their faith, for they saw their Messiah, the One who had come to be their Saviour.

We are also told that the shepherds immediately shared their discovery. The Good News was too good to keep. My friend, it is wrong to keep silent when we have met the Saviour. The shepherds "made known abroad the saying which was told them concerning this child" (Luke 2:17).

Luke continues by saying that the shepherds "returned, glorifying and praising God for all the things that they had heard and seen" (Luke 2:20). They went back to their common toil, but never to be the same. They had been transformed.

140

Yes, when you receive Jesus Christ as your Lord and Saviour, praising God becomes the very emphasis of your life. Jesus Christ makes the most common of tasks exciting. Glory and praise to God become as natural as breathing.

CONCLUSION

Have you experienced this kind of life? You can! By acknowledging that the Christ of Christmas came to be *your* Saviour from sin, and by committing your life to Him, you may know eternal life. Why not receive Him right now and make this Christmas the most dynamic and happiest you have ever experienced.

SIXTEEN

THE WISDOM
OF THE WISE MEN

Introduction

No doubt from your earliest recollections of the Christmas story, you recall hearing of the wise men who came to visit the newborn Christ Child. Each of us has sung many times the carols that tell their story. We can even visualize these imposing potentates riding their camels through the desert sands, dressed in their colorful kingly robes.

But who were they? And what do we really know about them?

Really, we do not know a great deal about these wise men. We are not sure who they were. We only have a general idea of where they came from. We can only surmise as to how they knew to follow the star in the heavens. In fact, we don't even know how many there were.

They seem to come out of nowhere, pay their respects to the Christ Child, and then disappear. Matthew's gospel gives us the record of their journey. "Now when Jesus was born in Bethlehem of Judaea in the days of Herod the king, behold, there came wise men from the east to Jerusalem, saying, Where is he that is born King of the Jews? for we have seen his star in the east, and are come to worship him" (Matt 2:1-2).

Who were these wise men? Probably, they were religious philosophers from Persia who, in their contact with the Jews scattered throughout the East, had become familiar with the Jewish Law and prophecies. For many years the report that a world conqueror would be born in Judea had been circulated throughout the Eastern nations. Many Gentiles of that day prayed for a "deliverer" to come, for they clearly realized that their heathen gods could not save them.

143

Two thousand years before, God had made a promise to Abraham, the father of the Hebrew people, which said, "In thee shall all families of the earth be blessed" (Gen 12:3). The prophet Isaiah, too, had elaborated on the blessing promised to Abraham when he wrote, "And the Gentiles shall come to thy light, and kings to the brightness of thy rising" (Isa 60:3).

Although these wise men were Gentiles, they obviously had a great interest in the fulfillment of God's promise to Abraham. They were intelligent and searching men, and they believed the Word of God as they had heard it.

But even though we are not given a great amount of information about these men, we can determine why they were called "wise men" simply by understanding what they did.

1. THEY FOLLOWED GOD'S DIVINE LEADING

The wisdom of the wise men centered first in the fact that they followed God's divine leading.

How they learned of the prophecy concerning the Messiah, we do not know. What we do know is that they believed that God would lead them to the Christ Child. It was natural that these wise men should be familiar with the heavenly bodies. Undoubtedly they had searched the skies for many days seeking a sign of the birth of the King. To their receptive minds, the guiding star was the finger of God moving across the heavens, and they followed that star.

Are you sensitive to God's leading? This truth has not changed from that day to this. The truly wise man is the one who follows the leading of God. These learned men from the East were not given a road map to follow; they were simply given a star. They followed the light they had, and God honored them for it.

Someone has said that, "the way to see far ahead in the will of God is to go ahead just as far as you can see." That is so true! God does not always outline our entire journey, but He does lead our every step.

144

The writer of Proverbs tells us that if we acknowledge God in all our ways, He will direct our path (Prov 3:6). God gave the children of Israel a cloud by day and a pillar of fire by night to follow. He gave the wise men a star to lead them. It is true that He does not deal with most of us that dramatically, but He has promised to go before us. If we are willing to take *one* step toward the Lord, He will take *two* steps toward us! Wise men today, as always, are those who follow divine leadership.

2. THEY RESPONDED IN FAITH

Second, the wise men were wise because they responded in faith.

I am sure that their friends must have thought these wise men were out of their minds. "Where are you going?" they were asked. "Well, we don't really know," the wise men had to answer. "We don't know who this new King is or where to find Him. We don't have any idea how long our journey will take or how much it will cost."

And I imagine the wise men were asked, "Well, why do you want to take this foolish and dangerous trip? Why are you going to all this trouble?" "Why?" the wise men must have replied. "Because we have heard a story from Scripture; we have seen the star in the sky; and we have felt a stirring in our souls."

Like Abraham of old, the wise men went out, not knowing whither they went. And wise men of every generation have done the same. William Carey, an English shoemaker, read our Lord's Great Commission. He realized the responsibility of taking the Gospel to every creature. In the face of severe opposition and ridicule, he traveled to that far-off land of India and labored seven years before he saw even one soul won to Christ. He worked relentlessly and translated the Bible into several languages. And he became known as the "father of modern missions."

David Livingstone demonstrated the same venture of faith as he pioneered with the Gospel message throughout the continent

145

of Africa. C. T. Studd, an all-star cricketer from Cambridge, England, forsook fame and fortune and poured out his life in missionary work. He, too, traveled by faith. When Jim Elliot and four other men were murdered by the Auca Indians, some were critical of their attempts to penetrate that savage people with the Gospel. "What a waste," some people cry. "How foolish to throw your life away for nothing." But when the book of God is finally opened, all of these will be listed as wise men, men who ventured forth in faith.

I wonder if you and I can say we have used the opportunities we have had. Have we demonstrated genuine faith? Have we been "wise men" or "foolish men"?

3. THEY WERE WISER THAN THE WORLDLY WISE

Third, the wisdom of the wise men was unique.

God's wise men are always wiser than worldly wise men.

After losing the star on their westward trip, the wise men decided to seek further information concerning the new King. Surely in Jerusalem they would be told where He could be found. They came saying, "Where is he that is born King of the Jews? for we have seen his star in the east, and are come to worship him" (Matt 2:2).

I imagine the wise men expected to find all of Jerusalem worshiping at the feet of this new King. But such was not the case. In fact, Matthew records, "When Herod . . . heard these things, he was troubled, and all Jerusalem with him" (Matt 2:3).

No one in the religious center seemed to be aware of the Messiah's birth. When the frightened Herod demanded of the chief priest and scribes where this Christ should be born, they had to go to the Scriptures. It was from the Old Testament prophecies that the religious leaders were able to determine that Christ would indeed be born "in Bethlehem of Judaea" (Matt 2:5).

But in spite of the fact that these learned men came up with the correct answer, in spite of their knowledge, these religious leaders never did find Jesus. The scribes and priests represented the wisdom of this world. They *knew* but they did nothing! The men from the East were God's true wise men. They believed His word and *did* something. They acted upon it. Their theology was scant, but their obedience was complete. And the Bible tells us that the same "star, which they saw in the east, went before them, till it came and stood over where the young child was" (Matt 2:9). God led them to the Christ Child. Heavenly wisdom is always far superior to earthly wisdom.

4. THEY WORSHIPED THE CHRIST CHILD

Fourth, the wisdom of the wise men was demonstrated in the fact that they worshiped the Christ Child.

In Matthew 2:10-11 we read, "When they saw the star, they rejoiced with exceeding great joy. And when they were come into the house, they saw the young child with Mary his mother, and fell down, and worshiped him."

Charles Lamb was once discussing the greatest literary characters of all time when the names of both William Shakespeare and Jesus Christ were mentioned. "The major difference between these two," said Charles Lamb, "is that if Shakespeare came into this room we would all stand in honor and respect. But if Jesus Christ were here, we would all humbly bow and worship Him."

The wise men had come a long way by faith. But more than that, they entered the house, fell on their knees, and worshiped the Christ Child.

Perhaps you, today, are just like the wise men, seeking to know the Lord. You may have come to the very brink of giving your life to Christ, but you have stopped short of that goal. You have acknowledged your need of a Saviour, but you have failed to enter into His open arms of love.

The Bible tells us that the wise men entered into the house, saw the child, and worshiped Him. They had journeyed by faith, and now they entered in and worshiped by faith.

So many in our world today say, "Show me, and *then* I'll believe." But God's way turns it around. He invites us to *believe,* and then we will see. Believing means seeing. The wise men believed God, and they were rewarded with sight.

But there is more!

The wise men not only worshiped the Christ Child, they presented gifts unto Him. The gold, frankincense, and myrrh were an indication of their love and adoration. This is the reason they had come. This is why they had journeyed so far. When a person has truly come to know Christ, the outpouring of gifts of love are sure to follow. This is what Christmas is all about. God's gift to us is His Son, Jesus Christ. And in return, God desires a gift of you: your heart, your life. The great hymn writer Isaac Watts has said:

> Were the whole realm of nature mine,
> That were a present far too small;
> Love so amazing, so divine,
> Demands my soul, my life, my all.

CONCLUSION

I wonder how far you have come on this journey of faith. Are you still searching and asking, "Where is He?" Or have you received the Saviour? Have you given your life to Jesus Christ the King?

Won't you today, with the wisdom of the wise men, accept Him as your Saviour and Lord?

SEVENTEEN

THE COSTLIEST CHRISTMAS

INTRODUCTION

Many people today are concerned about our growing preoccupation with Christmas giving and getting. Gifts keep getting more and more expensive. Increasingly the Christmas season seems swallowed up by shopping, wrapping and mailing packages, and sending cards.

Christmas sales in recent years have hovered at near-record levels. Retailers traditionally expect to conduct more than 15 percent of their annual business during the month of December. Many companies count on heavy Christmas sales to end the year in the black.

While many families this season will give useful gifts and probably less expensive items, stores like Nieman-Marcus say that shoppers seem more willing than ever to buy expensive gifts. These may range from boat cruises and mink coats to Chinese junks at $11,500 each, an adjustable mirror which will make the owner look as thin or rounded as he likes, or even a luxurious bathroom with gold-plated basin and fixtures.

Who will give the world's most expensive Christmas gift this year? What will it be, and how much will it cost? Will it be given by a king or prince or billionaire?

No one knows, of course, but we do know about the world's most costly gift—a gift with you in mind. It was given to the whole human race two thousand years ago. Nearly everyone knows at least a little about this costly gift. It was a child, born in a stable in Bethlehem and laid in a manger. His birth announcement was made from heaven by angels. Word of His coming was beamed by a very special star. Wise men from the East brought Him costly gifts.

No fact in history is so well attested as is the birth, life, and death of Jesus Christ. *Encyclopaedia Britannica* devotes more words to Jesus than to Aristotle, Cicero, Julius Caesar, or the great Napoleon. No life has been so carefully examined, so carefully noted. No life has reached down so many centuries with so great an impact on so many millions of people.

The most costly Christmas of all time brought the gift we need the most: a Saviour, the Holy Son of God. This is the Good News we read in Luke 2:10-11: "Fear not: for, behold, I bring you good tidings of great joy, which shall be to all people. For unto you is born this day in the city of David a Saviour, which is Christ the Lord."

A savior is one who saves. He does for us what we cannot do ourselves.

Joan of Arc was credited with saving France from the total domination of the British. In a similar way, the Duke of Wellington is credited with being the savior of Western Europe, because he turned back Napoleon at Waterloo.

But such great leaders have saved nations only from temporary perils, dangers outside themselves. Jesus saves us permanently from deadly foes within. Can Jesus Christ really save you from the effects of sin? That's an important question, the most important question of all time. Do you need what Jesus can give you? God says yes to both these questions. Around the world, an army of liberated men and women could stand and say, "Jesus has saved me from sins that once spoiled my life. He has made my life new."

Not one who has come to Jesus Christ in sincerity has ever been disappointed or let down. The young person hooked by dope, the "successful" man or woman tangled by pride and selfishness, the person enslaved by lust or bowed down by guilt— all these have found in Jesus Christ the very help they need.

God does not change. Several hundred years before Christ's

birth at Bethlehem, God made the promise recorded in Isaiah 1: "Though your sins be as scarlet, they shall be as white as snow; though they be red like crimson, they shall be as wool" (v. 18). God gave the greatest gift of history to keep that greatest promise of history.

In the Christmas story you remember that Joseph, the husband of Mary, was greatly troubled. "Fear not to take unto thee Mary thy wife," God told him in Matthew 1, "for that which is conceived in her is of the Holy Ghost" (v. 20). And then God added, "And she shall bring forth a son, and thou shalt call his name JESUS [the name means Saviour] for he shall save his people from their sins" (v. 21).

The greatest, most costly gift since time began is the Saviour. He bought and paid for the pardon God offers each one of us today. Only Jesus can save His people from their sins.

Why was God's gift so costly? There are three important reasons.

1. THE GREATNESS OF THE NEED

The world and its people's future were at stake. Sin had made havoc of God's creation. It had brought estrangement from its Creator. There were darkness, guilt, and the fear of death.

Seneca, the Roman philosopher, said, "All my life I have been trying to climb out of the pit of my sin, but I cannot and will not unless a hand is let down to lift me." Sin has gripped men's hearts so they cannot change themselves. Apart from Jesus Christ there is no hope, no help. Are you like that today? Unless you have received God's gift, the Bible says you are helpless and hopeless.

2. THE GREATNESS OF THE GIFT

Not only was the need so great, the gift was great! God gave His Son. "This is my beloved Son," He said, "in whom I am well pleased" (Matt 3:17).

The verse which is perhaps the best known in all the Bible is really a Christmas verse: John 3:16, "For God so loved the world, that he gave his only begotten Son." Why? "That whosoever believeth in him should not perish, but have everlasting life."

How much did it cost God the Father to send His Son to the cross for you? The Old Testament gives a beautiful, descriptive picture. Centuries before the birth of Jesus Christ at Bethlehem, God revealed Himself to Abraham, a man of faith. In Abraham's old age, God gave him a son and heir named Isaac. Then came a day when God asked this man of faith to sacrifice his son on Mount Moriah. Though God had other plans, so far as Abraham knew, he was to take the son he loved, travel to Mount Moriah, and offer him there on a lonely mountain altar. As we think of Abraham making that journey with his son, we can picture God's sorrow as Christ moved from Bethlehem to the cross.

But Abraham was spared. At the last minute, as he raised his hand to kill his son, God intervened. But God did not spare *His* Son. He suffered and died to save us from our sins.

3. THE GREATNESS OF THE COST

Read the inspired pictures of the suffering of Christ in Isaiah 53, Psalm 22, and Psalm 69. This great suffering on the cross was only part of the price He gladly paid.

Have you thought of what Jesus left behind, of what it meant for the eternal Son of God to be born in the form of man? He who had done no sin shared sin's effects: a human birth, the trials and sorrows of the life we know, hunger and thirst, fatigue and pain, even the pangs of death.

The Word of God sums it up like this: "Let this mind be in you, which was also in Christ Jesus: who, being in the form of God, thought it not robbery to be equal with God: but made himself of no reputation, and took upon him the form of a servant, and was made in the likeness of men: and being found in fashion as a man, he humbled himself, and became obedient unto death, even the death of the cross" (Phil 2:5-8).

Christ did this willingly for you and me. He says in John 10: 17 and 18, "I lay down my life. . . . No man taketh it from me, but I lay it down of myself." Again, in John 15, He says, "Greater love hath no man than this, that a man lay down his life for his friends" (v. 13).

Jesus Christ did not die for sins of His own or because He was the victim of circumstances. He came as God's supreme gift to you and me. What does this mean? It means that you dare not miss this greatest gift. The Bible asks this pointed question: "How shall we escape, if we neglect so great salvation" (Heb 2:3).

But it means *more.* The facts of the most costly Christmas remind us, first, that there are no limits to God's love. "Greater love hath no man than this, that a man lay down his life for his friends" (John 15:13). What more can God do to save you than He has already done?

The most costly Christmas reminds us of God's power. How could God be holy and forgive our sin? How could He take rebellious, sinful people like us and change our hearts and lives? God made all this possible through His great gift!

But the most costly Christmas reminds us of something else which holds a most serious implication. While God's love and power are great, His wrath and judgment upon sin are also real and fearful. If God gave His Son to save us from His judgment of sin, how fearful that judgment must be.

CONCLUSION

The story is told of a family that was experiencing hard times. The father was out of work. The mother had taken a job, but she was earning only a little. Christmas came, and somehow this family managed to have a happy time. There were the usual decorations and even a few small gifts. But everyone felt the financial pressure.

The day after Christmas, dad went out once more to look for work, and mother went back to her job. Meanwhile one of the children amused himself by rummaging through the colored paper and ribbon left over from the opened gifts. To his surprise, he found an envelope directed to his father. Later that night, his father opened it and found a generous check, a gift that somehow had been placed with the others, but was almost lost in the wrappings and ribbons of the Christmas season. For that family, the gift turned out to be the beginning of better things.

Could it be that you, too, have overlooked the really important gift of Christmas? Perhaps these moments together have been God's prompting to you to look through the odds and ends of Christmas. God's gift for you is here. Don't miss it. Don't wait to make it yours. Right now, wherever you are, you can receive the costliest gift, Jesus Christ the Saviour.

EIGHTEEN

MAKING ROOM
FOR CHRIST

Introduction

Where were you born? Most of us would reply by answering, "in a hospital." Some, perhaps, would say, "at home." And occasionally we even hear of an emergency birth in a plane or taxi cab. The circumstances of birth for most of us were very ordinary.

But two thousand years ago, a very uncommon birth took place. It was the birth of Jesus, the Son of God. It was a birth that literally changed the course of the world.

1. No room at Bethlehem

Luke's gospel tells us that the unusual birth of Jesus Christ took place in an animal stable. God incarnate was born in a stable, "because there was no room . . . in the inn" (Luke 2:7).

But, as unique as the birth of the Christ Child was, it really should have been expected. Centuries before, the Old Testament prophet Isaiah wrote, "The Lord himself shall give you a sign; Behold, a virgin shall conceive, and bear a son, and shall call his name Immanuel" (Isa 7:14).

Seven hundred years before Christ came to earth, the prophet Micah wrote, "But thou, Beth-lehem Ephratah, though thou be little among the thousands of Judah, yet out of thee shall he come forth unto me that is to be ruler in Israel; whose goings forth have been from of old, from everlasting" (Mic 5:2).

Throughout the Old Testament Scriptures, the birth of Jesus Christ is clearly predicted. The place of His birth, His name, His position, all were recorded hundreds of years before Jesus was born in Bethlehem.

From the account in Luke 2, we are given some insight into the secular setting that preceded the Saviour's birth. In that day,

Rome was the capital of the world, and Latin was the official language. Caesar Augustus, the supreme ruler of the Roman Empire, sat in his palace on the Tiber River. Luke 2:1 tells us that the emperor, wanting to establish a basis for taxation, decreed that a census was to be taken. This meant that every person in the empire had to be enrolled in his own city.

On the fringe of this great empire, in the little village of Nazareth, soldiers tacked up the order. And Joseph, a builder, an obscure descendant of the great king David, was obliged to go to Bethlehem, the city of David, to register.

Hundreds of years earlier, Micah had prophesied that Bethlehem was to be the place of Christ's birth. The Scriptures proclaimed it to be so. But when Mary and Joseph arrived in the city, there was no room. Of course there was plenty of room for the Roman soldiers who oppressed the people. There was room for the public officials who administered the census. There was room for the wealthy businessmen and merchants. But for Mary and Joseph and the Saviour, soon to be born, there was no room!

Oh, the sadness of those words, "No room in the inn."

In his book entitled *When Iron Gates Yield,* author Geoffrey Bull tells of spending Christmas Eve in a Tibetan inn, enroute to a communist prison camp. As he walked into the stable to feed the horses and mules, he says, "My boots squashed in the manure and straw. The horrible smell of the animals was nauseating, and I thought, 'to think Christ came all the way from heaven to some wretched, eastern stable, and what is more, He came for me.'"

How often we beautify the manger scene. We glorify the hay and straw, the animals, and the shepherds gathered around. And all the while we forget that the Son of God was made to lie in the feeding trough of filthy cattle, that God incarnate was subjected to such abuse and scorn. Why? Because there was no room in the inn or in the hearts of men.

Reginald Heber captured the true perspective of this when he wrote:

160

Cold on his cradle the dew drops are shining,
Low lies his head with the beasts of the stall.

Merson's painting entitled "No Room" depicts a scene of deep shadows, cold stars, a lonely street, and howling dogs, as a hard-hearted innkeeper closes the door and turns Mary away, saying, "No room here."

Yes, in the lowliest place in the world—a barn—the sinless King was born. For the Son of God, the Prince of Peace, there was no room!

2. NO ROOM—OF COURSE NOT!

But think of it another way. How could there have been sufficient room for the God-man? How could any earthly inn contain God? Whether an inn, a palace, or a city, no place is large enough to hold the God of the universe.

The apostle John declares, "In the beginning was the Word, and the Word was with God, and the Word was God. The same was in the beginning with God. All things were made by him; and without him was not any thing made that was made" (John 1:1-3). Jesus the God-man—the One who shared the glory of the eternal Father before the world was, He who was present in eternity past, He who created the world and hung the stars in place—how could there be room for Him?

The apostle also declares that it was this Son of God who "was made flesh, and dwelt among us." This is He who was born in Bethlehem's manger, "and we beheld his glory, the glory as of the only begotten of the Father, full of grace and truth" (John 1:14).

Yes, the God-man who said, "Let there be light," who spun the world out of nothing, who scooped out the valleys and piled up the mountains, He became an infant that day. And there was no room.

In one sense we say the whole world is too small to contain Him. But in another sense, we have experienced His habitation

161

within our souls. The songwriter says, "He's big enough to fill the mighty universe, yet small enough to live within the heart."[1]

3. Will you make room?

Do you have room for Jesus?

Consider this phrase in the conventional way. The Bible teaches us that there never was room for Jesus. From His lowly birth in a filthy stable to His burial in a borrowed tomb, there was no room.

As Joseph traveled to Bethlehem with Mary, I am sure he did not envision the problems he would encounter. Surely there would be room for a woman in this condition. No one would turn away an expectant mother soon to give birth to a child.

But as they approached the village that night, they could see that throngs of people had crowded into every nook and cranny. The hustle and bustle of business that first Christmas Eve crowded out the very Saviour of mankind.

How similar to the situation we find in our world today. People get so caught up in the commercialism of Christmas, they do not even see the Christ Child. To many, this day means nothing more than tinsel and gifts and Santa Claus, and that's all. There is no room for Jesus.

How tragic it was that night in Bethlehem! How tragic it is today!

But look a little farther. When the wise men came to Jerusalem looking for the Christ Child, they were questioned by King Herod as to where Jesus could be found. Using the guise of wanting to worship Jesus also, Herod asked the wise men to return when they had found where the young child was. But from that very moment, the wicked king began to secretly plot Jesus' death. For Herod, there was no room for the newborn King.

In Matthew 2:16 we read that when Herod realized the wise men would not return, he "was exceeding wroth, and sent forth,

---

1. Stuart Hamblen, "How Big Is God?" copyright 1958 by Hamblen Music Company, Inc. Used by permission.

and slew all the children that were in Bethlehem, and in all the coasts thereof, from two years old and under."

Herod could put out all the lights in Bethlehem, but he could not extinguish that shining star. Herod could still all the infant voices, but he could not silence the angels' singing. He could even kill all the young children, but he could not do away with the Son of God. Herod didn't want God to interfere with his personal plans. He tried to shut Jesus out of his life. He had no room for Jesus. But look on.

When Jesus first journeyed into Galilee to the city of Nazareth, there was again no room for Him. In Luke 4:29, we read that after Christ had preached unto them from the prophets, there arose a great wrath among those that heard Him and they "rose up, and thrust him out of the city, and led him unto the brow of the hill . . . that they might cast him down." His own countrymen rejected Him. They had no room for this carpenter's Son. They would not believe that He was from God.

Again in Luke 8, we find Jesus in Gadara casting out demons. And the account here tells us that when the whole multitude of people saw the power of Jesus, when they saw the demons rebuked, they were terrified and they "besought him to depart from them; for they were taken with great fear" (v. 37). They, too, had no room for Jesus!

Everywhere Jesus went, every time He preached, in every place He performed miracles, He met with opposition. Why? Because the people were unwilling to accept and believe that this was the Son of God. They could not allow this Prophet to interfere with their religious ritual and tradition. Their eyes were blinded. They had no room for Jesus.

What an indictment those words bring!

As Jesus entered into those last hours before the cross, He was so very alone. There was no one, not even the disciples, who had room for Him. As He prayed in the Garden of Gethsemane that night, He sweat, as it were, great drops of blood. He prayed and He suffered all alone!

Did you ever go through a period of time when you felt all alone? Jesus did. The Scriptures tell us that He had no place to lay His head. The rocks were His pillow; the ground, His bed. The wind was His comb, and He was all alone.

We at times can feel very lonely, and I'm sure that Jesus did too. But despite this fact, and despite the fact that we close ourselves off from Him, Jesus is still there waiting for us to make room for Him in our lives.

In Revelation 3:20, He says, "Behold, I stand at the door, and knock: if any man hear my voice, and open the door, I will come in to him, and will sup with him, and he with me."

He calls, but you must answer. He knocks, but you must make room for Him and open the door of your life.

God is all-powerful; He could force open your heart's door. But He does not. Jesus could have been born in a kingly palace. The Saviour could have summoned to earth His angelic armies to capture His tormentors. But He did not. And He never forces us to accept Him. He simply stands and knocks. Patiently He waits for us to respond.

Oh, what a wonderful time this would be for you to make room for Jesus. Someday, my friend, death will knock. Death comes on with rackless footsteps. It is inevitable and unrelenting. And when that day dawns, there will be no more opportunities, no more chances, to open the door of your life.

CONCLUSION

In his famous painting of Christ knocking at the door, artist Holman Hunt has purposely omitted from the door a knob or handle. Why? Because that is on the inside, and you, and you alone, can open the door to Jesus.

Two thousand years ago, on that first Christmas Eve, there was no room for Jesus. Throughout the centuries, men have rejected Him; they have turned their backs on His love. But you, today, have an opportunity to receive Jesus into your life. Why not make room for Jesus right now, and accept Him as your personal Saviour and Lord.

Book 2

SPECIAL
SERMONS
ON SPECIAL ISSUES

To that select company of
pastors who attend the flock
of God

with appreciation to
Jerry Rice, producer of "Moody
Presents," Wayne Christianson,
senior editor emeritus, *Moody Monthly,*
and Phil Johnson who have assisted
me in research and production

ONE

The Energy Crisis

In Chicago one cold January, when most residents were fighting the snow, a young Christian couple went shopping for a dream. After weeks of looking around, they finally placed an order for a car—a new Oldsmobile. In March it was delivered.

It was their first new car, and you know something of how they felt—at first. But now the world in which they drive has changed. Their dream has been spoiled as they have suddenly found themselves short of gas, in an energy crisis.

Remember the last time you ran out of gas? Perhaps the gas gauge was stuck, or you just forgot to look. But there you were with four wheels that would not move and no help in sight. These days the whole world appears to be out of gas, and there is little help in sight. We are in an energy "crunch" they tell us is getting worse.

What is your answer to all this? Are you bracing for the worst, or hoping for the best? Does the whole situation say something to you as a Christian?

THE REALITY OF THE CRISIS

There are some people who believe that there is no energy crisis. They believe the shortage is not real—that it is a gimmick contrived to raise our energy prices or it is another scheme to "gouge" the public. Others hold that the crisis is real, but temporary. They think new sources will be found. They are confident that technology will discover new and better ways to provide sources of energy.

In his book *The Energy Balloon,* Steward Udall, United States secretary of the interior from 1961 to 1969, contends that both views are totally unfounded. He believes the American public has been misled about the potential energy reserves, as well as about energy alternatives.

Perhaps a more realistic view is that the day of abundant energy is gone forever, and unless we find hard-nosed solutions, catastrophe could overtake us. The issues are controversial; the problems are complex. There are conflicting viewpoints. In all the welter of figures, claims, and warnings, it is very hard to find the facts.

But the problem is important. It affects our future and our very existence.

What is the real nature of our problem? To begin with, our country is dependent on various forms of energy, expecially petroleum, and our demand for oil and petroleum products is rapidly increasing. With only 5 percent of the world's oil reserves, the United States owns half the automobiles in the world. We use over half of the world's gasoline supply and participate in half of the world's air travel. Our demand for oil has doubled every fourteen or fifteen years.

To compound the problem, the supply of available oil is limited and shrinking fast. Richard H. Bube, chairman of the Department of Materials Science and Engineering at Stanford University, believes that domestic production of petroleum peaked in 1971. He points out that 75 percent of all known petroleum reserves are in the Middle East, where they will continue to be constantly threatened by international politics, and he expects that we will begin to actually run out of petroleum in about twenty-five years and out of natural gas in twenty years.

There is also another factor. Even should we assume we can import the oil we need during the next few years, the price may soon become prohibitive. Oil that was selling at less than two dollars a barrel at the beginning of 1970, cost more than thirty dollars in 1980, and the end is not in sight.

That is the situation—an escalating demand for energy beyond our own resources, plus a shrinking, costly world supply.

Our attitude as a nation toward energy has been somewhat careless. We are incredibly wasteful of energy. In the 1970s our country, with only 5 percent of the proved world reserves, was consuming 30 percent of the world supply. And we are using more today.

We waste our energy in many ways. I was surprised to learn that an ordinary 100-watt incandescent light bulb uses only 5 percent of its energy in giving light. The rest of the energy used makes heat, which, of course, is simply wasted. And did you know that pilot lights on kitchen stoves consume up to one-third of the gas used annually by the average gas range?

We also waste incredible amounts of energy in the things we throw away. Figures from the 1970s show that the United States threw away nearly six pounds of trash per day for every man, woman, and child. The figure may now be as high as eight pounds per day per person. Virtually all that trash represents a tremendous energy waste. We need to be concerned that every 365 days we throw away 40 million tons of paper products. That trash represents 600 million trees—trees that had to be cut down, cut up, and worked with in a number of ways, all of which consumed energy. And that is typical.

In the next fifty-two weeks we will throw away 10 million tons of iron, over 15 million tons of glass, 8 million automobiles, 100 million tires, and billions of cans.

Even power plants burning coal or oil are incredibly inefficient. More than 60 percent of the potential energy used in fuel is wasted before it is converted to electric power. Nuclear power plants are even more inefficient. They lose as much as 70 percent of the energy they could pass on, in terms of wasted heat.

But possibly our greatest energy waste comes on the open highway. More than 80 percent of our working population drives to and from work, and more than half have only one person to a car. Many of our cars use engines that give us only 20 percent of the energy they consume. Not a few are getting as little as ten to fourteen miles to the gallon.

Compounding this problem of wastefulness is our practice of stimulating demand for more energy. Good business demands that if I have oil, I not only sell it for the most that I can get, but I also try to influence people to buy more. Or if I have a product that uses energy—cars, air conditioners, or appliances—I sell as many as I can. So demand for energy is increased. And the public tends to buy beyond its needs, anyway.

Our use of energy, then, links with our way of making a living. We cannot cut back on energy use without affecting our business and our livelihood.

Stewart Udall and the coauthors of *The Energy Balloon* believe that answers to our energy problem, at best, will be slow and costly. We must lay aside our wishful thinking, tighten our belts, and prepare for a time of major adjustment. They believe that we must halt our waste of energy, drive smaller cars, and drive them less. They believe we must develop public transportation.

In any case, it is clear that we must watch our energy use at every point. We must conserve, recycle, and develop every possible source of alternate energy production. In short, we must change our present life-style.

Time alone will tell how effective those measures will be. An energy-hungry society will do its best to find an easier way, but for now there seems to be no other choice than those crucial, urgent changes in our way of life.

The Root of the Crisis

A closer look at our energy situation suggests that the shortage has its roots in spiritual issues. The crisis is a reminder that our generation needs the grace and help of God. The measures we have so far suggested are at best temporary, stopgap measures. They do not deal with the root problem, which is corruption in the human heart. The ultimate solution to the problems that have brought about the energy shortage is a return to the God of the Scriptures. The only answer to man's greed, wastefulness, self-indulgence, and pride is the redemption that is available in

Jesus Christ. God's Word says, "If any man be in Christ, he is a new creature: old things are passed away; behold, all things are become new" (2 Corinthians 5:17).

Man-made solutions often generate new problems. The 1979 nuclear emergency at Three-Mile Island near Harrisburg, Pennsylvania, provides a good example. With little or no warning, a man-made solution to our energy needs confronts us with an urgent safety problem. Looking at the situation broadly, nuclear power would seem to be an answer to our need for energy. But instead we find ourselves confronted with a more imminent danger than the energy shortage.

God's solutions, on the other hand, create no new problems. Proverbs 10:22 says, "The blessing of the LORD, it maketh rich, and he addeth no sorrow with it." The salvation God offers in Christ is a real solution, not a cover-up or a cop-out. The person who comes to Christ finds genuine answers, for Christ says, "I am the way, the truth, and the life" (John 14:6). As the way, He is the answer to man's lost state. As the truth, He is the answer to man's confusion. And as the life, He is the answer to man's fear of eternity.

In Christ, God offers man the only real answers to the attitudes that have led him into the energy crisis. And the offer is to anyone who will trust Christ and receive Him by faith. "But as many as received Him, to them gave he power to become the sons of God, even to them that believe on his name" (John 1:12).

OUR RESPONSE TO THE CRISIS

How should the Christian respond to the energy crisis?

I firmly believe there should be a Christian perspective of the world situation. The Christian trusts in God in the good times and in the bad. The Christian will look to God to bring him through the stormy seas that lie ahead. Our confidence is in the Lord, come what may. He is sovereign. He can be trusted.

It would be very easy to put the blame for the problems of the world on the United States of America. That would also be inaccurate and very wrong. The problem is *the sinful nature of man,* not his nationality. Energy is wasted in Tokyo as well as in New York. Bigger is better in Sao Paulo as well as in Chicago. The "good life" is sought after in Paris, London, Southeast Asia, and throughout the Orient. Wherever there are people there are greed, selfishness, dishonesty, and deceit.

But how should we respond?

1. *Recognize we are stewards of God's creation.* Adam and Eve were told to subdue and have dominion over all the earth (Genesis 1:26-28). We must exercise greater care over the resources that have been given to us.

2. *Stop wasting what we have.* Many of us have been wasteful. If all of us would turn off the water, fix the leaky faucet, or take one less trip, the demand for energy would be that much less all along the line. We are living in a day when *wasting energy* is as much an act of violence against the poor as refusing to feed the hungry.

3. *Develop a simpler life-style.* Each day almost a billion people lie down to sleep inadequately fed. A thousand million people hungry! I am sure we agree that this is tragic, but some how we feel helpless to do anything about it. So we compartmentalize our thinking. We put it out of the way. In effect, we turn it off. And we continue to do what we have been doing. We buy things that are convenient to find and to fix. We eat more than we need—not all of us, but many of us. Expensive packages and containers become trash, and on it goes.

As victims of an easy life-style, we have unthinkingly perpetuated a problem that is fast becoming a crisis. We need a fresh vision of God and our needy world, which in turn will produce a life-style worthy of God's calling. Our model is Jesus Christ Himself, who, though rich, became poor that through His poverty we might become rich (2 Corinthians 8:9).

4. *Display compassion for the whole world.* The love of Jesus Christ working in and through us should compel concern for the whole world. When we learn that what we have is *all out of proportion* to what other prople have, it should make us ill at ease, uncomfortable, motivated to take action, to do something. We dare not live selfishly. We must retrain our self-desires. As the

children of light, we must reach out in Christian compassion to the whole world.

Writing on ecology, Dr. Francis Schaeffer points out that exploitation comes basically from greed and haste. In the end, he says, those who take too much too fast find the problems they have created return full circle to themselves. As Dr. Schaeffer reminds us, the church is really God's living, small-scale demonstration of the world as it should be. We dare not live selfishly. We must be examples of those who see and face the issue clearly, retraining our self-desires. We should walk as children of light.

Finally, the energy problem should remind us that we are in a twilight world. Human solutions have human limitations. We need God's wisdom, and we need God's grace. The clouds over our world today remind us that men are but tenants on this earth. Our existence here is not an end in itself. We are bound for an eternal dwelling place.

Let me ask you an important question. Are you prepared for what is coming? I do not mean just the immediate future with the problems of an energy crunch. Are you prepared for eternity?

In John 5:24, Jesus said three highly important things. First He said: "He that heareth my word, and believeth on him that sent me, hath everlasting life." Did you catch that? He said he that hears and believes has everlasting life. That means that you can have everlasting life now—you do not have to wait for death to find out that you have eternal life. Second, He said that he that hears and believes "shall not come into condemnation." Think of that—a promise that he who hears and believes will not be judged.

Finally, He said that the one who hears and believes passes here and now "from death unto life." It happens now, and you can make sure of it in your own life.

TWO

Abortion: Throwaway Life—Can We Afford It?

When is human life expendable? The question seems to have an easy answer—never! There is no life not worth saving. Two persons, or fifty, or even an entire nation will team up to find a child lost on a mountain, rescue a miner trapped by an explosion, or free a terrorist's hostage.

And yet millions of lives are being written off, snuffed out quietly and efficiently with scientific expertise. In fact, in the United States in 1979 the legal act of abortion caused more deaths than heart disease or cancer.

A talented Italian journalist, Oriana Fallaci, has become the spokeswoman for millions of unhappy women in her book *Letter to a Child Never Born*. In her book Miss Fallaci debates aborting her illegitimate child because the baby will interfere with her career. Finally she decides against abortion, but loses the baby by miscarriage after willfully disobeying her doctor in order to take an assignment. In short, she loses the child by choice.

Miss Fallaci acquits herself. But she clearly joins the millions of women who are experiencing uneasiness about their "right" to have abortions.

THE EFFECTS OF ABORTION

Abortion was legalized by the Supreme Court in 1973, and since then the problem of "throwaway life" has not lessened. In fact, it has multiplied astoundingly. Today it presses on the

American conscience as have few other issues. And it should. More than 8 million legal abortions are on record in the United States in the six years since the Supreme Court upheld abortion as a right.

It is not easy to picture the bodies of 8 million babies. Imagine if you can, a procession of abortion clinic attendants, marching in single file, each carrying what moments ago was a live fetus. They pass by you steadily, one every other second. Picture the grim procession moving endlessly, day and night, twenty-four hours a day. You would have to watch for nearly six full months before 8 million babies could be carried by.

A *Moody Monthly* editorial asks, "Have we been sitting, Lot-like, in the seats of the scornful, in the gates of our individual Sodoms, quite at home, quite unruffled, even critical of those who are so easily alarmed about—babies?

If the blood of Abel—one innocent adult—cried out to God from the ground, how much more eight million babies since 1973?"

Let me put it another way. In the years since the Supreme Court legalized abortion, we have snuffed out a population considerably larger than that of Philadelphia. Dr. C. Everett Koop estimates that Japan has destroyed 50 million preborn children since abortion was legalized there in 1948. And the epidemic has spread around the world.

Many who justify this form of extermination do so on the grounds of safeguarding human rights—the rights of mothers to avoid the consequences of conception. Others have a vested interest—the fathers who want no further responsibility, or possibly the doctors and medical assistants who make abortions a rewarding business. Taxpayers, many of them unknowingly, finance approximately one-third of a million abortions annually.

The effects of this harvest of willful death are far greater than we think. We could well be moving toward a society of middle-aged and older people. The present generation is not replacing itself with younger life. Consequently, fewer and fewer workers will be left to support a growing population dependent on Social Security.

Columnist Joan Beck recently wrote, "Doubts about abortion are growing, not diminishing. A kind of collective uneasiness seems to be increasing in this country, not so much among those who have always opposed abortion as among some who welcome it and still support it."[1]

But most important, abortion is affecting our relationship with Almighty God. Few nations in history have so invited divine judgment while needing God's favor. What should the Christian's view of abortion be? Should we accept what has been termed "the American way of death?"

The Evils of Abortion

Many argue that abortion does not involve taking a human life. They say there is no proof that life begins until a child is born. In its historic *Roe* v. *Wade* decision, the United States Supreme Court concluded that it could not decide when human life begins—that the fetus may be destroyed "for any reason or no reason."

Many believe, however, that in the decision the Supreme Court overlooked overwhelming evidence. One aspect of that evidence was dramatized and documented in 1979 in a historic feature on CBS television. For the first time in history, television viewers coast to coast saw motion pictures of the human fetus in the womb. The pictures made plain that even at the age of forty days, a fetus in the womb has a beating heart, a slender spine, and a brain that is already sending out nerve impulses. The feature stressed that this was human life, each one a "life never seen on earth and never to be repeated."

Recently, *Time* magazine made a similar point. "Even in the earliest stages of pregnancy," the magazine said, "the embryo is amazingly baby-like. By the ninth week the fetus is kicking and wiggling. . . . Its sex can be recognized, and at one point it seems to be trying to shield its eyes from the lights of the camera."

Is a fetus only flesh? Dr. C. Everett Koop, well-known for his outstanding work in surgical pediatrics, has this to say in his recent book *The Right to Live: The Right to Die:* "Once there is the union of sperm and egg, and the 23 chromosomes of each are brought together, that one cell with its 46 chromosomes has all of the DNA (deoxyribonucleic acid), the whole genetic code that will, if not interrupted, make a human being just like you with the potential for God-consciousness."[2] He asks a crucial question, "At what point can one consider this life to be worthless and the next minute consider the same life to be precious?"[3]

Later in his book Dr. Koop, who is a Christian, says, "As recently as 1967, at the first international conference on abortion, a purely secular group of people said, 'We can find no point in time between the union of sperm and egg and the birth of an infant at which point we can say this is not a human life.' "[4]

It is this human life that is the victim of abortion. Some fetuses are removed from the womb by suction, in a mass of blood and tissue. Some are destroyed by scraping from the womb, and some are drowned in an injection salt solution. Still others are removed by surgery not unlike a Caesarian operation, and the fetus is left to die if it is not already dead. In every case, regardless of the means, a precious life is blotted out.

Some people are quick to point out that the Bible does not specifically speak out against abortion. But the Bible does not specify every sin. It does say, "Thou shalt not kill." And the Bible clearly speaks of human life as beginning in the womb. The mother of Samson was told that her child would be a Nazarite from the womb (Judges 13:5), the implication clearly being that his status as a person began before his birth. Psalm 58:3 says that the wicked are estranged "from the womb." The implication is that even as unborn babies they are living persons. Speaking of John the Baptist, Luke 1:15 declares that this great man of God would be "filled with the Holy Ghost, even from his mother's womb." Only a living person can be filled with the Holy Spirit.

So the nature of the human fetus, medical science, and the Word of God all testify that the tiny creature in the womb is a unique and living person. If that is true, no one can commit abortion without destroying human life.

The Errors of Abortion

That brings us to the real heart of the problem—wrong values that have been accepted by our society without regard to God's Word. What are some of those wrong values? First, there is *a wrong attitude toward human life.*

What is a human life? When God made man, He said, "Let us make man in our image, after our likeness" (Genesis 1:26). And the record goes on to say, "God created man in his own image, in the image of God created he him" (Genesis 1:27). Every human life, even in its fallen state, reflects to some degree the likeness of Almighty God. When man dares to take another human life, he lifts his hand in rebellion against the image of Almighty God. When Cain killed Abel, God said, "Thy brother's blood crieth unto me from the ground" (Genesis 4:10). The very universe records the violation of a human life.

God spelled out to Noah the seriousness with which He views the taking of human life. In Genesis 9:6, He says, "Whoso sheddeth man's blood, by man shall his blood be shed." And then He gives the reason for demanding such a penalty: "For in the image of God made he man." Never forget that God condemns the taking of human life and demands the ultimate penalty. Again and again the Bible tells us that judgment came to men because of blood guiltiness.

God judges nations, too. Israel—God's own people—was sent into captivity. Psalm 106:38 reminds us that this judgment came in part because the Hebrew people had dared to take the lives of their own children—a sin only a hair's breadth from the abortion we flaunt so openly today.

A second wrong value that gives rise to abortion is *a wrong emphasis on self.* Perhaps the most often heard argument for abortion is that the mother has the right to decide what happens to her own body. On the surface the argument seems reasonable. The mother is the one chiefly involved. Her future and well-being are at stake. But wait a minute. What about the child she

185

has helped conceive? What about the obligation to the human life already conceived? What about the future and well-being of the unborn child? Are not his rights to be considered?

God gave the sex relationship to strengthen the marriage bond and to bless the home with children. No privilege is more sacred than that of bringing a new life into the world. No privilege should be exercised more carefully. And it should be viewed as a holy responsibility.

The Word of God says plainly that sex is for marriage only. Abortion would virtually disappear tomorrow if it were not for the willful violation of God's great charter of marriage and purity. The abortion problem begins with a rebellion that says, "I will do as I please for pleasure. I reject the limits prescribed by God in favor of personal satisfaction."

And that is the essence of the wrong values of which we are speaking. The root of all wrong value systems is a rebellious attitude toward God.

To put one's will above God's will, one's rights above God's rights, is to rebel against the sovereign of the universe. You cannot seize sovereignty for yourself without challenging Almighty God. That is what Satan did in his fall. Isaiah 14 describes how Satan went from being God's highest angel to become the enemy and deceiver we know him to be. In verse 13 God, speaking to Lucifer (Satan's name before he fell), says, "Thou hast said in thine heart, I will ascend into heaven, I will exalt my throne above the stars of God. . . . I will be like the Most High. Yet thou shalt be brought down to hell."

When we flout the will of God, we are walking in the footsteps of a doomed and defeated Satan. We are not the Creator; we are His creatures. We are not God, but people subject to His will and wishes.

For generations our nation has pushed aside the Bible. We have defied the voice of God. We challenge Him at our peril. Pride and rebellion are deadly sins. Part of their harvest today is the tragic and bloody snuffing out of millions of tiny lives.

Although we have made abortion legal, although we have made

it respectable, although we have made it commonplace, the fact—the sin—is unchanged. Like Cain, we are daring to strike down human life, life with potential, life made in the image of Almighty God.

"But," someone will say, "is abortion *always* wrong?" "Always" is a broad and sweeping word. There are difficult questions we have not been able to touch upon in this brief chapter. For example, what about defective babies? What about abortion in the wake of rape?

Those are special circumstances that represent only a small fraction of the total number of abortions, and there are answers for even such problems. We can trust God with the hard situations in our lives if we set ourselves to do His will where it is clear. We cannot expect His help or blessing if we ignore His Word and set aside His precepts.

And God's will seems clearly to stand in opposition to the wanton destruction of precious lives.

The heart of the abortion issue is stated by R. F. Gardner in a booklet published by the *Christian Medical Society Journal.* He writes, "From the moment of conception the couple concerned have not the option whether a proffered gift be accepted, but rather whether an already bestowed gift should be spurned." That is the issue—what will we do with a human life that has been given to our keeping?

Meanwhile abortion, like all sin, is not standing still. The tide is rising fast. Judicial decisions continue to make abortions easy, even for teenagers and wards of local government. England is looking forward to abortion kits for home use, within a year or two.

In this country many believe that only an antiabortion amendment will change the situation. If so, let's get behind it.

I am well aware that few who read these pages have had or will have responsibility for the abortion crisis. But we are guilty if we fail to raise our voices in opposition. God's judgment is not far from any nation that complacently accepts the slaughter of its unborn babies. Once His judgment falls, it will be too late.

May we stop being neutral on this issue. If abortion is wrong, we cannot keep silent. Besides taking a stand, we need to help others realize what is happening—and put our influence as Christians where it will count.

NOTES

1. Joan Beck, *Chicago Tribune,* 31 January 1977.
2. C. Everett Koop, *The Right to Live: The Right to Die* (Wheaton, Ill.: Tyndale, 1976).
3. Ibid.
4. Ibid.

THREE

Is the Church Unfair to Women?

Is the church behind the times in its attitudes toward women? A growing number answer, "Yes!" Too long, they say, we have restricted women. It is time, and past time, for a change. And change, they believe, is on the way.

What should the Bible-believing Christian say about equal rights for women within the church? How should church leaders respond, and what should be the attitude of Christian women?

THE WORLD AND WOMEN'S RIGHTS—A CONTROVERSIAL ISSUE

Since 1963 when Betty Friedan published her book *The Feminine Mystique,* the battle for women's rights has touched virtually every aspect of our national life. Now it is touching the church, and it brings up a difficult question—are women underprivileged in the Christian church?

Some believe with fervor that they are. In 1976 that conviction prompted the Episcopal church to vote in favor of ordaining women. A minority of the group reacted in dismay. Two years later, a hundred parishes broke away to form a new denomination.[1]

In 1974 the ordination of women was the most important religious news story of the year, according to a vote of the Religious Newswriters Association. The move toward women's ordination outranked such headlined stories as the moral issues of Watergate, the world hunger crisis, and the sensational aspects of exorcism.[2]

Today the tensions concerning the role of women in the church are even greater. Church leaders are asking if we have been unfair to women. Books on the subject are being written. As women remove the barriers to once-forbidden secular occupations, some church leaders are upset because they believe the church is lagging far behind. They believe women are discriminated against by being denied positions of equal leadership in the church. What is the situation? Although the number of ordained women is on the increase, the total number is small. About seventy American church bodies permit ordination of women, but many of those are small denominations.

Fewer than 1 percent of American Baptist, United Methodist, Presbyterian, and Disciples of Christ clergy are women. Southern Baptists, the largest Protestant denomination, having over 35,000 churches, have fewer than twenty ordained women in the ministry.[3] In a number of other groups committed to the Bible, ordination of women is opposed.

The critics argue that churches are steeped in prejudice and that it is high time they become enlightened. On the surface, the arguments may seem convincing. Barring women from the ministry, it is argued, presumes inferiority and is rank discrimination. Women are proving themselves in every other line of work. Why should they not serve as pastors? Many women equal or outstrip the men in gifts and abilities. The church, we are told, is missing out by not letting them use their talents.

Some hold that the requirements for pastors outlined in the Scriptures have been grossly misinterpreted—that they merely reflect cultural prejudices of the day, or perhaps of the apostle Paul. Society sees a whole new world for women today, they argue. So should the church.

How should the church respond to such pressure? What shall we say to sincere, dedicated young women who want to serve their Lord?

Are there satisfying answers? I am glad there are.

As we turn to the Bible to see what it says concerning women and the church, we find today's pressures have arisen from several basic misunderstandings. First, there is a basic error in understanding the scope and nature of the differences between the sexes. The Bible nowhere teaches that men are superior to women, but it does teach that they are different.

God created the woman at a different time and in a different way. In creating woman, He did not make a carbon copy of what He had already made. He fashioned a personality and spirit that would complement man and supply qualities man lacked.

The tendency today is to assume that except for physical differences, men and women come from the same, unchanging mold. Therefore they are to be competitive. But that is not God's intent. God created men and women to work together, not to compete. But He gave them different functions.

Man is at his best as an initiator—when he plans, leads, risks, and strives. Woman is made to reach her greatest potential when she rests on man's provision and supports him in his efforts.

We commit a basic error when we try to sweep this difference under the rug. It may appear to succeed for a time, but in the end we violate something elemental in our inner structure.

A second mistake in thinking there should be equal authority for men and women in the church rises from failure to see the difference between one's status and his role. As men and women are different, so God has made clear that they were made for different functions. In the church, as in the home, men and women are called to serve in different ways.

The New Testament makes clear that administration is a man's calling. Women are called to assist, helping as only they can in accomplishing the work. Some administrators of the early church bore the title *elder*. Others were designated *deacon*. Qualifications spelled out for both offices make it absolutely clear that both were always men.

In harmony with this principle, the apostle Paul in 1 Timothy 2:12 plainly writes, "But I suffer not a woman to teach, nor to usurp authority over the man, but to be in silence." (He gives two reasons. First, woman was not created to be independent; she was created after Adam to be his helper. Second, the woman had been the first to give place to sin.)

And so God has assigned leadership in the church, as well as in the family, to the man. His office is not a badge of honor; it is a mantle of responsibility. Men make a mistake to think their headship makes them superior. Women make as serious a mistake to assume their role makes them in any way inferior.

Jesus Christ clearly showed His regard for women during His earthly ministry. He sought out the woman of Samaria. He spent much time in the home of Mary and Martha. Luke 8 speaks of "certain women" whom He had healed and who, in turn, "ministered to him of their substance."

It was to women that He first appeared after His resurrection. Women were present in the upper room as the disciples waited for the Holy Spirit, and they, too, were filled when the Spirit came.

As if to make their standing clear, Galatians 3:28 seems to say that there are no distinctions in status in Christ. Paul writes, "There is neither Jew nor Greek, there is neither bond nor free, there is neither male nor female: for ye are all one in Christ Jesus."

Of course Jews still are Jews, Greeks still are Greeks, slaves still are subject to their masters. But all have equal status with Christ who loved them and gave Himself for them. The ground is level at the cross. Women matter as much as men, but we are called to different tasks.

A third reason for thinking that women should have more leadership in the church grows out of failure to understand the nature of Christ's church. The church is not a human organization to be conducted like a secular business enterprise. It is not a democratic organization to be run by majority rules. It is a spiritual body composed of those redeemed by Jesus Christ, persons made new creatures and brought into personal union with the Savior. It is a living organism, a spiritual family. In fact, the apostle Paul in various places speaks of the church as "the household of faith," "the household of God," and "the house of God" (Galatians 6:10; Ephesians 2:19; 1 Timothy 3:15).

As head of His family, Jesus Christ is entitled to set over it whom He will. And Scripture makes clear that in the local church, as in the individual home, it is His will that men should plan, care for, and protect the local congregation.

In a recent *His* magazine interview, Elisabeth Elliot makes an interesting point. Positions of leadership in the church are not, she says, rewards for competence. They are not earned or assigned purely on the basis of ability. They are assigned sovereignly by God. Those who take positions of authority in the church must be ordained by God. And God's Word makes abundantly clear that it is His will to have men in positions of leadership.[4]

Do not be misled by arguments that the Scriptures are influenced by cultural bias. Second Timothy 3:16 teaches that all Scripture is given by inspiration. In other words, it came forth from God like His very breath. God Himself speaks through the Bible, and the thoughts conveyed are exactly what God wants us to know and follow. God would not allow Paul—or any other writer—to dilute the truth of Scripture by adding personal opinion or cultural bias.

And by the same token, we must not be guilty of diluting the truth of Scripture ourselves by trying to limit its clear teaching to an isolated cultural situation. And we must resist attempts by the world to force on the church the secular thinking of our day.

Christian Women and Women's Rights— A Consecrated Attitude

Many who argue that scriptural guidelines be set aside in favor of so-called equal rights fail to realize another fact—that Christian satisfaction comes not from title or position but from faithfulness in service.

From the church's early days, that kind of satisfaction has been experienced by women as well as men. Since apostolic times, women have found fulfillment in the church. In Romans 16, Paul writes of "Phebe our sister, which is a servant of the church which is at Cenchrea." Phebe found honor and fulfillment in effective service.

Paul also commends three women, Tryphena, Tryphosa, and Persis, who "did labor much in the Lord." In Philippians he speaks of Euodias and Syntyche as "fellow workers in the Lord." Priscilla, who ably reinforced her husband, Aquila, in instructing Apollos, is warmly commended by Paul. She knew how to minister—even to teach—in the authority framework of the Scripture.

Such ministry is possible for any women. But the usurpation of authority is forbidden women in the church. Women are not to attempt to rule either directly or by authoritative preaching or teaching. They are not to contend in church discussions.

But women can declare the gospel, teach where authority over men is not involved, witness, and carry the good news of salvation to the ends of the earth.

Sisters in Christ, do you want the blessing of God in ministry? Do you long to share in the work committed to the church? You can. But always remember the Bible pattern—God reserves authority for men. In all other places you can help as God allows. Do all you can within the framework of God's pattern. God will bless and make you fruitful beyond all that you could ask or think.

In some respects your gifts and insights may be superior to the men who are in leadership positions. Help and encourage them. Leaders are responsible to Christ for what they have to give. You are responsible for what God wants from you.

The well-being of God's work can be severely damaged when either men or women fail to recognize and fill the roles God has for them within His church.

The world has its ideas of who should lead the church. Those who do not understand will wave banners of new equality. They will minimize and rationalize. The world does not appreciate God's will or His purpose in the church.

But the Christian understands and knows God's way is best. We know that women are equal to men in God's sight and that

God merely reserves the right to assign roles in the church according to His wisdom and His will. We must resist the pressure to rebel against God's way.

NOTES

1. *Time,* 13 February 1978, p. 60.
2. Sarah Frances Anders, "The Role of Women in American Religion," *Southwestern Journal of Theology* (Spring 1976), p. 55.
3. Ibid.
4. Elisabeth Elliot, *His* (January 1978), p. 20.

FOUR

Is Capital Punishment Biblical?

"The issue that won't go away." That is how a national news magazine describes the capital punishment question. As recently as 1972, the United States Supreme Court decision in *Furman* v. *Georgia* invalidated existing laws providing for capital punishment. That decision gave new hope to over six hundred convicts in state prisons.

But the tide is turning again. Recent Supreme Court decisions have cleared the way for death sentences under certain conditions, and many states have new laws requiring capital punishment for certain crimes.

In 1977, there were few names better known across America than the name of Gary Gilmore, a man with a tragic past and facing a tragic future. The year began for Gilmore in a death cell in a Utah prison. Gary Gilmore had been condemned to die for murder, but other people had intervened on his behalf.

He himself demanded execution. Often it seemed, however, that he would be given a lighter sentence. On two occasions he tried to kill himself. At last he faced a firing squad, and his long case was closed.

Gilmore's execution was the first since June of 1967. In that month Colorado's gas chamber had been used to put to death Luis Monge for the murder of his wife and three of his ten children. During the intervening decade it seemed that the United States had closed the door on capital punishment for good.

In 1972 the Supreme Court struck down all the nation's death penalty statutes because they placed too much discretion in the hands of judge and jury. The court also voiced the judgment that the death penalty constitutes "cruel and unusual punishment."

Since then the pendulum has slowly swung back the other way. Why? One reason is that in the nine years from 1966 to 1975 the number of murders in the United States nearly doubled, rising from 10,900 in 1966 to more than 20,000 in both 1974 and 1975. Our lawmakers responded. During those nine years, thirty-six states enacted new captial punishment laws.

The Supreme Court modified its 1972 ruling by upholding death penalty laws for murder in three states and rejecting laws in two other states. It rejected statutes automatically imposing death for certain offenses, but approved laws that set standards for guiding juries.

But the real conflict is just starting. *U.S. News and World Report* recently stated, "Arguments over capital punishment are escalating to a feverish pitch." Opponents of the death penalty hope to create a national revulsion against what they see as a form of legalized killing. Others are prepared to battle for capital punishment laws as essential to the survival of our nation.

The issue is a serious one. On the one hand we have a rising tide of violence and death, an appalling disregard for human life. On the other hand, we face the responsibility of taking other lives in retribution.

THE DISPUTE OVER CAPITAL PUNISHMENT

How should Christians view the conflict? Is the death sentence a barbaric relic of the past? Or is it a vital safeguard to the welfare of our country? What does the Bible say on the subject?

The opponents of capital punishment are many and vocal. Abe Fortas, former associate justice of the United States Supreme Court, summed them up in an article entitled "The Case Against Capital Punishment," in *The New York Times Magazine,* January 23, 1978.

"Why," he asks, "when we have bravely and nobly progressed so far in the recent past to create a decent, humane society, must we perpetuate the senseless barbarism of official murder?" Mr. Fortas and those who hold his view point out that at least forty-five nations have abolished capital punishment.

He also underscores the difficulty of administering it fairly. Statistics show that only one out of seventy-five of those guilty of capital punishment crimes are finally brought to execution. And the poor and underprivileged, especially members of racial minorities, are more likely to be executed.

In addition, opponents of the death penalty contend with vigor that capital punishment does not cut down on serious crimes. Life imprisonment, they say, would serve as well.

Many disagree. A growing number of voices are being raised to defend the other side. In fact, a recent Gallup poll showed that 65 percent of those surveyed favored capital punishment. To remove the fear of execution, many believe, will inevitably invite an overwhelming tide of death and violence. To ban capital punishment would constitute another backward step toward permissiveness and anarchy.

Defenders of executions also make the valid point that life sentences in our times are rarely carried out. Many prisoners are too easily paroled. They insist that capital punishment is indeed a deterrent to serious crime.

THE DEMANDS FOR DIVINE JUSTICE

Does God have counsel for us on this subject? He does indeed. In fact, it is only in the light of the Bible that we can hope to find a reasonable and adequate answer. Let us look at the history of capital punishment in the Bible.

Where did capital punishment begin? What we call the death penalty today is virtually as old as the human race. The death penalty began in the times of Noah, when the total population of the world numbered only eight souls. God had destroyed a wicked and violent world civilization. In Genesis 9, we find God setting forth conditions under which human life would make a new beginning. One of His conditions is expressed in verse 6: "Whoso sheddeth man's blood, by man shall his blood be shed: for in the image of God made he man."

Here is the foundation for all human government. At its very base is the imperative for capital punishment. Man was made responsible for enforcing the sanctity of human life. Human life is sacred, not because we are great but because of the greatness of the God whose image we reflect. Notice again Genesis 9:6. "Whoso sheddeth man's blood, by man shall his blood be shed: for in the image of God made he man." The great crime of taking a human life is that we dare to desecrate the image of God. The one who takes a human life destroys something he cannot replace. He cuts off a potential he is powerless to fulfill. And God says the greatest crime of all is that the murderer dares to dishonor Almighty God.

And the human race has reached the place today where man destroys his fellow man without seeming qualm or question. Why? One important reason is that man himself has failed completely to enforce God's demand for capital punishment. There is little doubt that the swift, impartial execution of those found guilty of capital crimes would work to slow down their occurrences.

Let us be careful, however, of saying that God demanded capital punishment primarily as a deterrent. The scripture makes clear that God had a more important reason—the principle of simple justice. Dr. William H. Baker, of the faculty of Moody Bible Institute, has written a scholarly and thoughtful book in which he takes a careful look at what the Bible teaches concerning capital punishment. In *Worthy of Death,* he speaks of retribution, a term that means "the dispensing of reward or punishment according to the deserts of the individual."[1]

He writes, "Retribution is properly a satisfactor or according to the ancient figure of justice and her scales, a restoration of a disturbed equilibrium. As such it is a proper, legitimate and moral concept."[1]

When someone dares to snuff out the divinely given life of another person, he violates a principle of right and wrong as real as the law of gravity. And when God's laws are violated, retribution is demanded.

Strange to say, our so-called enlightened society today has virtually lost sight of the essential fact that ours is a world ruled by a holy God. Many cannot see that He is in control, but He is. Many of God's judgments pass unseen by man. Paul reminds us in 1 Timothy 5:24, "Some men's sins are open beforehand, going before to judgment; and some men they follow after."

God is not being hoodwinked nor is He being overpowered. Broken laws mean retribution. Although man may not fulfill his role, God will, in one way or another.

Some argue, of course, that capital punishment itself expresses irreverence for human life. They even say that to condemn a man to death is to violate the commandment "Thou shalt not kill." A closer look at the meaning of the original Hebrew, however, makes clear that the commandment is, "Thou shalt not commit murder." God is prohibiting individuals from acting in personal anger.

To act administratively in honoring God's law and making sure that it is kept is vastly different from an act of personal vengeance. Paul, speaking in Romans 13, reminds us that administrative power comes from God and acts by his permission. "For he is the minister of God to thee for good," he says in verse 4. "But if thou do that which is evil, be afraid: for he beareth not the sword in vain."

There are also some who say that God's Old Testament law has been rendered obsolete. They argue that Christ taught love and forgiveness. That is an inaccurate understanding of Christ's clear teaching. God is a God of love and compassion, but He is also a God of holiness and justice. Jesus said in Matthew 5:17, "Think not that I am come to destroy the law, or the prophets: I am not come to destroy, but to fulfil."

A little later in the same discourse He spoke specifically of the law that demanded death for death. "Ye have heard that it was said by them of old time," He said, "Though shalt not kill; and whosoever shall kill shall be in danger of the judgment" (Matthew 5:21). The "judgment," of course, is death, but He does not say such a punishment has been or will be suspended. Instead He says that even those angry with another without a reason are in danger of judgment as well.

The issue, very simply, is not whether we need capital punishment for a deterrent to crime, although a case might be made to show that it is indeed a powerful deterrent. And the issue is not whether capital punishment is being administered fairly. If it is not, we need to take steps to assure justice in the fear of God. The real issue is not whether we find the administration of capital punishment comfortable or pleasant. Punishment is never pleasant, but it is needful.

The Christian is concerned *primarily* with obeying the commands of God, a God not of anthropomorphic imagination, but the "High and Holy One" who gives *laws*, not recommendations, requires obedience, not requests cooperation.

We should also remember that capital punishment is, indeed, a deterrent in the sense that *the criminal executed has been effectively deterred* from committing another capital crime.

The issue is whether we will accept or ignore the clear mandate of God. We cannot deny that the world in which we live is steadily growing more violent. In the world and in our nation men are trying to edge God out of the picture.

As a nation, little of what we say or do is based on the Word of God. We have largely rejected God's counsel in government, in business, in schools, and in the family. And we are paying the price.

Will we fail to recognize that God has the first and the last word? We can brush His commands aside, but we must bear the consequences. As Christians, we ought to see the alternatives clearly, pray, and then speak out as those who understand and are committed to the will of God.

NOTES

1. William H. Baker, *Worthy of Death* (Chicago: Moody, 1973), p. 83.

FIVE

Alcohol:
America's Most Costly Luxury

America has many luxuries—large and lavish homes, sleek cars, recreational vehicles by the thousands. But there is something more costly than all those. In terms of total cost—death, sickness, crime, and accident—our greatest national luxury is the use of alcohol.

Some Christians favor the use of alcohol beverages in moderation, whereas other believers insist on total abstinence. Some believe it is possible to drink alcoholic beverages without damaging their Christian testimonies, and others that the only safe rule is total abstinence.

In a recent book titled *Drinking,* Jack B. Weiner brings together a striking series of related tragedies. True stories, these all happened within a few days' time, in places all over the country. The first tragic event took place in Calumet, Oklahoma, several days before Christmas. A nineteen-year-old youth finished drinking a bottle of shaving lotion, then staggered into the corner of an abandoned garage. There, in a drunken stupor, he methodically used a razor blade to slash the artery of his wrist. In thirty minutes he was dead. Later that evening in Denver, Colorado, six hundred miles northwest, a middle-aged woman lapsed into an alcoholic blackout. When she came to, her baby boy had suffocated in his crib.

Still farther north and only hours later, a father of three

children in Great Falls, Montana, choked to death on a three-inch piece of sirloin steak. He had been drinking and failed to cut his steak properly.

The following morning, two thousand miles due east, in Augusta, Maine, a mother and her two young girls were rushed to a hospital for emergency treatment of serious burns. The mother, a widow, had passed out while drinking. Unnoticed, her cigarette dropped down between the cushions of the couch. The blaze that followed almost took three lives. We cannot deny that the world in which we live is steadily growing darker. In the world and in our nation men are trying to edge God out of the picture.

As a nation, little of what we say or do is based on the Word of God. We have largely rejected God's counsel in government, in business, in schools, and in the family. And we are paying the price.

Will we fail to recognize that God has the first and the last word? We can brush His commands aside, but we must bear the consequences. As Christians, we ought to see the alternatives clearly, pray, and then speak out as those who understand and are committed to the will of God.

Although widely scattered, those tragic happenings all had a common cause—the use of alcohol. They are but samples of the tragedies that take place every twenty-four hours of every day across the nation, month after month.[1]

THE REALITY OF THE LIQUOR PROBLEM

From coast to coast, in communities large and small, alcohol leaves destruction in its path. Half of all homicides in the United States and one-third of all suicides are alcohol related.[2] Nearly half the 5.5 million arrests a year in this country involve persons who have used alcohol.

Alcohol is our number one killer on the highways—a factor in some 25,000 deaths and 200,000 injuries each year.[3] Narcotics experts tell us that, notwithstanding marijuana, heroin, and all the rest, alcohol remains the chief drug problem in America.[4] It also constitutes the primary health problem of our nation, a

208

problem that is getting worse.[5]

Researchers at George Washington University say there may be as many as 9 million alcoholics in the United States—nearly one in every twenty persons—plus many millions more on the verge of serious drinking problems. Jack Weiner insists the figure is somewhere between 15 and 20 million.

It is estimated that one out of every ten workers, managers, and executives in the United States suffers from alcoholism.[6] The price tag for lost time, accidents, and related consequences of employee alcoholism has soared to a colossal $15 billion yearly.[7]

Only one thing is more amazing than the ruin left by alcohol, and that is our national unwillingness to get rid of it and free our people from its curse. Statistics tell us that the United States is consuming an annual average of 2.7 gallons of alcoholic beverages for every person fourteen or older in the country. That is no trivial amount. It measures out to 21 fifths of 86-proof whiskey, plus 12.6 fifths of wine, plus 12.5 cases of beer a year for every male and female fourteen years and older in our country.[8]

The Reasons for the Liquor Problem

Why do we permit the misery liquor brings? There seem to be two main reasons. First, some people like the thrills that come with drinking. And nothing—not all its tragedy or cost or misery—can make them give it up. The second reason our nation gives alcohol its unholy place is our insatiable lust for profit. Retail sales of alcoholic beverages for one recent year totaled $32.5 billion. From that our government claimed $9.5 billion in federal, state, and local taxes.[9]

Despite the tragic aftermath of liquor's place in our society, many moral people like to think that the answer to the problem simply lies in moderation. The liquor industry itself joins in this persuasive chorus. "If people would only learn to drink sensibly," they say, "there would be no liquor problem." However, the very nature of alcohol is to weaken the will to drink with moderation.

Recently, in a midwestern Sunday school, a teacher who had been an advocate of drinking in moderation made a startling admission. Only hours before, one of his former public school mates had ended his life by jumping from a twelfth-story hotel window. It was the tragic climax to years of giving in to alcohol. The teacher told the class, "My friend and I thought we could stop. We never dreamed he would become an alcoholic. I think I'm to blame."

Alcohol is no respecter of persons. It could touch you or someone that you love. Once alcoholism picks a victim, prevention is too late.

Observers tell us that although per capita consumption of alcohol has leveled off in recent years, more young people are becoming regular drinkers, and more women are drinking now than in the past.

Meanwhile we are learning that the effects of even moderate drinking can be more serious than we think. Studies recently presented at the quadrennial International Conference on Birth Defects in Montreal give strong indication that even moderate drinking by a pregnant woman—as little as two to four drinks a day—may damage an unborn baby's brain for life.[10]

THE REMEDY FOR THE LIQUOR PROBLEM

In the face of facts like these, what should be the Christian's stand concerning social drinking? Let us remember that one becomes a Christian only by repentance and faith in Jesus Christ, not by any works of righteousness. Faith in Christ makes us new creations with new goals and aims and standards. The Holy Spirit indwells us, and He makes the changes that show that we are Christians.

Some Christians assume that because they have been saved by grace, conduct does not matter. Some even believe that living with a principle of total abstinence constitutes a form of legalism and somehow negates the fact that they have been saved by grace.

But that is a wrong idea of Christian liberty. There is no reason the person saved by grace should not restrict himself to please the Lord who saved him.

The apostle Paul recognized the importance of that principle.

In 1 Corinthians 8, he speaks concerning his right to eat meat that had been offered in heathen temples. In verse 13 he writes, "If meat make my brother to offend, I will eat no flesh while the world standeth."

I see four basic reasons why the Christian should voluntarily abstain from social drinking. First, the Bible suggests that abstinence is a sound position for the earnest Christian. Someone will say at once, "But doesn't the Bible speak of drinking wine? Didn't Jesus drink wine? And the apostle Paul wrote to Timothy, 'Drink no longer water, but use a little wine for thy stomach's sake . . .' " (1 Timothy 5:23). It is interesting that Paul had to urge Timothy to take a *little* wine. That seems to imply that he was not used to taking any wine.

Wine drinking *is* often mentioned in the Bible. However, our English translations make no distinctions between words denoting different kinds of wine. In some cases, especially in the New Testament, the references are to sweet, unfermented wine.

Although the Bible nowhere says one cannot drink wine, it does condemn excess. "Woe unto them that are mighty to drink wine," says Isaiah 5:22, "and men of strength to mingle [or mix] strong drink." Proverbs 20:1 likewise warns, "Wine is a mocker, strong drink is raging: and whosoever is deceived thereby is not wise."

It is interesting to note, however, that God required total abstinence for those in close relationship to Him. Leviticus 10:9 forbids the use of wine to priests who ministered in the Tabernacle. Wine was likewise forbidden to those under special vows to God as Nazarites (Numbers 6:3).

Should the New Testament believer be less holy than those separated to God in Old Testament times? Peter writes, "But as he which hath called you is holy, so be ye holy in all manner of conversation; because it is written, Be ye holy; for I am holy" (1 Peter 1:15-16).

Paul writes, "Let us walk honestly [or decently], as in the day; not in rioting and drunkenness, not in chambering and wantonness. . . . But put ye on the Lord Jesus Christ, and make no provision for the flesh, to fulfill the lusts thereof" (Romans 13:13-14).

But some will say, "Did not the Lord Jesus Christ turn water into wine?" He did, indeed. One must remember, of course, that He was providing the accepted refreshment of the day.

Although Bible scholars differ, there is no absolute evidence that the wine He made had intoxicating qualities. The narrative in John 2 makes a point that the wine He made was distinctive in its taste, clearly different from that provided earlier by the hosts. In this, our Lord's first miracle, illustrating the newness of the life He gives, it is debatable that Jesus would provide a wine that would intoxicate.

A second reason for abstinence is the role and character of alcohol in our modern world. Liquor today, especially in our country, is the partner of excess and evil. Overall, the brewing, sale, and distribution of liquor is a monstrous evil in which no Christian should want to have a part.

One cannot drink without giving endorsement to a baneful custom and a conscienceless enterprise. It is unthinkable that a Christian should contribute to an industry that deals in death, misery, and the ruin of countless lives. A very pointed command is given in 1 Thessalonians 5:22: "Abstain from all appearance of evil," or "from every form of evil." One cannot argue that drinking is a harmless custom when millions are alcoholics.

What are the present-day associations of alcohol? Can we find any that are good or uplifting or honoring to God? Social drinking is at best a "detente" with the god that holds millions in bondage. And, as Paul asks, "What fellowship hath righteousness with unrighteousness? and what communion hath righteousness with unrighteousness? and what concord hath Christ with Belial?" (2 Corinthians 6:14-15).

A third reason for abstinence is that drinking, even in moderation, can be destructive to one's personal Christian life. Alcohol is harmful to the body. The great inventor Thomas Edison said, "To put alcohol in the body is like putting sand on the bearings of an engine. It doesn't belong." Centuries earlier,

William Shakespeare spelled out the same essential truth when he wrote, "Alcohol is a poison men take into the mouth to steal away the brain."

Medical research is showing that alcohol not only has an immediate, short-range effect but also inevitably brings about long-range damage to the human system. Brain cells die when alcohol is taken into the bloodstream. Heart, liver, and kidneys are also permanently affected. If you are a Christian, your body is the temple of the Holy Spirit. You should not defile or damage it by subjecting it to liquor.

Not only is alcohol detrimental to the body, it also is spiritually and morally degrading. Even moderate drinking cannot but fog the mind and cloud the spirit.

Finally, a Christian should abstain for the sake of others, especially those who may be influenced by his example. Experience shows that for every dozen people who choose the path of social drinking, one will become an alcoholic before ten years have passed. Three others will teeter on the brink, becoming problem drinkers.[11] Eight out of every dozen social drinkers succeed as moderate drinkers, but four others will fail, and one of them will drop off the precipice of addiction. There is no telling which ones will be affected.

In the light of such facts, Romans 14:21 speaks to us pointedly. "It is good neither to eat flesh, nor drink wine, nor anything whereby thy brother stumbleth, or is offended, or is made weak."

Your decision on this issue is crucial. There are no signs that our national alcohol problem is getting better. It is getting worse. Not only men and women, but children and youth are deeply affected. The liquor industry aims to bring its products into every home and family in the United States. Estimates indicate that American breweries, wineries, and distilleries will spend from $500 million to 1 billion dollars in advertising this year. Government and business, by and large, are sympathetic to the liquor industry.

It seems clear that the only safe principle for a Christian is total abstinence from alcoholic beverages in any form. In light of the cost, in terms of lives, property, and health, alcohol is a luxury we cannot afford.

NOTES

1. Jack B. Weiner, *Drinking* (New York: Norton, 1976), pp. 2-3.
2. Ibid., p. 3.
3. *Christianity Today,* 6 November 1970, p. 28.
4. "Drinking Plateau Reached?" *The American Issue,* January-February 1977, p. 3.
5. *Christianity Today,* p. 28.
6. Weiner, p. 42.
7. Ibid., p. 41.
8. "Drinking Plateau Reached?" *The American Issue,* p. 3.
9. *Reader's Digest,* February 1977, p. 163.
10. Joan Beck, "Even Social Drinking by a Woman Can Harm a Fetus," *The Chicago Tribune,* 26 August 1977.
11. Walter S. Krusich, "Alcohol: Headache Around the World," *Moody Monthly,* December 1972.

SIX

The Question of Civil Disobedience

Verdict: *Peter and John, guilty of civil disobedience.* These unauthorized preachers, after healing a lame man, stirred the people by attributing the miracle to Jesus Christ and by proclaiming the resurrection. Furthermore, Peter boldly accused the religious leaders of being responsible for the crucifixion of Jesus Christ. For such crimes Peter and John were sentenced to jail.

Verdict: *John Bunyan, guilty of civil disobedience.* The author of *Pilgrim's Progress* failed to attend the Church of England and persisted in preaching without proper credentials. Therefore, he was found guilty of breaking the king's laws. Arrested three times, Bunyan spent thirteen years in jail for such crimes.

Verdict: *Martin Niemöller guilty of civil disobedience.* During World War II, this German pastor stood before Hilter and declared, "God is my Führer." For this crime he was removed from his pulpit and placed in a concentration camp.

THE APOSTLES AND CIVIL DISOBEDIENCE

The issue of civil disobedience is not new. For centuries Christians have been caught between giving their allegiance to God and obeying the laws of man. Ever since A.D. 30, when the Jerusalem hierarchy desperately tried to silence Peter and John (Acts 5), Christians occasionally have been forced to disobey some of man's orders. Peter and John refused to be silent in the face of a

217

threatened jail sentence. These first preachers of the gospel had received their authority from Jesus Christ Himself; but because they lacked the necessary papers and approval from the authorities of their day, the Jerusalem leaders were determined to stop them. They thought Peter and John were too irregular. They did not fit the established order of the day; they were transformed nonconformists.

The priests in charge of the Temple were disturbed by these men because the priests desired things to be done in a certain way. Money changers selling their doves were allowed, but children of God lifting their voices in unrehearsed praise were out of order. The Sadducees, one sect of religious leaders, did not believe in a resurrection, and they were determined to stop anyone preaching about the subject. And miracles were stirring people up. All this was dreadfully irregular.

The apostles were arrested late at night. The authorities knew that if they made their arrest during daylight hours, the public might protest. So they were careful to carry out their challenge of God's Word under cover of darkness.

But the Word of God cannot be bound. The apostles had unquestionable power behind them. It must have dismayed the authorities that the evidence was so incontrovertible. When the lame man stood before them whole, they could not deny that power.

What made the disobedience of the apostles legitimate? Supernatural power caused them to speak. And that same kind of supernatural power should characterize every Christian. The work of the church is ministering to people. We are to find people who are lying at the gate, excluded from our worship; to lift them up; and to make them worshipers of Jesus Christ. The church will convince no one of its right to speak unless it can point to changed lives in men and women. The world wants to see miracles.

Another thing that upset the authorities was the apostles' persistence. The hierarchy was used to seeing people melt in their presence. Those priests even bent the Roman officials to their

218

wills. But the simple boldness of the apostles was shocking. There was only one way to stop them—forbid them by law to preach. Then if they persisted, they could be jailed.

But the religious leaders forgot that the believers lived by a higher authority. Said Peter, "We ought to obey God rather than men." When civil law opposes God's clear commandments, we are obliged to obey God. There are times when it is right to disobey the laws of men.

THE BIBLE AND CIVIL DISOBEDIENCE

But there are also times when it is wrong to disobey human authority. A few more examples from the Scripture will illustrate the distinction.

Exodus 1 tells of an Egyptian ruler who ordered the death of every Hebrew male child. Verse 17 says, "But the midwives feared God, and did not as the king of Egypt commanded them." Jochebed, the mother of Moses, engaged in civil disobedience when she hid her child in a basket among the reeds in the river. Hers was not mere rebellion, however; it was obedience to the will of God.

Consider Daniel 6 and the law of Darius that "whosoever shall ask a petition of any God or man for thirty days . . . he shall be cast into the den of lions." Daniel, fully aware of the law, disobeyed it. Daniel "went into his house . . . and prayed and gave thanks before his God, as he did aforetime" (Daniel 6:10). Daniel too disobeyed the king's law. But his desire was not to express rebellion—it was to be in conformity with God's clearly revealed will.

Jeremiah criticized the government of his time so severely that he was jailed and called a traitor to his nation. But the substance of his criticism was the Word of God. He was not motivated by a desire just to disobey.

What is the other side to the question? The Scriptures speak clearly concerning the Christian's responsibility to obey his government. First Peter 2:13 tells us, "Submit yourselves to every ordinance of man for the Lord's sake: whether it be to the king, as

219

supreme." "Let every soul be subject unto the higher powers. For there is no power but of God: the powers that be are ordained of God" (Romans 13:1). Peter and Paul are saying that no civil power exists except by God's permission. Therefore, whoever resists civil power resists God's ordinance, unless the civil power demands disobedience to a clear commandment of God's Word.

The story of the rebellion of Korah and a band of Israelites is found in Numbers 16. The government of the day was a theocracy, and Moses was God's chosen civil leader. When the people rebelled against the authority of Moses, God judged them with sudden death, because Moses, the civil leader, represented God's authority. A rebellion against him constituted a rebellion against God.

Now, of course, the problem is to reconcile what may be apparently contradictory instructions of Scripture. On the one hand, we are to view the authority of civil government as God-given authority. On the other hand, we are not to obey any civil laws that contradict God's Word. That is a difficult problem to many Christians today.

THE CHRISTIAN AND CIVIL DISOBEDIENCE

Here are conflicts some of our brothers and sisters in Christ have faced in recent years:

Christians in China during the communist takeover suddenly found themselves under a law that forbade them to gather for religious services. Yet the Bible commanded them not to forsake the assembling of themselves together.

A family of Christians living in Germany during Hitler's time had to decide whether to turn over Jewish neighbors to the secret police, or defy the government and hide them.

A pastor in Russia was given the choice of jail if he continued to preach against the atheistic doctrines of Communism, or freedom if he would merely teach the sections of Scripture that would not conflict.

A believer in Christ living in Cuba had to decide whether he would join a revolutionary movement to overthrow the godless government of Fidel Castro.

A young Christian, a citizen of the United States, believed that his country was involved in an unjust war. He was being drafted, and others encouraged him to resist the draft because of his moral convictions.

Some guidelines in deciding what to do in difficult situations like those should help us.

First, disobedience, if necessary, must be without violence. To be violent or to hurt someone is contrary to the teaching of the Word of God. The riots that shake our country are violent and evil. Such demonstrations are perpetrated by extremists who have no use for the laws of God.

Second, the law being disobeyed must be clearly contrary to the Word of God. We cannot disobey merely as a matter of preference. Peter and John are examples. They were commanded by their Lord to bear witness to the things they had seen and heard. The command of the authorities to be silent was clearly in conflict with God's word to them.

Many young men who have resisted the draft in recent years have disobeyed simply because they feel no obligation to serve their country. But others believe God's Word specifically teaches that Christians should resist military service. Their stance as conscientious objectors is a matter of genuine conviction. Each young person must decide these matters in light of the Spirit's teaching in the Word of God. And the laws of the United States provide for honest, conscientious objectors.

Third, disobedience must not be a general rebellion against civil government as a whole, because all governments (both good ones and bad ones) fall within God's permissive and directive will. Peter and Paul lived and served while wicked Nero held sway, yet both commanded believers to be submissive to the government. The direct teaching of Scripture requires respect and submission to government (Romans 13:1-7; 1 Peter 2:13-17).

Henry David Thoreau wrote, "It is not desirable to cultivate a respect for the law, so much as for the right." But, we must ask, who decides what is right? The government may make a mistake, but so may the people. If seven people disobey, that is one thing. But if seven million disobey, that is anarchy.

Finally, Christians must be willing to bear the consequences of disobedience to civil authority. Peter and John were so committed to Jesus Christ that they were willing to suffer ridicule, jail, and death to get out the gospel. They willingly accepted the punishment that resulted from their disobedience.

The Scriptures are clear that ordinarily the commandments of God and the commandments of government are not in conflict. They also establish that God is the Lord of the Christian's conscience. However, for the most part, obedience is in and disobedience is out. If we are forbidden to bear witness to salvation in Christ, we must disobey that command. If we are ordered by authorities to do evil in the sight of God, we must disobey.

But there is much that can be done without disobeying! Christians in the United States are blessed with freedom and possibly more governmental tolerance than any other nation in history. Our government was established with freedom of religion as one of its fundamental principles, and we still largely enjoy that freedom.

One of the greatest threats to today's church is that it will get sucked into the spirit of rebellion that seems to prevail in our age. Already some formerly sound religious groups have become major exponents of worldwide revolution. There is nothing that resembles such rebellion and arrogance in the teachings of Christ or in the example of the early church.

Civil disobedience is sometimes called for. Those occasions are rare, and it must be done humbly, prayerfully, and wisely, in accordance with God's Word.

SEVEN

The Christian School Versus the Public School

Today there is a fresh, new breeze in the troubled world of education. And it is coming from the Christian school. In a day when most educators are worried, Christian schools are showing vigor and new promise.

Even the prestigious *Wall Street Journal* recognizes that. Recently, sandwiched in with columns of stock quotations and national and business news, was a report from Southern Pines, North Carolina.

Because the teaching in the schools was inferior and conflicted with pupil's religious beliefs, some parents from Calvary Christian Church pulled their children out of the public school system. Their congregation built its own school. Christianity and the basic skills of reading, writing, and arithmetic are being taught by the school's twelve teachers and learned by its student body of 125 pupils.[1]

The report continues for more than a full column. It notes that the number of Christian schools is steadily growing. One estimate places the number of interdenominational Christian schools at 5,000. By 1990 Christian schools will outnumber public schools if current growth trends continue.[2] A specialist with the United States Office of Education says that Christian schools are the fastest growing segment in private education today.[3]

Why have Christian leaders and parents across the land chosen to enter the field of education? There is a price to pay, of course. Each new Christian school involves a tremendous cost in terms of study, prayer, personal sacrifice, and money. The answer is the growing concern of thoughtful Christian parents for the course of public education. The secular outlook in schools today, they believe, demands an alternative for Christians.

I do not want to be misunderstood. We live in a day when the American public is all too prone to condemn and criticize. There are thousands of conscientious and dedicated people deeply involved in our public schools. Among them are many dedicated Christians. They deserve our thanks and appreciation for their important contributions. However, trends in the field of education are such that the Christian parent must at least consider the possibilities of a Christian education. Let me suggest four issues to be considered in regard to the question.

THE DIRECTIVE: PARENTS ARE RESPONSIBLE FOR EDUCATION

Who is responsible for the task of education? The Bible clearly says God assigned that job to parents. Speaking of His commandments, God says in Deuteronomy 6:7, "And thou shalt teach them diligently unto thy children, and shalt talk of them when thou sittest in thine house, and when thou walkest by the way, and when thou liest down, and when thou risest up." If God has given you children, your task will not be complete until they have the best and most adequate preparation to meet the tests of life. We dare not casually pass along our task to others, without being certain what they are teaching our children.

Send your child to school today, and by the time he receives his high school diploma you will have delegated 16,000 hours of time to outside teachers. At the very least, you need to be concerned about how all those hours are used.

THE DISAPPOINTMENT: PUBLIC SCHOOLS ARE FAILING

Deuteronomy 6 tells us that the prime concern of education should be not the skills of life, important as they are, but a grounding in the fear and knowledge of God. Secular education writes off that obligation completely.

Education without God tends merely to teach the young how to make a living. It teaches them culture and the arts as a means of enjoying life, but it does not teach them wisdom. It does not teach them how to make vital life decisions.

A study of education will clearly show that educators through the centuries have taught succeeding generations to be man-centered. God, for the most part, has been forgotten and even opposed. That is especially true today. In 1963, the Supreme Court ruled that Bible reading and prayer in the public schools are not constitutional. The ruling then was new, but the spirit behind it was not. For centuries we have been moving down the road toward excluding God and the Bible from public education.

The most serious effect of the 1963 decision is not that it cuts off children from prayer and Bible reading. Prayer and Bible reading can and should be done at home. Rather, the ruling says, in a way no young person can misunderstand, that God and faith have no essential place in education.

Surely that is one of the most basic points of failure in our public education system. It shouts that faith in God and reliance in the Bible are add-ons in the process of education. They are not really needed.

That is one reason for the growing number of Christian schools. Many parents believe that God should not be barred from education. But there are other reasons. One is the parent reaction to the rising tide of violence in our public schools. Violence in the schools has more than tripled in this decade. Some 70,000 teachers are physically assaulted in schools each year, not to mention assaults of students.[4] Parents naturally fear for the safety of their children. But beyond all that, they know that schools today are schools of lawlessness, permissiveness, and often violence.

There is a growing feeling that our secular schools are failing in their basic job of teaching the essentials. Each year taxpayers foot an education bill in excess of $144 billion, then watch helplessly as Scholastic Aptitude Test scores plummet.[5]

For all our national stress on education, surveys from time to time show distressing percentages of the functionally illiterate. Colleges complain that high school graduates come to them inadequately prepared to read and write. Average scores for Scholastic Aptitude Tests in math are down 10 percent from fifteen years ago. School effectiveness varies greatly, of course. But many parents have taken their children from public schools to place them in Christian institutions because of disappointment in the learning situation. In a report for the Center for the Study of Democratic Institutions, Dr. Robert M. Hutchins charges that our education institutions are not imparting "the arts of reading writing, speaking, listening and figuring."

The content of what public education is teaching also troubles many thoughtful Christians. Pupils are not only subjected to teaching that excludes faith in God and the Bible, but they are indoctrinated in what one Christian educator calls the "deadly duo" of evolution and humanism.

Dr. Paul A. Kienel, executive director of the Association of Christian Schools International, lists eight significant humanistic assumptions inherent today in our public education:

1. Man is supreme. If this is true, there is no higher power.
2. Man evolved from lower forms of life. Consequently, there was no act of divine creation.
3. Man is an animal. Therefore, he cannot have a soul.
4. Man is inherently good. He does not need a Savior.
5. Common practice sets the standard. This, of course, is the assumption that whatever the majority does, must be the thing to do. If this is true, there are no moral absolutes.
6. Criminals are merely antisocial. The implication here is that lawbreakers have a problem, but they are not really sinners.
7. The term maladjustment explains all adverse human behavior. In other words, there is no such thing as guilt.
8. Finally, secular education assumes that bad environment is to blame for evil. If this is true, man himself is not responsible.[6]

Those are assumptions interwoven in every facet of secular

228

education—in English and literature, in government and sociology, in biology and general science. They are transmitted not only in textbooks, but also by the personal views of the majority of teachers, who were trained and indoctrinated in secular institutions where humanism reigns.

Christian parents object to specific teachings of certain textbooks—books that have socialistic and communistic viewpoints. They object to salacious literature. Parents can protest, of course, but as a minority their voice is seldom heard.

THE DIRECTIVE: A COMPLETE BIBLICAL EDUCATION

Those are some of the many reasons Christian parents especially are turning away from secular education today. And there are equally important reasons they are finding Christian schools effective. Let me first of all dispel an illusion. Often the public assumes that Christian schools give all their time to teaching the Bible itself. That is not true.

Christian schools are schools, not Sunday schools or Bible classes, although the Bible is read and often memorized. Pupils and teachers pray. They study and relate as Christians. Pupils focus on the familiar basic subjects. They learn reading, math, writing, history, science, and other subjects required for college preparation. They meet prescribed basic educational standards.

In general, Christian schools tend toward fewer frills than our secular education system—fewer courses that border on the hobby level and far-out lines of specialization. Extracurricular activities are more limited; pupils give more time to serious learning.

This may explain, for example, the record set recently by eighth graders enrolled in schools affiliated with the Association of Christian Schools International. These students in 1,200 member schools scored twelve months above the national average on the Stanford Achievement Test.[7]

Although the situation may vary from school to school, many parents believe their children are getting better teaching in Christian schools than in the public system. Discipline is better maintained; children learn respect for the law and order. They learn to work and study. Classes tend to be smaller than in public schools, so children receive more personal attention. The *Wall Street Journal* quotes Perry King, a biology teacher at a Christian school in North Carolina. "I have ten students in my biology class," he says. "I can give them as much attention as they need. I can discipline them if I need to. If they don't learn in this situation, we just don't have an excuse."[8]

Christian schools must meet state standards for teachers. Teachers often have to teach more subjects and are usually paid less than teachers in the public schools. But more of those who teach in Christian classrooms are there because they want to serve.

The great distinctive of Christian schools, however, lies in their overall approach to education. God is not ignored but is made the center of all learning. Children are taught to make important judgments, to choose the right, and reject the wrong. The Christian school attempts to turn the searchlight of the Scriptures on every aspect of education. The Bible becomes a guide for discerning truth, a help in choosing what is good.

History, geography, science, social studies, and all the rest are presented in the light of Bible teaching. Most Christian schools do not ignore the theory of evolution, but they study it as a theory, not as a fact. They learn to see its fallacies. They see the wonder and meaning of creation.

The place of the Bible in this kind of Christian school is the same as the place of the Bible in the Christian life. It is a discerner, a yardstick, an evaluator. Psalm 119:105 says, "Thy Word is a lamp unto my feet, and a light unto my path." Hebrews 4:12 says, "The word of God is quick and powerful, and sharper than any two-edged sword, piercing even to the dividing asunder of soul and spirit."

Secular education has laid the Bible aside—even banned the Bible—and is walking in the dark. Christian schools are setting education on its feet by restoring the Bible to its proper place.

THE DOUBT: DO CHRISTIAN SCHOOLS ISOLATE CHILDREN?

Some people say that Christian schools are fine—but. And one of the biggest objections they raise is the charge of isolation. Christian schools, they say, shut up children in an unreal world. They will emerge as hothouse plants, unable to cope with the secular world in which they have to live.

But that is a weak objection. Students at Christian schools do not enter a monastery. They live and play with non-Christian children in their neighborhoods, meet others on the streets and at places of recreation. They watch television and listen to the radio. Inevitably they read comics, see the same magazines, and come under many of the same influences as students in secular schools.

Meanwhile, their teachers in their Christian schools are realistic people. Their concern above all, is to help their pupils cope with the world as they will find it. Dr. Roy W. Lowrie, Jr. writes in a pamphlet on this subject, "The Christian school does shelter students. It shelters them from the prevalence of drugs, lack of discipline, sexual promiscuity, situational ethics, disrespect for authority, drinking, occultism, atheism and agnostic values.

"[But] as a professional educator, and . . . a father, I earnestly believe that kind of sheltering . . . is highly desirable."[9] With that I thoroughly agree.

Christian schools—well-conducted Christian schools—are friends of Christian parents today. Christian schools provide the kind of education that the Bible says our children need. If you are not already involved in a Christian school situation, perhaps it is time at least to investigate.

What kind of education are your children getting? What kind of textbooks are they studying? What kind of teachers shape them for tomorrow? Do you know?

NOTES

1. *Wall Street Journal*, 7 December 1978.
2. Dave Raney, "Public School vs. Christian School," *Moody Monthly*, September 1978, p. 44.

231

3. *Wall Street Journal*, 7 December 1978.
4. Raney, p. 44.
5. Ibid.
6. Paul L. Kienel, "Do Christian Schools Care About Discipline," *Christian School Comment*, April 1973. Used by permission.
7. *Wall Street Journal*, 7 December 1978.
8. Ibid.
9. Roy W. Lowrie, Jr., "Are Christian Students Too Sheltered?" Pamphlet. Christian Schools Today, 464 Main Road, Newton Square, PA 19073.

EIGHT

The Problem of Homosexuality

The most explosive issues of our day are those that have their roots in human rights—the right to basic freedom, the right to education, the right to work, the right to worship as I may feel led. But should I have the right to do something you are convinced is morally wrong?

That is the crux of what is called the "gay rights" issue. Across the land, pressure is increasing to give homosexuals access to jobs of every kind, the right to be accepted as foster parents, and even the right to marry each other. Beneath it all is the insistence that the public change its thinking about the validity of the homosexual pattern.

The Conflict of Homosexuality

A forty-year-old mother from Dallas believes she is a victim of discrimination. She is divorced but wants custody of her eleven-year-old son. A few years ago, a jury decided against her because she is a homosexual, living with a woman companion.

Gay organizations and the National Organization for Women came to her defense. Her newly published book is being filmed for television as a network movie. Meanwhile the mother and her living companion are traveling around the country raising funds for legal appeals.

She says, "They didn't prove I was an unfit mother. The issues are the right to privacy, due process, and the separation of church and state. I'm a very Christian person, but I learned in eighth grade civics that laws aren't supposed to be based on the Bible."[1]

Can a person be a good parent and still be a homosexual? Can a homosexual be a Christian? What should be our attitude as Christians toward the homosexual life-style? Equally important, what should be our attitude toward persons in the grip of homosexual practices? What does the Bible have to say about the issue?

More and more we are hearing about the issue of gay rights. Only a few years ago Anita Bryant was projected into national prominence–condemned by some and praised by others—for her successful efforts in opposing a gay rights ordinance in Dade County, Florida.

Twenty years ago a discussion of homosexual rights in our society would have been unthinkable. Today, however, the pros and cons of gay acceptance are very much an issue. Many people—including some who say they are Christians—accept homosexuality as a legitimate alternative life-style. In the next few months and years the country will be obliged to make decisions on many of these issues.

A great deal of uncertainty is evident. Some time ago, *Time* magazine in an essay "The Homosexual in America" made this discerning comment:

> Beset by inner conflicts, the homosexual is unsure of his own position in society. . . . A vast majority of people retain a deep loathing toward him, but there is a growing mixture of tolerance, empathy or apathy.[2]

Society is torn between condemnation of the homosexual and compassion for him, the article continued. The deviate's plea is that he be treated just like everybody else, yet it is known that he is not like everybody else.[3]

In simple terms, a homosexual is one evidencing sexual desire toward a member of the same sex, men with men or women with women. It may express itself merely in preference for intimate companionship. More often it involves a sexual act. Psychologists tell us that one may yield to homosexual tendencies occasionally or often. Others may follow the homosexual pattern for all or most of their lives.

The first question to be faced is whether homosexuality is wrong, as most of us have been instructed. The answer, quite simply and on the authority of God's Word is—yes, it is.

The big push of homosexuality today is to defend its practices as just another life-style. To buttress that position, homosexuals offer an amazing array of arguments. They say that homosexuals are born with their sexual preferences, just as others are born with heterosexual preferences. They cite the fact that sodomy is widespread, even common, and that when carried on in private it is no one's business but their own. They argue that other kinds of sexual indulgences are condoned or overlooked. In fact, within the past dozen or fifteen years the whole emphasis of homosexuals has been to defend the validity of their practice and press for what they call "gay rights."

Says one psychiatrist, "It is clear that it is becoming increasingly unpopular in the movement to ask or be asked the old question, 'Why are we what we are?' The trend is, unmistakably, to reject this question as arbitrarily posed, very possibly unanswerable, and most important of all, immaterial."[4]

The same authority goes on to say, "The homosexual is coming more and more to regard himself as in no way inferior because of his homosexuality, or homosexuality as in no way inferior to its counterpart as a valid mode of human self-expression; and he is expecting that society will eventually come around to a similar view."[5]

Today homosexuals are highly organized, having a network of regional conferences and a national clearinghouse to facilitate exchange of information. A national legal defense fund exists, and lawyers are instantly available to press the battle for gay rights wherever a need arises.

THE CONFUSION OF HOMOSEXUALITY

In all this, the Bible inevitably has come under sharp attack. Some homosexuals say the Bible should have no place in setting moral standards. Others seek to show by Scripture that the Bible itself justifies the homosexual life-style.

No Christian should be deceived. The Bible clearly tells us that homosexuality is without defense. Genesis 19 describes the homosexual lusts of the men of Sodom, which led to destruction of that city.

Homosexuals cite Ezekiel 16:49, which mentions Sodom's other sins—"pride, fulness of bread, and abundance of idleness," as well as failure to help the poor and needy, but forget that the next verse goes on to say, "and they . . . committed abomination before me; therefore I took them away." So clearly is Sodom's destruction linked with the practice of homosexuality that the term *sodomy* today still has a single meaning.

The Levitical law expresses God's principles of righteousness. Here, in Leviticus 18:22, God's commandment says, "Thou shalt not lie with mankind as with womankind; it is abomination." The fact that that is followed by a commandment against sexual acts with animals suggests the unthinkable nature of the homosexual relation.

There are other prohibitions in the Bible against homosexuality. One of the most revealing New Testament statements is in Romans 1, which tells how men once knew Almighty God, but turned from Him to idols. The passage goes on to say that because men gave up God, God in turn gave up men to "uncleanness through the lusts of their own hearts, to dishonor their own bodies between themselves."

Could this be homosexuality? The following verses make the fact too clear to miss. "For this cause God gave them up unto vile affections; for even their women did change the natural use into that which is against nature; and likewise also the men, leaving the natural use of the woman, burned in their lust one toward another, men with men, working that which is unseemly" (Romans 1:24, 26-27).

Does that mean that homosexuality is a curse on especially godless men? That is not what the Bible is saying. Paul *is* saying that homosexuality was brought into the race because man turned from God. It is one of many sins—and others are enumerated in the closing verses of the same chapter.

Homosexuality, like alcoholism, cursing, or violence, gets its hold on an individual in many different ways. The only ultimate solution is the blood of Jesus Christ.

If homosexuality is sin, then man is ultimately responsible, not just for the sin but for rejecting deliverance from that sin through faith in Jesus Christ. And that is what the New Testament says in 1 Corinthians 6:9-10.

"Do you not know that the unrighteous shall not inherit the kingdom of God? Do not be deceived; neither fornicators, nor idolaters, nor adulterers, nor effeminate, nor homosexuals, nor thieves, nor the covetous, nor drunkards, nor revilers, nor swindlers shall inherit the kingdom of God" (NASB*).

Homosexuality is a serious and offensive sin. But by far its worst effect is that it, along with other sins, can keep a man or woman outside of heaven forever. Today there are millions of homosexuals in our country—some believe as many as 20 million. The degrading effect is beyond our understanding. But the tragedy above all else is that they are letting their lust come between them and the blessing of salvation.

Genesis 4 tells how the world's first murderer, Cain, turned his back on God and occupied himself with other things. He built a city. He had a family. Soon his descendants were wrapped up in making a go of life without the help of God. They developed ranching interests. Some became musicians. One became a skillful metal worker. They built a great society, but they built it without God.

There is not much doubt that numbers of homosexuals today will go on building a society of their own. They may even get what they call "gay rights." But it will be a society walled off from God.

THE CURE FOR HOMOSEXUALITY

Let us be careful of our thinking, however. There is a remedy for homosexuality, and God has put it in our hands. After

---

New American Standard Bible.

declaring in 1 Corinthians 6:9-10 that no homosexual can inherit the kingdom of God, Paul goes on to say in verse 11, "And such were some of you: but ye are washed, but ye are sanctified, but ye are justified in the name of the Lord Jesus, and by the Spirit of our God."

What is this saying? The Word of God is telling us that although no one can hang on to homosexuality and still be accepted by Almighty God, some former homosexuals in the church at Corinth had found deliverance. They had entered a brand new life by faith in Jesus Christ.

We must be careful however about thinking that we can merely tell a homosexual to get right with God and expect him to become a Christian. Homosexual desire grips the heart and life with a strength and fury beyond anything most of us have ever experienced. Much love and prayer and concern are always needed. Much patience, too, and possibly much counseling. But the power of Jesus Christ does have the ultimate answer.

Is our attitude toward homosexuals really representative of Christ? Can we find the grace to love the sinner while we abhor the sin? Can we accept the person, yet keep from giving ground to desires and practices that are evil?

I believe in certain rights for homosexuals. They have the same rights as other men and women bearing an awesome weight of sin to share in the power of the gospel.

William Barclay writes, "The proof of Christianity [in Corinth] lay in its power. It could take the dregs of humanity and make men out of them. It could take men lost to shame and make them sons of God. . . . No man can change himself, but Christ can change him."

The church today is in the world at a time of desperate need. We must resist the adversary, but we must hold out the hope of life and deliverance through Christ to those who will be lost without it.

NOTES

1. "A Lesbian Mother Still Fights to Regain Custody of Her Son," *Chicago Daily News,* 10 August 1977.
2. *Time,* 21 January 1966, pp. 40-41.
3. Ibid.
4. Foster Gunnison, "An Introduction to the Homophile Movement." Pamphlet. (N.p., 1967), p. 28.
5. Ibid., p. 29.
6. William Barclay, "The Daily Study Bible," *The Letters to the Corinthians* (Philadelphia: Westminster, 1956), p. 60.

NINE

The Unseen Faces of Communism

What philosophy of government has risen to power in our twentieth century by consistently deceiving its citizens? What system was the first to use hostages as weapons against its enemies? What political party has in less than a century mushroomed from a mere handful of loyal supporters to a worldwide movement?

The answer to those questions is one word—Communism. Communism deceives. Communism oppresses. Communism marches beneath the banner of an empty hope. Yet the shadow of Communism falls on half of our world at this moment. What should we know about Communism?

Seven Russians and their families will always remember April 27, 1979. On that date, five Soviet dissidents, all of them under sentence in Russian labor camps, arrived in Kennedy International Airport in New York to begin life as free men. A few hours later, two convicted Russian spies, each under sentence for buying United States military secrets, were put on a plane bound for Moscow. The Russian spies were released in exchange for the freedom of the five.

Among those given their freedom in the exchange were Ukrainian Baptist pastor Georgi Vins and human rights activist Alexander Ginsburg. What a strange exchange! Two convicted spies for the freedom of five of that country's citizens—men who wanted to leave.

Something is seriously wrong in a country where passports for dissidents must be purchased by exchanging them for spies. Something is wrong when refugees must by the thousands stream from countries that boast of the people's rights. And yet every year new countries pick up the communist banner. "Liberation" is their cry. "We want a people's government!"

THE DOMINATION OF COMMUNISM

From the standpoint of growth, Communism is a success. In three-quarters of a century, Communism has grown from nothing at all to become a system that controls the lives and fortunes of more than 1.5 billion people.

The movement began at the turn of this present century when Vladimir Ilyich Lenin established the movement known as Bolshevism in Russia. In 1903 the movement had only seventeen supporters. In 1917 Lenin was able to take control of Russia's millions with only 40,000 in his party. By 1928 there were forty-six communist parties with 1.6 million members. Today there are more than one hundred different parties with a total membership of 60 million people.

In recent years, two things have happened. First, there has been a Communism explosion! More and more countries have joined the communist block of nations. Second, Communism has become a many-sided movement. Whereas once the Soviet Union was the undisputed model of the communist state, Communism now seems to follow a number of different patterns. The Soviet Union is at odds with China. Eastern European countries like Yugoslavia have made clear that they want to forge their own communist regimes. In other countries, like Spain and Italy, Communists are content to carry on as one of several political parties.

The apparent fragmentation puzzles many in the West. Is the communist movement breaking up? Is this a hopeful sign? The best answer seems to be that although Communists want independence from one another, they have a common aim—the conquest of the world. Aleksandr Solzhenitsyn bluntly states that a nation's very life is often destroyed so that Communism can implement its ideals. Chinese Communism is no better than the Soviet variety. To think for a moment that relief is actually reaching the starving people of Cambodia is naive. The army and government of the Heng Samrin regime are receiving all the benefits.[1]

Few non-Communists today really understand Communism. They assume that Communism involves government ownership of land and factories, but in other ways, communist thinking is like our own.

That is not the case!

THE DOCTRINES OF COMMUNISM

An Australian doctor, Dr. Fred Schwarz, was stunned by the tactics of the Communists in his homeland years ago. As a result, he began an intensive study of Communism and for more than twenty years has headed the Christian Anti-Communist Crusade in Long Beach, California. Today he is still interpreting Communism and pointing out basic facts that everyone should know.

Keep in mind that the Communism we know today is a fusion of the thinking of German philospher Karl Marx and the organizing genius of Russian leader Vladimir Ilyich Lenin. Every committed Communist today in Russia, China, Vietnam, or Africa claims to be a Marxist-Leninist. What do Marxist-Leninists believe?

First, they believe that society around the world is engaged in a great ongoing struggle. It is not a conflict between nations, between right or wrong, or between God and Satan, but between the interests of two classes of people. One class is made up of those who get their wealth by owning and managing property. The other is the class that makes a living by hiring out as laborers.

Communists believe that if you are born in the owner-manager class, you will have one set of principles and instincts, and they will never change. Or, if you are a member of the worker class—the *Proletariat,* they call it—you will have a different set of qualities. Marxists are convinced that the property-owning class has its heart set on bigger profits. Workers they say, on the other hand, struggle for the highest possible wage.

As Communists see it, conflict between the classes is inevitable. They believe the laboring class is bound to win. One day the working class will overthrow the owning class, establish a dictatorship, and dominate the world.

The second important teaching of Communism is that the communist party is the means of speeding up that proletariat victory. To that end they make the communist party a small, well-disciplined, and highly committed group. If you are a communist party member, you are expected to be ready to do anything for the party—work, steal, lie, or give your life if necessary. No sacrifice is too costly or too great. Relatively few Russians are members of the communist party. Two hundred fifty-eight million people are controlled by fewer than 16 million party members—about 6 percent. That is shocking, isn't it?

But party members do not control the communist party. The party controls its members. This is the way it works. At the grass roots, the communist party in every area is organized in small, compact groups. They meet in a home, in a school, or a farm, or in a factory. Each local unit elects a representative to send to the district party council. Party members have no control over the council member they elect. The district council meets and discusses and votes—usually on the recommendations from the council higher up. Once a vote is taken, it becomes binding on every member of the council. Delegates then go back to tell the groups below what the higher council has decided.

Each council sends a representative to a higher body. Each council in turn receives its orders from above. Decisions made by the highest body become binding on every party member. Ultimately, one man becomes the leader-dictator—a Brezhnev or a Castro. In practice, the "people's government" becomes an empty phrase. No other party organization is permitted in a communist country. The communist party holds a tight monopoly on every phase of the nation's life—business, labor, education, army, police. There is no other leadership. There is no other voice.

A *third communist doctrine is that religion is a purely man-made institution.* Communists are materialists—only the material world is real. In other words, they say man is a material machine. He is shaped by his experience, according to the class in which he was born.

Because they hold this to be true, Communism promises that when its program has been carried out and the class conflict ended, the flaws in human nature will quickly disappear. Man will be a perfect creature. No communist country has ever achieved this goal, but it is the party's dream and promise.

Meanwhile the Communist would argue that there is no good or evil in itself. Lying, sabotage, even murder are good if they help to speed the party goal of worldwide revolution. Anything that hinders the revolution, on the other hand, is evil.

A *fourth teaching of the Communists is what they term "dialectical materialism."* In simplest terms, it means that they believe in a material universe in which progress comes through crisis. Communists therefore believe that revolution—or more exactly, a series of violent changes, is essential for winning the war against the capitalistic society. That can best be accomplished, they believe, by a succession of advances and retreats.

In the words of Dr. Schwarz, "It is impossible to judge the goal of communism merely by the direction in which they are moving at any given time. The objective is fixed, it does not change. The direction of progress towards the objective reverses itself all the time." A favorite communist technique in a given country is to find some cause—some real or fancied injustice—and rally support in the interests of that cause. In Russia, the communist slogan was Bread, Peace, and Land. Accordingly, in 1917, while coming to power, they distributed land to millions of peasants. In 1928, however, when they had consolidated power, they deprived the peasantry of the land that they themselves had given.

THE DECEPTION OF COMMUNISM

Communism is an evil system, a system to be feared. It is a system rooted deeply in untruth. It promises "people's government," but it gives dictatorship. It denies man's need for God, yet promises to save mankind by revolution. It is deceptive, yet clever and implacable. It changes methods constantly, but it does not change its course.

Today the Communists have conquered more than one and a half billion people on our planet. In addition, they have programs operating in practically every country. Why? To win the world for Communism.

Nikita Khruschev in his day of power said, "Although I am sixty-nine years old and do not have much longer to live, nevertheless I hope to live to see the day that the Red flag covers all the earth."

But you as a Christian ask, What can we do? First, we should stop helping Communism. That does not necessarily mean a breaking off of normal diplomatic relations, but rather a halt to policies that strengthen the communist movement.

Consider the ties sustained by business interests in the United States. Lenin is quoted as predicting that western capitalists "will compete with each other to sell us goods cheaper, and sell them quicker, so that the Soviets will buy from one rather than from the other. . . . They will bring [these goods] themselves," he said, "without thinking about their future."

Aleksandr Solzhenitsyn, the Russian exile and Nobel-Prize-winning author now living in this country, says that is exactly what has happened. The major construction projects in Russia's initial five-year plan were built exclusively with American technology and materials. And now we are beginning to do the same thing in China. Lenin predicted that our greed would result in this.

Another alliance is the one that links our government with theirs. We gave diplomatic recognition to communist Russia in 1933 and entered into a military alliance during World War II, even when Stalin was executing an estimated 40,000 persons every month. Solzhenitsyn reminds us that when the war was over, we gave the Soviet Communists unlimited aid and virtually unlimited concessions. Since then we have let Communists swallow up one country after another around the world. Afghanistan is only the most recent of scores of nations the Communists have taken over.

It is a serious thing to strengthen the hand of one who is intent on doing evil. The Bible warns against alliance with the wicked. The principle of 2 Corinthians 6:14 applies to nations as well as individuals: "Be ye not unequally yoked together with unbelievers."

But there is another potentially more effective thing each of us can do—and this is crucial. We must give ourselves to building a strong and spiritually alive America. Communism expects America to give up eventually, because we have lost the will to resist. They want to bring us to the point where we will no longer sacrifice for freedom. It is a burning, searching question whether the day is approaching when our nation will soon reach the point of believing the slogan Better Red than Dead. As things stand now, it seems we are marching toward defeat. We need to open our eyes, to be valiant for the right, to renew our faith in Jesus Christ and our commitment to His ways of righteousness.

Can America resist? Pray and live and work and witness to the end that our country may turn to God, that we may recover ourselves from self-indulgence and sin and unbelief, that we may stand in the coming day of crisis.

NOTES

1. "Solzhenitsyn on Communism," *Time,* 18 February 1980.
2. Fred Schwarz, "What is Communism?" Published lecture series. Christian Anti-Communism Crusade, Box 890, Long Beach, CA 90809

TEN

Divine Healing

Is there such a thing as divine healing today? That question is being asked by thousands of people who long for relief from physical sickness. Physical and mental afflictions are common to most of us. Why does God permit His children to suffer? Is illness necessary? Can God heal? Does God heal today? Is it always God's will to heal? What does the Bible teach about healing? Those are some of the questions that I will try to answer.

In the New Testament epistle of James we are reminded that God cares about our afflictions. He is deeply interested in our needs. If any believer is afflicted, says James, "let him pray" (5:13). He also reminds us that when we pray, God "giveth to all men liberally" (James 1:5). Our God is all-loving, all-powerful, all-wise, and He wants the best for His children. God really cares about our needs.

In James 5 we find that this caring God is concerned about our emotional needs. Verse 13 reads, "Is any among you afflicted? Let him pray. Is any merry? Let him sing psalms." The word *afflicted* refers to the difficult experiences of life, and especially the depression and anxiety we encounter because of them. "Is any among you suffering?" James is saying. "Let him pray." What are we to do with the great needs of life? James tells us to bring them to Jesus Christ. Whatever else we do, we are to share our joys and sorrows with the Lord Jesus and talk them over with the loving Father who hears and responds to our afflictions.

Sometimes the problems of life appear to be more than we can handle. In our grief we hardly know where to turn or what to do.

Matthew 14 records such an incident. John the Baptist was brutally murdered. Matthew says of John, "And his head was brought in a charger, and given to the damsel: and she brought it to her mother. And his disciples came, and took up the body, and buried it, and went and told Jesus" (Matthew 14:11-12).

What a traumatic, heartbreaking experience! John's disciples were shattered. What were they to do? They lovingly picked up John's body and carefully buried it and went and told Jesus.

Heartaches of one kind or another come to each of us. And we, too, must turn to Jesus in our hour of grief. It is comforting to realize that He understands our sorrow.

Isaiah described the Lord as "a man of sorrows, and acquainted with grief" (Isaiah 53:3). Jesus as the God-man knew what it was like to be weary. At times He even had no place to lay His head. He knew what it was to be lonely, what it was like to suffer intense pain and even death. Always remember that we have an Intercessor who understands and is touched with our sorrows, our pain, and grief.

But there are not only sad days in life. There are also glad days. Gladness is a wonderful emotion. James asks, "Is any merry? Let him sing psalms" (James 5:13). Happy or sad, cheerful or tearful, James tells us to relate everything to God through prayer and praise. Praise is as much a part of prayer as are petitions. The word *praise* in its various forms is found over five hundred fifty times in the Bible. Paul told the believers at Philippi, "Rejoice in the Lord always: and again I say, Rejoice" (Philippians 4:4). Praise should become habitual.

We find prayer to be an important solution to our emotional needs. But we find in James 5:14-15 that prayer is important to our physical needs as well. "Is any sick among you? let him call for the elders of the church; and let them pray over him, anointing him with oil in the name of the Lord: And the prayer of faith shall save the sick, and the Lord shall raise him up; and if he have committed sins, they shall be forgiven him" (James 5:14-15).

Notice what is *not* taught here. *James is not teaching that all sickness is a direct result of sin.* The word "if" in verse 15 suggests that some sickness is not the direct result of sin. As we study the gospels, we find that even Jesus' disciples were confused about the relationship of sin to sickness. In John 9:2-3, the "disciples asked [Jesus], saying, Master, who did sin, this man, or his parents, that he was born blind? Jesus answered, Neither hath this man sinned, nor his parents: but that the works of God should be made manifest in him." The blind man's illness was not a punishment for his or anyone else's sins. It had a greater purpose—that Christ might glorify the Father by healing the man.

At times, sickness *is* a result of sin. Some of the Corinthian Christians were careless concerning the Lord's table, and Paul wrote to tell them, "For this cause many are weak and sickly among you, and many sleep" (1 Corinthians 11:30). In Mark's gospel, Jesus ministered to the man sick of the palsy. First He forgave his sin, and then He healed his body. Jesus forgave his wickedness and then relieved his weakness.

There is no doubt that at times sickness is a direct result of sin, but it is a serious mistake to assume that *all* sickness is because of unconfessed sin. To accuse a sick person of sin is the kind of judgment no human being is capable of making. James 5:14-15 certainly does not teach that all sickness is caused by sin.

Neither is James condemning the use of medicine for healing. Some people believe and teach that we should have nothing whatsoever to do with the medical profession. They assert that consulting doctors or using medicine, hospitals, or other human means reveals a lack of faith in God. But the Bible does not teach that. In fact, many scholars would suggest that the anointing oil of verse 14 was actually used as medicine in Bible times. That seems often to be the case in biblical accounts of illness and treatment. For example, Luke's gospel tells how the good Samaritan applied oil to the wounds of the man he found on the road to Jericho. Also, much of the historical literature of that day confirms that oil was used as a healing medicine.

But whether or not James is referring to the use of medicine, we do find that there are many references to medicine throughout the Bible. In Proverbs 17:22 we read, "A merry heart doeth good like a medicine." Luke was a member of the medical profession. In Colossians 4:14, Paul refers to his co-worker as "Luke, the beloved physician." We find that Paul even prescribed some medicine himself. Writing to timid Timothy, who was suffering from stomach trouble (possibly an ulcer), the apostle suggested that he "drink no longer water, but use a little wine for thy stomach's sake and thine often infirmities" (1 Timothy 5:23).

Actually, Jesus Himself settled the entire controversy. In Matthew 9:12 Jesus said, "They that be whole need not a physician, but they that are sick." Jesus was saying that sick people need a doctor.

So James is neither teaching that all sickness is caused directly by sin, nor condemning the use of medical procedures in seeking healing. What is he teaching?

SOME POSITIVES

First, he is teaching that God is able to heal. There is no doubt as to our faith in that statement. It would be foolish to deny that the all-powerful God who created us can just as easily repair our bodies if that pleases Him. Without any question, God is able to heal the body.

Second, James is teaching that God does heal. Few believers would question God's present activity in the area of healing. The Bible clearly records the exercise of God's power in the healing of the sick. Jesus Himself healed multitudes while He was here on earth and has healed others during the centuries that have elapsed since He ascended to heaven.

Even in my own life, I have experienced God's miraculous healing power. During my junior year at the Moody Bible Institute I was stricken with a malignant tumor. For weeks I was confined to a hospital bed. I experienced two operations and

254

thirty radium treatments. My doctor told me that I might not live and if I did, the hope of having children was only remotely possible.

Right there in my hospital room I prayed, "O Lord, this bed is my altar of consecration. My life is in Your hands. I yield myself to Your will alone. I know You are all-powerful and can do absolutely anything. Thy will be done."

That was more than thirty years ago. God did a healing work in my life that even amazed the doctors. I believe I am living proof that God is able to heal, and He does heal in many instances.

SOME INTERROGATIVES

But, we must ask, *Is it always the will of God to heal?* I realize that there are some brothers and sisters in Christ who answer, emphatically, yes. They contend that it is God's will to heal all sickness—that only sin, or lack of faith, keeps us from being healed. They say that when Jesus Christ atoned for our sins on the cross, He brought about deliverance from all our infirmities.

We agree that Christ's death brought about deliverance. His death did purchase our deliverance from the infirmities of sin. But nowhere in the Scriptures do we find the promise of complete freedom from physical infirmity until Jesus Christ comes again to reign. It is in that day of full redemption that "God shall wipe away all tears from their eyes; and there shall be no more death, neither sorrow, nor crying, neither shall there by any more pain: for the former things are passed away" (Revelation 21:4). In that day we shall know full deliverance from our illnesses.

Some suggest that if we only have enough faith, we can be healed now of all sickness. But that is a difficult position to try to defend from the Scriptures. To argue that the healing of our infirmities depends on our faith would suggest, it seems, that if our faith were great enough, we would never have to die.

Romans 8:22-23 appears to contradict this position. "For we know that the whole creation groaneth and travaileth in pain together until now. And not only they, *but ourselves also,* which

255

have the firstfruits of the Spirit, even we ourselves groan within ourselves, *waiting for the adoption, to wit, the redemption of our body"* (italics added). Paul continues to verse 26, "For we know not what we should pray for as we ought: but the Spirit itself maketh intercession for us." And in verse 27 he writes, "And he that searcheth the hearts knoweth what is the mind of the Spirit, because he maketh intercession for the saints according to the will of God." If the indwelling Holy Spirit prays for our infirmities according to the will of God, who are we to pray any other way?

God may grant healing if, in His wisdom, that is best. But He may allow His children to suffer. Suffering does not necessarily indicate a lack of faith on their part, nor does it indicate a lack of love on God's part. Sometimes we learn more of God's way in sickness than in health, and often we glorify Christ more in suffering than in health.

The apostle Paul was one whom God used greatly in spite of physical affliction. Paul was apparently half-blind. He had to dictate his letters because he was unable to write except in a huge scrawl. To the church at Corinth he wrote, "Lest I should be exalted above measure through the abundance of the revelations, there was given to me a thorn in the flesh, the messenger of Satan to buffet me, lest I should be exalted above measure. For this thing I besought the Lord thrice, that it might depart from me. And he said unto me, My grace is sufficient for thee" (2 Corinthians 12:7-9). Three times Paul prayed for physical deliverance. God's answer was, "My grace is sufficient." Paul understood that it is not always God's will to heal.

We might also ask, "What does James mean by 'the prayer of faith'?" Personally, I do not believe that the prayer of faith refers to ordinary prayer, no matter how good and earnest it may be. On one occasion Paul had to leave his sick friend Trophimus behind. Paul was a man of great faith, and surely he must have earnestly prayed for his afflicted friend. Apparently, the "prayer of faith" cannot be prayed simply at will. It is my conviction that the faith necessary to pray the kind of prayer James is speaking of is given of God in certain cases to serve His purposes and to accomplish

His sovereign will.

Can God heal our afflictions? Yes, He is able, and He often works powerfully in the lives of some of His children. But is there healing for us all? No, not until the day we receive our glorious resurrected bodies. Until that day, we must daily submit ourselves to the will of God—nothing more, nothing less, and nothing else.

> My Jesus, as Thou wilt! O may Thy will be mine;
> Into Thy hand of love I would my all resign.
> Thro' sorrow or thro' joy, Conduct me as Thine own;
> And help me still to say, My Lord, Thy will be done.
>
> My Jesus, as Thou wilt! All shall be well for me,
> Each changing future scene I gladly trust with Thee.
> Straight to my home above I travel calmly on,
> And sing, in life or death, "My Lord, Thy will be done."
>
> Benjamin Schmolck

ELEVEN

How to Keep the Faith

Christian institutions, like people, are born to live and serve. But, like individuals, they are susceptible to death. The mortality rate of Christian schools is especially evident when we look at the early history of our country. Some of America's oldest and most prestigious colleges and universities began as virile Christian institutions. But the light of Christian testimony flickered and went out.

Harvard College was founded in 1638 with a special view of training pastors. Until 1700 more than half its graduates went into the ministry. The early Harvard handbook set out the knowledge of God and Jesus Christ as the principal end of life. But by 1869, spiritual Harvard lay on its deathbed, as the university was presided over by an enemy of the Christian faith.

Yale, from its beginning in 1701, was more conservative. In 1795 its president addressed students on such subjects as "The Bible Is the Word of God." In 1825 a Yale gospel group traveled about the country in evangelistic ministry. But Yale's once evangelical stance has long since disappeared. Fifty-four percent of a recent graduating class said they had no belief in any God.

Dartmouth College was founded to train men as missionaries to the American Indians. Princeton in its early days insisted that the faculty be "convinced of the necessity of religious experience for salvation." Yet both soon left their orthodox paths and secularized. Many other well-known schools had similar beginnings—and similar fates.

As once-Christian schools became secularized, churches and individuals stepped into the breach. They established new Christian schools and training institutions. Of these, the greater number have drifted from their original moorings. The mortality rate is high, even today.

How can a Bible-believing school maintain a faithful stand in these turbulent times? The question is important to every church and every Christian, for tomorrow's leaders—pastors and Christian workers, as well as laymen—are being shaped by the Christian schools of today. No Christian school falls by itself. It brings down other organizations with it. With no exception I know of, every professing Christian group floundering in the quicksand of unbelief today can trace its trouble to the failure of its schools.

How can our Christian schools be conserved for the Christian ministry? There is no easy answer. But let me suggest some possible guidelines that may help us fight "the good fight of faith" (1 Timothy 6:12).

KNOW THE FAITH

First, if we are to keep the faith, we must know the faith. It must be virile and well-defined. We cannot safeguard a nebulous, shibbolethlike shadow, hidden in a closet.

The great evangelist George Whitefield once asked a coal miner in Cornwall, England, what he believed.

"Oh," the miner replied, "I believe what my church believes."

"And what does your church believe?" the evangelist inquired.

"Well, the church believes what I believe."

"But what do you both believe?" Whitefield persisted.

Still the miner would not be cornered. "We both believe the same thing," he retorted.

An elusive faith can never be defended. The Word of God tells us that we are to "be ready always to give an answer to every man that asketh [us] a reason of the hope that is in [us] with meekness and fear" (1 Peter 3:15).

The foundation of our faith is the Word of God. Speaking

seventy-five years ago, Dr. Benjamin Warfield warned: "The Word of the living God is our sole assurance that there has been a redemptive activity exercised by God in the world. Just in proportion as our confidence in this Word shall wane, in just that proportion shall we lose our hold upon the fact of a redemptive work of God in the world."

Our faith rests in the inspired Word of God. The Moody Bible Institute's doctrinal statement reads, "The Bible, including both the Old and the New Testaments, is a divine revelation, the original autographs of which were verbally inspired by the Holy Spirit."

God's Word makes the same claim for itself. "All scripture is given by inspiration of God, and is profitable for doctrine, for reproof, for correction, for instruction in righteousness: That the man of God may be perfect, throughly furnished unto all good works" (2 Timothy 3:16-17). The expression "given by inspiration of God" means "God-breathed." God is the source of the Scripture; it comes from Him, just as if it were His breath, in such a way that it is His own expression word for word. "For the prophecy came not in old time by the will of man; but holy men of God spake as they were moved by the Holy Ghost" (2 Peter 1:21). If *all* Scripture is inspired, no Scripture is uninspired. *Verbal inspiration* means that the very *words* of Scripture are God-breathed. Our faith rests upon the *inerrant* Word of God. To quote Dr. Alfred Martin, "Because some people have tried to restrict the infallibility of the Bible only to the area of faith and morals, it is also helpful to use the word *inerrant* in describing it. When we say that the Bible is inerrant, we mean that there are no errors of any kind whatever in it. 'That is *infallible* which makes, or is capable of making, no mistakes; that is *inerrant* which contains no errors' [*Webster's Collegiate Dictionary*]. The Bible is both infallible and inerrant."

William Lyon Phelps of Yale, sometimes called the most beloved professor in America, said, "I thoroughly believe in university education for both men and women, but I believe a knowledge of the Bible without a college course is more valuable than a college course without the Bible." If Christian schools are to keep the faith, we must have the same attitude—an attitude of total trust in the Word of God.

AFFIRM THE FAITH

It is not enough, however, to know the faith. We must consistently affirm the faith. Biblical Christianity is contrary to the natural man, and it cannot be maintained without constant struggle. We must fight the good fight of faith.

Not only must the faith be affirmed before opponents, but it must be reaffirmed among ourselves as well. Deuteronomy 6 sets a pattern for the family that must be followed by all believers. Notice the fourfold command from Scripture: "And these words, which I command thee this day, shall be in thine heart: And thou shalt *teach them* diligently unto thy children, and shalt *talk of them* when thou sittest in thine house, and when thou walkest by the way, and when thou liest down, and when thou risest up. And thou shalt *bind them* for a sign upon thine hand, and they shall be as frontlets between thine eyes. And thou shalt *write them* upon the posts of thy house, and on thy gates" (Deuteronomy 6:6-9, italics added).

God's people were to know the faith, to teach the faith, to talk the faith, to live the faith, and to write the faith for all to see. But even after all that, they were warned, "Beware lest thou forget the Lord" (v. 12).

How can a Christian institution affirm the faith? First, by making known its doctrinal stand so that no one can miss it. We at the Moody Bible Institute do this annually in our catalog and, as much as possible, in other public statements. We feel a deep responsibility to make known the essence not only of what we are but also of what we believe and teach.

Second, a school can affirm its faith by stressing it among faculty, administration, and students. Once a year every person in a key position at Moody Bible Institute—teachers, administrators, even our trustees—re-reads our doctrinal statement thoughtfully and seriously, signing it to show his recommitment. Members of our faculty and staff are chosen in the light of their attitudes toward our doctrinal position as much as on the basis of their educational qualifications. Prospective faculty members are carefully interviewed by our director of personnel, our dean of education, and the president. We review their eschatology (theology of end times), their attitude toward Christian separation, and their commitment to personal soul winning. Preventive medicine is far less costly than emergency treatment later.

Often schools have drifted because, in seeking to improve academically, they have sacrificed the heart of their original commitment to Jesus Christ and a needy world. Our goal is academic excellence coupled with personal faith, commitment to and love for Christ.

We expect our faculty and staff to reaffirm the faith in their personal lives and work as well as in the classroom. As president, I attempt to do that in our weekly chapel sessions, in which we touch on the basic themes of Christian life and ministry. I also recall the events that led to the founding of our school.

Once every year I speak on how to lead a soul to Christ, how to know the will of God, and the importance of a daily quiet time. I also speak on our view of the church and on our position as servants of the church. We see these truths as basic. In repeating them we reaffirm our faith.

Why do schools drift? Because of individuals. And individuals drift because they lack a stated purpose. The person who has no target is not likely to shoot many arrows. The uncommitted mind is the drifting mind.

A school must not only make known its doctrinal position; it must enforce it as well. Harvard College, now Harvard University, for example, permitted freedom in matters of theology. It also failed to set any kind of standards of spiritual commitment for its officers. True, such measures will not always prevent drifting. Andover Theological Seminary attempted to require conformance to the Westminster Confession, only to have this requirement set aside by court ruling. Princeton, on the other hand, seems to have been overpowered as a result of granting degrees to non-Christians. Eventually pressure from secular-minded alumni forced the school to desert its evangelical thrust.

We do not apologize for our doctrinal statement or try to hide it. We publicize it. When asked, "Where does Moody stand?" I am happy to say, "Moody Bible Institute stands where we have stood since our inception. We have not altered our theological stance in any way, nor do we intend to do so." By the grace of God, we want to walk humbly, yet courageously, in the steps of those men who have gone before—men like Moody, Torrey, Gray, Houghton, and Culbertson.

Our message is the tried and proved gospel of Jesus Christ. Our passion is to see lost people converted and added to the family of God. Our motive is the constraining love of Christ. Our attitude is that of faith in a living Savior who delights to do abundantly above what we ask or think. Our method is serving people. In all these things we unashamedly affirm the faith.

Undergird the Faith

But more than doctrine is involved. *A Christian school must also undergird the faith.* The New Testament word for "church" is *ekklesia,* which means "called out ones." A truly Christian institution, by its very nature, is called out to a superior life-style. We believe that a position of separation is essential to keeping the faith. Students may complain occasionally about rules and regulations, but if nothing else, they are a reminder that the Christian's life-style is different.

Conformity to the world would merely show that we were drifting. We are mindful of the emphasis of Romans 12:2 brought out with special clarity in the Phillips translation: "Don't let the world around you squeeze you into its own mold." We reject the pressure to conform to this world.

We also undergird our faith by a positive program of training. Christian separation is separation *from* the world and *unto* Jesus Christ. Such separation demands cultivation of the inner life. We strive to encourage the devotional life through a daily quiet time. Throughout the year we try to make ours a climate conducive to spiritual growth.

Share the Faith

Finally, we must share the faith. An organization that does not share the faith will ultimately not keep the faith. A Christian organization must share the faith for the same reasons that constrain the individual Christian to do so.

We must share the faith, first of all, because of our knowledge. Paul declares in Romans 1:14, "I am [a] debtor." We owe the world a debt because of what we know.

Some years ago Dr. Jonas Salk discovered the final phases of the polio vaccine. He had a means of freeing the world from the suffering and pain caused by the dreaded disease polio. Suppose he had decided to withhold that lifesaving vaccine. Such action would have been criminal.

In the same way, Christians have the truth that can free people from the power of sin. Can we sit idly by and watch people die in sin without giving them the good news that Christ died for them? Of course we cannot—if we really accept the truths of God's Word. We must share the faith because of our knowledge.

Second, we must share the faith because of our blessings. Like the lepers of 2 Kings 7:9, we should remind ourselves, "We do not well: this is a day of good tidings, and we hold our peace." Contrary to the view of many people today, the world does not owe us a thing. But believers owe the world an intelligent, loving presentation of God's good news.

The Old Testament prophet Ezekiel presents an answer to the question "Why share the faith?" Listen to the Lord's words to him.

> When I say unto the wicked, O wicked man, thou shalt surely die; if thou dost not speak to warn the wicked from his way, that wicked man shall die in his iniquity; but his blood will I require at thine hand. Nevertheless, if thou warn the wicked of his way to

turn from it; if he do not turn from his way, he shall die in his iniquity; but thou hast delivered thy soul. [Ezekiel 33:8-9]

God is telling Ezekiel that he has the privilege and responsibility to warn people. Failure to sound the warning would result in his being held accountable. The same principle applies to Christians today. We must share because of our blessings.

Third, we must share the faith because of the Great Commission. "Go ye into all the world" (Mark 16:15) applies to us. William Carey read Matthew 28 and was burdened for a perishing, unbelieving world. He thought, "Does this commission of Jesus apply to me? Does God really want me to go as a missionary to share the good news?" Carey decided to share his burden for witnessing with the local ministerium. The presiding pastor sternly rebuked young Carey and informed him that when God wanted to save the heathen, He would do it without his help. In spite of that rebuke, William Carey responded to the commission given by Jesus. He accepted his responsibility to share the good news and became a missionary to India.

Just as God the Father sent His Son into this world, so God the Son sends each of us to communicate His love. This divine succession brings to us an awesome responsibility. "As my Father hath sent me, " said Jesus, "even so send I you" (John 20:21). We must share the faith because of the Great Commission.

Finally, we must share the faith because of our position. "We are ambassadors for Christ . . . we pray you in Christ's stead, be ye reconciled to God" (2 Corinthians 5:20). It is sobering to realize that God is making His appeal to the lost world through you and me. Charles B. Williams translates 2 Corinthians 5:20 powerfully: "So I am an envoy to represent Christ, because it is through me that God is making His appeal. As one representing Christ, I beg you, be ye reconciled to God."

With that awesome position, we are very much responsible. Each Christian is either a good ambassador of Christ or a poor one, but we cannot escape the fact that we are ambassadors. In the light of that staggering truth, accept your position with great care. We must share the faith because of our position.

The great preacher Alexander Maclaren pointed out that "Christianity is the only religion that has ever passed through periods of decadence and purified itself again. Men have gone back to the Word and laid hold again of it in its simple omnipotence, and so a decadent Christianity has sprung up again into purity and power."

I believe that is true. But what tragic loss there has been where those entrusted with keeping the faith have failed, especially in Christian schools. Again and again, such collapses have been responsible for tragic attacks against the church, attacks made from within.

We have a charge to keep, and with God's help we must be faithful. Each generation must in turn fight the good fight of truth and keep the faith. The only way is loyalty to the Word of God and to Jesus Christ, the living Word. By God's grace and with His help, no generation need fail nor falter. In our day we must keep the faith.

TWELVE

A Call for National Renewal

Some historians have told us that we are living in the closing hours of a dying culture. Many of our world's great cities are threatened by corruption and violence. The dark clouds of war hover dangerously over the Middle East. Red China, now a major power, appears anxious to display its muscles. Russia has flagrantly committed open aggression and seems to be daring the world to react. In many places, common sense and reason have been replaced by mob rule.

Morality in the United States is virtually nonexistent. Crime is on the increase. Most of our universities have become centers of humanism and secularism. Poverty and illiteracy predominate in many areas.

The late J. Edgar Hoover said, "We face the twin enemies of crime and Communism. Crime and moral decay are eating at us from within. And Communism stands ready to pick up the pieces."

Amid all this, a large segment of the church of Jesus Christ has adopted the spirit of this age and is apostate. Situation ethics and the "new morality" have been encouraged, and the masses are blinded to God's truth, God's will, and God's redemption. We desperately need a national call to repentance. It is no secret that we need help. But few realize that our hope as a nation lies in the hands of God's people.

When Seneca, the Roman philosopher and teacher, warned his day of the weakness of the Roman Empire, people laughed at him. To Roman citizens living in the glitter of success, inspired by their magnificent buildings, tree-lined avenues, gushing fountains, and triumphant arches, Rome was unbeatable. Rome was the eternal city.

It seemed absurd to think that war, taxation, crime, race riots, subversion, and apathy would prevail. But Rome fell—the impossible happened.

And now, the causes for the fall of Rome are increasingly prominent in our society! Divorce is bulldozing the family to ruin; for every three marriages in the United States, there is one divorce. Taxes are climbing steadily, and inflation continues to eat away at our standard of living. Pleasure is an obsession to the majority of people. In 1970 a total of 80 billion dollars was spent for national defense. Religion is in a state of compromise and sleep. The five fundamental reasons for the fall of Rome are now glaringly evident in our nation.

Several years ago Roger Babson, newspaper journalist, stated in an article that the measure of the strength of a nation is the intellectual and spiritual growth of its people, not its monetary gains. In fact, material prosperity often leads to the ruin of a nation. The only movement that will save a nation is a spiritual revival, because people are then more interested in serving, in seeking strength rather than security, and in pursuing character more than profit.

That is very upsetting, isn't it? But if we honestly face ourselves and our national condition, there is hope. We need divine help! We need national repentance. We need a spiritual revival.

What Revival Is Not

Unfortunately many people seem to have a false idea of what revival is. Revival is not large crowds. All of us have witnessed large religious gatherings where thousands attended, but by no stretching of the definition could that be called revival. Revival is not great preaching. As a boy, I listened to the great George Truett. I had never heard such preaching, but that was not revival. Revival is not even people's being converted. Where genuine revival exists, people usually are converted. But in the true sense of the word, revival is not the salvation of the lost.

WHAT IS REVIVAL?

Then what does the word *revival* mean? The word *revival* comes from two Latin words: *re*, which means "again," and *vivo*, which means "to live." The literal meaning is "to live again." Charles Finney, the great evangelist, defined revival as "a new beginning of obedience to God . . . just as in the case of a converted sinner, the first step in a deep repentance, a breaking down of heart, a getting down in the dust before God, with deep humility and a forsaking of sin." J. Edwin Orr simply calls revival "times of refreshing from the Lord."

Revival in the spiritual realm is to love Jesus Christ in a new and significant way. To be revived is to regain spiritual consciousness.

GOD'S PRESCRIPTION FOR REVIVAL

About once a year I come down with a severe head and chest cold. Immediately I phone my doctor. He, in turn, gives me a good prescription. If I act and do what the prescription requires, I am fine within a few days.

The Bible contains a divine prescription for revival. It is God's medicine for moral and spiritual sickness, and it is found in 2 Chronicles 7:14. "If my people, who are called by my name, shall humble themselves, and pray, and seek my face, and turn from their wicked ways; then will I hear from heaven, and will forgive their sin, and will heal their land." God promises to do His part in revival, but it is conditional. Let us review together the ingredients of God's prescription.

Look first at the words *"If my people, who are called by my name."* Do you know where revival begins? Revival begins with the people of God. Have you received Jesus Christ as your Savior? If so, you are God's child. God is your Father, and you are part of God's wonderful family. Revival begins in the lives of those of us who are in God's family.

Some time ago I concluded a study in the book of Jonah. Let me share with you what I discovered. When Jonah repented of his rebellion, his indifference, and his prejudice, God caused the people of Nineveh to repent. The greatest obstacle to the conversion of Nineveh was not to be found in Nineveh. It was not the sin and corruption of the Ninevites, although those were great. It was not the graft-ridden police force of corrupt politicians. It was not the false cults and religions. The biggest obstacle to the salvation of Nineveh was found in the heart of a pious, prejudiced man named Jonah. There was no deceitfulness in all of Nineveh like the deceitfulness in Jonah's heart.

Jonah was the key to the salvation of Nineveh. And God's people are the keys to the spiritual climate of our nation and the world. That means that you and I have a big responsibility. Revival starts with us, and if it is to come to our nation, it must come through us. God's prescription for revival begins with a humbling of the individual.

The second step to revival is found in the words, *"If my people . . . shall humble themselves."* Take a look at this word *humble*. It means "not proud," or "not arrogant, but modest, broken." The message of James 4:6 is powerful: "Wherefore he saith, God resisteth the proud, but giveth grace unto the humble."

Have you ever had to work with someone who really made life difficult for you? He resisted every idea you had and everything you said. He fought you at every turn. Things were not comfortable, were they? Can you imagine anything as helpless and hopeless as having Almighty God resist you? Are we proud people? Brokenness and humility are key steps in meeting God's prescription for revival. Paul prayed with tears day and night. David Brainerd, suffering a slow, painful death from tuberculosis, interceded for the souls of the American Indians. Dr. William Culbertson, former president and chancellor at Moody Bible Institute, would often say to us in chapel, "Walk humbly before God." His life was an example of his words.

Approximately 3 billion people on our earth need to see the power of God displayed! God tells us that we are the key to our nation's spiritual condition. Revival begins with God's people, with individuals. The theme of our day is the mass man. We live in a day of computers and collectivism. But here we see that God deals with the individual. "Revive *me*, O Lord," is our plea.

Self-examination on the part of the Lord's people is imperative. As long as Christians are unbroken, unconcerned, unimpressed, and unforgiving, revival cannot come. We must say with Elihu, "If I have done iniquity, I will do no more" (Job 34:32).

There is a third ingredient in God's prescription, and that is prayer. Second Chronicles 7:14 says, *"If my people . . . shall . . . pray."* You ask, For what shall we pray? Through the prophet Hosea, God said, "Break up your fallow ground: for it is time to seek the LORD (Hosea 10:12). Fallow ground is dry ground, unproductive ground. We need to pray that we might become productive Christians, instruments fit for the Master's use.

Job was a good man, yet he was not released from his captivity until he prayed for his miserable comforters. Prayer has a boomerang effect; it blesses the one who does the praying.

We need to pray for revival in our hearts, in our schools, in our churches, and in this nation. Our prayers should be definite. We need to pray for complete yieldedness to the Holy Spirit. God through Zechariah said, "Not by might, nor by power, but by my spirit" (Zechariah 4:6). Complete dependence upon the Spirit's leadership is the only method.

Revival has always found power through prayer. Go back with me through the centuries to A.D. 30. The city is Jerusalem. The evangelist is a bold, untutored fisherman named Peter. The occasion is a Jewish holiday when Jews and God-fearing Gentiles have gathered from all over the known world. Peter powerfully proclaims Jesus Christ. Three thousand people receive Christ that very day. The secret of the harvest was the power of the Holy Spirit activated by the prayers of God's people.

Move on. The year is 1872. The city is London, and the evangelist is a relatively unknown YMCA worker from America, D. L. Moody. On a Sunday evening, Moody is preaching in a North London church. He asks those who have decided for Christ to stand. During the past few days, over four hundred people have made decisions for Christ. Ultimately thousands came to Christ through the ministry of Moody. What was the cause? God's people were praying.

God wants to start with you and me. Do you want Him to revive you? Can you pray, "Here I am, Lord. You're the Potter; I'm merely the clay. Begin Your revival in me right now. Change me. Make me usable, and let me aid in bringing revival to our world."

God's formula continues: *"If my people . . . shall . . . seek my face."* To seek God's face is not a quick "Lord bless me, my wife, and our two children." It demands determination, steadfastness, singleness of heart, and perseverance. John Welch, the Scottish preacher, felt that a day was misspent if he did not spend eight to ten hours in prayer for the needs of his congregation. Once when the English writer John Ruskin was trying to complete a book and did not want to be distracted, he published a notice: "John Ruskin is totally engaged in completing a book and therefore unable to answer calls or correspondence. Consider him dead for the next three months."

We need to seek God's face with that kind of determination and perseverance!

God gives the final step: *"If my people . . . shall . . . turn from their wicked ways."* When ancient Israel finally dealt with the sin of Achan, there was victory. For them to turn from what was wrong meant repentance. As long as David continued in sin, he lacked fellowship, power, and the blessing of God. He was a liability rather than a asset. Then, he faced his sin, confessed it, and repented fully. Restoration began only after repentance. When the early church dealt with Ananias and Sapphira (Acts 5), it started to move ahead again. The same thing will happen in our lives when we deal with our sin.

Repentance is often difficult because many times we are not sensitive to our sin. Sin is smothered and camouflaged in our day. Sin has been driven underground. These days few people experience true conviction. Instead of repenting and confessing sin, they visit a psychiatrist who shows them how to lay the blame for their guilt on an austere father or an overprotective mother, or tells them that they act the way they do because they were underprivileged or overdisciplined in childhood.

But sin has never changed, and we have to learn to face it openly and honestly. God hates sin! God's message to us is *Repent*. In fact, the last word of Jesus Christ to the church was not, as many think, the Great Commission. The Great Commission is the program for the church, but the message of Christ to the churches of Revelation 2 and 3, in reality Christ's final message to the church, was "repent."

Now, let me be exceedingly practical. What can we as individual citizens and Christians do? How can we obey God's command to turn from our wicked ways? First, we can develop the desire to know Jesus Christ better. We should have a holy dissatisfaction. The contented Christian is the sterile Christian. Paul said in effect, "Jesus arrested me on the Damascus road. Now I want to lay hold of all that for which I was arrested by God." We too ought to be thoroughly dissatisfied with our spiritual posture.

Second, we should pray for a change in our lives. I think of Jacob's wrestling with God. He wanted blessing. He would not be denied. Throw your entire life into the will of God. Seek God's very best.

Third, we must commit ourselves to obedience. If we pray for revival and neglect witnessing, we are guilty of hypocrisy. To pray for growth and neglect the local church is absolute foolishness. To pray that we will mature, and then neglect the Word of God is incongruous. We must put ourselves in the way of blessing through obedience.

Fourth, our repentance must be complete. "Create in me a clean heart," David sobbed in Psalm 51:10. For a whole year David had been out of fellowship with God. But he confessed his sin; he turned from his sin; then he could sing again; he could write again; he could pray again. His repentance was total and without reservation.

Fifth, we need to make the crooked straight. If we owe debts, we must pay them, or at least have an understanding with the people we owe. Zacchaeus said, "Lord, the half of my goods I give to the poor; and if I have taken any thing from any man by false accusation, I restore him fourfold" (Luke 19:8). As much as possible, he made the crooked straight.

Sixth, we should develop a seriousness of purpose. It is not easy to keep off the detours, but we should let nothing deflect the magnetic needle of our calling. If there is anything that is a Trojan horse in our day, it is the television set. We must beware lest it rob us of our passion and purpose.

Finally, we have to major in majors. The Christian life requires specialists. We need to have a singleness of heart and purpose. Jesus said in effect, "Be a one-eyed man" (cf. Luke 11:34-36). Paul said, "This one thing I do" (Philippians 3:13). Too many of us burn up too much energy without engaging in things that bring us nearer to God. We must refuse to rust out. Let us start sharing our faith; let us make ourselves available. Let us back our decision with our time and talent and dollars. And let us ask God for great faith in Him. We must begin to expect great things.

Notice what God promises to do if we obey according to 2 Chronicles 7:14: "Then will I hear from heaven, and will forgive their sin, and will heal their land." If God's people will meet the conditions, then God promises to hear, forgive, and heal our land. If we do our part, God will do His part. May we humbly seek God's forgiveness and then give ourselves to be a channel of blessing to our beloved nation.

The Greek word for man is *anthropos,* "the up-looking one." We are to look up, but we are also to hook up. James 1:6 says that we are to ask "in faith, nothing wavering. For he that wavereth is like a wave of the sea driven . . . and tossed." God is saying, "Come alive!" He is saying, "Look up; hook up!" May we realize there is human responsibility and human opportunity. Let us stir up the gift that God has planted in us and seek the outpouring from heaven that our nation so greatly needs!

R. A. Torrey, the second president of the Moody Bible

Institute, often shared God's formula for national recovery: Revival in a church or community is brought about by Christians getting right with God, then praying for revival till God answers that prayer, and finally making themselves available to be used in God's service in winning others to Christ.

Today we call upon each Christian in our beloved nation to meet these conditions. Are *you* willing to pay the price?

THIRTEEN

What Makes a Nation Great?

"It was the best of times: it was the worst of times . . ."

Charles Dickens used those thought-provoking words to open his famous novel *A Tale of Two Cities*. Although they described Europe in the early eighteenth century, they could properly be used to picture our United States today.

We live in the best of times and the worst of times. Scientifically, we have seen fantastic advances. Man has attained such speed in travel that he now looks forward to exploring the solar system. He has split and fused the atom, which has given him the key to enormous unleashed power. The field of communications has literally exploded. First there was the human voice, then writing, then the breakthrough of the printing press, then radio, and now, worldwide television—even live television from the moon. Our world today is indeed a global village.

The technical advance has reached much farther than we realize. Some time ago I was in the jungles of the Yucatan Peninsula to study the ruins of the ancient Mayan civilization. In the middle of nowhere I came upon a one-room, thatched-roof hut with a television antenna proudly pointing toward the sky. "Do you see what I see?" I asked my associates. We entered the very simple one-room house and found a modern television set!

Yes, in many ways these are the best of times. But in other ways they are the worst of times. Technology has brought a host of benefits, but it has also brought its difficulties.

Take one of our more simple problems, for example. We live in rectangular boxes we call houses. They keep heat in and hold cold out. But inside the boxes it is too warm for food; so we build another rectangular box to keep food cold inside the box we made to keep us warm. But inside the box for food it gets too cold for butter; so we make another box to keep the butter warm.

Although advancing civilization has provided solutions for many problems, it has created many others. Along with heart transplants, computers, and supersonic travel, it has also given us nuclear warfare, the problems of the pill, and the tragedy of abortion.

A traveler today can circle the globe in a matter of hours, but millions of people are confused about the directions of their daily lives. Illegal drugs infest our youth cultures from junior high school through college. Crime is rampant in our streets. Corruption spreads like creeping mold from Washington to Watsonville.

One of our great historians, Arnold Toynbee, writes of nineteen major civilizations that have existed since man began to structure government. Of the nineteen, no more than five remain. Our Western civilization is among them. Today we are asking with growing concern, "Will it survive?"

A former secretary of the Department of Health, Education and Welfare, John W. Gardner, has written some probing books concerning the life and death of civilizations. In one of them, *No Easy Victories,* he writes powerfully:

> Back of every great civilization, behind all the power and wealth, is something as powerful . . . a set of ideas, attitudes, convictions and the confidence that those ideas and convictions are viable.
>
> No nation can achieve greatness unless it believes in something—and unless that something has the moral dimensions to sustain a great civilization. [1]

Then Gardner goes on to cite this illustration:

> In Guatemala and southern Mexico one can observe the Indians who were without doubt the lineal descendants of those who created the Mayan civilization. Today they are a humble people,

280

not asking much of themselves or the world, and not getting much. A light went out![2]

A light went out! What light? And what made it go out? What is the light that sets apart our Western civilization? Do we really know? If we do not, how do we know that it, too, will not flicker and go out?

Alexis de Tocqueville, the famous French political philosopher, visited America when this nation was very young, to find the secret of our greatness. He traveled from town to town, talking with people and asking questions. He examined our young national government, our schools, and our centers of business, without finding the reason for our strength.

Not till he visited the churches of America and witnessed the pulpits of this land "aflame with righteousness" did he find the secret of our greatness. Returning to France, he summarized his findings with this word of warning: "America is great because America is good, and if America ever ceases to be good, America will cease to be great."

Was de Tocqueville right? If America's strength lies in her goodness, our light is going out. It is time we ask ourselves what is true greatness, what has been our light, and what has made it burn with brightness?

Contrary to the thinking of many, greatness is not measured in muscles or missiles. It is not calculated in silver or gold. It is not found in the things that we can see and handle. And because true greatness is measured in unseen qualities, it appears unspectacular and it is tragically neglected.

Greatness is a quality of the inner person. Greatness is found in what we are rather than in what we have. Greatness is a quality of the heart and mind and soul! The Bible gives much insight here. If I were to ask you to name the greatest person pictured by the Word of God, excluding Jesus Christ, whom would you name?

Perhaps you would think of Moses the lawgiver, or Joshua the deliverer of Israel. Or you might choose Mary the mother of Jesus, or Paul the greatest missionary of all time.

But what of John the Baptist?

Jesus identified John as the greatest person who had ever lived until that time. "Among those that are born of women," He said, "there is not a greater prophet than John the Baptist" (Luke 7:28). John's greatness, in fact, had been foretold. Before his birth an angel had said of him, "He shall be great in the sight of the Lord" (Luke 1:15).

Look closely at the life of John the Baptist and you will find specific qualities of greatness. Those same qualities must characterize our lives if our nation is to continue to be great. What are those qualities?

HUMILITY

First, John reflected a spirit of humanity and service. One day a very important committee from Jerusalem came to visit John. Because of his eloquence and popularity, they asked, "Are you the Messiah?"

John answered honestly, "I am not. . . . I am the voice of one crying in the wilderness, Make straight the way of the Lord" (John 1:21-23). He was saying, "I am not the way; I am only the one who shows the way." John walked modestly.

The very next day something exciting happened to John. Jesus came to the Jordan to be baptized. John was amazed. "Baptize you?" he said. "I have need to be baptized by You, and do You come to me?" (Matthew 3:14, NASB). Before that John had said, "One mightier than I cometh, the latchet of whose shoes I am not worthy to unloose" (Luke 3:16). Later, he said of Jesus, "He must increase, but I must decrease" (John 3:30). Powerful John the Baptist served in humility.

Not long ago a national news magazine devoted forty-four pages to the subject of leadership. Many educators and statesmen were quoted concerning their insights as to the essence of leadership. Some defined it as charisma, talent, or know-how, but no one suggested the definition given in the Bible: that of humble service.

Jesus said in Matthew 18:4, "Whosoever therefore shall humble himself as this little child, the same is greatest in the kingdom of heaven." He also declared this principle after His disciples began to argue about rank in their group. "Whosoever will be great among you," He told them, "let him be your minister" (Matthew 20:26). Concern for the good of others is a virtue that made America great. The capacity to care for others and to serve is what gives life significance.

Jesus Christ not only taught humility and service, He also lived it. "For even the Son of man came not to be ministered unto," He said, "but to minister, and to give his life a ransom for many" (Mark 10:45).

In John 13:4-5 we read that Jesus rose from supper "and laid aside his garments; and took a towel . . . and began to wash the disciples' feet." The son of God in humility served men. The symbol of greatness is not necessarily an eagle or a sword or a dollar sign; a more appropriate symbol would be a towel.

In the book *The Ugly American* an Asian journalist writes, "Poor America. It took the British a hundred years to lose their prestige in Asia. American has managed to lose hers in ten years."[3] The book in general gives the impression that we are loud, ostentatious, self-centered, and, worst of all, proud and haughty.

George Washington, kneeling in prayer at Valley Forge, tells us something about the heartbeat of the founders of America. We need to remember that the method of all leadership is humble, modest service. What else makes a nation great?

HONESTY

Second, John possessed integrity and courage. Proverbs 11:3 sets out the importance of this quality: "The integrity of the upright shall guide them: but the perverseness of transgressors shall destroy them." Simply put, honesty builds but dishonesty destroys.

For many years Dr. Madison Sarratt taught mathematics at Vanderbilt University. Before giving exams he would say, "Today I am giving two examinations—one in trigonometry and the other in honesty. I hope you will pass them both. If you must fail one, fail trigonometry. There are many good people in the world who can't pass trigonometry, but there are no good people who cannot pass the examination of honesty." Honesty is the name of the game. Yet many in our land are sick with the disease of dishonesty.

John the Baptist possessed integrity and courage. Jesus said of him in Matthew 11:8, "What went ye out for to see? A man clothed in soft raiment? Behold, they that wear soft clothing are in king's houses." No, John was not a weak, flimsy reed, but a rock. He was not a soft, permissive, wishy-washy, spineless wonder, but an honest man. To those who were false and dishonest John the Baptist said, "O generation of vipers, who hath warned you to flee from the wrath to come?" (Matthew 3:7).

I am afraid that ours is the day of the placid pulpit and the comfortable pew. Dante said, "The hottest place in hell is reserved for those who, in time of crisis, preserved their neutrality." May God grant us integrity and courage.

Noah Webster defines honesty as "honorable; characterized by integrity and straightforwardness in conduct, in thought, and in speech." Integrity means "soundness of moral principle and character."

But our country is not known for its soundness of moral character. White-collar crime costs this nation $40 billion every year. Our nation's hotels and motels spend $500 million per year just to replace items carried off by guests, and one first-class New York City hotel replaces 2,000 towels each month. Shoplifters in Illinois get away with some $800 million worth of merchandise each year. The FBI says that this kind of stealing has increased 221 percent since 1960. Exodus 20:15 needs to be heard across America: "Thou shalt not steal."

In 1973, for the first time in the thirty-six year history of the All-American Soap Box Derby competition, a winner was disqualified for cheating. He forfeited his first-place trophy and a $7,500 college scholarship when X-rays disclosed that an electromagnet and battery had been rigged in the nose of his vehicle, giving him extra starting impetus. Said the county prosecuter: "It's like seeing apple pie, motherhood, and the

American flag grinding to a halt!" Without doubt we are witnessing an erosion of integrity!

John the Baptist was straight. John told his generation, "Bring forth fruits for repentance" (Matthew 3:8). John said, "Every tree which bringeth not forth good fruit is hewn down, and cast into the fire" (Matthew 3:10). John called for repentance and righteousness. One day John stood before the most powerful person in the nation, King Herod. This man had seduced his brother's wife, Herodias, and was living in open immorality. Courageously John said, "It is not lawful for you to have your brother's wife" (Mark 6:18, NASB). That is the type of courage and truth we need today.

When John Huss was about to be burned to death, they asked him to give up his teachings. Huss answered, "What I have taught with my lips, I now seal with my blood." That is courage!

The signing of the Declaration of Independence took courage. When Charles Carroll signed his name, some asked, "How will anyone know which Charles Carroll is meant among all those with that name?"

"Well, let there be no mistake," said the courageous patriot, and he signed in bold letters, "Charles Carroll of Carollton."

In the final chapter of his book *Profiles in Courage* the late President John F. Kennedy wrote:

> Without belittling the courage with which men have died, we should not forget those acts of courage with which men . . .have lived. The courage of life is often a less dramatic spectacle than the courage of a final moment; but it is no less a magnificent mixture of triumph and tragedy. A man does what he must . . . —in spite of personal consequences, in spite of obstacles and dangers and pressures—and that is the basis of all human morality.[4]

Courage and honesty are marks of true greatness. These make the light of a civilization burn brightly! The question is, Can we restigmatize dishonesty and magnify honesty?

Third, John the Baptist possessed purity and faith. From birth John was set apart to live a moral life. John was a good man. The prophecy concerning him was: "He . . . shall drink neither wine or strong drink; and he shall be filled with the Holy Ghost" (Luke 1:15). John knew about purity, goodness, and discipline. He lived in the wilderness and ate locusts and wild honey. His purpose was to direct men to Jesus Christ. John had a reason to live. He was the forerunner of Christ. He was the one who showed the way to the Lord Jesus, and he lived his life and carried out his mission in purity.

Will Durant, one of today's most respected philosopher-historians, said, "The greatest question of our time is not Communism versus individualism, not Europe versus America, not even the East versus the West; it is whether men can bear to live without God. Can civilization hold together if man abandons his faith in God?"

Psalm 11:3 asks the question, "If the foundations be destroyed, what can the righteous do?" In his book *Man's Search for Himself,* Dr. Rollo May quotes Friedrich Nietzsche, who wrote a parable about the death of God. It is a haunting story about a madman who ran into the village square shouting, "Where is God?" The people around him did not believe in God; they laughed and said that perhaps God had gone on a voyage or emigrated. The madman then shouted, "Where is God? I shall tell you! We have killed Him—you and I—yet how have we done this? . . . Who gave us the sponge to wipe away the whole horizon? What did we do when we unchained this earth from its sun? . . . Whither shall we move now? Away from all suns? Do we not fall incessantly? Backward, sideward, forward, in all directions? Is there yet any up and down?"[5]

Nietzsche was not calling for a return to conventional belief in God, but his story serves to point to what happens when a nation loses its center of values. "If the foundations be destroyed, what can the righteous do?"

George Bernard Shaw, a critic of the Christian faith, wrote, "This I know—men without religion are moral cowards. The cause of Europe's miseries was its lack of religion."

Voltaire, the French infidel, is reported to have said in connection with achieving a regulated society, "If there were no God, it would be necessary to invent Him."

All these men, although we would reject their overall philosophies, were right in one regard. According to the Bible, nations fall because they turn from God and from His Word. They attempt to build an adequate way of life by their own efforts and without regard to God. The cycle of rise and collapse that we see in history is the inevitable result.

But there is an alternative; there is hope. Our country does not need to fall. If the cause of collapse is turning *from* God, the remedy lies in turning *to* God. Can we do this? Yes. First we can cry out to God for help in returning to Him. Three times in Psalm 80 the writer, in a seeming agony of urgency, seeks this kind of favor. "Turn us, O God," he pleads, "and cause thy face to shine; and we shall be saved." We need God's help and mercy even to seek Him. We who belong to God must ask Him to send revival to His people. Lukewarm, half-hearted, apathetic Christians are the greatest obstacle to renewal in our country.

As individuals we can commit ourselves anew to honesty and integrity. We can seek a spirit of humility and genuine readiness to serve. We can speak out for higher standards of morality, contending for the truth in every circumstance and situation. But especially we can ask God to help us proclaim Jesus Christ as God's eternal Lamb, who alone can meet the need of cleansing from sin and the new birth.

We must reach individauls with the message of the gospel. That is God's way, His program for our age. What, after all, are dying civilizations but the sum total of dying individual lives? Never underestimate what God can do through you as an individual. But you must begin by letting Him make you a Christlike person, a man or woman with a quality of holy life that cannot go unnoticed.

That was the characteristic Woodrow Wilson noted in the great evangelist D. L. Moody. Speaking at Princeton University before he became President of the United States, Mr. Wilson said of Moody:

> I was in a very plebian place. I was in a barber's shop, sitting in a chair, when I became aware that a personality had entered the room. A man had come quietly in upon the same errand as myself and sat in the next chair to me. Every word he uttered, though it was not in the least didactic, showed a personal and vital interest in the man who was serving him; and before I got through with what was being done to me, I was aware that I had attended an evangelistic service, because Mr. Moody was in the next chair. I purposely lingered in the room after he left and noted the singular effect his visit had upon the barbers in that shop. They talked in undertones. They did not know his name, but they knew that something had elevated their thought. And I felt that I left that place as I should have left a place of worship.[6]

God can do great things through consecrated individuals, through yielded lives. Ask Jesus Christ to light the light that makes our nation great. Ask Him to begin with you right now.

NOTES

1. John W. Gardner, *No Easy Victories* (New York: Harper & Row, 1970), p. 13.
2. Ibid., p. 16.
3. William Lederer and Eugene Burdick, *The Ugly American* (New York: Fawcett, 1971), p. 144.
4. John F. Kennedy, *Profiles in Courage* (New York: Harper & Row, 1964), p. 216.
5. Rollo May, *Man's Search for Himself* (New York: Dell, 1973), p. 54.
6. As quoted in John McDowell, *Dwight L. Moody* (New York: Revell, 1915), pp. 38-39.

FOURTEEN

Why Christians Need the Poor

"When you have enemies like hunger, poverty, and disease," declares a young man from Bangladesh, "you have no choice but to fight. You fight to be born and fight to stay alive!" The battle of poverty goes on and on. Most of us, the world would say, are among the winners. But what should Christians do about the poverty of others?

WHO ARE THE POOR?

Mattie Schultz is a white-haired widow, now ninety-one years old. She is the kind of person you would expect to keep a well-filled cookie jar for children who call her "grandma."

Yet, just last summer in her home city of San Antonio, Texas, she was lodged overnight in jail. The charge was shoplifting. She was accused of taking $15.04 worth of ham, sausage, and butter to keep from starving.[1]

Within a few days after newspapers and television stations had told her story, offers to help came pouring in. But the fact that such a thing could happen reminds us that in spite of all our relief and help programs, the poor are still among us.

Not many years ago, shortly before the Christmas season, a little paperback book appeared. It was filled with thumbnail sketches of the poor for whom there would be no Christmas. The poor spoke for themselves. They told how it felt to be without such things as underwear, soap, and toothpaste when the world around exchanges presents.

By virtually every standard, ours is the most affluent country in the world. We spend billions on relief and welfare. Yet millions among us know the ache of poverty. In 1964 President Lyndon Johnson, as part of his dream for what he called the "Great Society," declared unconditional war on poverty. But poverty did not disappear. In 1976, after spending hundreds of billions of dollars to fight poverty, the country was told by the Census Bureau that more than one in every ten Americans must be considered poor.[2]

Overseas the pinch of poverty is worse. *Time* magazine, not long ago, declared that nearly thirty out of every one hundred persons worldwide barely keep from starving. Millions struggle for existence on a per capita income of less than $200 a year! The World Food Council tells us that a third of the children in the world die of malnutrition and disease before they have five birthdays. Each year 100,000 children go blind because of lack of vitamin A in their early diets.[3] Shocking, isn't it?

WHY DO WE HAVE THE POOR?

Why are things like that still true today? Why is it that society, in spite of all its resources, has never solved the poverty problems? There are a number of reasons. One obviously is individual differences. Some poor people are strong, aggressive, clever—even ruthless. Some are less capable. Some encounter adversity. Health may fail, accidents may strike, opportunities may be denied. Great numbers begin this life as underprivileged people, never rising above the disadvantaged group.

More important, the Bible seems to say that God allows the poor among us to test our compassion for our fellow men. Do we really love the poor? Will we help in their need? Our response to poverty reveals our attitude.

Some have wrongly assumed that to be poor is a sign of God's disfavor. That is not true. God loves the poor and cares for them. He hears their cry. He sees and judges those who wrong them in their weakness. Speaking of the poor, the psalmist says, "The Lord is his refuge" (Psalm 14:6). God sees and cares and intervenes. God "setteth . . . the poor on high from affliction," says Psalm 107:41, "and maketh him families like a flock."

Likewise, the Word of God teaches that God will bless those who reach out to help the poor. "Blessed is he that considereth the poor," we read in Psalm 41:1. "The Lord will deliver him in time of trouble." On the other hand, we invite God's judgment if we ignore the needs of the poor. Proverbs 21:13 declares, "Whoso stoppeth his ears at the cry of the poor, he also shall cry himself, but shall not be heard."

If God loves the poor, if He is concerned about their needs, if He leaves the poor among us to prove our love and compassion, we as Christians cannot ignore the poor.

How Can We Help the Poor?

The question is not whether Christians should help the poor, but *how?* Some contend that we should find some way to redistribute wealth and thus wipe out all poverty.

I do not see that as Christ's will or as an answer to the ultimate poverty problem. To be sure, Christ taught that Christians are not to hoard riches. He taught that we should share. Nothing in Scripture, however, suggests that Christians can or should change the world's economic structure itself or eliminate poverty. On the contrary, Jesus clearly taught that poverty goes with this present evil world. "Ye have the poor with you always," He said in Mark, chapter 14.

Christ's principle of ministry to the poor is that it be done from a heart of genuine compassion. In His Sermon on the Mount in Matthew 6, Jesus taught not only that helping the poor should be done—He said, *"When* ye do alms," not "if"—but also that it should be done without fanfare. Christ regarded giving to the poor as normal.

Just what was Christ's program for the poor? It included justice, for the whole of Scripture sets that standard. But beyond that, He urged compassion and simple sharing. Such sharing demands awareness of need.

In the Old Testament economy of God, poverty was not wiped out, but the poor were given special protection. A poor worker

293

was paid each day. If a poor man borrowed, giving his robe as security, the garment was to be returned before the owner needed it for warmth that night. Persons who sold themselves as servants were freed each seventh year. If lands were sold, they could be redeemed by relatives. If not redeemed, they automatically reverted to their former owners every fifty years in the Year of Jubilee.

Anyone willing to work was assured of food to feed his family. It could be obtained by gleaning in fields, where produce was left deliberately for that purpose. The Old Testament book of Ruth describes how Ruth and her mother-in-law, Naomi, lived on such gleanings.

In New Testament times, the Jewish poor were less protected by laws. The duty of giving alms, however, was acknowledged and encouraged. Jesus often spoke of giving to the poor. The record of the early church is filled with references to Christian compassion for the poor, especially to fellow believers. Widows without support were cared for by the church, as seen in Acts 6:1 and 1 Timothy 5:9, 16. The poor were a subject of special concern at the first church council in Jerusalem. Paul mentions them in Galatians 2:10, where he writes that church leaders desired "that we should remember the poor." And then he adds, "The same which I also was forward [eager] to do."

Christians have always been God's special channel of mercy to the poor. But we should not lose sight of the fact that God blesses us as we carry out this ministry.

WHY SHOULD WE HELP THE POOR?

The poor are good for Christians in at least three ways. *First, the presence of the poor prompts us to exercise compassion.* How selfish and self-centered we become when we think just of ourselves! The presence of the poor is a constant challenge to be concerned about the needs of others.

Christians have been called out to demonstrate God's love. The needs of our world are our concern. God's love is to be shown in tangible, practical ways. John writes in 1 John 3:17, "But whoso hath this world's good . . . and [closes his heart against him], how dwelleth the love of God in him? . . . Let us not love in word . . . but in deed and in truth." John is speaking here of love for fellow Christians. But Christian love is to reach beyond the confines of church membership.

So Paul wrote the church in Thessalonica, "The Lord make you to increase and abound in love toward one another and toward all men" (1 Thessalonians 3:12). As the church ministers to the poor, inside its membership or outside, it demonstrates God's love.

Jesus taught that the will of God can be summed up in two great commandments—love God and love your neighbor. If we would do the will of God, we must have compassion on the poor.

Second, the presence of the poor gives us opportunity to prove that Christ has touched our hearts and made them new. Helping the poor, especially when it costs in time and money, is not a natural instinct. Instead, our old sin natures prompt us to look the other way. Compassion, on the other hand, is an evidence of an inner work of grace.

The apostle James speaks of faith and works. Real faith produces works. Our acts are proof of faith. The Christian who helps the poor proves beyond the shadow of a doubt that he shares the life and love of Christ.

Third, the poor give Christians opportunity to lay up heavenly treasure. "He that hath pity upon the poor lendeth to the LORD," says Proverbs 19:17. "And that which he hath given will he pay him again." To give to the poor for Jesus' sake is to invest money in heaven. Not only is such treasure safe from moth and rust, but it helps our hearts to be fixed on heaven as well. "For where your treasure is," Christ said, "there will your heart be also." It is not just a duty for the Christian to help the poor. In the wisdom of God, helping the poor is a blessing and a privilege.

There is a practical side to helping the poor. How should a church reach out? The first concern of any church is for the poor among its members. Does some fellow Christian struggle under the burden of inadequate housing? Has sickness brought financial crisis? The church can help in such a situation. Are children in need of clothing? Is someone out of work? The church should be concerned. Many churches have special funds for providing material help. Often these can be used to relieve a needy situation.

But individual Christians also have an obligation. If I see a need within my power to meet, I have no right to turn away. God will help me if I share in love and trust that God will meet my needs as I give generously to others.

We dare not turn our backs on the world's needs. The apostle James warns in James 2:15-16, "If a brother or sister be naked, and destitute of daily food, and one of you say unto them, Depart in peace, be ye warmed and filled; notwithstanding ye give them not those things needful to the body; what shall it profit?"

That is the attitude of the world, not the outlook of the Christian. The Christian is to love, to care, and to show compassion, even at the cost of sacrifice.

Could there be someone in your church who needs more or better food? Someone who needs to see the dentist or be fitted for glasses? Does some family need warmer winter outfits for their children? It may be your opportunity to minister—perhaps your chance to win a blessing.

The same principles hold for those we encounter outside the circle of church membership. If we see a need and it lies within our power to be of help, we have responsibility to help. The person involved may be a neighbor down the street. Or we may share in some united effort to help the disadvantaged in a worthy way. Neither the church as a body nor individual Christians can turn away from need, wherever it may be.

And then there is the yawning chasm of worldwide need. The church as a whole, and every member of the church, can have part in helping somewhere in our world. The need is so great that we cannot respond to every need, but we can help generously with some. Jesus told his disciples, "Freely ye have received; freely give." Our first and great obligation, of course, is to share the

Bread of Life. But we cannot withhold the bread of material aid when it lies within our power to give it.

Jesus told two parables that may help us see our obligation. The first, recorded in Luke 16, was about a rich man and a beggar. The rich man, Jesus said, lived out his life in luxury. In time he died and went to hell—not merely because he had been rich, of course, but because he had been satisfied with riches and had looked no further. The poor man had lived out his life unnoticed at the rich man's very doorstep.

The parable teaches the folly of trusting riches, but it also should remind us that the poor are all around us. Like the rich man we can shut them out, or like Christ we can help them in compassion.

The other parable is the story of the Good Samaritan. Three travelers in succession saw a man in a desperate plight. He had been robbed, beaten, and left beside the road to die. Two of the men who passed by the victim professed to be religious. But they did not want to get involved. The third, a Samaritan, took the time and trouble to help. He bound up the wounds of the injured man and brought him to a place of safety. He even arranged to pay his bills until the victim was back on his feet.

The church collectively and Christians as individuals have been called to be good neighbors. We cannot prevent the tragedies of life that leave poor people by the wayside. Nor can we help them all. But we can help some of the needy—those that are within our reach.

Let us recall the two kinds of attitudes—the rich man lived a lifetime indifferent to the beggar on his doorstep; the Samaritan in a moment of opportunity chose to make himself a blessing. God's call to us is to be like the Good Samaritan. We need to be willing to share salvation and material aid with our fellowmen.

NOTES

1. *Chicago Tribune,* 21 July 1979.
2. *Newsweek,* 9 October 1978, pp. 54,56
3. *Chicago Tribune,* 4 December 1978.

Book 3

SPECIAL
SERMONS
ON THE FAMILY

With warm appreciation to
Herman Braunlin
E. Brandt Gustavson
James A. Gwinn
Donald E. Hescott
Lawrence E. Pearson

Special gratitude is extended to
Phil Johnson, who has assisted
me in research and editing.

ONE

The Dangers of an Unequal Yoke

Divorce in America is reaching epidemic proportions. Almost half of the marriages begun each year end in divorce before the fifth anniversary. In the high population areas of our nation the number of divorces granted annually exceeds the number of marriages performed. And the statistics on divorce are growing worse.

A common excuse for divorce is incompatibility—inability to meet the needs and expectations of the partner. Marriage is bonding, a uniting of two different persons; and compatibility is vital for harmony in the union. But a biblical marriage requires more than just physical or emotional compatibility. Spiritual compatibility is also required, because marriage is a spiritual union as well as a physical, mental, and emotional one. And it is my conviction that the sense of incompatibility that is often felt between marriage partners is at its root *spiritual* incompatibility—the inability to have oneness of mind in spiritual matters.

Of course, spiritual incompatibility is likely when two unbelievers marry, because without faith in the authority of the Word of God, there is no basis for spiritual unity. But when a believer marries an unbeliever, spiritual incompatibility is inevitable.

There seem to be few things as clear in Scripture as the teaching that a believer should not marry an unbeliever. But despite the clarity of God's Word and the evidence from actual experience that such marriages involve risk, marriages between Christians and non-Christians occur today with greater frequency than ever. And the divorce rate for such couples continues to rise at a staggering rate; divorce between couples of differing faiths occurs three times as often as divorce between members of the same faith.

The thrill of loving and of being loved temporarily minimizes all obstacles to a mixed marriage. The excitement of the wedding plans, the beauty of the ceremony, and all that goes with marriage and the anticipation of a new life temporarily carries the young couple along on the assumption that all will be well because their love is so deep it can conquer any problem. But reality soon manifests itself, and the problems of what God's Word calls an unequal yoke cannot be pushed aside.

The effects of a marriage between a Christian and a non-Christian are many and far-reaching. What are some of those effects? I would like to examine them from three perspectives.

THE UPWARD EFFECTS

First, let us look at *the upward effects*. How does marrying an unbeliever affect a Christian's relationship with God?

One of the obvious effects of a mixed marriage is carelessness about the things of God. That is understandable! The believer often drops his church connections and grows increasingly indifferent, silently at first, but more openly as time passes. What causes such a decline?

Remember that, at its root, a believer's marriage to an unbeliever is defiance of God and His order. The clear command of God is that a believer should not be "unequally yoked together with unbelievers" (2 Corinthians 6:14), and marriage to an unbeliever is an example of such an unequal yoke. A marriage that begins in rebellion to God can hardly expect His blessing.

Olivia Langedon was a believer. But she was in love with a young author, Samuel Clemens (whom we know as Mark Twain), and he was not a believer. In fact he was a skeptic. But she felt that her love for him was great enough to overcome any obstacles, and besides, she was a good influence on him. So she married him.

At first it seemed to be working, but as the years went by he showed more and more antagonism to her beliefs. One day as she was reading the Bible aloud, he strongly protested, "I don't believe the Bible. I can't sit here and listen to it."

Not only was there no unity of faith between them, but his unbelief produced a paralyzing effect on her until her faith was destroyed as well! After many years, while they were passing through days of sorrow, Mark Twain tried to comfort his wife. "Olivia, if it comforts you to lean on the Christian faith, do so."

"I can't," she said. "I haven't any left."

A mixed marriage can mean loss of faith as well as loss of fellowship with the heavenly Father. When we behave contrary to His direction we forfeit the possibility of a close walk with the Lord.

Not only that, but God is not glorified in a mixed marriage. Marriage is presented in the Bible as a sort of divine object lesson—a picture of the relationship of Christ and the church. Marriage of a believer to an unbeliever corrupts the purity of that lesson. Christ's union with the church is perfect, flawless. A marriage between two believers pictures that unity, with the potential of perfect spiritual, emotional, and physical unity. But a marriage involving a believer and an unbeliever cannot illustrate perfect unity, and so it cannot bring glory to God.

Second, what are some of *the inward effects* of mixed marriages? What is the effect on a believer when he chooses to unite in marriage with an unbeliever?

A lady who asked to speak to me concerning marriage was deeply moved as she related her story. "Before our marriage John attended church with me and showed signs of spiritual interest. He promised to make a spiritual decision after our marriage, but he never has. During our eight years of marriage he has never attended church. He shows nothing but bitterness toward anything spiritual in the home. My children are not being trained. Our home is not a reflection of heaven. My heart is broken. If only I had obeyed the Scriptures!"

Not long ago a man came to my office to tell me of his broken marriage. "Why didn't someone warn me of those things?" he said. "I never dreamed we'd have so many differences."

And aside from the heartache and bitterness that can grow out of a mixed marriage, there are some very serious spiritual consequences for the believer who marries an unbeliever. Those consequences are inescapable for several reasons.

One of the primary reasons is that the marriage of a true believer and an unbeliever lacks common ground of purpose. Amos wrote, "Can two walk together, except they be agreed?" (Amos 3:3).

Because the unbeliever will not rise to a life of faith, the believer must bow to a life of unbelief. On the Lord's day one wants to worship with the Lord's people while the other wants to sleep. The believer wants to give to God's work, and the unbeliever maintains that they cannot afford to do so. Sunday is a holy day to the believer but a holiday to the unbeliever. Times of crisis come, and they are not able to pray together. The unbeliever may even despise the convictions of the believer and ridicule his faith.

All of that can put a strain on the spiritual activities of the believer and therefore weaken his relationship with the Lord. He begins to neglect God's Word, because spending time in the Word is frowned on by the unbelieving mate.

Guilt feelings can build and grow, both from the guilt of marrying out of God's will and from the guilt of neglected spiritual responsibilities. The believer's prayer life is adversely affected. He may become severely depressed, as many have who have married out of the Lord's will. Or he may become resentful of the Lord or of other Christians and in the end forsake fellowship with other believers altogether.

The Outward Effects

Finally, what are *the outward effects* of a mixed marriage? What effect on a believer's spouse, his children, his family, his in-laws, and those around him can result from marriage to an unbeliever?

The Bible speaks of a few people who willfully disobeyed their parents in choosing a life partner. Esau, it seems, delighted in disobeying his parents. According to Genesis 28:8, Esau saw "that the daughters of Canaan pleased not Isaac his father," yet he had deliberately chosen a wife from among them. He treated his parents' wishes with contempt, and the whole family and his offspring for generations paid bitterly for his sin.

Samson likewise flouted the counsel of his parents, and as a result his entire family was engulfed in sorrow. The curse of God falls upon those who have no concern for parental guidance, and the effects of their sin touch everyone around them.

For the believer blessed with a believing mother and father, a mixed marriage is only a source of sorrow both to himself and to his parents. The unbelieving mate frequently destroys all the fruit of the believing parents' loving labor in the spiritual growth of their child, and it can hardly be expected that they will respond favorably to the unbelieving son- or daughter-in-law. That results in a strain of the family relations, which is a source of grief in itself.

Children are the biggest losers in mixed marriages. Any church affiliation they might have is usually superficial. Because of the lack of agreement in principles between the parents, discipline tends to be inconsistent, and the child can become confused. There is no unity of conviction, and thus there is continual conflict.

In the law of Moses, the children of Israel were forbidden to yoke the ox and the ass together. Why? The ox and the ass were very different in size, strength, and temperament. To yoke them together was not only unfitting but unfair as well. Both suffered discomfort from the unequal yoking, and they could not work well together. It is possible that that is what Paul had in mind when he wrote to the Corinthians urging them to stop being yoked together with unbelievers. For a believer to be yoked in marriage to an unbeliever is cruel. Marriage between a believer and an unbeliever is a poor working relationship and a source of injury and anguish to both partners.

God forbade the Israelites to marry outsiders, "for they will turn away thy son from following me that they may serve other gods," (Deuteronomy 7:4). Marrying an unbeliever is the same as marrying his unbelief.

Soft words and mellow phrases are often used to make it sound better, but the truth is that people who do not think the same on vital spiritual issues have no business getting married! They cannot be together for long without both becoming very unhappy.

It is generally true that if a young man or young woman will not receive Christ before the wedding, he or she will not do so after the honeymoon is over.

The time to deal with the question of marrying an unbeliever is before becoming involved with one. If you are single, perhaps you should purpose, as many dedicated Christians have, not to date anyone who is not spiritually compatible with you.

The wife of Matthew Henry, the renowned Bible commentator, was the only daughter of a wealthy merchant. When Matthew Henry sought permission to marry her, her father refused. He said that while Matthew was polite, scholarly, and nice, he was a stranger to the family. "Why, I don't even know where he comes from," insisted the father.

"True," replied the daughter, "but I know where he is going and would like to go with him."

Apparently her father saw the point and granted his permission for the marriage. She had her priorities straight. She understood that spiritual compatibility was far more important than any other requirement for a prospective mate. When two people truly love the Lord with all their hearts and love each other, God's blessing will go with them.

Make sure that the life partner you choose is a believer who sincerely wants the will of God. Make Christ the center of your wedding plans. Determine to do His will, to be obedient to Him, and to build your family around Him.

"But," you may be saying, "the problems you have mentioned describe our home exactly. My mate is not a believer. I have disobeyed God. My spiritual fervor is diminished. I am a defeated Christian because of it, and I would give anything if I could undo the damage I have done. Is there hope for me?"

Yes, thank God, there is always hope. God has promised to forgive our sin if we confess it. We may still have to live with some of the consequences of our sin, but we do not have to be defeated.

Purpose to yield your life more completely to God.

Determine to love your mate more than ever and pray regularly for his or her conversion. God will multiply His grace to you if you truly seek His best for you and submit fully to His will.

TWO

Wanted: Christian Parents

Several years ago an eminent sociologist and author made an amazing prediction. The day might come, he said, when parents would let experts raise their children. We would see newspaper advertisements like this:

> Why let parenthood tie you down? Let us raise your infant into a responsible, successful adult. Class A Pro-family offers: father age 30, mother, 36, grandmother, 67. Uncle and aunt, age 30, live in, hold part-time local employment. Four-child-unit has opening for one, age 6-8. Regulated diet exceeds government standards. All adults certified in child development and management. Bio-parents permitted frequent visits. Telephone contact allowed. Child may spend summer vacation with bio-parents. Religion, art, music encouraged by special arrangement. Five year contract, minimum. Write for further details.

That prediction, by the way, was made by Dr. Alvin Toffler in his best-selling book *Future Shock*.[1] Another prominent author, Ferdinand Lundberg, in *The Coming World Transformation* made a similar prediction. He claims that the family as we know it is near the point of extinction.[2]

And there is some troubling evidence that in the past few decades there has been a serious decline in the traditional family. The divorce rate is soaring, homosexuality is touted as an alternate life-style, and in a large number of American families, because both the mother and the father work, the children are left at home alone to run the house.

Of course, Bible-believing Christians deplore those developments. We believe that God's standards for the family are absolute and that the family is essential to the survival of our nation. In fact, the very turbulence of the times in which we live makes the ties of home and family more important than ever. And although writers and commentators are boldly saying that conventional marriage has seen its day, and although permissive sex abounds, the marriage commitment and a stable home life remain first choice for the great majority of young people.

Better than anyone else, you that are parents know why that is true. Although it costs a great deal to establish and carry on a home, no other pattern of life can provide so much love and joy and genuine satisfaction. God has made the family an institution whose foundations are love, satisfaction, and mutual service. And when that institution passes away, it will mark the end of our existence as a people.

Why did God establish the family? Why is the family unit so crucial? Why could not the same love be shared in a different environment? What is it about the conventional family that God uses? I am persuaded that God designed the family for several reasons, but one of the primary reasons is the challenging task of caring for, nurturing, and training children—a task that could not be adequately fulfilled by any other means than the conventional family.

No other calling is more crucial. Great men in places of leadership make far-reaching decisions in government, science, and business. But parents set the course of a whole new generation! What an opportunity! And what a responsibility!

Each child is eternally important. That little human life God gave you at the birth of that tiny child will continue on, in heaven or in hell, forever. In his brief life on this earth he will leave a trail of blessing or a trail of ruin. And before he leaves this globe, he in turn will play a part in shaping the generation still to come.

The calling of a mother or father is the most important calling on earth. If you are a parent, your responsibility to your children is more important than your job, your hobbies, or anything else you could spend your life on. And parenting never has been a greater challenge than right now. The storms that lash and batter the family today have never been more violent. You ask, What can we do? Is there any hope? How can we fortify our homes? Can we prepare our children for what is ahead?

Yes, God's Word does give us some guidelines. In fact, if we go as far back as the Old Testament book of Deuteronomy, we find that even when God gave Moses the law, He had a word for the parents. Listen to the Word of God from Deuteronomy 6:5-9:

> And thou shalt love the LORD thy God with all thine heart, and with all thy soul, and with all thy might.
>
> And these words, which I command thee this day, shall be in thine heart:
>
> And thou shalt teach them diligently unto thy children, and thou shalt talk of them when thou sittest in thine house, and when thou walkest by the way, and when thou liest down, and when thou risest up.
>
> And thou shalt bind them for a sign upon thine hand, and they shall be as frontlets between thine eyes.
>
> And thou shalt write them upon the posts of thy house, and on thy gates.

In that passage, I see three guidelines for parenting, and they all deal with the Word of God.

LOVE THE WORD

First, to be successful parents, we are told, we must *love the Word of God.* Love for God includes love for His Word. "Love the Lord thy God," it says, "and these words . . . shall be in thine heart." You cannot love God unless you love His Word, and you cannot love God's Word unless you truly love Him.

Centuries later than Moses, Jesus said that this is the most important commandment in all the Bible, and it certainly is the foundation on which we must build our families.

Notice that we are to love God with all our heart, soul, and mind. "Your heart" means your spirit—that part of you that is able to worship and have a relationship with God. "Your soul" includes the rest of your immaterial being—your mind, emotions, and will. And "your might" refers to your physical being, or your body. What this verse is saying is that our love for God and for His Word must consume every part of our being—body, soul, and spirit.

Love results in obedience. Jesus said, "If a man love me, he will keep my words . . . He that loveth me not keepeth not my sayings" (John 14:23-24). The greatest thing you as a parent can give to your children is an example of loving obedience to God and to His Word.

Paul wrote to Timothy of the faith that had been in his grandmother, Lois, and in his mother, Eunice (2 Timothy 1:5). In the same epistle Paul reminded Timothy "that from a child thou hast known the holy Scriptures, which are able to make thee wise unto salvation through faith which is in Christ Jesus" (2 Timothy 3:15). Timothy had a grandmother and a mother who loved the Word of God, and Paul was reminding him that that was the greatest heritage he had. Timothy went on to become one of the greatest leaders in the early church.

TEACH THE WORD

But it is not enough just to love the Word of God. David

318

loved the Word of God, but that did not make him a good parent. We must also *teach the Word of God.* We cannot expect our children to find the right way by themselves. God's Word reveals the way to salvation, security, and satisfaction, but each generation must be shown. They must be taught the Word of God.

Deuteronomy 6:7 says, "Thou shalt teach them diligently unto thy children." As parents it is not enough just to love and honor God ourselves. We must also teach our children, both with our lives and with our lips.

You cannot begin to teach your children too soon or repeat your teaching too often. The command is to speak about God's Word "when thou sittest in thine house, and when thou walkest by the way, and when thou liest down, and when thou risest up." God is saying to teach your children in every situation of life—morning, noon, and night. When you are at home, when you are driving in your car, while picnicking in the park, when you tuck them in at night, when they get up in the morning, teach them! Teach them!

Teach your children that God is the Creator, that He loves them, that He answers prayer. Teach them that wrong is wrong and right is right, and that sin destroys and separates. Teach them that we reap what we sow, and that the wages of sin is death. Teach them that Christ died for their sins according to the Scriptures and that He was buried, and that He rose again the third day. Teach them that whosoever believeth in Him should not perish but have everlasting life. Teach them diligently.

At least five times in slightly different ways the Bible says that the fear of the Lord is the beginning of wisdom. What a powerful phrase! The child in your home may become a brilliant scholar, he may receive degrees and honor and fame. But if he does not learn to know and honor God and His Word, he will grope and tumble and stumble through life as a failure and as a fool.

319

Only God's Word applied to the life has the power to cleanse and deliver and give light. In Psalm 119:9, the psalmist asks, "Wherewithal shall a young man cleanse his way?" And then he answers, "By taking heed thereto according to thy word." Teach your children *how* to apply the Word to their lives.

Happy is the young man or young woman whose parents have taught him to allow the Word of God to correct and shape his life. Long after that father and mother have stepped aside, the Bible will reprove him and guide him.

Paul wrote to Timothy and reminded him that he had known the Word of God from his childhood. Then he made this poignant observation: "All scripture is given by inspiration of God, and is profitable for doctrine, for reproof, for correction, for instruction in righteousness" (2 Timothy 3:16). That means that the ministry of the Word of God in a person's life is a ministry of discipline.

What is discipline? My dictionary defines it as "training that corrects, molds, or perfects the mental faculties or moral character." Discipline, my friend, involves shaping and correction. It takes place only when the person involved can subject himself to another's authority. Hebrews 12:5-6 says, "My son, despise not thou the chastening of the Lord, nor faint when thou art rebuked of him: For whom the Lord loveth he chasteneth, and scourgeth every son whom he receiveth."

Parent, are you teaching your children that they cannot expect to call all the signals in their lives? Can they accept authority? They will have to learn eventually, but so many learn too late!

And are you teaching your children that they must be saved from their sin? By far your greatest responsibility as a parent to your child is to lead him to personal faith in Christ as his Savior. Do not assume that because he has gone to Sunday school and church, to summer camp or Bible club, to vacation Bible school or to a local Christian school, that he has personally accepted Christ as his own. You cannot afford to be afraid or ashamed to talk to him personally about it.

KEEP THE WORD

Finally, Deuteronomy 6:8-9 says that it is our responsibility as parents to *keep the Word of God*. We are to bind the Word on our hands, put it as a frontlet between our eyes, and put it at the entrance to our houses. Traditional Jews bind their arms and foreheads with phylacteries when they pray, and put mezuzahs on doorposts because of this verse. But I am convinced that the meaning of the verse goes far deeper than that.

Binding the Word on our arms signifies the *practice* of God's Word. Deuteronomy 6:8 is saying that whatever our hands do, they should be guided by the Word of God. The Bible gives us direction as Christian parents. We are to learn from the examples in it, obey the commands in it, and follow the guidelines in it. In doing so we not only serve as examples to our children, but we bring glory to God as well.

Keeping the Word of God as a frontlet between our eyes suggests the *presence* of the word. We are to keep it ever before us, out in front where we can see it, and let it be a reminder and a guide to us.

Do you remember the call of Moses? God wanted him to lead His people out of slavery in Pharaoh's Egypt. Moses was overwhelmed. Perhaps you feel the same way when you think of your responsibility as a parent. Despite forty years of the best training Egypt offered, Moses felt inadequate.

God's answer to Moses was all that he needed. He promised him His presence. "Certainly I will be with thee," He said (Exodus 3:12). Later in the life of Moses, at a time of great discouragement, God renewed that promise to him.

God will help you to be an effective, faithful parent, and if you are a believer, you have the promise of His presence. But look at what Paul wrote to the Colossians. "Let the word of Christ dwell in you richly in all wisdom" (Colossians 3:16). That is just like saying, "Let God's Word be a frontlet between your eyes." You have the assurance of God in your life, because His Spirit dwells in you. But does His Word dwell in you richly in all wisdom? If the presence of God gives confidence, the presence of His Word, dwelling in you richly, can multiply that confidence.

As a parent, you need to memorize the Word of God. You need to meditate on it regularly. You must let it dwell in you richly, and let it be as a frontlet before your eyes to remind you of God's presence and to give you guidance.

Binding the Scriptures on our arms signifies the practice of God's Word. Letting it be a frontlet before our eyes suggests the presence of God's Word. And writing it on our gates and doorposts shows the *prominence* of God's Word.

Parent, how prominent is the Word of God in your life? What is the testimony of your home to those that see it from the outside? Is the Word of God written on your gates and doorposts? I don't mean that you necessarily need to put a sign with a Scripture verse on your door. What I mean, and what I think Deuteronomy 6:9 teaches us, is that the testimony of God's Word should be so prominent in our lives and families that when an outsider sees us, one of the first things he should be able to tell is that our family reveres the Word of God.

What is the testimony of your life? What is the testimony of your family? Do you love the Word of God? Do you teach the Word of God? Do you keep the Word of God? If so, you are the kind of parent America needs.

A Christian home must have Christian parents who are sensitive to the Spirit of God and the Word of God. Perhaps you need to receive Christ as your Savior yourself. Perhaps you need to commit yourself to a new loving obedience to the Word of God. Will you not do it today?

1. Alvin Toffler, *Future Shock* (New York: Random House, 1970), pp. 216-17.
2. Ferdinand Lundberg, *The Coming World Transformation* (Garden City, NY: Doubleday, 1963), p. 295.

THREE

How to Fight the World— and Win!

Henrietta Mears correctly observed that God does not always choose great people to accomplish what He wishes, but He always chooses a person who is yielded to Him. Do you want God to use you as a parent to accomplish great things in the lives of your children? Then *you* must be yielded to Him.

In the eyes of the world a parent committed to Christ may not always be great. But in the eyes of the Lord, in the eyes of their children, and in the eyes of those who know them best, they are persons without equal. Their lives are marked by love and unselfish service.

But mothers and fathers in our times bear heavy burdens. The pressures against Christian homes have never been greater. Many wonder if they can counterattack or even hold the line. How can the Christian family resist today's heavy pressure to compromise biblical standards?

The *opposition* to the traditional family and its values today is overwhelming. But the *opportunities* for the family and for growth in the family are tremendous, too. As I study the New Testament, and especially the life of the Lord Jesus, I see three encouraging truths for today's Christian families.

The first truth that encourages me about today's families is *the pattern we have for living in a Christian home,* and that pattern is the Lord Himself in His submission.

Some time ago I read a short account of a very human happening. A family was planning a full-day treat for Mother on her birthday. She was to have the entire day to herself, to do whatever she wanted. The father and children would cook the meals and clean the house while Mother relaxed.

They had planned a picnic. The whole family would go to a nearby lake to spend the day. The son would join some friends in water skiing, and the daughter would play tennis. Mother could rest and read while father tried out the new fishing rod he had received for Christmas.

When the day arrived, however, the family was taken up with getting ready. So Mother got breakfast ready for everyone. Then, after she had helped them find their things and loaded the car, there was only enough room in the car for three.

That was all right, Mother said. She would not mind the day at home. She would have peace and quiet and probably get more accomplished than if she went to the lake. The family agreed. After all, Mom was only going to read and relax, and she could do that as well at home as at the lake. Maybe better.

While the family was gone, Mother tidied up the house a bit. She ironed her daughter's dress for that evening, picked up the father's suit at the cleaner, did a couple of loads of laundry, did a few other odds and ends that had needed doing for some time, fixed supper for the family, and even baked herself a birthday cake.

There were a few presents at Mother's plate for dinner, and everyone agreed that she was the greatest. Someone suggested that this was the nicest birthday she had ever had.

Mother, reflecting, had to agree that indeed it had been one of the nicest, most meaningful birthdays she could remember.

Why was that birthday such a special one? Because that mother derived her satisfaction in the family from her loving, submissive service to others.

Christ Himself was an example of that kind of service to others. Think for a moment what Christ came into this world to do. The world He entered at Bethlehem was black as night. Just as it does today, sin seemed to reign supreme and unchallenged. When Jesus was yet a little baby, Satan moved King Herod to try to take His life. As Jesus prepared to minister, the "establishment" was solidly against him—priesthood, government, and even the predominant attitude of the people. It seemed that everyone and everything was against Him.

But He "was the true Light" (John 1:9), and He shined in the darkness of those days. Remember who Jesus is. He is God (John 1:1), but He became man (John 1:14) and humbled Himself even to the point of dying on the cross for sins that He had not committed (Philippians 2:8). Jesus' entire life was marked by a humble service to others, and His example is our pattern for family living, whether we are mothers, fathers, or children.

Notice some significant observations we can make about the way our Lord approached the task that was before Him. First, He was totally yielded to the Father's will. "I seek not mine own will," He said in John 5:30, "but the will of the Father which hath sent me." His Father's will was seldom easy, but the Lord was determined to do it just the same. "My meat," He said, "is to do the will of him that sent me, and to finish his work" (John 4:34). His very sustenance was the Father's will. Obeying God was what kept Him going.

Second, to do God's will, He was submissive even to the ones who mistreated Him. Peter, who spent the entirety of

Christ's public ministry with Him, writes a remarkable thing in his first epistle. He says that when Jesus was reviled, He "reviled not again; when he suffered, he threatened not; but committed himself to him that judgeth righteously" (1 Peter 2:23). Jesus submitted Himself to others, even when they abused Him!

Look again at 1 Peter 2. Verse 21 says that Christ's sufferings and the way He responded to them were "an example, that ye should follow his steps." We are called and commanded to follow the same example of submission that Jesus showed, submitting to men and committing Himself to God.

Ephesians 5 makes the same point. Verse 21 says that we are to submit ourselves to one another in the fear of God.

No Christian family can be successful unless the example of submission is followed by every member. No other human relationship is as basic as that of the family. And unless submission is practiced in the family, the family relationships will fail. And if we fail in the relationships of the family, we will fail in every relationship of life.

The Moody Bible Institute sponsored family-life conferences across the nation for several years. In almost every conference the same problems surfaced in the families of those who responded. The problems began in relationships between members of the family, and they seemed universally to spread to other areas of life.

If I could sum up one great truth that would help a family make giant strides toward success in fighting both the internal and external pressures of today's world on the family, it would be this: learn the importance of loving, submissive service to one another.

Many magazines and books today are filled with counsel for parents and families. Some of it is constructive. But most of it is frighteningly destructive. Most of the advice falls short because it fails to recognize that most family conflict is essentially a spiritual problem. The real foes of the family today are not social change or even permissiveness. The real foes of the Christian family are the same as the foes of the Christian: the world, the flesh, and Satan himself, which all work together to stir up pride in the Christian. And the only answer to that pride is the loving, serving, submissive mind of Christ (Philippians 2:5-8).

THE POWER FOR THE CHRISTIAN HOME—JESUS' LIFE

A second truth that encourages me about the potential of Christian families today is *the power we have for living in a Christian home,* and that is the very life of Christ.

As God Himself, Jesus had unlimited power. Hebrews 1 tells us that He is the creator of the universe. His power is infinite. But did you know that while He was here on earth, Jesus did not use that power? Every miracle He ever did, every healing He ever performed, was done in the Father's power. Jesus said, "The Son can do nothing of himself" (John 5:19), and, "I can of mine own self do nothing" (John 5:30). Not only was Jesus yielded to the Father's will, but He was dependent on the Father's power as well.

Again and again, Jesus stressed the same important fact. "The words that I speak unto you I speak not of myself," He claimed, "but the Father that dwelleth in me, he doeth the works" (John 14:10).

By the same token, the Christian is not to live in his own power but in the power of Christ. The great apostle Paul, who did so much for the Lord, gave the secret of his effectiveness. "I am crucified with Christ," he wrote. "Nevertheless I live; yet not I, *but Christ liveth in me*: and the life which I now live in the flesh I live by the faith of the Son of God" (Galatians 2:20, italics added). The power for his life was not Paul's own, but it was the resurrection power of the Lord Jesus.

The truth that the Lord Jesus is the empowerment for the

Christian's life and obedience to God runs throughout the New Testament. Paul said, "I can do all things through Christ which strengtheneth me" (Philippians 4:13).

Parent, if you are a believer in Christ, you are not alone. Christ dwells in you through His Spirit, and He has promised that He will never leave you nor forsake you (Hebrews 13:5). He is your power to live and to lead your family. You have a tremendous task and an overwhelming responsibility. But God did not give it to you without the enablement to do it.

Are the influences of this world on your family more than you can handle? God does not expect you to handle them in your own power. But you, too, can do all things through Christ, who will strengthen you. He will be your power to have the kind of family that meets God's high standards.

The Promise for the Christian Home— Christ's Presence

A third truth that encourages me as I think about the tremendous opposition to and opportunity for the Christian family is *the promise we have for living in a Christian home.* I am speaking of the promise of Christ's presence. We have already seen Christ's promise in Hebrews 13:5. "I will never leave thee, nor forsake thee." Look now at another verse of Scripture. In Colossians 1:27, Paul writes that Christ in us is "the hope of glory."

John taught that Christ was the embodiment of God's glory. In John 1:14 he wrote, "And the Word was made flesh, and dwelt among us, (and we beheld his glory, the glory as of the only begotten of the Father,) full of grace and truth." Do you wish to have a family that reflects the glory of God? Do you want your family to live by God's grace and truth? Christ's presence among you is your hope, or promise, of the glory of God.

You can have a family that redounds to the glory of God if

you understand the truth of His presence. He is an unseen member of your family. He never sleeps or fails or falls short in His blessings. You are laborers together with Him, and your family is just a part of an even bigger family—the family of God.

What does His presence mean to your family? Does the knowledge that He is there affect what you talk about? What you watch on television? How you treat each other? How you treat guests in your home?

Are outsiders who come into contact with your family aware of His presence there? Is your home really different from other homes because of the presence of the Lord? Does His presence make your mealtimes different? Do you share together as a family in prayer and in God's Word?

And is Christ truly the head and the center of your family? Are you sensitive to His will, and do you seek His guidance? Is His Word the final authority in your family's decisions and disagreements?

If we truly recognize and respond to the presence of Christ in our families, it will make an impact on our daily lives.

But perhaps Christ is not in your family. Perhaps you have never really trusted Him as your Savior. "But as many as received him," says John 1:12, "to them gave he power to become the sons of God, even to them that believe on his name." Unless you have been born again, you are not in His family. And if you are not in His family, He is not in yours.

My friend, will you trust Him today and receive His offer of free forgiveness of sins? He died for your sins that you might live for Him, and He offers eternal life to you as a gift, freely, if you will accept it by faith (Romans 3:24-25).

Truly the family of today is suffering. Its exact status is in dispute. According to the 1976 report of the United States Census Bureau, more than 1,300,000 unmarried couples are living together in our country.

On the other hand, a lead article in the magazine *Changing Times* says that the picture is better than many think. "When the smoke clears," says the magazine, "most authorities expect that the family will still occupy the central position in most people's lives."[1] As proof, the article cited a survey of nearly 200,000 college freshmen at 366 schools across the country. Of these, more than half listed "raising a family" as one of the most important goals of their lives. Most put raising a family ahead of financial success and all other goals.[2]

If raising a family is such a priority in so many people's lives, why aren't they more successful at it? Because without Christ, there really is no hope for any family. Without His submission as our pattern we are left with our weakness and insufficiency. And without His presence as our promise, we are left with our hopelessness and confusion.

No family can be a success without Christ. How is your family doing?

1. "What Future for the American Family?" *Changing Times* 30, no. 12 (December 1976): 10.
2. Ibid., p. 9.

FOUR

God's Pattern for Parents

The average family in America today enjoys a higher standard of living than ever before. However, there are many disturbing signs that the family faces serious problems. The failure of the home is a definite threat in our world today. Laymen and educators alike are expressing concern over the health of this basic institution of our society.

Dr. K. E. Appel of the University of Pennsylvania states that the family is in a state of serious crisis. And he suggests some reasons for the crisis.

First, he says, *the family is seriously fragmented.* It does not hold together any longer than circumstances compel it to do so. As long as it is expedient, or as long as the marriage satisfies selfish personal needs, it stays together, albeit sometimes only in name.

In this permissive age in which we live, some people look upon the institution of marriage simply as a convenient way for a man and a woman to live together. And if marriage is not convenient, often they live together anyway. The media seems to delight in publishing shocking statistics and predictions about marriage. For example, the *London Observer* printed a headline some time ago that asked, "Are We the Last Married Generation?" In the accompanying article, British psychologist James Heming, a member of England's official Marriage Guidance Council, predicted that engagements are doomed and weddings will soon be something of the past.

Of course we disagree with such predictions, but the fact that they are widely being made says something about the state of marriage.

The truth is that marriage is God's provision for the family, which He ordained from the beginning, even before Adam sinned. Some have always violated the biblical ideal of the family and marriage. But now God's structure and plan for the family is being neglected and ignored by many.

In an article in *Moody Monthly* magazine, Christian psychologist Dr. Lacey Hall reminds us, "The Christian needs to realize what is happening to the family if he is to understand the forces shaping his own home, his own children, the families in his church and the homes in his neighborhood."[1]

Second, Dr. Appel suggests that a reason for the crisis in the home is that *the average family is rootless,* having few ties of tradition or history. Since the beginning of the post-World-War II era, America has been on the move. Twenty percent of the population changes its place of residence annually. Industry and business demand people who will move. One third of all families with husbands under thirty-five years of age move each year.

Dr. Lacey Hall suggested that such mobility is changing the roots of the home. When the family moves, he said, it has to adjust to new housing, new schools, and new friends. And the strain that is put on the family relationships can lead to deep feelings of insecurity and instability. He quoted a book that compared such mobile families to young trees grown at a nursery with shallow roots for easy transplanting. Such trees, he said, cannot withstand the storms.[2] Many of today's families are not equipped to weather the storms of today's world.

As a result of all this rootlessness, many families today have lost all sense of orientation. Some wives really are not certain whether they want to be wives and mothers, husbands are not sure whether they want to be husbands and fathers, and children are not given the opportunity to experience childhood in a well-ordered and secure home.

Security is vital to a family. It seems obvious that the first requirement for a unified and happy family is a sense of belonging for every member. And yet, today's families have largely lost any sense of unity or security between family members. The result is a loss of harmony and an abundance of personal conflicts.

Many of the responsibilities that really belong in the home have been taken over by other agencies, such as the school, local clubs, and even the church. The result is that today families are made up of individuals who have little time for each other because their lives are so wrapped up in their own activities.

In many homes the husband, wife, and children all come and go as they please—often failing even to check in. In such an atmosphere genuine communication is impossible, and the family structure breaks down.

Yes, the family today is seriously in need of help.

And let's remember that although the Christian home is different, it is not automatically exempt from those problems. Even the Christian family is adversely affected by the many crises of our society. Never before has there been such a gaping need in the average Christian family as now.

Is there help for the Christian home today? What does God's Word say about it?

I am convinced that the only hope for the problems of any family is to be found in the Word of God. As I look at God's Word, I see three steps that must be taken by the parent who would follow God's pattern for family living.

REPENT OF YOUR SINS

Some time ago a mother shared with me her heartache concerning a married son who had committed suicide.

"Apples do not fall far from the trees," she said, as she spoke of the problems her son had experienced. She told how he had capped a fast romance with a speedy marriage. He had not had time to get to know his wife, and she had not had time to get to know him. Their romance and marriage had been too hasty. Potential problems had just been brushed over until after the honeymoon.

Soon his wife had discovered that he was a heavy drinker. He was emotionally immature, totally lacking any sense of responsibility. He was no more reliable than a cracked barometer. He was really a poor marriage risk!

But she had viewed marriage as a kind of reform school. She thought that after the wedding she could be a good influence on him and work on his faults. Needless to say, it did not work. Such an arrangement never works. It is the testimony of most married couples that after marriage a person's faults are the same, and often more intense.

Shortly after the birth of the couple's first child he deserted the family, and the marriage ended in divorce. Five years later he was dead—a victim of his own hand.

"He was just like his father," said the mother. "Apples do not fall far from the trees."

That mother's grim words reminded me of some fundamental Bible truths, especially that we always reap what we sow (Galatians 6:7). "Be sure your sin will find you out," says Numbers 32:23. You cannot sin without suffering the consequences of your sin. Therefore, if you want to follow God's pattern for the family, you must first *repent of your sins.*

The Old Testament book of Exodus tells about the children of Israel as they traveled through the wilderness. There, as they pitched their tents around Mt. Sinai, God gave them His immutable law. In explaining the very first commandment, God made this remarkable statement: "I the LORD thy God am a jealous God, visiting the iniquity of the fathers upon the children unto the third and fourth generation of them that hate me" (Exodus 20:5).

Moses was so impressed by that statement that he repeated it in Exodus 34:7. And years later, when the children of Israel wavered between fervor and fear, Moses recalled those exact words in Deuteronomy 5:9. They were unforgettable to Moses. He had seen God write them upon the tables of stone, and they were indelibly etched also upon the table of his heart. Those words were terrifying then, and they are terrifying now! They mean that our children can reap the results of our sins unto the third and fourth generation.

Every second a baby is born into this world. They are emotionally, physically, and morally capable of developing into mature, happy, well-adjusted adults, by the grace and power of God. Yet most people grow up to become just the opposite—miserable, unhappy, and frustrated. Why? I am convinced that it is largely due to the sins of the parents.

God's Word says, "Be not deceived; God is not mocked: for whatsoever a man soweth, that shall he also reap. For he that soweth to his flesh shall of the flesh reap corruption; but he that soweth to the Spirit shall of the Spirit reap life everlasting" (Galatians 6:7-8). And we are not the only ones who reap the consequences of our sins; our children reap them also.

Yes, apples do not fall far from the trees. George Gordon, Lord Byron, the famous English poet, is an example of one who reaped the sins of his parents. Humanly speaking, he had everything going for him. He was handsome, witty, intelligent, and gifted—and yet his life was a tragedy. At the age of thirty-six he wrote his final poem:

> My days are in the yellow leaf;
> The flowers and fruit of Love are gone;
> The worm, the canker, and the grief
> Are mine alone!

Neither glacier, mountain, torrent,
Forest or cloud can lighten the weight
Upon my heart, or enable me to lose
My wretched identity.

> "On This Day I Complete My
> Thirty-Sixth Year"   [Stanza 2]

Byron's ancestors, as far back as they can be traced, were violent, passionate, and unrestrained in their morals. And Byron lived as his parents lived. He openly violated all standards of morality and righteousness. He inherited his parents' sins.

He left unforgettable poetry, but Lord Byron also left an unforgettable example of what happens to children whose spiritual welfare is neglected by careless parents. He died a tragic death at a young age.

But look again at Exodus 20:5. It says that the sins of the parents are visited to the third and fourth generation of *them that hate God*. It is my conviction that the grace of God is extended as well to the children of sinning parents who repent of their sins. Of course, the children are not automatically saved because of the faith of their parents, but many of the effects and judgments for their parents' sins are removed from them when the parents turn to God in repentance.

Do you want to do what you can to assure that your children will not have to suffer the effects of your sins? Repent—turn from your sin to the Lord and seek His forgiveness. Confess to your children any sins that you may have committed against them. And purpose to serve God both as an example to your children and as a minister to them. The Lord may use your life to help reverse some of the consequences of your sin on your children.

RETURN TO THE BIBLE

A second step that you can take to realign your family

with God's pattern is to *return to the Bible.* There is no easy way—no shortcut or magic formula—to build a happy home. God's Word is clear when it instructs parents to bring up their children in "the nurture and admonition of the Lord" (Ephesians 6:4). A successful home must be built on the foundation of the Word of God.

God instructed the parents of Israel to teach and instruct their children in the precepts of Jehovah. Deuteronomy 6:7 says, "Thou shalt teach them *diligently* unto thy children" (italics added). The diligent teaching of the Word of God is the fundamental requirement for a successful, God-honoring home. It is God's plan for the family. The reading, studying, and memorizing of God's Word are essentials that cannot be overlooked.

A family that is not built on the foundation of God's Word will not stand. But you cannot hope to bring your family into focus with God's Word unless your own life is already meeting the standard. Repenting from past sins is good, but it is not enough. You must determine to obey God's Word from now on. You must be the example of obedience to God in your family.

And if you are to teach your family the Word of God, you must know it. Too many parents are biblically illiterate. Do you study God's Word regularly? If not, you will not be much of a teacher to your children.

RESPOND TO THE LORD

A third step to take in bringing your family into harmony with God's pattern is to *respond to the Lord.* Be sensitive to the will and direction of the Lord in your life. Parents, of course, must set a good example for their children to follow. Proverbs 22:6 says, "Train up a child in the way he should go: and when he is old, he will not depart from it."

The Old Testament tells us about Absalom, the third son of David. He was a man who had every opportunity to

341

become something for God. But his father was not a good example to him. When David fell into sin with Bathsheba, Absalom surely knew about it. Apparently, that one poor example was enough to undo all David's prior teaching and example. Absalom reflected David's desire for self-gratification. Law meant nothing to him. He lived only for what he could get in the way of immediate results.

Absalom killed his brother for ravishing his sister. Then he conspired to overthrow his father, David. As David's soldiers went out after him, David pleaded with them to deal gently with the boy. But Absalom died in his rebellion—a victim of the sins of his parents.

Others in the Bible show the danger of parental insensitivity to the Lord. The sons of Noah, the daughters of Lot, the children of Jacob, of Eli, and of Samuel all give examples of the folly of failing to respond to the Lord.

Parent, if you are not sensitive and submissive to the will of God, your children will follow your example. They will be unresponsive to your authority as well as to God's. That is the natural law of sowing and reaping.

Are you willing to repent of your sin, return to the Bible, and respond to the Lord? Does the spiritual well-being of your family mean that much to you? It is a price to pay—or rather, seed to be sown. And you will reap the fruit of whatever seed you sow.

Remember the assessment of Dr. Appel? He said that family problems are caused by fragmentation in the family, by a lack of family roots, and by a lack of communication. Repentance from sin is the only way to heal the conflicts caused by fragmentation. A return to the Bible is the only way to restore the sense of solidity and stability caused by the loss of our roots. And a proper response to the Lord is the only answer to the loss of harmony caused by the breakdown in communication that has taken place in our families—because God's love and forgiveness are the only

342

answers to the broken relationships and shattered bonds in our families. What will your response be?

1. Cited in "The Christian Home," by Gene A. Getz, Moody Manna Series (Chicago-Moody, 1967), p. 1
2. Lacey Hall, "What's Happening to the American Family?" *Moody Monthly* 67 (July-August 1967): 26
3. Ibid.

FIVE

Train Up a Child

Horticulturist Luther Burbank warned long ago, "If we had paid no more attention to our plants than we have to our children, we would now be living in a jungle of weeds." Unfortunately there are many homes in our world today that resemble jungles instead of gardens. Juvenile delinquency continues to rise as parents are forced to reap what they have sown.

To bring up a child in this world is a tremendous responsibility. There is no bigger job than that of being a faithful and dedicated parent. The rearing of our children is one of the most important jobs we will ever engage in. We must do it carefully and prayerfully.

Dr. Payson said, "What if God should place a diamond in your hand and tell you to inscribe on it a sentence which should be read at the last day and shown there as an index of your thoughts and feelings. What care, what caution you would exercise in the selection!" That is exactly what God has done. He has placed before you the immortal minds of your children, less perishable than the diamond, on which you are inscribing every day and every hour by your instruction, by your spirit, by your example, something that will remain and be exhibited for you or against you at the judgment!

And yet, in spite of the tremendous responsibility, many parents today leave the instruction of their children to chance. Recently a brokenhearted father confessed to me, "I've spent more time training my dog than I have my sons." What a tragedy!

Many of the ten thousand runaway children in this country each year can be traced to homes in which little parental love and concern was demonstrated. Almost all juvenile delinquency is the result of parental neglect. A juvenile court judge in New York said, "When I retire I'm going to write a book and call it *Why I Hate Parents.*" Asked why he said that, he replied, "Because of my disgust with parental failure to assume their primary job—the care of their children."

A youth in Chicago who has already been in trouble with the law stated, "The only reason I know what my mother's face looks like is because my family gets together on Thursday evenings for one hour—from seven to eight P.M. The rest of the week, my mom and dad are running a thousand directions." No activity that robs children of parental care and companionship, no matter how important that activity might seem, is worthwhile.

God has ordained the family structure as we know it, and one of its primary purposes is for the training of children. Proverbs 22:6 clearly shows a parent's responsibility to his child. "Train up a child in the way he should go," it says, "and when he is old, he will not depart from it." *You* must teach them. You cannot leave the job to the school, the church, or the babysitter. It is your responsibility as a parent.

There are at least three character qualities that you must teach your children if when they are old they are to follow the way you have taught them.

TEACH YOUR CHILDREN TO BE DILIGENT

First, you should teach your children to be *diligent.* A leading law enforcement officer of a previous decade charged our society with substituting indulgence for discipline, pleasure for duty, and money for morals. As one who dealt with criminals and knew the criminal mind, he placed the blame for the growing menace of youth crime largely at the door of the parents. He cited as the heart of the problem parental "negligence, indifference, personal greed, and bad example." His words ring true today as we see an even further deterioration of the family.

In his book *Rome, Its Rise and Fall,* Phillip Van Ness Myers speaks of the disintegration of the Roman family as part of the reason for that great empire's collapse. Myers wrote, "The typical Roman family consisted of the father . . . and mother, the sons, together with their wives and sons, and the unmarried daughters. . . . The most important element or feature of this family group was the authority of the father."[1]

The historian continues, "It would be difficult to overestimate the influence of this group upon the history and destiny of Rome. It was the cradle of at least some of those splendid virtues of the early Romans that contributed to the strength and greatness of Rome, and that helped to give her the dominion of the world."[2]

But something happened. The stability of Roman family life did not last. By the end of the second century, Roman fathers, says Myers, had "yielded to the impulse to become far too complacent. Having yielded the habit of controlling their children, they let the children govern them, and took pleasure in bleeding themselves white to gratify the expensive whims of their offspring. The result was that they were succeeded by a generation of idlers and wastrels."[3] They failed to teach their children diligence.

Parents, you must teach your children diligence both by example and by precept. Teach them diligence in their responsibilities in the home, in the neighborhood, and at school. Teach them diligence in prayer. Teach them diligence in the study of God's Word. Teach them diligence in all things.

I am convinced that laziness and a lack of sense of purpose among today's young people are the greatest causes of their personal problems. If you have not taught your children to work, you have not taught them anything of value.

Eli is an example of a man who failed to teach his sons diligence. He was the high priest and a judge of Israel, and his sons worked in the Tabernacle. Or rather they occupied their time in the Tabernacle, supervising the offerings. First Samuel 2:12-14 tells us that they had devised an unlawful method of taking the people's sacrifices for their own personal use.

Those sons had followed the example of their lazy father and gone even further in their evil. They were desecrating the very sacrifices it was their duty to oversee. Eli had failed to teach them diligence.

God spoke through a prophet to Eli, condemning him for his failure to train his sons in the way they should go. "Wherefore kick ye at my sacrifice and at mine offering, which I have commanded in my habitation; and honourest thy sons above me, to make yourselves fat with the chiefest of all the offerings of Israel my people?" (1 Samuel 2:29). God blamed Eli for the sin he had allowed his sons to commit, and He said that it was really idolatry, or honoring Eli's own sons above God!

Failing to teach your children diligence is a serious sin against God as well as against your own children.

TEACH YOUR CHILDREN TO BE OBEDIENT

In our permissive society with its emphasis on children's rights, we seem to have forgotten that the child's direct command from God is to honor and obey his parents. And it is your responsibility to your child to teach him to be *obedient*. Obedience does not come naturally. Rebellion does, but obedience must be taught to a child from the very earliest age. And, parent, the responsibility to teach your children obedience falls not on the teacher, not on the babysitter, not on the neighbors, not on your youth pastor, but on you.

The apostle Paul, under the direction of the Holy Spirit, wrote, "Children, obey your parents in all things; for this is well-pleasing unto the Lord" (Colossians 3:20). Why should children obey? Because the Bible teaches that it is well pleasing unto the Lord. God is pleased with obedience. But there is another reason. Obedience will be necessary all through their lives. My dear father would often say to his six children, "Children, learn to obey the laws of this home, and the laws of the school, state, nation, and God will be easy to obey." Obedience to authority pleases God not just in the case of children in the home but for employees on the job, for citizens under the government, for students in a school, and even for members of a church.

In Ephesians 6:1 we read, "Children obey your parents in the Lord: for this is right." Why should children obey? Because it is right. Built into every divine and human institution are patterns of authority. Everyone, no matter what his position in life, is under authority. It is God's order. "The powers that be are ordained of God" (Romans 13:1). Obedience is right.

Luke 2:51 tells us that Jesus was subject to His parents in all things. If Jesus, the eternal Son of God, was subject to His earthly mother and father, surely it is right for every child to obey his parents.

In order to learn obedience a child needs discipline at times. The Bible emphasizes that. "He that spareth his rod hateth his son: but he that loveth him chasteneth him betimes" (Proverbs 13:24). "Chasten thy son while there is hope, and let not thy soul spare for his crying" (Proverbs 19:18). "Foolishness is bound in the heart of a child; but the rod of correction shall drive it far from him" (Proverbs 22:15).

The writer of the book of Hebrews calls attention to the same truth. "Now no chastening for the present seemeth to be joyous, but grievous," he writes. "Nevertheless, afterward it yieldeth the peaceable fruit of righteousness unto them which are exercised thereby" (Hebrews 12:11).

Someone has said that everything in the modern home is controlled by switches these days—except the children. The predominant feeling seems to be that children must not be restrained but given free release of their impulses. Some say that restraint may cause the child severe damage in his personality.

Dr. Jules Henry, a prominent St. Louis sociologist and author of *Culture Against Man* (New York: Random Vintage, 1963), charges that our society's permissiveness has turned our nation from being parent-centered to being child-centered. He correctly points out that permissiveness "leads to the destruction of gratitude and the elimination of guilt." Even more serious, "Where there is no concept of punishment," he says, "there is no concept of right or evil."

In debunking the theory that restraint harms a child, the doctor points out that most of the men who have been great leaders throughout history grew up in environments of strict discipline. Most of our own country's founders and leaders, he says, "grew up under firm fathers and mothers and under teachers whose prime pedagogical instrument was the birch rod."

Dr. Henry carefully explains that he is not calling for the "cat-o'-nine-tails and the straight jacket" treatment, but, said he, "There is a strange confusion nowadays in the minds of parents between authoritarianism and authority, and hand-in-hand with this confusion had gone the notion that the old-fashioned firm and commanding parent was somehow psychopathogenic."

It is my conviction that most youngsters, even those who are rebellious against adult authority, are actually seeking a strong hand of guidance. Discipline that sets definite boundaries of right and wrong for a child, discipline that demands his obedience, actually is a source of security to him. Several years ago the *New York Mirror* listed ten suggestions for parents who would like to take measures against juvenile delinquency. All of the suggestions were offered by boys who had been in trouble with the law. Paraphrased, they are:

1. Don't always give us our way.
2. Be firm but fair in discipline.
3. Make us feel wanted.
4. Teach us to work and get along with others.
5. Deal with and punish infractions of the family rules.
6. Listen to our side in arguments.
7. Carefully monitor our friends.
8. Don't let us stay out late at night.
9. Don't spare the rod.
10. Give more time to family-centered activities.

Eli failed in this respect, too. He did not teach his sons obedience. First Samuel, chapter 2, tells us that his sons were defiling the Tabernacle by having illicit relations with the women that assembled there. In response to such a great evil, Eli offered his sons a weak rebuke. "Nay, my sons," he said in verse 24. "It is no good report that I hear: ye make the LORD's people to transgress."

Eli's sons were grown men, but their attitude and behavior show that they had not learned obedience in their childhood. And if Eli's words to them are any indication of how he dealt with them as children, it is no wonder. He rebuked them, but he did not demand their obedience. He did not take steps to see that they were corrected, and he failed in his responsibility both as a father and as the high priest.

You can teach your children diligence and obedience and still fail in your greatest responsibility. You must teach them to be *reverent*. You must teach them to honor the Lord, His Word, and His ways.

Diligence is your child's responsibility to himself, and obedience is his responsibility to others, but reverence is his responsibility to the Lord, and that is the greatest responsibility of all.

Reverence is not just praying before meals. It is not just attending church regularly. It is not just reading the Bible or talking about spiritual things. It includes all those things, but it is more.

True reverence grows out of a heart devoted to the Lord. Genuine reverence is possible only in one who is a child of God. And your first step if you would teach your children reverence is to lead them to personal faith in the Lord Jesus Christ.

A disturbing thing in many Christian families today is that mothers and fathers are afraid or uneasy in talking freely to their children about the things of the Lord. Read Deuteronomy 6:6-9 about the parents' responsibility to speak freely of the things of the Lord and teach them to the children. We ought to instruct and encourage our children in the things of the Lord in every situation of life.

Look at some biblical examples of godly parents. Abraham was the friend of God, the Bible tells us. And God said of him, "I know him, that he will command his children and his household after him, and they shall keep the way of the LORD, to do justice and judgment" (Genesis 18:19). Abraham did not fail in his responsibility to teach his family reverence for the ways of the Lord, and look at the beautiful illustration of obedience and submission we have in Isaac, who allowed his father to bind him and place him on the altar of sacrifice!

Joshua led his entire family in the way of righteousness. He said, "As for me and my house, we will serve the LORD" (Joshua 24:15). He correctly assumed the responsibility for the spiritual leadership of his children.

Cornelius also "feared God with all his house" (Acts 10:2). His was one of the first Gentile families God brought into the church, and the testimony of his family's acceptance by God made great progress in the uniting of the Jewish and Gentile factions of the church.

But here again, Eli failed in his responsibility. As high priest in Israel, he had a position of spiritual leadership over the entire nation. But he could not even fulfill his spiritual responsibility to his own family! He failed to teach his sons reverence.

First Samuel 4 tells of the culmination of the sins of Eli's sons. Because they had not been taught diligence, they had desecrated the offerings of God. Because they had not been taught obedience, they had defiled the Tabernacle of God. And now, because they had not been taught reverence, they despised the Ark of God.

The Philistines had defeated Israel in a battle, and the irreverent, superstitious sons of Eli took the Ark of the Covenant into battle. The Ark belonged in the Most Holy Place in the Tabernacle, and even the high priest was not to enter there except once a year on the Day of Atonement. The Ark symbolized the presence of God and was the dwelling place of God's glory.

But Eli's sons had never learned reverence for the things of God. They intruded into the Holy of Holies and took the Ark with them into battle. As a result they were killed, the Ark was taken, and the glory of the Lord departed from Israel.

Parents, our task is immense, our responsibility is great. May God give us the wisdom and strength to do our job well. We must set an example of diligence, obedience, and reverence to God in all phases of our lives.

Does the thought of your responsibility overwhelm you? Look to God for the strength and wisdom to fulfill it. Make Christ the Lord of your life and of your family, and begin to train up your children in the way that they should go.

1. Phillip Van Ness Myers, *Rome, Its Rise and Fall* (Philadelphia: Richard West, 1901), pp. 11-12.
2. Ibid.
3. Ibid.

SIX

Handmaid of the Lord:
A Mother Chosen by God

One of the fundamental doctrines of Christianity is that Jesus existed from eternity past. John 1:1 tells us that He "was God." Do not ever get the idea that His origin was at His conception in Nazareth. That was merely the beginning of His life on earth. As the Son of God, the second Member of the Trinity, He had always existed.

Hebrews 1 tells us that Jesus was at work in the creation of the world. He "laid the foundation of the earth; and the heavens are the works of [His] hands" (Hebrews 1:10). But He came into this world "to seek and to save that which was lost" (Luke 19:10). He was "made flesh" (John 1:14) that He might dwell among us and die for us.

God could have chosen any woman in the world to be the earthly mother of Jesus. But He chose Mary. Have you ever wondered why? She was a unique person, the one among millions that God selected to bring His Son into the world. She was blessed of God and highly favored. I believe the reason God chose her can be traced to three outstanding characteristics in her life.

PURITY THAT GREW OUT OF A CHASTE LIFE

First, Mary demonstrated *the purity that grows out of a chaste life.* The village of Nazareth, where Mary lived and grew up, lay in the path of the caravans that traveled from Capernaum to the seaports. As in every generation, there undoubtedly were women in that town who became involved with the traveling men. But not Mary. Mary was pure.

Of course there could not have been unfaithfulness of any kind in Mary. Otherwise God could not have chosen her. The words that came to her from Gabriel echoed full approval. "Fear not, Mary: for thou hast found favour with God" (Luke 1:30). Some of the great masterpieces of art that picture this great event show the angel presenting Mary with a lily. The lily symbolizes Mary's purity.

Luke 1:27 says that Mary was a virgin. I know that there are many today who reject that teaching. They attempt to do away with the supernatural reality of Christ's birth by suggesting that Jesus was born of a natural, human union. But to deny the virgin birth of Jesus is plainly to call God a liar.

Centuries before the angel appeared to Mary, the prophet Isaiah had written, "Therefore the Lord himself shall give you a sign; Behold, a virgin shall conceive, and bear a son, and shall call his name Immanuel" (Isaiah 7:14). God through His holy Word required that the mother of the Messiah would be a virgin—pure, chaste, and holy.

Luke goes to great lengths to defend the doctrine of the virgin birth. He states that she was a virgin (1:27); then he quotes Mary's own statement that she was a virgin (1:34); and then he reports the angel's confirmation that she was a virgin (1:35-37). Luke understood that the doctrine of Christ's virgin birth was essential to the Christian faith. For without the virgin birth we have not only an impure Mary, but a human Jesus and a faulty Bible as well.

His supernatural birth through a chaste virgin was necessary for the sinlessness of the holy Son of God.

When Mary received the angel's announcement, she was

overwhelmed. "How shall this be," she said, "seeing I know not a man?" (Luke 1:34). Mary was engaged to Joseph (Luke 1:27), but they had not yet come together as husband and wife. Imagine her amazement when the angel told her that she was to have a child!

The angel reassured her. "The Holy Ghost shall come upon thee," he said, "and the power of the Highest shall overshadow thee: therefore also that holy thing which shall be born of thee shall be called the Son of God" (Luke 1:35).

Then the angel gave Mary proof that her child would be without a human father. What was the proof? "Thy cousin Elisabeth, she hath also conceived a son in her old age; and this is the sixth month with her, who was called barren. For with God nothing shall be impossible" (Luke 1:36-37).

What was the angel saying? That if God could cause Elisabeth to conceive, He could do anything. If Elisabeth and Zacharias could have a child at their age, Mary could have a child without a human father. Nothing is too hard for the Lord.

Mary went to visit her cousin. When Mary and Elisabeth met, Elisabeth knew immediately that Mary was singularly blessed of the Lord. "When Elisabeth heard the salutation of Mary," Luke tells us, "the babe leaped in her womb; and Elisabeth was filled with the Holy Ghost: and she spake out with a loud voice, and said, blessed art thou among women, and blessed is the fruit of thy womb. And whence is this to me, that the mother of my Lord should come unto me?" (Luke 1:41-43).

This is yet another testimony to the purity of Mary. Elisabeth's blessing was an acknowledgement that her chaste, pure cousin was indeed blessed by God to be the human mother of His Son.

But to say that Mary was pure is not to say that she was any different from you or me in regard to her sin nature. Mary was not sinless. Jesus was, but not Mary. She was a person just like you and me. She, like all human beings had "sinned, and come short of the glory of God" (Romans 3:23). To be sure, she was pure, chaste, and holy, but only because she had responded to God in faith. We do not worship Mary; we worship her Son, who alone is sinless.

SUBMISSION THAT GREW OUT OF A HUMBLE HEART

Another significant characteristic in the life of Mary that led to God's choosing her was *the submission that grows out of a humble heart.*

Luke tells us that "the angel came in unto her, and said, Hail, thou that art highly favoured, the Lord is with thee: blessed art thou among women" (Luke 1:28). What was Mary's response to such a blessing? "She was troubled at his saying, and cast in her mind what manner of salutation this should be" (Luke 1:29).

What would your response have been to such praise from an angel? What would mine have been? We probably would have been flattered. But Mary was troubled and confused. She was humbled.

I want you to notice her amazing humility. When the angel finished his startling announcement that she was to be the mother of the Messiah, she beautifully replied, "Behold the handmaid of the Lord; be it unto me according to thy word" (Luke 1:38). What a beautiful response! "Lord, I'm your servant. Whatever You want, I want." What submission! Mary could have hesitated or even rebelled. But she did not.

Have you ever considered what it cost Mary to be the mother of Jesus? It cost her her reputation. It almost cost her Joseph.

Think of what Mary must have felt. *What will I tell people, since I have no husband? And what will I tell Joseph?* How overwhelmed she must have been!

But also think of what Joseph must have thought. When

360

he heard about Mary, he must have been disturbed by doubt. Mary had not told him how she had come to be in this condition. From Matthew's account, we learn just how upset Joseph was. Matthew 1:19 states, "Joseph . . . being a just man, and not willing to make her a publick example, was minded to put her away privily." Joseph, himself being a righteous man, was going to divorce her quietly, as was his prerogative under the law.

But God intervened, and "while he thought on these things, behold, the angel of the Lord appeared unto him in a dream, saying, Joseph, thou son of David, fear not to take unto thee Mary thy wife: for that which is conceived in her is of the Holy Ghost" (Matthew 1:19-20).

Joseph was satisfied, but what do you think Mary's neighbors thought? And what do you think the relatives thought? How much abuse do you think Mary suffered because of her submission to the Lord?

What else did it cost Mary to obey the Lord? Look at the prophecy of Simeon. When Jesus was just eight days old, His parents took Him to the Temple to be dedicated. In the Temple there was an old devout man by the name of Simeon, who had received a promise from the Holy Spirit that he would not die before he saw the Messiah. When he saw the baby Jesus, he knew that the promise had been fulfilled. He turned to Mary and said, "Behold, this child is set for the fall and rising again of many in Israel; and for a sign which shall be spoken against; (Yea, a sword shall pierce through thy own soul also,) that the thoughts of many hearts may be revealed" (Luke 2:34-35).

How was a sword to pierce through the soul of Mary? Imagine how she must have felt when she saw the multitudes reject and ridicule her son. What do you think she felt when He was accused of being demonic and in league with Satan? And imagine what must have gone through her heart as she stood by and watched Him be crucified. She saw them drive the nails into His hands, she saw His beaten and battered face, and she heard His cries from the cross. Surely a sword pierced through her soul!

Yes, it cost Mary a great deal to be submissive to God. Think also of the inconvenience to both Mary and Joseph. Not only were they talked about and persecuted, but some time after the birth of Jesus, they were forced to take Him to Egypt to avoid an attempt by Herod to kill Him. Mary and Joseph were never wealthy. When Jesus was dedicated at the Temple, they had to offer the offering of the poor (Luke 2:24). Even in His death, the Lord had to make provision for Mary so that she could live after He was gone. She was too poor to live without outside help (John 19:26-27). She had paid a very great price for her obedience to God.

And yet isn't that the same submissive spirit the Lord demands in all of us?

DEVOTION THAT GREW OUT OF A DEDICATED MIND

Finally, I see in Mary *the devotion that grows out of a dedicated mind.* Mary knew her Bible. And she loved the Word of God. Although she was very young, possibly still in her teens, Mary was a devout person. She knew the Scriptures well. She had studied the Law and the Prophets.

Her song, which we know as "The Magnificat," refers to portions of Scripture from 1 Samuel, the Psalms, Isaiah, Micah, and Exodus. It is a very beautiful passage.

> And Mary said, My soul doth magnify the Lord, and my spirit hath rejoiced in God my Saviour. For he hath regarded the low estate of his handmaiden: for, behold, from henceforth all generations shall call me blessed. For he that is mighty hath done to me great things; and holy is his name. And his mercy is on them that fear him from generation to generation. He hath showed strength with his arm; he hath scattered the proud in the imagination of their

362

hearts. He hath put down the mighty from their seats, and exalted them of low degree. He hath filled the hungry with good things; and the rich he hath sent empty away. He hath holpen his servant Israel, in remembrance of his mercy; as he spake to our fathers, to Abraham, and to his seed for ever. [Luke 1:46-55]

What a beautiful expression of faith, coming out of a mind totally dedicated to the Lord! It is true that Mary could have been given those words, without any forethought on her part, by divine inspiration. But I believe that they came out of her life of familiarity with the Word of God. What she had studied and pondered in her heart broke out in glorious praise. Mary had saturated her mind and life with the Scriptures. Her mind was full of the treasure of the Word of God.

What makes me think so? Because as I see the life of Mary I notice that one of her outstanding characteristics was her inclination to ponder the things of God. She was not an idle talker. She was not a waster of time. Because she came from an environment of poverty, she had to work hard to see that the needs of the family were met. But she spent her spare time meditating on the things of the Lord.

Remember the story of when Jesus' parents went to Jerusalem for the Passover? They left, and no one noticed that Jesus, who was just a boy at the time, was not with the group. When they returned and found Jesus in the Temple, He asked, "How is it that ye sought me? wist ye not that I must be about my Father's business?" (Luke 2:49).

Jesus' parents, the Bible tells us, did not understand the meaning of His words. The account concludes with this poignant statement: "But his mother kept all these sayings in her heart" (Luke 2:51). What a privilege was hers, to be so intimately related to the Son of God! And Mary treasured up all His words and meditated on them. She was a devout, modest, worshiping mother.

Why did God select Mary? We have seen three reasons. He chose her for her purity and chaste life. He chose her for her submission and humble heart. And He chose her for her devotion and dedicated mind.

Think about those same three characteristics in terms of the Lord Jesus. He was pure. Hebrews 7:26 tells us that He was "holy, harmless, undefiled, separate from sinners." It is the consistent teaching of Scripture that Jesus was totally pure and without sin. He was also submissive. Philippians 2:8 tells us that He became obedient unto death. His submission was total. And He was devoted. He rose up early to pray. He said that His meat was to do the Father's will. His devotion to the Father was total.

It is interesting to think that the One who was totally pure, totally submissive, and totally devoted to God the Father saw examples of those same three characteristics in His earthly mother from the time He was an infant. She was a good mother for the One who was God in the flesh.

And Mary is an example of the kind of mothers we need today.

We need mothers who will teach their children purity, submission, and devotion. We need mothers who will be examples to their children. We need mothers like Mary.

And yet, let us not forget that Mary, too, was a person with needs. She was a woman in need of a Savior (Luke 1:47). And she recognized her need. Mary will be in heaven not because Jesus was her child, but because Jesus was her Savior, Lord, and Redeemer. Is He yours?

SEVEN

Hannah: The Mother Behind God's Man

We are living in a changing world!

Motherhood, the American flag, and apple pie used to be known for their stability and nationwide appeal. Today, however, the price of apples is up, the flag is down, and motherhood is abused.

Yes, motherhood has fallen on hard times. Television makes fun of mothers, children often treat their own mothers with scorn and contempt, and even many women these days ridicule the old values of the housewife and mother. Career-minded, "liberated" young women are admired and respected in our society, and motherhood is not even considered as an option by many young girls.

But we have a need today for mothers who will guide and guard the home. It is a high and holy calling and one with much potential for great influence either for good or for evil. Motherhood is a tremendous responsibility.

Good mothers are the key to happy homes and a great nation. Through the years, the mother has been a stabilizing force in the shaping of history. Several years ago, a nationwide survey was conducted by the University of Michigan. Thousands of girls between the ages of eleven and eighteen were questioned regarding their personal and social ambitions. When asked what they would like to be in adult life, a surprising 80 percent expressed a desire to be like their mothers.

It has been said many times that no other force in the life of a son is as strong as the influence of a mother, and the testimony of millions of sons bears this out. Napoleon said, "The future destiny of the child is always the work of the mother. Let France have good mothers and she is bound to have good sons."

"The mother is the one supreme asset of the national life," said President Theodore Roosevelt. "She is more important by far than the successful statesman, businessman, artist, or scientist."

Many famous men have been greatly influenced by their mothers. George Washington's mother was a patriotic and religious woman. Her son became the father of his country. Lord Bacon's mother was a woman of superior intelligence and deep piety. He reflected her character in his own. Sir Walter Scott's mother was a great lover of poetry and literature. He became one of the finest poets of all time.

In contrast, Byron's mother was proud, contentious, and violent. He became a social misfit and died at a young age. Nero's mother was greedy, lustful, and a murderess. He became one of the worst tyrants and mass murderers the world has ever seen. Without a doubt mothers influence their children for good or for evil.

So often the traits of the mother are passed on to the children! Children learn by observation, and they learn mostly from their mothers, because they have more time to observe their mothers than anyone else.

Susannah Wesley was a great Christian mother. Despite the fact that she had nineteen children, she found time to give each child an hour's religious instruction each week. She taught her children to love God and to honor the Bible. One of her sons, John Wesley, became the founder of the Methodist movement. Another of her sons, Charles Wesley, was one of the most prolific hymnwriters the church has ever seen. His songs are a heritage the church enjoys widely today, and both Charles and John claimed that they owed a great deal to their mother.

No less a man than Abraham Lincoln said, "All that I am, or can become, I owe to my angel mother." What a tribute!

In the Old Testament, in 1 Samuel 1, we see a beautiful picture of a good mother. Hannah lived in a day when, as a nation, Israel was in bad shape. The conditions closely resembled the corruption and disorder of today. The nation's leaders had failed. Gideon and Samson, the spiritual leaders, were nothing more than memories. Patriotism was nil and morals were low. The heroes were all dead, and the prophets were yet unborn. The nation was stumbling, and a spiritual rebirth was desperately needed.

Hannah, we are told, came from a little town called Ramathaim-zophim. It was just a wide spot in the road. The biggest thing about it was its name. And yet in that little obscure village, God had a mother. And He would eventually have His servant.

God so often uses the small people of this world to bring about His divine purposes! And so it was with Hannah. God would take this obscure woman, build her character through trials and hardships, and use her to have an instrumental part in His dealings with the entire nation.

The influence of Hannah is still felt today. She was a great mother, and her story is an inspiration to mothers everywhere. There are three events in her life that show her greatness as a mother.

HER PRAYER

The first event in the life of Hannah that demonstrates her greatness as a mother is her *prayer*. Hannah was a praying woman. She was a woman of sorrow. She had been denied the crowning glory of every Hebrew woman—the privilege of motherhood. She was childless. For years she had prayed for a son. She longed to take her own son to Shiloh on the yearly pilgrimage to the Tabernacle for worship. And now, still with no child, her disappointment was more than she could bear.

The Scriptures tell us that she was deeply disturbed. She came from a devoted but divided family. They went to worship at the Tabernacle every year at the appointed time (1 Samuel 1:3). But there was not harmony in the home. Elkanah, Hannah's husband, had another wife. Polygamy was sometimes practiced in Old Testament times, but it was a violation of God's principles. Jesus made clear that from the beginning it was God's design that one man should marry one woman and that they should remain married (Matthew 19:3-6). Those who violate God's principles of marriage suffer the consequences, sometimes in strained relationships.

And the relationship in Elkanah's home were severely strained. Peninnah, Elkanah's other wife, teased Hannah because of Hannah's childlessness (1 Samuel 1:6). Hannah "was in bitterness of soul," the Bible tells us in 1 Samuel 1:10, "and [she] prayed unto the LORD, and wept sore."

Hannah's response to Peninnah's teasing was not a personal attack, but prayer to the Lord. She was a devout, godly, praying woman, and she turned to the Lord in earnest, fervent prayer.

Here was a woman totally yielded to God! First Samuel 1:7 tells us that her desire for a son was so great that while they were at the Tabernacle she gave up eating to pray. She prayed with tears, and she prayed silently. Her prayers were so intense that Eli, the high priest, thought that she was drunk! Her lips were moving, but no sound was coming out (1 Samuel 1:13), and as Eli watched the intensity of expression and anguish on her face, as he saw her lips moving and the tears running down her face, he thought she must be drunk.

That says something to me about Hannah's dedication. Even the high priest in those days of spiritual drought could not tell the difference between devotion and drunkenness! Apparently he had never seen anyone pray with such fervor, and that is a sad statement on the spiritual climate of those days.

Hannah refused to let the spiritual atmosphere around her be the determiner of her consecration to the Lord. Eli's wicked sons ran the Tabernacle and had made it a place of immorality and thievery. But Hannah came, unaffected by all the corruption around her, and poured out her heart to God in prayer.

Here was Hannah, just a simple woman from a simple family in a small village, coming to Shiloh, then the spiritual capital of Israel, to seek the Lord in prayer. And her dedication to the Lord and the faith that she evidenced made her head and shoulders above anyone else in the nation. And God was to use her in a very great way.

Her Promise

A second event in Hannah's life that shows her greatness as a mother is her *promise.* Look at Hannah's promise to the Lord in 1 Samuel 1:11. "And she vowed a vow, and said, O Lord of hosts, if thou wilt indeed look on the affliction of thine handmaid, and remember me, and not forget thine handmaid, but wilt give unto thine handmaid a man child, then will I give him unto the Lord all the days of his life, and there shall no razor come upon his head."

Hannah's desire for a son was not just for what she could get out of it. She longed for a son, but she longed for a son that she could dedicate to the Lord. With the eyes of faith, she saw what God could do with a small child dedicated to Him. And she wanted a son—not to bring glory to herself, but to bring glory to God.

Her request was for a man child. She did not want just a healthy child, but specifically a boy. Why? A girl would have sufficed if all she wanted was to stop Peninnah's mocking. But that was not Hannah's primary motive in asking for a child. She wanted a child who could serve God by working in the Tabernacle, and only a boy would do.

Yes, Hannah had plans for this boy. He would be God's child, not hers and Elkanah's. He would serve in the Tabernacle and work for God all the days of his life. Furthermore, he would live the life of a Nazirite all his life.

A Nazirite was a man who had taken a vow to serve the Lord and be set apart especially for Him. Numbers 6 tells us the requirements for a Nazirite. He would be separate from wine and strong drink. In fact he would not eat grapes, raisins, or any other product of the grapevine. He would not shave his head or allow a razor to touch the locks of his hair. And he would not touch any dead body or any other thing that would make him ceremonially unclean. He was to be holy, separated, fully dedicated to God. But ordinarily his vow was for a limited period of time, such as a few weeks or months. And he himself made the vow to become a Nazirite.

Hannah's son would be different. His dedication to God would be for life. It would not be a matter of choice for him. He would be dedicated before he would be old enough to decide for himself. He was to be the Lord's unique possession.

Many people today dedicate their children to God in infancy. But Hannah dedicated Samuel before his birth—even before his conception. What tremendous faith she displayed!

It is interesting to note that Hannah assumed the responsibility for her son's spiritual welfare. Modern parents often are content to wait and let their children decide for themselves at an older age. They do not urge them or encourage them to accept the claims of Christ personally. What a tragic mistake! The worst thing that we can do to our children is give them the impression that surrender to the Lord is optional.

HER PAYMENT

The third event in Hannah's life that shows us her greatness as a mother is her *payment*. It was a sacrifice for Hannah to pray to the Lord. Prayer always involves sacrifice. It was a greater sacrifice for her to promise her son. But the greatest sacrifice was when it came time to pay her vow.

Hannah had prayed diligently to the Lord for a son, and God answered her prayer. God listened to Hannah's cry. He seemed to say, "I have found my kind of mother, and now I shall have my kind of man." He took this simple, uneducated, plain woman, and He answered her prayers.

Hannah would be out of place among the wealthy or elite. She was not the kind that is listed in the society pages. But she made the V.I.P. list of heaven, and God honored her with a son.

Hannah had made a promise to God. Within a few short years the time came for her to give Samuel back. During all those years as she nursed him, cared for him, loved him, watched him grow, she never forgot her vow to the Lord, and she never wavered on whether to pay it.

Hannah was made of the stuff of which martyrs are made! I can just see her gathering clothes, assembling all the provisions for the journey. Her heart is both sad and glad. She occasionally looks down at little Samuel and listens to his childish words. She would miss him very much. But he was the Lord's, not hers to keep.

Hannah gave Samuel up at a very young age. First Samuel 1:24 tells us that he went to the Tabernacle to live as soon as he was weaned. From what we know of the culture of that time, Samuel was probably five years old when he left home. Arriving at the house of the Lord, Hannah greeted the attendant and gave him Samuel and his little bundle of clothes. The moment of parting had come. Hannah gave her little boy one last hug and turned around and walked the lonely road homeward.

Her words are an inspiration: "I have lent him to the LORD; as long as he liveth he shall be lent to the LORD (1 Samuel 1:28). And so she paid her vow.

What a beautiful picture is Hannah of a mother yielded to God! She gave her son to the Lord—not to things, not to society, not even to her country. She gave him to God!

Who can know the ways of God? God uses this woman's barrenness, her family conflicts, and her heartaches to drive her to her knees. She sought God's will completely and by faith dedicated her little son to Him. And God used that boy in a great way to benefit the entire nation.

Mothers, is your commitment to God's will like Hannah's? Are you consecrated to the Lord yourself, and are you willing to consecrate your children? Are you willing to dedicate your child to God, knowing that He may take him away from you? Do you seek God's will for your child, knowing that he may be called to serve the Lord on a foreign mission field far away from you? Is your love for the Lord that strong? And is your love for your child that strong? God's will is not always easy, but it is always best.

And mothers, is your life an example of sacrifice and dedication, as was Hannah's? Samuel grew up in the house of Eli, which certainly was no good influence for him. Eli was lazy, lackadaisical, and lenient; and his sons were immoral, ungodly, and crude. But the example of godliness Samuel had seen in his mother in those early years never left him. He grew up to become a wise and good leader for Israel, and a man of God.

Are you that kind of influence for your child?

And children, does your life speak well of the example of

your mother? Augustine, the great church Father and theologian, had a mother that devoted her life to his Christian upbringing and his conversion to Christ. In his early years it appeared that her efforts had failed. Augustine lived carelessly. He flouted moral restraint and actively rebelled against God. But one day he was brought to his senses and remembered his praying mother and the Word of God. He was gloriously converted and became a champion of the faith.

There once was a young lady who ignored the claims of Christ. She laughed at her mother's prayers and turned her back on her mother's God. She seemed to be headed for an eternity without God. There came a day, however, when she was moved to pen these words:

> I grieved my Lord from day to day,
> I scorned His love so full and free.
> And though I wandered far away,
> My mother's prayers have followed me.
>
> I'm coming home, I'm coming home,
> To live my wasted life anew,
> For mother's prayers have followed me,
> Have followed me the whole world through. *

Some of you had Christian mothers who prayed for you. They have prayed for years, but as yet you have not come home. You have refused to give your life to the Lord Jesus Christ. Perhaps your mother has already gone to heaven. She is there waiting for you, my friend. Do you intend to prepare for the final homecoming? Will you receive Christ right now? He knocks, He calls, but you must open your life to Him.

*Lizzie DeArmond, "Mother's Prayers Have Followed Me." Copyright 1912 by B. D. Ackley (c) Renewed 1940, The Rodeheaver Co. Used by permission.

EIGHT

God's Power for Faithful Mothers

Several years ago a very unusual letter came to the office of *Moody Monthly* magazine. It read:

Dear Magazine Publishers,

If you ever have a Mother of the Year contest, I feel that you should pick my mom.

The reason is because my mom is one mom that really cares about me. My mom disciplines me when I'm bad and is nice to me when I'm good, and she works every day from morning to night, and when she comes home, she's in a good mood, when most mothers aren't.

My mom is one mom that needs something to live about and be proud of. I sure love my mom and I want her to lead a beautiful life; and most of all I want to be proud of her. So, please, could you make her mother of the year? Thank you.

Sincerely, Paul

That is all. There is no street or address. There is not even named a town from where it was sent. But it's just as well because we do not have a Mother of the Year contest. How could we ever choose? In God's eyes as well as in the eyes of their families, many sincere, godly mothers are mothers of the year.

To mothers are entrusted the most precious of God's creation—children. They have the responsibility, shared with the fathers, to train up the children in the way that they should go. To parents more than anyone else is given the opportunity to raise children in the nurture and admonition of the Lord. And the influence of the mother certainly is felt.

Every year for the parents is the year that counts. Next year may be too late. The little lives in your sphere of influence must be nurtured, protected, guided, and pointed to Jesus Christ right now! Today's opportunities may not remain for tomorrow.

But God knows all that. He sees and cares. He is infinitely concerned about mothers and their needs. How do I know? The Bible tells me so. The mothers in the Bible show by their lives that God makes special provision for the special needs of mothers. Let's look at the messages in the lives of several Bible mothers.

EVE—GOD'S POWER TO DEFEAT SATAN

Eve was the first mother and the mother of the entire race. Motherhood for Eve must have been a frightening thing. No one had ever been a mother before, and she and Adam had just lost everything because of sin. Satan had beguiled Eve, she and Adam had disobeyed God, and all creation had been placed under a curse. Adam and Eve had lost their right to live in the Garden of Eden. They could no longer walk and talk with God, and death for them was a certainty.

But as we look at the life of Eve, we see *God's power to defeat Satan*. Satan had appeared to Eve as a serpent and had tricked her into leading Adam into sin. God had told them that the consequences of disobedience would be death, but they had disobeyed anyway, and God pronounced a curse on them.

But with the curse was a promise, and that was the promise of a deliverer. Genesis 3:15 records God's curse on the serpent, Satan. "And I will put enmity between thee and the woman, and between thy seed and her seed; it shall bruise thy head, and thou shalt bruise his heel."

My friend, do you see the importance of those words? Although Eve had been the instrument of Satan in the human downfall, she would have a part with God in the redemption of the human race. Her motherhood would ultimately mean Satan's defeat. A child born to her would become the deliverer who would crush the head of the serpent and defeat Satan.

Eve realized that. Perhaps that is why she named her first son "Cain," or "gotten one," adding, "I have gotten a man from the LORD." It seemed that she thought he was the promised deliverer. Of course, we know that God's promise was not to be fulfilled directly through Eve but through one of Eve's descendants, Mary of Nazareth. Her Son, Jesus, truly crushed the head of Satan, completely defeating him, and, as Colossians 2:15 tells us, openly triumphing over him in His own death and resurrection.

But Eve was a vital link in the line that at last led to Jesus Christ our Savior. Her motherhood demonstrates God's power to defeat Satan. God uses people. And for each person He sends into the world, He needs a mother. And He needs mothers that are godly.

Think of how God defeated Satan's working in Eve. He dealt with her *sin*. Genesis 3:21 tells us that the Lord God made clothing of animal skins for Adam and Eve. It is my belief that God's purpose in that was only partly to give Adam and Eve a covering for their nakedness. They had made their own clothing by sewing together some large leaves (verse 7). But in using animal skins, God had to slay some animals. Adam and Eve surely witnessed that event, probably the first time blood was shed for any purpose.

Hebrews 9:22 tells us that without shedding of blood there is no remission of sin. The shedding of blood was God's first lesson to man in the doctrine of atonement. Those animal skins made a covering for Adam and Eve, but the deaths of the animals by the shedding of blood made a covering for their sins. And that is what atonement is—a covering for sins.

But God dealt also with her *sorrow*. And her sorrow was great. She surely had sorrow over her sin and loss of fellowship with God. And God Himself had promised her sorrow in childbearing. But He also had, through childbearing, given her a reason for hope. A redeemer was coming. The redeemer that was to come, the Lord Jesus Christ, did more than just cover sin—He took it away. So God's provision dealt with their sin.

Satan had tried to destroy mankind, but instead he was destroyed himself. And Eve's life stands as a testimony to the power of God to defeat Satan.

JOCHEBED—GOD'S POWER TO OVERRULE CIRCUMSTANCES

Look now at the life of another mother. Jochebed, the mother of Moses, shows us *God's power to overrule circumstances*. Like Eve, Jochebed became a mother at a time of great sorrow. The king of Egypt, where Jochebed lived, had issued an order to the Egyptian midwives that when an Israelite boy was born, he should be killed (Exodus 1:16). It was the first major persecution of the Jewish people.

Jochebed, an Israelite woman, feared God, and she trusted God. When a son was born to her, she hid him for three months (Exodus 2:2). And when she was no longer able to hide him, she put him in the river among some weeds and sent his sister to watch to see what God would do. Hebrews 11:23 gives us some wonderful insight into what was in Jochebed's heart as she hid her son at the river.

First, it was an act of faith. Jochebed was confident that

God who was able to overcome Satan also was able to overrule circumstances. Hebrews 11 tells us that she acted in faith.

Second, notice that she was not afraid of the king's commandment. For three months as she did her best to conceal the existence of her little son, she was not afraid. Her faith in God gave her confidence. She worshiped a God who was able to overcome circumstances, and the king's commandment was nothing compared to God's power.

Look how God overruled the negative circumstances for Jochebed. First, Moses lived. Despite the king's order and his all-out campaign to destroy the Israelite boys, Jochebed was able to keep her son.

Also, Moses not only lived, but he lived in luxury as well. God had His hand on this little baby, and even though he was marked for death by Pharaoh, he lived. And what is more, he lived in Pharaoh's own household! Exodus 2:5-6 tells us that Pharaoh's own daughter found the baby Moses and took him home to care for him.

That is the way God works. Man can shake his fist in defiance of God; he can attempt to thwart God's purposes; and he can even take stringent measures to see to it that he has his way instead of God's. But in the end, God always overrules the circumstances, and Pharaoh ends up with the one he was so determined to kill living in his own household.

Have you considered what it meant to Moses to be raised in Pharaoh's house? He had access to all the finest things in Egypt. He had the finest education that could be had. He walked among prime ministers and governors. And his exposure to all that gave him the best training for leadership that the world could offer.

But that is not all God did to overrule the circumstances. He made it possible for Jochebed to stay with her son! God rewarded her faith by sovereignly ordaining that when

Pharaoh's daughter sought a nurse for the boy, Jochebed was the one that was chosen. What a wonderful God we have who can overrule every circumstance!

BATHSHEBA—GOD'S POWER TO CHANGE A LIFE

Finally, look with me at the life of yet another mother: Bathsheba, the mother of Solomon. You know the sordid story of Bathsheba and David's sin with her. It all began with a look. David lusted after Bathsheba, committed adultery with her, had her husband killed, and then married her. The record of that sin is one of the saddest chapters in all the Bible. But the whole story of Bathsheba is the story of *God's power to change a life.*

David and Bathsheba had an illegitimate child, who died soon after he was born. Second Samuel 12:24 tells us that after the death of that child, Bathsheba bore to David another child, whom they named Solomon. And the Scripture adds these meaningful words: "and the LORD loved him."

Why does the Scripture make it a point to say that the Lord loved Solomon? It is the Holy Spirit's way of letting us know that God's forgiveness of David and Bathsheba was complete. God had blotted out their sin, and He would remember it no more. This new child born out of their union was to have the blessing and love of God in a special way.

And God did bless Solomon. Out of all David's sons, it was Solomon who was chosen to occupy the throne in Israel after him. He was blessed with wisdom by the Lord, and he was used of the Lord to write three books of Scripture. One of those was the book of Proverbs, most of which was penned by Solomon. Look at the last chapter of that book.

Proverbs 31 begins, "The words of king Lemuel, the prophecy that his mother taught him." Many Bible students believe that Lemuel was actually Solomon, and that

"Lemuel" was his mother's pet name for him. The chapter is a collection of the advice his mother gave to him. She advises him on matters of morality, judgment, and the proper behavior of kings.

Where did Bathsheba get such wisdom? How did one who sinned so outrageously have the insight and understanding to advise the king on matters of morality? I believe that God had transformed her life. She was not the same weak-willed woman that had committed adultery with David.

Look especially at the final twenty-two verses of Proverbs 31. Beginning with verse 10 he describes the virtuous woman. Do you think Solomon would have taken seriously his mother's advice about women if she herself did not exemplify those qualities? I feel that the description in Proverbs 31 is a description of Bathsheba, and it is a wonderful demonstration of God's power to change a life.

The relationship that began as adultery ended with God's approval and blessing. God was able to take man's sin and work it unto His own glory. And because David and Bathsheba sincerely repented of their sin, He was able to transform two lives for His glory.

Mothers, can you identify with these Bible mothers? Perhaps you see Satan working hard to influence and corrupt your children. Then look at Eve, and see God's power to defeat Satan. Or perhaps you can see the circumstances of life threatening your family with problems. Then remember Jochebed, and see God's power to overcome circumstances. Maybe you feel inadequate as a mother. Perhaps your faith, or your relationship to the Lord are not what they ought to be. Or maybe some sin from your past life haunts you with feelings of guilt. Then look at Bathsheba, and take note of God's power to change a life.

God is omnipotent. His power can defeat Satan, overcome circumstances, and change lives. There is nothing that can come in the way of your responsibilities as a parent that God's power cannot overcome. The key is faith.

Eve displayed faith when she allowed God to provide clothing and a sacrifice for her. She could have persisted in the way she had begun, sewing flimsy clothing out of fig leaves for herself. That clothing was adequate as a covering, at least for a while. But it could not do anything for her sin, and it lacked the permanence that God's provision of animal skins gave. It represented man's good works, which just never are good enough.

But Eve responded to God in faith. She put aside her own works and accepted God's clothing of righteousness. That was an act of faith.

Jochebed displayed faith when she hid her son. As we have seen, she was not afraid of Pharaoh's power. She acted in faith, and God responded by giving her more than she could have asked for or wished for.

Bathsheba, too, showed faith. In coming to God for forgiveness, she was coming in faith. By faith was the only way she could come. She could not offer to do anything to atone for her sin, because it is "not by works of righteousness which we have done, but according to his mercy he saved us" (Titus 3:5). No person can earn forgiveness from sin by good works. It must be accepted by faith.

And God honored Bathsheba's faith. She is one of three women listed in Matthew's genealogy of our Lord (Matthew 1:6). Through David and Bathsheba came the line that was to bring the Messiah, God's anointed Deliverer, the Lord Jesus Christ.

Mother, will you respond to God in faith? Will you by faith receive the power you need to fulfill your responsibilities as a mother?

Children and fathers, the invitation is open to you, too. God will supply your needs. And you must trust Him for it—you cannot work for it. "For by grace are ye saved through faith; and that not of yourselves: it is the gift of God: not of works, lest any man should boast" (Ephesians 2:8-9). The Lord is calling you today. "My calling is a holy one. Trust me and do not be afraid."

NINE

What It Takes to Be a Good Father

Some people say that any man can be a father. It's a job, they say, that takes very little talent. The facts, however, show that the rate of failure at fatherhood is higher than in any other occupation. Being a father is actually a colossal job that most people underestimate.

What does it take to be an adequate father? How do you measure up? Is it true that being a father is the most important job a man can have? I believe so.

And I believe that being a father is not a part-time job. The man that would be a true father, a father that does his job well and fulfills his responsibilities, must work at it full time. And there are not many full-time fathers these days.

In a recent book, Dr. Charlie Shedd describes an interesting experience.[1] He was on board a plane jetting to Los Angeles. In the seat beside him sat a well-dressed, young-looking man. He was absorbed in a magazine article on teenagers and the current drug problem. There were pictures, too, of what drugs can do to people.

When he finished the article, the young man closed the magazine and stared into space. Apparently forgetting those around him, he half-spoke, half-whispered what seemed to be a prayer.

"Oh, God—I wonder why! I suppose nobody knows."

And then he added quickly, "But if a father can make the difference, I sure want to make the difference!"

Dr. Shedd could not pass by the young man's concern. He learned that the young man so burdened about his role as a father was a successful businessman—a salesman for a well-known firm. He had a wife and three fine children. Success in business seemed written in his future. But there was nothing higher on his agenda for the years ahead than to be an effective father—a father that would "make the difference."

The Bible makes it clear that the ideal pattern for every home and family is built on a godly father. The father is the dominant figure in the family, and his role is vital. The Bible repeatedly implies that to be without a father is the greatest of afflictions for a family. God Himself is moved to pity the fatherless. Hosea says, "In thee the fatherless findeth mercy" (Hosea 14:3). The psalmist wrote, "He relieveth the fatherless and widow" (Psalm 146:9).

But even worse than a home without a father is a home in which the father fails to fulfill his role. And there are many these days. Maybe they are too busy. Maybe they are careless. Or maybe they do not see the full dimensions of a father's task. Whatever the reason, one of our greatest needs today is for fathers to fill their roles and do it full time.

Looking at God's Word, I see three main needs in a family that the father has a duty to give his full time to supply.

PROVISION FOR THE FAMILY

The first need of every family, and probably the most obvious, is the material need. The full-time father's duty is to supply *provision for the family.*

Not very many fathers fail here. We may not give them all they would like, but we take pride in giving them all we are able. The Bible says that is the way it should be. First

Timothy 5:8 says, "But if any provide not for his own, and specially for those of his own house, he hath denied the faith, and is worse than an infidel."

Providing is a great privilege for the parent. Paul writes, "For the children ought not to lay up for the parents, but the parents for the children" (2 Corinthians 12:14).

A man who does not do his best to provide the material needs of his family commits a great sin. In the words of the Bible, he is worse than an unbeliever. No greater charge could be hurled at anyone.

But perhaps the greater danger for most of us today is that we sometimes provide beyond our real needs. A father can set his family's standards of material wants too high. He can lead his children to want and expect too much by overstressing the importance of money. The wise father will not infect his family with the love of money, which Paul says brings many sorrows. His counsel to Timothy in 1 Timothy 6:8 is, "Having food and raiment let us be therewith content."

But the father's duty to supply provision for the family does not stop with material needs. More important, but often completely forgotten, are such spiritual and emotional needs as love, training, a positive example, encouragement, and spiritual leadership.

The father is the spiritual leader of the family—or he should be. In 1 Timothy and Titus, Paul gives lists of qualifications for elders and deacons—the men who have spiritual authority over the church. And each time, the qualification that heads the list is the requirement that he be a good spiritual leader in his own family.

Consider the word *father*. There is no more important word in any language. God even uses the word to describe Himself and His relationship to His people. The word speaks of life itself, of love and patience, of discipline and strength and refuge. All those are things God provides for us—and we must provide them for our earthly children.

Fathers, your responsibility to be a spiritual leader to your family cannot be overstated. You stand symbolically in the same position over your family that God stands in over His people. You actually represent God to your family! You have given your children life, and now you must give them what they need for spiritual growth.

Do you give your children the training they need in the Word of God? If you don't, who will? No one else has the opportunities or the influence that you have in the spiritual training of your children, and you must fulfill your duties.

Training in righteousness includes not only the whats and the hows of life, but the whys as well. The Bible is your textbook, and you can teach it only as well as you can exemplify it in your life.

You must teach your children to respond to authority. The boy or girl who has learned to love and obey his parents has taken the first step toward obeying and trusting God. God's Word makes it clear that discipline is vital. "Correct thy son, and he shall give thee rest," says Proverbs 29:17. "Yea, he shall give delight unto thy soul."

It is easy to be a permissive father, but it is costly beyond words. Proverbs again reminds us, "He that spareth his rod hateth his son: but he that loveth him chasteneth him" (Proverbs 13:24).

You also must provide love for your children. One of the basic human needs is love. Love assures your children that they really matter. Your love is an anchor of security that tells them they are really important to you, no matter what may happen.

Give your children the kind of love God shows to His children. Beware of giving the kind of love that loves only when they are pleasing you. God's love is not the kind of love that asks something in return. It is a love that loves even when we are undeserving. But God's love also firmly and lovingly corrects and rebukes.

Fathers, do you love your children? And do you spend time with them? You may think you have good reasons for making your business a priority over your children, but God can see through the flimsiness of them—and so can your children. There is no substitute for spending time with them, for being interested in their interests. They do not need the things you can buy them half as much as they need you. Your work is not more important than your children. And that goes for pastors and others in Christian work.

PROTECTION FOR THE FAMILY

A second need that every father has a duty to supply is *protection for the family.* Again, the father has the same role over his family that God has over His people. God protects and nurtures his children, and every father has that same responsibility.

Few fathers fail to provide physical protection for their families. It would be hard to find a father who, if someone came into his house threatening his children with physical harm, would not fight to the death to protect his family. That sense of duty seems to be engraved in our very nature. We look with utter contempt on a man who does not provide for his family's material needs, but we would respond in anger and disgust to a man who would not protect his family from physical harm.

And yet physical dangers are not the only things that threaten our families and children today. The spiritual dangers that confront our modern homes are overwhelming. Fathers, do you seek to provide spiritual protection for your family?

How can you protect your family spiritually? First, you must set an example of spiritual strength and stability. If Satan can get a foothold in your life, he will have a foothold in your family. Be yielded to the Lord. "Resist the devil, and he will flee from you" (James 4:7). Arm yourself with the spiritual armor of God listed in Ephesians 6. Is your breastplate on right? More important, do you have the right helmet? Are you familiar with your offensive weapon, the Word of God? If there is one weak point in your armor, you and your family are unnecessarily exposed. Protect your family!

How else can you protect your family? Be sure that they are not exposed to dangerous teaching. Be sure that the church you go to teaches and believes the Word of God. Be alert to what comes into your home via the television. And train your children in the truth.

PRAYER FOR THE FAMILY

Finally, every father has a duty to supply *prayer for the family*. Are you praying for your children? How much that prayer can mean!

Job was a praying father. Job 1:5 tells us that Job made it a habit to pray for each of his children. What a great thing it is to have a praying father!

David prayed for Solomon, and his prayer launched him into the pinnacle reign of the Old Testament. Under Solomon's kingship, the nation of Israel gained heights of glory and wealth never again attained. It began with a father's prayer.

Fathers, one of the greatest sins you can commit against your children is the sin of prayerlessness. God has committed your children to you, and part of your responsibility is to pray for them. You are to punish them when they do wrong and praise them when they do right, but pray for them at all times.

The time you spend in prayer for your family is rich. It benefits you as you draw nearer to the Lord with your heart's burdens. And it benefits your family as God answers your prayers and you see their growth.

Paul was a father. Not a physical father but a spiritual

one. All the churches he had begun, all the people he had won to the Lord, were his special children. Look through his epistles and see how many times he assures his spiritual children that he does not cease to pray for them. He understood that one of the responsibilities inherent in spiritual leadership is the duty to pray for those under that leadership. And he set a good example for all fathers to follow.

Yes, being a father is a full-time occupation. And its rewards can be rich. John wrote about his spiritual children, "I havs no greater joy than to hear that my children walk in truth" (3 John 4).

Sometimes there are effects of our influence that we may never know. Brooks Adams kept a diary from his boyhood. One special day when he was eight years old he wrote in his diary, "Went fishing with my father; the most glorious day of my life." Throughout the next forty years of his life, he never forgot that day he went fishing with his father; he made repeated references to it in his diary, commenting on the influence that day had had on his life.

Brooks' father was an important man; he was Charles Francis Adams, the United States' ambassador to Great Britain under the Lincoln administration. Interestingly, he too made a note in his diary about the fishing trip. He wrote simply, "Went fishing with my son; a day wasted."

Of course, the day was not wasted; its value may well have proved to make it one of the most wellspent days in his life. No one can measure the influence of a man on his children, and that is all the more reason to take the job and its responsibilities seriously.

Fathers, are you providing for your children? Are you really giving them all that they need? Are you protecting them? And are you praying for them? May God help you to be a full-time father.

1. Charlie Shedd, *Smart Dads I Know* (New York: Sheed and Ward, 1975), pp. ix-x.

TEN

Filling a Father's Shoes

If you were asked to name the world's hardest job, what would you say it is? Serving as president of the United States? Heading up the United Nations? Serving Jesus Christ somewhere as a missionary or pastor?

Each of those choices could be defended. But I believe that an even harder job than any of those is being a good parent. And today I'm thinking especially of the work of the father. I want to tell you why a father's job tops nearly every other. And if you are a father, I want to suggest some insight into what your job is and how you can do it better.

In a new book, *The Effective Father,* Gordon MacDonald describes an exciting moment while canoeing with his son in a treacherous stretch of rapids. "The river was a boiling white," he recalls, "running furiously, smashing around and over rocks, here and there climbing to gunwale-high waves. Our "survival" depended upon being able to pick a route back and forth across the river that would avoid . . . tipping over and losing everything—especially our pride as great wilderness explorers.

"Then it happened! A water-soaked tree . . . caught the shoekeel of our Grumman canoe. . . . In an instant we were upside down in freezing water." Apparently the incident had a happy ending. Both canoeists emerged unhurt and in due time were afloat again, a little more careful and a little wiser. MacDonald saw the experience as an illustration of the perils the average father faces most of the time. A father must make decisions—right decisions—and he dare not make them in a state of confusion or panic or bewilderment. A father, like a person steering a canoe, must always be ahead of the upcoming situation. The effective father, says MacDonald, must look downriver in the life of his family, preparing to make good decisions. His job is to keep the family dry.[1]

You can be a good father, but faith and good intentions are not enough. Even a godly man can be a failure as a father. Samuel, David, and Aaron are some men in the Bible who show that that is true.

The Bible, in fact, tells of many who failed in their task as fathers. Isaac was partial to Esau. You cannot read of his home life without sensing that he failed in raising his sons.

Jacob in turn was a failure. Genesis 34 tells of a crisis in his family in which he failed to act at all. As a result, an entire community perished.

Eli failed to guide his sons into a walk with God, and his house came tumbling down around his ears.

Solomon's son was weak and foolish, a living reminder that even this wisest of men was a failure as a father.

The question of the failure of so many fathers in the Bible is a troubling one. Why did they fail? And how can we fathers today avoid the same kind of failure? Consider with me three important questions about fatherhood.

WHAT IS A FATHER?

The first question is, *What is a father?* A father is a parent, a partner in transmitting human life. He is a protector and a provider. He also is a teacher sharing knowledge and instruction about living in our world.

Being an effective father is a staggering responsibility. It is one thing to guide your own footsteps; it is quite another to guide someone else's.

Many fail as fathers simply because they underestimate their task. They think that if they can pay their bills and make everyday decisions, the long-range plan will come out all right. But often—very often—it simply does not work that way, and the rate of failure among the fathers may well be higher than that of any other occupation.

When someone is needed to fill a place in a business organization, the company makes out a job description. A job description for a father could read something like this:

> The father must be a man of vision, strength, and character, capable of leading an in-service training organization that will in time reproduce parents like himself. He must carry on his training at all age levels. He must be able to cooperate effectively with the helpmate of his choice, give advice and counsel as needed, and provide spiritual help and leadership. He must care for his own personal problems, prepare his own budgets, and maintain good public relations. He must be a qualified service and repair man. He must be willing to do whatever is needed, twenty-four hours a day, 365 days a year.
>
> Finally, he must provide his own salary as well as the financial needs of the entire organization.

Now that's a job description! But it only begins to spell out the real responsibilities of an effective father. Surely no other calling is as demanding. A father must transmit to his children God's basic revelation—that we are God's creatures, accountable to Him in all we are and do. He is the source of right and justice in the home. he must be an arbiter, a leader, a provider, a teacher, and a counselor.

Examine the role of the father closely, and you begin to see a tiny likeness to God's own role with reference to the human race. As God in His infinite wisdom loves and rules and provides for all creation, so the human father is to nourish, protect, and guide his little family. David clearly perceived that likeness when he wrote Psalm 103. Verse 13 of that psalm says, "Like as a father pitieth his children, so the LORD pitieth them that fear him."

The Lord Jesus spoke of God as "your heavenly Father."

The point, of course, is not that father has rights and powers superior to those in his family, although in many ways he does. But the real truth is that he must use his position to minister to his family's needs. He is their protector and provider. They are guarded by his love.

As the one in authority over your family, as the one responsible to provide for them and protect them, you are God's representative to them. That, of course, is not to say that God does not deal directly with them—He does. But in many ways, God deals with those in your family through you—through your authority, through your example, and through your leadership. Thus the child who has a faithful, godly father learns what God Himself is like as he sees the father in the home. He first learns the principles of love and faith and obedience to God within the context of the family circle.

Your children will base their concept of God on what they see in you. Studies show that those who have had fathers who were irresponsible or unfaithful to their duties in the family often have a great deal of difficulty trusting God. They tend to think of God in the context of their father's examples, and as a result, their perception of God is marred.

On the other hand, those who have known loving, faithful, concerned earthly fathers tend to find it easier to develop and maintain a close relationship with the heavenly Father.

Put another way, what I am saying is that you should develop the kind of relationship with your children that you wish them to have with God.

A second question we want to examine is, *Why is a father?* Why does a family need a father? What is the father to do? Of course this is a basic issue. We have already listed some of the duties of a father, and if time allowed we could make an even more extensive list. But I want to look closely at three basic functions that encompass all the duties of a father.

The family without a father faces a very grave hardship. So important to the family is the father that the Word of God regards the lack of the father as a great calamity. In such a situation, however, God makes special provision for the family; He says that He Himself will step into the breach to protect and meet the need. "Thou art the helper of the fatherless," says Psalm 10:14. And Psalm 146:9 declares: "The LORD preserveth the strangers; he relieveth the fatherless and widow."

Why is the father so vital? What functions are there that he must perform that no one else can perform? First, he is to steer or *guide his family.*

Biblically, the family is not designed to be a loose or headless organization. God is a God of order. Ephesians 5:23 says, "The husband is the head of the wife, even as Christ is the head of the church: and he is the saviour of the body." Not only is the father the head of the wife, but he is the head of the family in its entirety as well.

The family is not a democracy. Its authority is vested in a person, and that person is the father. And his authority is derived from God, who is the beginning of all authority.

But with his authority goes a great amount of responsibility. In Ephesians 5, as well as in every other passage that speaks of the father's authority, it is clearly taught that husbands and fathers are not to rule for personal advantage, but for the well-being of the family.

The key word is *responsibility.* As a father, when you view your position, you are to see your responsibility, not your authority. No father who is worth his salt will throw his weight around or demand personal homage. He is there to serve, and his motivating power is the love of Jesus Christ. He recognizes that his position makes him a minister to his family, not one to be ministered to by them. He is there not to demand but to deliver. He is the Lord's representative.

Jesus taught that same truth, and He applied it to every position of authority. Not only that, He exemplified it in His own life. Matthew 20:26-28 says, "But it shall not be so among you: but whosoever will be great among you . . . let him be your servant: Even as the Son of man came not to be ministered unto, but to minister, and to give his life a ransom for many."

Another basic function of a father is to shape or *mold his family* through teaching. He does not do all the teaching, of course—the mother may do much of it—but the father is to oversee all the training that his children receive. He must see that they get the teaching that they need, and he must see that the teaching that they get is the right kind.

That involves many things—personal skills both major and minor, the training received at school, and fun and practical things like sports and hobbies. A father teaches attitudes as well. He builds in his children respect for authority and law, reference for God, a good attitude toward work, respect for human life, concern for one another, and a sense of responsibility.

A father is shaping the lives around him for the complexities of daily living in our confusing world. He should teach love for God and faith in Christ. He must bring his children to the Bible, teach them what it says, what it means for them, how to apply it in daily life, and how to study it for themselves. Remember that, as the Bible often says, the fear of the Lord is the beginning of wisdom.

Fathers, it is your responsibility, and a very large one, to monitor closely the things your children are learning at school. You are seriously damaging your child if you are allowing him to be taught at school values that contradict the values he is taught at home, especially if you let that teaching go unchallenged. If at all possible, you should send your child to a school whose teaching you can endorse. If your child receives six hours of humanistic indoctrination each day at school, it will almost certainly make an impression on him.

Of course, it may not be possible to send your child to a school where biblical values are taught. There may be no such school in your area. If that is the case, your job in teaching your child is even more important. You must be absolutely familiar with the things your child is taught in school, and you must know sound, reasonable, and biblical responses to those things he will learn that are not right. Remember, what he learns is your responsibility. God holds you accountable.

A third basic duty of the father is to *seek God's blessing for his family.* He must pray.

Father, you are the priest of the home. You are the spiritual leader. If you do not pray for your family, who will?

Possibly the cause of more friction in family relationships, the cause of more failure in the home, and the cause of more defeat in the family is the prayerlessness of our parents.

We have examined the overwhelming responsibilities of the father. How can any father approach his duties without first approaching God in prayer? Listen, fathers, we cannot do our job alone. We dare not leave God out of our families. We cannot afford the sin of prayerlessness.

How Is a Father?

A final question about fatherhood we need to ask is, *How is a father?* You may ask, How can any man, given his natural failings as a human being, ever hope to succeed in the massive job of being a father? I can give you the answer in one sentence:

You will have to be like God!

That, you may say, is not an easy answer. And you are right. There is very little about fatherhood that is easy. But in saying that you must be like God, I am not saying anything that puts success in fatherhood out of your reach. You *can* be like God!

I am not saying that you can be perfect and sinless, of course. And I am not saying that you can be all-powerful or all-knowing. But I am saying that you can, and you must, have all the characteristics of God working in your life. You will have to be just, loving, wise, patient, merciful, self-giving, tender, and a lot of other things. And God can enable you to be that kind of father.

You remember that I said that you are God's representative to your family. God does not ask you to represent Him without giving you the wherewithal to do it. But you must let Him do it for you and not try to transform yourself.

The first step is to receive Christ as your Savior. Let God reshape your life through the salvation that is in Christ. You need *a new birth*. Jesus said to Nicodemus, "Except a man be born again, he cannot see the kingdom of God" (John 3:3). Do not try to slip beyond this point, for it will never work. You must know Christ before you can have His blessings for your family.

Paul wrote, "If any man be in Christ, he is a new creature: old things are passed away; behold, all things are become new" (2 Corinthians 5:17). He will make you a new creation, and only He can do it.

Once you have made that initial step, you will need *communication with the Lord* every day. I have already mentioned the importance of prayer for your family. But now I am talking about prayer for your own personal spiritual needs. And I am talking about reading God's Word daily to get His guidance and wisdom and understanding. You'll need renewal every day.

Make it your business, and one of your priorities, to get alone with God each day and read His Word and pray. It is sheer folly to attempt to undertake the huge task of parenthood without proper daily preparation.

Finally, you'll need *commitment to the task*. Ask God to make you a dedicated father. Make it your unswerving purpose to honor God in the way you lead your family.

Are you in a good church that believes and teaches the Bible and honors the Lord Jesus? If not, that should be one of the first tasks you dedicate yourself to.

Are you a committed father? Do you represent God well to your family? The shoes of a father are big shoes to fill. Won't you today trust God for the wisdom, power, direction, and skill that you must have to fill those shoes? Or are your needs more basic? Do you need to yield to the Lord and accept Christ as your Savior? You can do it right now.

Fathers, our is a huge responsibility, and we cannot wait to come to terms with it. Make your surrender to the Lord complete today.

1. Gordon MacDonald, *The Effective Father* (Wheaton, Ill.: Tyndale, 1977), pp. 139-40.

ELEVEN

Guidelines for a Christian Marriage

Recently I received a letter from a California housewife in which she described her troubled marriage. "Our home," she wrote, "is in total uproar. My husband and I are fighting constantly. I am a nervous wreck and unable to sleep at night. I cannot go on like this."

Unfortunately those words are echoed in millions of homes around the world. Many marriages today are in trouble. In fact, modern marriage is deeply in trouble.

Almost forty years ago, sociologist Pitirim Sorokin predicted, "Divorces . . . will increase until any profound difference between socially sanctioned marriages and illicit sex-relationship disappears. . . . The main sociocultural functions of the family will further decrease until the family becomes a mere incidental cohabitation of male and female, while the home will become an overnight parking place."[1]

Although those words have yet to be fully realized, it is not too difficult to see the very real possibility of their complete fulfillment in the immediate future. There is no mistake—marriage is in trouble!

Today, nearly one in every four marriages ends in divorce before the tenth anniversary. In fact, in some densely populated areas of the country, the divorce rate is as high as 70 percent.

In addition to the soaring divorce rates, attitudes about the family are changing. As far back as 1970, a majority of teenagers and adults were becoming disillusioned with the importance of the family. A Harris survey in that year indicated that a majority of persons questioned believed that the family had declined in importance in the previous ten years. That opinion was expressed by 52 percent of the teenagers and 64 percent of the adults surveyed.

In a book entitled *The Death of the Family,* radical sociologist David Cooper calls for the abolition of the family.[2] Modern tensions and demands on individuals, he claimed, have rendered the family unworkable.

And many Americans are experimenting with alternate life-styles. Communal living, homosexual marriages, short-term marriages, live-in agreements, and other alternatives to marriage that were socially unacceptable only a few years ago are now rapidly gaining in acceptance and popularity. As the family deteriorates, more and more young people experiment with such harmful and unscriptural life-styles. And our society turns its back on marriage and the family in what seems to be an alarmingly widespread movement.

Psychiatrist Dr. Thomas P. Malone predicts that, before long, marriage will universally be on a short-term, contract basis. An article that appeared several years ago in *Ladies' Home Journal* quoted Dr. Malone: "A lot of people nowadays . . . think it is idiotic to put two people together at the age of twenty and expect them to be happy for fifty years. What we may shortly be talking about is a three year contract."[3] Dr. Malone concludes by predicting that we will soon be seeing a greater acceptance of trial marriages.

And his predictions seem to be taking shape. Already in several state legislatures, bills have been introduced that would put marriage on a contractural basis. All that would be needed to dissolve the marriage would be the mutual consent of the two partners.

In the midst of all these frightening developments, what can the Christian do? Are there any biblical guidelines for Christian marriage? How can a Christian young couple avoid marital problems that lead to divorce? Even a casual examination of the Bible reveals that it has many things to say concerning marriage. I would like to sum up all those things in three guidelines for a Christian marriage.

MARRIAGE IS A PERMANENT RELATIONSHIP

First of all, and foundational to a biblical understanding of marriage, is the truth that *marriage is a permanent relationship*. In Mark 10:6-7, Jesus said, "From the beginning of the creation God made them male and female. For this cause shall a man leave his father and mother, and cleave to his wife." And then in verse nine we read, "What therefore God hath joined together, let not man put asunder."

Christian couple, your marriage is a sacred union, a work of God, and to dissolve that union is to fall short of what God wants. Many young couples today enter into the marriage relationship with the idea that if it doesn't work out, they can get a divorce. A marriage built on that kind of attitude is doomed before it even begins.

The key to understanding the permanence of marriage is to realize that God planned for man and woman to be together. Marriage is a provision of God for man. He has ordained it, and He designed it to be permanent. In the Garden of Eden, God said that it was not good for man to be alone, and He designed a helper for him. God did not work out a trial marriage for Adam. He did not arrange a short-term contract. When God brought Adam and Eve together, they were to be one flesh forever.

Even in today's wedding vows something about the permanence of marriage is included. Usually both the husband and the wife pledge their love to one another "for

407

better or for worse, for richer or for poorer, in joy and in sorrow, in sickness and in health, *as long as we both shall live.*" That is God's plan, and you dare not say those vows without heartfelt meaning.

If you are planning a marriage, my advice is that you frankly discuss with your future mate the seriousness of the plans you are making. Have an understanding that marriage is permanent, and divorce is never an option for you. If you feel that that is too confining, then you had better not get married.

And if you are already married and have never confronted this issue, I suggest that you get together with your spouse and talk it over. Agree to abide by your sacred vows and keep your marriage permanent. Covenant together never to discuss divorce as a possible solution to your problems. God's will for you is that you remain married.

MARRIAGE IS A HARMONIOUS PARTNERSHIP

A second biblical guideline is that *marriage is a harmonious partnership.* The Bible speaks of the union of the husband and wife as harmonious. Jesus said, "And they twain shall be one flesh: so then *they are no more twain,* but one flesh" (Mark 10:8, italics added).

I have never known of a broken marriage where the husband and wife had enjoyed a true partnership that had been harmonious and mutually sacrificial. But God established marriage to be just that, and His Word gives strict guidelines about how to keep harmony in the home.

Did you know that the relationship of the husband and wife is similar to the relationship of Christ and the church? In his letter to the Ephesians, Paul writes, "The husband is the head of the wife, even as Christ is the head of the church" (Ephesians 5:23). Christ's relationship with the church certainly is a harmonious relationship, isn't it?

Each of the partners in a marriage has a role, and his

understanding that role and fulfilling it is vital to harmony in the marriage. What is the role of the husband? Husbands are to love their wives, "even as Christ loved the church and gave himself for it" (Ephesians 5:25). The husband is to display a *sacrificial love,* the kind of love Christ demonstrated for the church.

What is the role of the wife? "Wives, submit yourselves unto your own husbands, as unto the Lord" (Ephesians 5:22). The wife is to display a *submissive love,* the same kind of love she responds to the Lord with.

I want you to notice something with me. The husband is told to sacrifice for his wife, and the wife is told to submit to her husband. Both duties involve giving, not receiving. Marriage is a giving relationship. The husband is not to demand submission from his wife, and the wife is not to demand sacrifice from her husband. Marriage is not a set of demands for the partner, but a life of service to the partner.

If the husband loves his wife as this passage teaches, he will not think of his wife as a servant to be ordered around. He will see her rather as a partner and friend, someone with whom to share his dreams—someone to give his life for.

And if the woman is submissive to her husband as this passage also teaches, she will not demand his attention, service, and material goods all the time. She will lovingly seek to minister to him.

And so marriage works beautifully as a mutually sacrificial system, each ministering to the other's needs, and asking nothing in return. And this is marriage as God intended it—a harmonious partnership.

Why are there so few marriages that work like that? The reason is selfishness. Most couples today get married for what they can get out of it. People come into marriage looking primarily for companionship, security, gratification of desires, or position. And although all of those things are desirable, they are not the primary function of marriage.

409

Marriage is sacrifice, giving, ministering, working, and yielding. And the selfish heart has little room for ideas like those.

Today we are faced with the women's rights movement, minority rights movements, and even a widespread children's rights movement. We are conditioned by our society to demand our rights. But such an approach will not work in marriage. Remember, marriage is not a set of demands, but a life of service.

Many today have misread the issues. We are told by some that the biblical standard for women is unfair, that it makes the women inferior to the man. But the issue is not one of superiority and inferiority; it is an issue of the proper position. The wife is not superior or inferior to the husband, and the husband is not superior or inferior to the wife, any more than the head is superior or inferior to the rest of the body. The husband and wife, the Bible says, are like a head and a body. The head cannot function or exist without the body, and the body cannot function or exist without the head. But they have completely different functions.

In the same way, the husband and wife have separate but complementary functions. They cannot function apart from each other, but their roles *are* different. To make that an issue of superiority or inferiority is a terrible error.

The wife that tries to usurp her husband's role as head of the family destroys the marriage. And the husband that would exchange roles with his wife is guilty of abdicating a God-given responsibility. Harmony cannot exist in the marriage where God's plan for marriage is shunned.

Marriage Is a Spiritual Companionship

But there is a truth that is even greater than the truths that marriage is a permanent relationship and a harmonious partnership. And that is the biblical teaching that *marriage is a spiritual companionship.*

Christian marriage should be a companionship where each helps the other to grow in Christ. The Bible tells us that in the marriage relationship, the husband and wife become one. It is my conviction that that speaks not only of a physical union, but of a spiritual union as well.

We talked about the issue of inferiority and superiority. If anyone in marriage is superior, it is the Lord Jesus Christ Himself. He is a partner in a biblical Christian marriage. In fact, He is the center of the home, and around Him everything else revolves. In that sense, the home is a reflection of heaven.

How do I know that? In Matthew 18:20, Jesus said, "For where two or three are gathered together in my name, there am I in the midst of them." And that certainly applies to a Christian marriage, entered into in Christ's name.

Christian couple, do you understand the significance of that? Christ's presence is in a special way permanent in your home. Your home is His dwelling place, and He is there to fellowship with you, lead you, and minister to your needs. Do you live in your home in a way that recognizes His presence?

If the marriage relationship is to be a true spiritual companionship, the husband and wife must have a regular time of spiritual devotions. I mean a time of fellowship and prayer and study together in God's Word. It does not have to be a lengthy time, but it is vital that the husband and wife cultivate a spiritual companionship together.

Through the years I have counseled with many troubled families, and inevitably I have found that the homes with the problems are the homes without God's Word. Recently I read of an eighteen-year old boy who was arrested on charges of armed robbery. As he was questioned it was learned that this boy's parents were Christians. His father was a prominent deacon in the church. His mother taught a Sunday school class, and the whole family attended church regularly. When asked why he, a boy from a background like that, got into so much trouble, he replied, "My folks may be active church members, but we certainly don't have much of a Christian home! I never once have seen my parents pray or read the Bible."

What a shame! Is that true in your home, friend?

A Christian marriage demands Christian living. It demands a commitment—a serious commitment—to the Lord and to His will. It demands obedience. And you will discover, I think, that the saying is true—families that pray together stay together.

Yes, we are living in frightening times! Moral attitudes are changing so rapidly that it is impossible to predict the future. The marriage and the home that are not founded on God's Word are on shaky ground! But in a time of moral decay, in a day when it seems there is no certain standard, it is reassuring to know that God's standards are secure. God's Word is true and trustworthy, and it never changes. Not only that, but it works, as well. It is the only solid foundation on which to build our homes and marriages.

The writer of the book of Hebrews said, "Marriage is honourable in all" (Hebrews 13:4). Marriage, my friend, is God's plan and purpose for mankind. Is your marriage what it ought to be—a permanent relationship, a harmonious partnership, and a spiritual companionship? Are you living according to God's plan? Are you building your home on the foundation of God's Word?

If not, why not today let Christ take control? Surrender your life to the Lord Jesus. Let Him be the center of your home from this day forward.

1. Cited by Joan Cook in "Marriage," *Ladies' Home Journal,* September 1971, p. 192.
2. David Cooper, *The Death of the Family* (New York: Pantheon, 1970), p. 63.
3. Joan Cook, "Marriage," p. 197.

TWELVE

How to Have a Happy Home

"Our parents never have time for us," said a teenager being interviewed. "They're always too busy."

"Kids are not like they were when I was young," a parent was overheard to say. "Today they are brash, defiant, rebellious, and immoral. What have we come to?"

In this day of failing families, broken homes, teenage crime, open immorality, and drug abuse, one can see a great deal of truth in both the comments of the teenager and those of the parent. And we can indeed wonder what we have come to. Why are things this way? It is my conviction that at the root of most of society's problems is the real problem of families that are failures.

It is not supposed to be like that. The home is to be a happy place, a place of security, a place of fond memories, where we learn as children how to live as adults in our world.

The home was ordained and established by God. It is the first institution He ordained and the building block of all other God-ordained institutions—nations, churches, cities, or races. In the Garden of Eden, God united Adam and Eve in marriage and blessed the first home. Marriage is not merely for convenience or conventionality; it is God's plan for the happiness of all people. It is lifelong, not temporary. It is God-given, not manmade. It is a duet, not a solo. It is a partnership, not a tug of war.

And it is a relationship where two people are either happy or unhappy.

Who determines whether your marriage is happy or unhappy? You do. Not your in-laws, not your friends, not your children, not even your spouse. You alone are the one who has the power to make your marriage either a happy one or a miserable one. And you determine it by the way you respond to tribulation, which is inevitable in any marriage.

And yet, it seems, many people are not willing to sacrifice and yield to assure a successful marriage and a happy home. There are now almost a million divorces each year in the United States. From broken homes often emerge disillusioned young people with warped ideals. They in turn have families that fail, and so on. The collapse of the home is probably the greatest threat to our world future. Unless there is a return to the biblical patterns for marriage, the family, and the home, our entire civilization faces certain extinction.

Do you want to have a happy home? Do you want to have a family that honors God, lives harmoniously, and is successful? God's Word tells you how. And I would like to look at four ingredients in a happy home.

DISCIPLINE

The first is *discipline.* And by that I mean both self-discipline and parental discipline for the children. The chief value of discipline of any kind is orderliness. If your home is not united, if it is disorganized and fragmented, then your home is suffering from a lack of discipline.

First, you are to discipline yourself. How are you at *personal discipline?* Do you leave things lying around the house? Do you leave things undone until later, and then have to do them at the last moment? Are you able to control your appetites? Parent, if you are not disciplined yourself, you will not be able to discipline your children effectively.

But there are more important things in personal discipline than picking up your socks and being ready to go somewhere on time. Those things involve discipline in the practical realm. Discipline is vital in the spiritual realm, too.

Your walk with the Lord requires discipline. Paul wrote to Timothy, "Study to shew thyself approved unto God" (2 Timothy 2:15). That word "study" means "give diligence" or "be disciplined." The word *disciple* comes from the same word as *discipline.* It takes diligence and discipline to walk with the Lord.

Discipline is required if you are to have a regular daily quiet time. Establishing times of regular prayer requires discipline. In fact, almost everything you must do as a Christian requires discipline, including giving, church attendance, Bible study, and witnessing.

Lack of personal discipline in the home can cause conflicts. Duties are left undone, important things are forgotten, bad habits are accrued, all because of a lack of personal discipline. And all those things become sources of conflict in the family.

Parental discipline also is important in the home. By that I mean that the parents should discipline the children. Children should be trained to do right and punished when they do wrong. The book of Proverbs has much to say about proper discipline for a child. Proverbs 13:24 says that strict discipline is proof of a parent's love. "He that spareth his rod hateth his son: but he that loveth him chasteneth him betimes."

Proverbs 19:18 says much the same thing. "Chasten thy son while there is hope, and let not thy soul spare for his crying." And Proverbs 23:13-14 adds, "Withhold not correction from the child: for if thou beatest him with the rod, he shall not die. Thou shalt beat him with the rod, and shalt deliver his soul from hell."

417

Why is that? Proverbs 22:15 says, "Foolishness is bound in the heart of a child, but the rod of correction shall drive it far from him." A child is born with a sin nature, with an inclination to do wrong, and proper discipline is one way to lead him away from the evil toward the good.

What is the proper way to discipline a child? The Scriptures are quite clear that corporal punishment is the best way. But you must never inflict injury on a child.

Never strike a child in anger. It is important that he understand that his punishment is just that—a punishment, not a vent for your anger. Before you punish the child, talk to him. Make sure he understands what he is being punished for.

And never let your discipline become a weapon to get even with your children. Paul wrote, "Fathers, provoke not your children to anger, lest they be discouraged" (Colossians 3:21). Discipline must always be done in love. And disciplining your children gives you some of the best opportunities you will have to *en*courage them. Don't waste those opportunities.

DEVOTION

A second ingredient in the happy home is *devotion*. I am referring to devotion to each other as well as devotion to the Lord.

Loyalty is one of the sadly lacking elements in our homes today. Children fight with their brothers and sisters; fathers fight with mothers; and parents fight with their children. God did not ordain the family to be that way.

A spirit of devotion, of love and loyalty, should prevail in our families. The family unit is just that—a unit. And if it is to function properly, in unity, there must be a sense of loyalty.

Why has our devotion to one another in our families dissipated? Because we have forgotten how to serve one another. A family, like a church, is primarily giving, not receiving. Harmony cannot exist in an environment where each person is demanding, always asking, forever taking, constantly being ministered unto and never ministering. And yet that is exactly the situation we have in many families today. How can we expect to have happy homes?

Yes, we have forgotten the great truths of submission and yielded rights. Read Philippians 2 to see the Lord's example of submission. He gave up everything for the sake of others. And that is what we must do if we are to know happy homes.

But perhaps more important than devotion to each other is devotion to the Lord. God designed the family to be a spiritual body. Just like the church and the nation of Israel, one of the main functions God designed it for is corporate worship. The family, then, must be devoted to the Lord.

Your family should belong to a church where the Bible is believed and taught, where Christ is honored, and where you can serve the Lord together. And you should be actively involved in the work of the church. You should attend regularly. You should support the church with your gifts, prayers, and service. There is very little that you can do to unify your family as much as active membership in a sound local church will do.

And your family should meet together for fellowship in the Word of God daily. If your family is too busy to do that, you are too busy. Some families do it at mealtimes; others do it before bedtime; and others do it early in the morning. When you do it does not matter as much as the fact that you must do it. You do not have to spend a long time in family devotions. In fact, just a few minutes in the Word of God and prayer will probably be more effective than a longer period of time, especially if you have a wide range of age difference in your family.

And your devotions should include something for

everyone. If you have little children in your family, be sure to explain the Scriptures in a way they can understand. Devotions together should not be boring but an exciting adventure.

What can *you* do to give your family a greater sense of devotion to one another and to the Lord? There is no substitute for honest, heartfelt devotion in the family.

DISCUSSION

A third ingredient in a happy home is *discussion*. Interviewed members of broken homes consistently point to one cause of failure more than any other, and that is a lack of communication. Do you have open lines of communication in your home? Are your children free to come to you with their problems, no matter how trivial they may seem to you, with the confidence that you will listen with understanding and be able to offer good advice? Few parents can honestly answer yes.

In our busy society with its accelerated pace, one institution has suffered more than any other, and that is the home. Parents are too busy for the children, and the children are too busy for each other.

I began this message with a quotation from a teenager who complained that his parents were just too busy. That statement is echoed daily by millions of children throughout our nation. And their parents never seem to hear their pleas. They somehow think it is the other parent that is guilty. But I urge you to examine your own home life objectively. How much quality time do *you* really spend with your children?

I am not talking about the time you sit around watching television together. That seldom provides an opportunity for discussion or communication. And yet the average American family watches four to six hours of television daily. That does not leave much time for communication.

Another obstacle to communication in many homes is the fact that both parents work full time, leaving the children either with a babysitter or alone at home. No wonder the kids feel neglected!

What does God's Word say? That "children are an heritage of the LORD" (Psalm 127:3), and they dare not be neglected! God has given us our children, and they are our greatest responsibility.

Parent, if you do not have time to spend with your children, you had better rearrange your priorities. Perhaps you are involved in too many activities, or perhaps you watch too much television. Or maybe you should even settle for a simpler life-style and not work so many hours. But you must have time to spend with your children, and you must have open communication in your family.

DETERMINATION

A fourth ingredient in a happy home is *determination*. You cannot have a happy home unless you want it so badly that you are willing to make sacrifices for it. You must be determined that your family is going to be harmonious, united, successful, and happy.

Living in a family is a great privilege. The home is a kind of foretaste of heaven, where Christ is the center, and worship, fellowship, and unity revolve around Him.

But living in a family is a great responsibility, too. It is an opportunity to minister, to sacrifice, to serve, and to grow. And growth in the family takes determination.

At the beginning I said that how you respond to tribulation determines whether you will be happy in marriage. That truth can be applied to the wife, husband, child, or any member of the family. Trials are inevitable. Especially in an environment of close relationships like the family. Conflicts between family members will arise. How will you respond to them?

421

Did you know that every tribulation that comes to you is allowed by God and is an opportunity for growth? That is the teaching of both James and Paul. James wrote, "My brethren, count it all joy when you fall into divers temptations; knowing this, that the trying of your faith worketh patience. But let patience have her perfect work, that ye may be perfect and entire, wanted nothing" (James 1:2-4).

And what is patience's perfect work? Paul wrote, "We glory in tribulations also; knowing that tribulation worketh patience; and patience, experience; and experience, hope: And hope maketh not ashamed; because the love of God is shed abroad in our hearts by the Holy Ghost" (Romans 5:3-5).

The perfect work of patience in us, then, includes such qualities as confidence, assurance, and the overflowing love of God in our hearts. What better provision could there be for a happy home life?

So you must be determined to respond to tribulations in the home in the proper way. Do not demand your rights. Do not render insult for insult, an eye for an eye and a tooth for a tooth. Respond as Christ would, with love and a willingness to suffer—even wrongfully, if need be, to minister to the needs of the other.

Does your home have those four ingredients: discipline, devotion, discussion, and determination? If so there will be no division. There will be no dissension. There will be no destruction. There will be no dissolution. But there will be new direction and a new dimension of happiness and harmony in the home.

Why not yield today to the lordship of Christ and determine in your heart that you will make the necessary sacrifices to assure that your family life will be a happy and prosperous one?

THIRTEEN

Beautiful, Happy Wives and Mothers

In our last message we looked at the ingredients in a happy, successful, harmonious home. Those vital ingredients were discipline, devotion, discussion, and determination. You may be thinking that there are very few truly happy homes in our country, and unfortunately that seems to be true.

Why is it that a harmonious and unified family is such a scarce commodity? My feeling is that our families have violated God's established order. Husbands and wives have tried exchanging roles, parents have abdicated responsibility, and children have actually taken over the reins in many families. And it is not working.

The divorce rate continues to soar, juvenile delinquency is ballooning to the point that actually more than half of the crimes that are committed are committed by children, families are dissolving, and America is suffering because of it. Our entire society is in turmoil over issues such as abortion, homosexuality, women's rights, and children's rights. And at the heart of all those issues is God's order for the family.

God has established the family, as we have seen, and He has given detailed instructions in His Word concerning the proper order in the family. The husband has the role of leadership, the wife has the role of helper, and the children have the role of trainees in the art of living. The husband is the *leader,* the wife is a *laborer* together with him, and the children are *learners.* And thus the home works harmoniously, as each does his part to sacrifice, give, and minister to the others in the family.

But our society has rejected the Lord's order of the family, and as a result, it is suffering. The only answer to many of the problems and weaknesses of our nation, I am convinced, is a return to God's standard for family living. We can expect no great national renewal until we return to God's Word and put its principles to work again. The source of our strength as a nation always has been the strength of our individual families. We cannot continue to reject God's principles and remain a nation for very long.

I would like to examine closely what God's Word has to say about the Christian wife in a happy home. What is her role, her ministry to the family? What does she need to fulfill that role adequately? How can you, Christian wives, assure that your homes will be happy, successful homes, built on the foundation of the Word of God and operating after His pattern?

I would especially like to examine four words that describe a godly wife and mother.

SUBMISSION

The first of those four words is *submission.* Paul wrote to the Colossians to describe the roles of family members. "Wives," he said in Colossians 3:18, "submit yourselves unto your own husbands, as it is fit in the Lord."

That is not a popular concept in our society today. Some say that it makes the woman inferior to the man, which simply is not true. Others say that it is unfair, asserting that marriage and the family should be a democracy. And still others claim that it is a cultural thing, to be understood in the context of the Colossian culture in the first century and not applied to today.

But the fact remains that the biblical instruction to wives is that they be submissive. Paul says the same thing in Ephesians 5:22, with a different twist, "Wives, submit yourselves unto your own husbands, *as unto the Lord*" (italics added). Paul says here that submission ought to be as unto the Lord. In other words, the wife is to submit to her husband just as she would to God Himself! There is no softening of the language here, either.

Why does God demand submission from the wife? Because it is His plan. It is the order of creation, Paul says in 1 Corinthians 11:8-9. Man was created first, and then woman. In fact, woman was taken from man. And God designed that the woman was to be under the authority of the man. Again in 1 Corinthians 11, Paul says, "But I would have you know, that the head of every man is Christ; and the head of the woman is the man; and the head of Christ is God" (verse 3). He says the same thing in Ephesians 5:23: "For the husband is the head of the wife, even as Christ is the head of the church."

God has established a definite progression of authority through the Lord Jesus to the husband. That means that when God reveals His will to the family, He does it through the father. God will not usurp His own lines of authority and speak to the wife where He has not spoken to the husband. Therefore, the wife is to be submissive to her husband just as she would be to God, because God has ordained the husband's authority.

This is not a question of superiority of either the man or the woman. Both are superior in their respective positions. No one would suggest that a child is in any way inferior to his parents just because he is under their authority. And the wife certainly is not inferior to her husband although she is under his authority.

Some women, because of personality traits, find it more difficult to be submissive than others do. Nevertheless,

God's order for every family is that the wife yield to the authority of her husband.

And there is nothing more beautiful than the submissive wife who conducts herself according to the Word of God. She does not stifle her own personality or creativity; she fulfills it according to God's will. Therefore she is the one who truly attains her fullest potential.

Wife, do you feel that submission to your husband is too confining? Do you chafe under the idea that you must yield to his authority? If so, you need to learn to trust God in a deeper way. There is no substitute or alternative to His plan for your family, and you must learn to submit to God as well as to your husband.

SERVICE

A second word that describes the godly wife is *service*. Proverbs 31:13-21 describes a godly woman who lives a life of service to her family.

> She seeketh wool, and flax, and worketh willingly with her hands.
>
> She is like the merchants' ships; she bringeth her food from afar.
>
> She riseth also while it is yet night, and giveth meat to her household, and a portion to her maidens.
>
> She considereth a field, and buyeth it: with the fruit of her hands she planteth a vineyard.
>
> She girdeth her loins with strength, and strengtheneth her arms.
>
> She perceiveth that her merchandise is good: her candle goeth not out by night.
>
> She layeth her hands to the spindle, and her hands hold the distaff.
>
> She stretcheth out her hand to the poor; yea, she reacheth forth her hands to the needy.
>
> She is not afraid of the snow for her household: for all her household are clothed with scarlet.

And verse 27 adds, "She looketh well to the ways of her household, and eateth not the bread of idleness."

Here is a description of a woman whose life is spent in loving, faithful service. That is God's plan for all wives. Notice that the woman described here serves her husband, she serves her children, she serves the poor and needy, and she even serves her own servants. What a message about her love!

The woman that serves her family is following the example of the Lord Jesus, who came not to be ministered unto but to minister. There is no higher calling and privilege for the Christian wife and mother.

There are voices in our nation that call for the woman to assert herself. "Demand your rights," they say. "You have served and submitted long enough. Demand liberation from the chores of a housewife, and reach your full potential." The implication is that the woman who gives her life in service for her family is a second-class citizen, an underling who never quite makes it.

But I want you to notice that the woman described in Proverbs 31 is a woman who has reached the peak. Her service in the home has brought her a sense of personal fulfillment and the attainment of her highest potential. And her husband and children recognize it (Proverbs 31:28-29).

Women, service to your family is the highest calling to which you can rise. No career, no hobby, no occupation outside the home so fulfills God's purpose for a wife and mother. Are you a serving woman?

SACRIFICE

Closely related to service is a third word that describes the godly wife, and that is *sacrifice*. Real service demands sacrifice. The woman in Proverbs 31 sacrificed her sleep, her time, her money, and her strength to meet the needs of her family.

Every position in the family calls for submission, service, and sacrifice. But perhaps no position demands so much sacrifice as that of the wife and mother. From the painful experience of childbearing on, the life of a mother is one of sacrifice. There is not a mother worth her salt that does not know and cherish nights of sacrificed sleep with a sick and crying child. Mothers sacrifice their time, their strength, and sometimes even their own health to care for the needs of their children.

The wife and mother sacrifices to make the home attractive. She sacrifices to do the laundry, cook the food, care for the children, and care for her husband's personal needs.

Yes, the life of a Christian wife in a happy home is one of sacrifice. But it is a satisfying life. The woman who sacrifices knows exactly what the Lord meant when He urged us to lose our lives in order to find them. The loving sacrifice of a Christian mother and wife gives her life a depth and richness and meaningfulness that cannot be had in any other way.

And that is the idea of the fourth word that describes a godly wife.

SECURITY

Security. There is no sense of security quite like that of a woman whose husband and children rise up and call her blessed. She is secure in the knowledge that her husband loves her. She is secure in the knowledge that she perfectly fulfills God's will for her. She is secure in the love and fellowship of her home.

Have you known women like this? Surely you have. Their faces radiate with an inner glow. Wherever they go, they are a testimony to the wisdom of God's plan and pattern for the home. Their deep security can be sensed in everything about them. They know the spiritual security of a right relationship with the Lord, and they know the emotional security of a right relationship with their husbands. They are truly glorious.

It is frightening to realize that our nation seems to be headed at a breakneck pace in totally the other direction. Women seem to be making a mass exodus from the home. One-third of our total work force is made up of women (well over 20 million). Many of those are mothers and wives who have left home for a career, seeking security and a sense of accomplishment in a job.

Listen to this shocking statement. Dr. Jeanne Binstock, professor of sociology at the University of Massachusetts, states that in twenty years, mothers will be "a mere specialty group in the United States"—like plumbers, auto workers, or engineers. "We . . . need to demand," says Dr. Binstock, "that the ancient occupation of motherhood fall into disrepute, and that women commit themselves to other occupations. Women must be liberated to enjoy the fruits of other occupations, whether they want to or not."

Surprised? You shouldn't be. That is just an echo of what many men and women have been screaming now for years. And more women take up the cry every day. Our nation is headed in a direction that is frightening. And the ones who will suffer most are the women. Real security can come only through obedience to God's plan and purpose. When motherhood falls into disrepute, as it already has in some circles, the possibility of genuine security and happiness for women will be destroyed.

Christian wife and mother, are you living the life of a godly wife? Are you submissive, serving, and sacrificing? And are you secure in your position? God wants you to be.

FOURTEEN

Husbands at the Helm

There is perhaps no failure as widespread and tragic as the failure of husbands and fathers. Ignorance, apathy, and rebellion against God's will have led to the abdication by many husbands of their authority and responsibilities. In millions of homes across our nation, the father is no more than a breadwinner, a live-in paycheck who, in some cases, merely supplements the income of the wife. He has no authority, and he wants none because he fears the responsibility that goes with it. He is content to devote his time to his career, letting his wife and children fend for themselves in regard to their spiritual and emotional needs.

In other homes the father is a domineering, demanding man who abuses his wife and children and sees their existence as being merely for the gratification of his desires. The ideas of sacrifice and service are totally foreign to him. He is self-centered, egotistical, and unconcerned about the needs of his family and his responsibility to them.

In our last message we examined some of the characteristics of a godly wife and mother. In this message we look at the responsibilities of the husband.

It is apparent from the state of families in our nation that something is dreadfully wrong. Families are falling apart, children are torn between parents in the tangled web of divorce, and problems like child abuse and battered wives are steadily on the increase. How much of those problems are the fathers' fault? Quite a bit.

It is my opinion that the responsibility for a godly, successful, happy home lies chiefly with the father. He has been designated by God as the one responsible for the leadership of the family, and so he is responsible for the way the family is led. No matter what influence may threaten the family, be it an influence from the inside or one from without, the father is the one responsible to deal with it and counteract it. Fathers, listen closely! If you would have godly, harmonious homes ordered after God's pattern, you must take the initiative. You must assume the leadership because it has been given to you by God.

The first thing, then, that you must understand is your position. You cannot assume the role God has established for the husband and father unless you know what it is. The Bible very clearly points out the responsibilities of each family member. The home was ordained by God. It was the first and most important unit of human government, and it is both the foundation and the building block out of which all other divine institutions are constructed.

And God gives explicit instructions about how it is to operate, not the least of which are the duties of each family member.

God's instructions to family members are found in Colossians 3:18-21. "Husbands," writes Paul in verse 19, "love your wives, and be not bitter against them." And that is the first of three characteristics of the godly husband and father I would like to examine today.

HE IS A LOVER

He is a lover. By that I do not mean what you may think I mean. He is romantic with his wife, to be sure, but he loves her with a sacrificial love that goes deeper than romantic love. When Paul wrote the same thing to the Ephesians, he added one idea: "even as Christ also loved the church, and gave himself for it" (Ephesians 5:25).

The love of a husband is to be a giving, sacrificial love, like the love of Christ for His church. And what did Christ give for the church? "Himself," Paul reminds us. The depth of Christ's love and sacrifice for the church cannot be sounded, and it is representative of the kind of love and sacrifice a husband is to have for his wife. Without that immeasurable, totally committed, giving kind of love, there is not the divine spark in marriage God intended it to have.

How is a husband to love his wife? If he truly loves his wife, he will be considerate and kind. He will be compassionate and tender and never hard or harsh. Love is not rough and tough, rude and crude; it is generous, courteous, and kind.

Look at the characteristics of godly love in 1 Corinthians 13:4-8:

> [Love] suffereth long, and is kind; [love] envieth not; [love] vaunteth not itself, is not puffed up,
>> Doth not behave itself unseemly, seeketh not her own, is not easily provoked, thinketh no evil;
>> Rejoiceth not in iniquity, but rejoiceth in the truth;
>> Beareth all things, believeth all things, hopeth all things, endureth all things.
> [Love] never faileth.

Is your love for your wife and family like that? Is it patient, kind, generous, self-depreciating, humble, well-behaved, serving, and pure?

What was the kind of love Christ showed for the church? Its real essence was the spirit of unselfishness. Jesus had existed in the form of God from eternity, but He did not consider that position something to be grasped for personal pleasure. He was willing to lay it aside to become a man and die even the lowest form of death for mankind (Philippians 2:5-8).

Husband, if your love for your wife and family is a

435

reflection of that kind of love, you probably are experiencing a happy home. Men, do you see this truth? We are not here for personal gratification. The family is a service organization, and our duties involve doing, not demanding; sacrificing, not being served; and giving, not getting. The family does not exist to serve the father; he exists to serve them.

Are you aware of your family's needs? Are you demonstrating a serving, sacrificial love as you seek to meet those needs?

HE IS A LEADER

A second characteristic of a godly husband is that *he is a leader.* Paul wrote to the wives in Ephesians 5:22, "Wives, submit yourselves unto your own husbands, as unto the Lord. For the husband is the head of the wife, even as Christ is the head of the church: and he is the saviour of the body." In those instructions to the wives, Paul conceals, almost subliminally, a message to the husbands. Along with the truth that the husband is the head is the emphasis of the truth that as head, he is responsible to nurture and protect. Christ is the head of the church, Paul says, *and the savior of the body.* And just as He used His position of leadership for the more important function of ministry, so a husband is to use his position as head of the household as an opportunity to be a servant.

Husband, what do you see when you look at your position? The authority? No—the responsibility. The greatest thing to understand about being head of your home is the truth that with that position comes an overwhelming responsibility.

You are responsible to provide for your family's needs—not just their material needs, but their emotional and spiritual needs as well. You are responsible to nurture your family, to protect them from any kind of harm. You are responsible to teach your children, to train them in the way of righteousness and the Word of God. But most of all you are responsible to take the spiritual leadership.

Spiritual leadership in the family is a responsibility that probably more fathers abdicate than any other. Many a father, unsure or insecure in taking his place at the spiritual helm of the family, gives that responsibility to the wife or just neglects it altogether.

Perhaps this is at the heart of all paternal failure. It is the one area that is more easily attacked than any other, because it involves the most time, labor, and concern. But it also is one of the least externally visible of all parental duties.

Father, if you are going to fulfill your role as the spiritual leader of your family, it will involve a tremendous sacrifice in terms of time spent alone with the Lord in His Word and in prayer. Your private devotional life is vital to your family's spiritual well-being. Your personal walk with the Lord is more important to your family than anyone else's, because God uses you, as the spiritual leader, to deal with your family.

Spiritually, it is often true that as the father goes, so goes the family. Joshua spoke for his family. "As for me and my house," he said, "we will serve the Lord" (Joshua 24:15). The Philippian jailer's whole family believed and was saved because of his faith (Acts 16:34).

On the other hand, think of the many fathers in the Bible who saw their families corrupted or destroyed because of carelessness in their spiritual lives. Noah, Lot, Eli, and David all are examples of men who failed in their personal spiritual lives and saw their families bear the fruit of their failure.

It is sobering to realize that our responsibility to our families is of that magnitude. Certainly the job of being head of a home is not easy! The extent of our responsibility is awesome.

437

But our responsibility goes far beyond our personal spiritual lives and extends to the lives of the individuals in our family as well. One of the requirements for an elder in the church is that he have "faithful children not accused of riot or unruly" (Titus 1:6). "Faithful" in that verse means "believing," and it places the responsibility for the spiritual condition of the child squarely on the shoulders of the father.

Fathers, you are responsible for the spiritual health of the individuals in your family. That is part of your responsibility as a leader. And yet most fathers do not even know very much about the personal spiritual lives of their children. If you are going to fulfill your complete responsibility to your family, you are going to have to be able to communicate effectively with them about spiritual matters. That will involve spending time with them— quality time, discussing the things of the Lord.

Yes, leadership is an awesome responsibility. It is not something that happens on its own. It involves hard work. And that brings to mind the third characteristic of a godly husband.

HE IS A LABORER

The truly godly husband is a *laborer.* There is no room for sloth in the business of fatherhood. Paul wrote to Timothy, "If any provide not for his own, and especially for those of his own house, he hath denied the faith, and is worse than an infidel" (1 Timothy 5:8).

There is no question that Paul was speaking primarily of the material provision a father should provide for his family, but the father's provision for the family goes much further than that, as we have seen. A father must labor to supply every need of his family, and again, that involves a great sacrifice.

Are you beginning to get the idea? The father's duties are

all sacrificial. He does them asking nothing in return. He gives and yields, and sacrifices, and then he does it some more.

The father is a laborer. He is a laborer *for* his family. But he is a laborer *in* his family as well. The father works to assure that there is harmony in the home. His is not an easy job. All that he does must be done with wisdom and fairness and understanding.

And he also is a laborer with his family. Their goals are his goals. He provides encouragement, incentive, and correction when needed. He prays with the family, worships with the family, and studies with the family. He must be sympathetic, patient, reasonable, and diplomatic. He must see clearly where the family is going and be able to give direction.

And above all, he must understand that he is a laborer *among* his family. The Christian father must be an example. He must represent what he expects his children to become.

I heard of a father who returned home from work to hear his small son and daughter quarreling, yelling, and threatening one another. It appeared that they were about to come to blows.

"What's wrong with you kids?" he demanded.

Frowns turned to smiles. The little boy tilted his chin and said, "Nothing. We were just playing Papa and Mama."

I hope that father hung his head in shame. We must realize just how influential our lives are on our children. They see us more clearly than anyone out in the world. And it is imperative that we give them a good example.

That is the way it should be in the Christian home. Daily Bible reading and prayer should be as regular as meals. The father should be the head of the house—a lover, a leader, and a laborer.

May your home be built on the solid and unchanging standard of God's precious Word.

Book 4

SPECIAL SERMONS

ON
MAJOR BIBLE DOCTRINES

To dear friends who have been a source of inspiration and strength over the years:

Herrmann and Lydia Braunlin
James and Karen Gwinn
Ronald and Marion Kerr
George and Ruth Mak
John and Jan Prins
William and Carol Sweeting
Norman and Amelia Sweeting
Robert and Betsy Wiker

ONE

The Bible—God's Own Word

It was my heritage to be born into a home where the Bible was read, revered, believed. I remember that as a child I accepted it as God's Word, because that was the viewpoint of my parents. As I grew older I became aware of arguments against the Bible offered in the name of science. My confidence was shaken, and I began to waver.

Soon I had to confront the issue. Was I to believe the Bible as unique, the Word of God, or was it just another book?

Perhaps you face the same questions. Perhaps you have wondered, *How far can I trust the Bible? Can I find a sure answer?*

The need is urgent. At no time in history has there been a greater longing for a definitive blueprint to guide our thinking. Men everywhere are looking for authoritative answers to the problems of contemporary life. Does the Bible provide such answers?

Let me say with absolute confidence, it does! The Bible is God's own Word to us. It gives sure and timeless answers to our complex problems and is the only source of truth worthy of our faith. How do I know? Let me give you several reasons.

First, *the Word of God is inexhaustible.* Lewis Sperry Chafer, founder of Dallas Theological Seminary, said, "The Bible is not the sort of book a man would write if he could, or could write if he would." The depth of the richness of its truth is not possibly of human origin. Its beauty, unity, honesty, and purity stand together as testimony to the divine origin of the Scriptures.

Poet John Dryden realized that. He wrote,

Whence, but in *Heav'n,* cou'd Men unskill'd in arts,
In several Ages born, in several parts,
Weave such *agreeing Truths?* or *how,* or *why*
Shou'd *all* conspire to cheat us with a *Lye?*
Unask'd their *Pains, ungrateful* their *Advice,*
Starving their *Gain,* and *Martyrdom* their *Price.*

Religio Iaici

It is absurd to suggest that a book having the depth and unity of the Scriptures could have been written by men. The Bible was penned by some forty different writers over a period of more than fifteen hundred years. Its sixty-six different books were written in three different languages. Yet its message is a comprehensive revelation of God's dealings with men through the ages, perfect in its unity and absolutely consistent with itself throughout. One would think that with so many different human authors and with such a lengthy time span from its beginning to its completion, the Bible would be filled with confusion, chaos, and a tangle of contradictory ideas and opinions. But the Bible is free from all that. Why? Because those human authors, "holy men of God [,] spake as they were moved by the Holy Ghost" (2 Peter 1:21). Harmony and purity prevail in the Scriptures from the first word to the last.

And that unity makes its inexhaustible depth even more amazing. There are a number of themes throughout the

Bible—themes such as the love of God, man's failure and sin, redemption, judgment, righteousness, and sacrifice. The richness of truth throughout God's Word is further testimony to the fact that it is indeed a supernatural book—inspired by God.

Men have given their lives to the study of the Bible, only to testify in later years that they had not begun to sound the depths of truth in it. Truly no man has. Even the cumulative efforts of biblical scholars over the centuries have barely scratched the surface of the riches in God's Word.

The Bible contains revelation about subjects on which men could only speculate. It tells of the creation of the universe, the origin of man, the fall of Satan, and the workings of the spirit world. It gives information about the future; and many of its prophecies have already been accurately fulfilled. It is the only infallible source of information about the end of the age.

Yes, the Bible is inexhaustible. Mere men could not have written it had they wanted to.

THE BIBLE IS INDESTRUCTIBLE

Another proof that the Bible is God's Word is the fact that it is indestructible. No other writing in the history of man has outlasted such fierce criticism as has the Bible. Throughout the centuries it has been subjected to the fiery blast of unbelieving criticism. But even as Shadrach, Meshach, and Abed-nego rose out of the flames of Nebuchadnezzar's furnace, so the Bible has emerged unscathed from the mocking and criticism that has been heaped upon it.

The enemies of God have always tried to get rid of the Bible. But they have failed. In the days of Jeremiah the prophet, King Jehoiakim tried to destroy the Word of the Lord by casting it into leaping flames. Immediately the Lord said to Jeremiah, "Take thee again another roll, and write in it all the former words that were in the first roll, which Jehoiakim the king of Judah hath burned" (Jeremiah 36:28). The infidel king tried to destroy God's Word, but all his efforts were vain. In fact, he was destroyed for his unbelief. But today the Bible stands.

"The grass withereth," wrote Isaiah, "the flower fadeth: but the word of our God shall stand forever" (Isaiah 40:8, NSRB*). The Hebrew word translated "stand" is *yaquam*. Its literal meaning is "rises to stand." It is the picture of something that has been beaten and broken and yet, in spite of all, rises to stand.

Henry V of England considered Bible reading a crime and passed a law that threatened death or loss of property to anyone caught reading a Bible. But his decrees could not shorten its life by one minute or lighten its weight by one ounce. The Bible traveled more roads, spoke in more languages, and knocked at more doors than any other book in that day, and it continues to do so today.

Unbelievers during the eighteenth century mocked the Bible and predicted its death. Thomas Paine, author of "Common Sense" and "The Age of Reason," said of the Bible, "I have now gone through a wood with an axe, and felled trees. Here they lie. They will never grow again." But he was wrong. The Bible stands.

Jean Jacques Rousseau, Voltaire, and Robert Ingersoll all predicted that the Bible would become obsolete in their lifetimes. They are all long dead, but the Bible still stands.

William E. Gladstone referred to the Bible as "the impregnable Rock." He was right. The Bible stands.

Critics have attacked the Bible from every angle. Some have claimed that it is inconsistent. But they have yet to demonstrate any insurmountable contradiction. It is almost ludicrous to read some of their claims and see the lengths to which desperate men will go to try to discredit the Bible.

Some critics have maintained that the biblical record is

*New Scofield Reference Bible.

not historically accurate, but time and again archaeology has upheld the Bible account, and the critics' history books have had to be rewritten.

Science has never successfully challenged the Word of God, although unbelieving scientists have manufactured theories that attempt to discredit biblical accounts. Scientific discoveries, even in this century of the explosion of scientific knowledge, have overwhelmingly supported the accuracy of biblical accounts, and the serious Bible student cannot help but be impressed with the scientific accuracy and lack of superstitious error in biblical language. Secular science textbooks have to be updated, but the Bible stands, unchanged from the beginning, a testimony to the wisdom and power of God.

THE BIBLE IS INFLUENTIAL

Another evidence that the Bible is the Word of God is that it is so influential. No book in the history of mankind has had the impact on civilization that the Bible has had. "England has two books," said Victor Hugo, "the Bible and Shakespeare. England made Shakespeare, but the Bible made England."

Great ethical systems, governments, legal concepts, humanitarian movements, social programs, educational concepts, and philosophies have had their roots in the teachings of the Bible. A leading law enforcement official of a previous generation said, "It is quite impossible to believe that progress along the road to righteous living may be accomplished without the guidance of the Bible. It is the source of spiritual food, the solution of life's problems, and the inspiration for Christian living."

The Bible has changed the lives of millions of people. It exudes an unprecedented and unequaled influence on the hearts of men. William Biederwolf said, "There are many important books in this world, but did you ever hear of any book that controlled lust or brought unholy people to a

451

place of purity and respectability? Did you ever hear a man say, 'I was a failure, a wretched misfit, but I read a book on botany, and thanks be to botany, my life has been changed, my habits are broken, and peace now reigns within'? Did you ever hear a man say, 'I was a beast of a man and worse as a husband, and then I studied a little geology. I got a hammer and started chipping on the rock, and thanks be to geology my brutality was changed to kindness, my cruelty to love, and I have had a song of joy in my heart from that day on'?"

Yet the Word of God has amazing transforming power. It has transformed criminals, political leaders, scientists, bankers, laborers, religious leaders, housewives, and people from every walk of life.

I know the transforming power of God's Word firsthand. I have tasted it. I can testify to what it has done for me. I have taken the promises of the Word of life and applied them to my heart, and I have found that they are true. They have transformed my life.

There are questions I cannot answer, and problems I cannot totally resolve, but I know that the Bible is indeed the Word of God because of the supernatural impact it has made on my life. I can say with the blind man in John 9: "One thing I know, that, whereas I was blind, now I see" (John 9:25).

Perhaps you too have experienced the transforming power of the Word of God. If not, God invites you to "taste and see that the LORD is good" (Psalm 34:8). Accept His Word by faith, "for the word of God is [living], and powerful . . . and is a discerner of the thoughts and intents of the heart" (Hebrews 4:12). It will transform you.

The Bible Is Inescapable

Another proof of the Bible's authenticity is the urgency of its message. *The Word of God speaks to every man, and its words are inescapable.* The message of the Bible is such that it cannot be ignored. It must be accepted or rejected. There is no middle ground. "He that is not with me is against me; and he that gathereth not with me scattereth abroad," said Jesus (Matthew 12:30).

Think about that for a moment. Jesus is saying that neglect is the same as outright rejection, and even opposition! He is urging each of us to confront His inescapable claims and decide where we stand. We cannot ignore God's Word.

Consider for a moment the teachings of the Bible. Romans 3:10 says, "There is none righteous, no, not one." Romans 3:23 says, "For all have sinned, and come short of the glory of God." Isaiah 53:6 teaches the same truth, "All we like sheep have gone astray; we have turned every one to his own way." These verses all show that every one of us has a need—we are guilty before God. We have sinned, and as Romans 6:23 says, "The wages of sin is death." The Bible destroys the humanist's rationalization about the goodness of man. Man is not basically good, gaining favor with God because of his brilliant achievements. He is a sinner in need of redemption. That is an inescapable claim of the Word of God.

But the Bible also is full of inescapable invitations. Isaiah 55:1 says, "Ho, every one that thirsteth, come ye to the waters, and he that hath no money; come ye, buy, and eat." And Revelation 22:17, one of the last verses in the Bible, is a similar invitation: "The Spirit and the bride say, Come. And let him that heareth say, Come. And let him that is athirst come. And whosoever will, let him take of the water of life freely."

You see, Jesus Himself bore the punishment for our sin, and the Bible teaches that "whosoever believeth in him should not perish, but have everlasting life" (John 3:16). God's inescapable invitation is the invitation to receive eternal life as a gift. You cannot earn or purchase eternal life, but you can receive it freely by trusting the Lord Jesus.

Have you responded to the inescapable claims of God's Word? The writer of Hebrews asked, "How shall we escape, if we neglect so great salvation?" (Hebrews 2:3). The danger is not only in rejecting the Word of God, but in neglecting it as well. You do not need to openly reject the claims and invitations of Scripture to suffer condemnation; all you need to do is neglect them. Remember, Jesus said, "He that believeth not is condemned already" (John 3:18). God's judgment is inescapable; Christ's invitation is inescapable; the warnings of the Bible are inescapable. Respond to them today.

THE BIBLE IS INERRANT

Finally, *the Word of God is inerrant*. Great battles have been fought among theologians in recent years over the subject of the inerrancy of God's Word. Amid all the controversy, I fear that one point may be obscured—never has anyone been able to demonstrate the slightest error in the Bible in its original autographs.

We know of numerical errors that have filtered into copied manuscripts, and recent scholarship has corrected many errors in translation of the Bible into English. It is generally conceded that there are places where copyists have inserted verses both intentionally and by mistake, but those are all errors that may be called human errors, and they have all slipped into copies of the Scriptures after God's work of inspiration was complete.

We believe that the Bible in its original autographs, as it was given by inspiration from God to man, was entirely without error. There were no statistical errors, no numerical errors, no historical errors, no scientific errors, and no geographical errors.

Critics of the Bible have always claimed errors. Until

454

relatively recently it was popular among unbelieving critics of the Bible to claim that Moses could not possibly have written the Pentateuch because, it was asserted, writing did not exist during the time of Moses. But archaeology proved the critics wrong and the Bible accurate.

That did not silence the unrelenting critics, who have claimed at various times that the Bible is in error in its descriptions of the Hittite culture, the size of Nineveh in the days of Jonah, and the geography of Palestine in the days of the judges. Again archaeology has upheld the accuracy of the biblical accounts in those and literally scores of other instances. The Bible has yet to be shown to be in error. History, science, and archaeology have consistently upheld the inerrancy of the Scriptures.

Yes, we can say with confidence that the Bible is the Word of God. It is inexhaustible, indestructible, influential, inescapable, and inerrant. It is worthy of our highest reverence. But more important, it is worthy of our unquestioning obedience. Its commands are God's commands. Its power is God's power. Its truth is God's truth. And its principles are God's principles. It alone can transform your life. It alone can guide your footsteps. It alone can free you from sin. And it alone can give you life.

To doubt the Bible is to question the veracity of God. To disobey it is to challenge the authority of God. And to ignore it is to reject the grace of God.

What will you do with the Word of God? Will you make it a lamp to your feet and a light to your path? Will you let it give you peace instead of pain? Will you let it give you life and power and victory over sin? Will you study it and master it, obey it and let it master you?

TWO

What Is God Like?

What is your concept of God? Whether accurate or not, your idea of God will determine your behavior, your outlook on life, and your destiny in this world and the next.

In his book *The Knowledge of the Holy,* A. W. Tozer says, "The most portentous fact about any man is not what he at a given time may say or do, but what he in his deep heart conceives God to be like."[1]

What do you conceive God to be like? Some would say that to believe at all in a personal God requires a giant leap of faith—but I am convinced that belief in God is a far more reasonable position than atheism. Nature, the personal experience of literally billions of people, and something innate in the heart of man all testify to the existence of God.

How can we know what God is like? The Bible tells us that we cannot know God through human wisdom. We can see evidence of His existence in nature, and we can even discern some of His character in what we see around us. But for a fuller understanding of what God is like, we must look to special revelation—the written Word of God, the Bible—and to the incarnate Word of God, the Lord Jesus. Both sources give us a clearer glimpse of God than we could see anywhere else. Jesus said, "He that hath seen me hath seen the Father" (John 14:9).

Speaking to the woman at the Samarian well, Jesus implied two characteristics of God. "God is a Spirit: and they that worship him must worship him in spirit and in truth" (John 4:24). Look at those characteristics and the attributes they suggest.

GOD IS SPIRIT

First, *God is a spiritual being.* He is not confined to a body that can be seen and touched. His presence cannot be detected with the senses. He is present in the material world, but He transcends it. Several of God's attributes relate directly to the fact that He is a Spirit Being.

Second, *God is omnipresent.* Unlike a being with a physical body, which can be only in one place at a time, God can be everywhere at once. In Psalm 139, David wrote, "Whither shall I go from thy spirit? or whither shall I flee from thy presence? If I ascend up into heaven, thou art there: if I make my bed in hell, behold, thou art there" (Psalm 139:7-8).

Jeremiah wrote in his prophecy, "Am I a God at hand, saith the LORD, and not a God afar off? Can any hide himself in secret places that I shall not see him? saith the LORD" (Jeremiah 23:23-24). Of course no one could hide himself from the presence of God, for God is everywhere.

God's omnipresence is a tremendous source of encouragement to the believer. It means that God sees what happens to us, and He is there in the midst of our trials. It means that we can pray to God wherever we are, and He is there to hear us. It also means that, although we may be out of fellowship with the Lord for a time, we can never be out of His presence. He is there.

A closely related attribute of God is that *He is omniscient.* In addition to being everywhere, He knows everything. He knows our thoughts, He knows our feelings, He knows our fears, and He knows our needs. Psalm 139 is a hymn exalting God for His omniscience. "O LORD, thou hast searched me, and known me," wrote David. "Thou knowest my downsitting and mine uprising, thou understandest my thought afar off. Thou compasseth my path and my lying down, and art acquainted with all my ways. For there is not a word in my tongue, but, lo, O LORD, thou knowest it all together. Thou hast beset me behind and before, and laid thine hand upon me" (Psalm 139:1-5).

God knows the past, the present, and even the future. His wisdom and knowledge are infinite in their scope. He is able to devise perfect ends and to achieve them by perfect means. He cannot fall short. He cannot make a mistake.

By His infinite wisdom He created the universe. By it He willed and wrought salvation. By it He has prophesied things to come. And by it He understands and loves us more than we can know.

It is a comfort to know that He cannot be taken by surprise, He cannot make mistakes, and He cannot be wrong. He is omniscient.

In addition to that, *God is omnipotent.* The Bible tells us that He is eternal and self-existent. He was not brought into being by someone else, and He is not the least bit dependent on any other being. He is superior to all others in every way, and everything else that exists is His creation. He is the source of all power and authority. There is nothing consistent with His nature that He cannot do. "With God all things are possible" (Matthew 19:26).

It is, of course, impossible for us to conceive such infinite power. We have difficulty enough thinking in terms of the metric system. So we can only dimly conceive the meanings of terms like *omnipotence* and *omnipresence* and *omniscience.* Those words go beyond our ability to understand, and yet they are inadequate to convey the dimensions of God as revealed in His Word. He is infinite in every way, and nothing is too hard for Him to do.

God is a spirit. He is omnipresent, omniscient, and omnipotent. But there is yet another spiritual attribute of God that many people never think about. And that is *He is immutable.* He never changes. There is never the slightest variation in His essence or character. He is perfect, so He cannot change for the better or for the worse. "I am the LORD," says Malachi 3:6, "I change not."

Very little in our world is unchanging. The economy is unstable, world politics are in a constant state of flux, and scientific development changes the way we live all the time. But God is the same as He was in the beginning. His nature, His essence, and His character are unchanging.

GOD IS TRUTH

Look again at Jesus' words to the woman at the well in John 4:24. "God is a Spirit," He said, "and they that worship him must worship him in spirit and in truth." The fact that God must be worshiped in truth implies that God is a moral being. He has moral attributes, and since He is God and since He is immutable, His attributes are absolute and cannot be broken or violated. What do I mean by moral attributes?

First, *God is holy. Holy* means "set apart" or "separated." God is separated from sin. He cannot be touched or defiled by sin. He is perfect in holiness and perfect in all that He is and does. Angels in heaven cry, "Holy, holy, holy," in worship at His throne. The word itself speaks of awesome perfection.

It was God's holiness that caused Daniel, a righteous man, to fall on his face as he confronted a vision of the eternal God. "There remaineth no strength in me," he wrote in Daniel 10:8. "For my comeliness was turned . . . into corruption, and I retained no strength." Isaiah saw the same truth. When he saw the Lord, "high and lifted up" (Isaiah 6:1), he was filled with sudden realization of his own sinfulness, and he cried, "Woe is me! for I am undone" (v. 5). Later he wrote "But we are all as an unclean thing, and all our righteousnesses are as filthy rags" (Isaiah 64:6). Even the best things about man seem evil and dirty when compared with the absolute holiness of God.

How hopeless and helpless we would be, how utterly unable we would be to meet God's standard of holiness if we had to be dependent on ourselves! Yet God says to His people, "Be ye holy; for I am holy" (1 Peter 1:16). And He offers you and me the holiness of His Son through simple faith in Him.

A second moral attribute of God is that *He is just.* That means that everything He does is fair and righteous and good. Saying that God is holy means that He is separated from sin. Saying that He is just means that what He does is characterized by perfect righteousness. Every act of God is a righteous act. His commandments are righteous. His standards are righteous. His punishments are righteous. His rewards are righteous. He is perfectly righteous. He cannot violate His righteousness or allow it to be violated.

A remarkable passage in Romans 3 deals with the importance of God's righteousness in regard to man's salvation in Christ. In verses 22-24 the apostle Paul describes how God through faith in Christ justifies, or legally declares righteous, a believing sinner. In other words, the most sinful person that trusts in the Lord Jesus is seen by God to be perfectly righteous the moment he believes. Verse 25 tells us that such a thing is possible because Christ died and paid the price for our sin with His blood. His death, we are told, was a declaration of the righteousness of God. Verse 26 concludes with these amazing words: "That he might be just, and the justifier of him which believeth in Jesus."

What that means is that God's righteousness required the

death of the Lord Jesus to pay for the sins of man. A perfectly righteous God cannot simply overlook man's sin and accept sinning men into His fellowship. And man cannot himself make atonement for his sins. But through the death of Christ on the cross God made a way that He Himself could pay the price for sin without compromising His own righteousness.

God is holy. He is righteous. And also *He is faithful.* God's faithfulness is an attribute closely related to His immutability. It means that God cannot violate His Word. He cannot renege on a promise. "He cannot deny himself" (2 Timothy 2:13).

God's faithfulness is not contingent on man's faith. Second Timothy 2:13 says, "If we believe not, yet he abideth faithful." God will not fail to fulfill perfectly all His promises. The Christian's assurance is deeply rooted in the faithfulness of God.

"God is faithful," wrote Paul to the Corinthian church (1 Corinthians 1:9). He is faithful to finish the work that He has begun in you (1:8-9), and He is faithful to deliver you from the power of temptation (10:13).

The whole of the Bible is a testimony to the faithfulness of God. God is still fulfilling His promises to the children of Abraham. He fulfilled His promises to Moses, to David, to the prophets, and to the apostles. He is fulfilling His promises in the lives of millions today. We can testify with them that God indeed is faithful.

God is gracious. That God is a God of grace is seen throughout the Word of God. God's grace is His favor and goodness and power to those who deserve His condemnation. Man's sin is a direct challenge to God's authority and righteousness, but God in His grace can elect to show favor to those who sin.

He did so with Adam and Eve. God's word to Adam was that he should not eat of the fruit of the tree of the knowledge of good and evil, "for in the day that thou eatest thereof thou shalt surely die" (Genesis 2:17). But the man and his wife disobeyed the Lord, and both ate the forbidden fruit. That was the first sin, and it constituted rebellion against God and a challenge to His power, to His holiness, to His authority, and to His righteousness.

But what was God's response to Adam's sin? It was a response of grace. Adam and his wife did die spiritually that day, and they desired to hide from the presence of God and cover their nakedness. God graciously dealt with them, made them clothing, and gave them a promise of redemption. He could righteously have responded in anger with judgment, but instead He responded in grace.

The Lord Jesus fulfilled God's promise of redemption, and He was the embodiment of God's grace to man. He came to seek and to save the lost. He came to heal, to release captives, and to demonstrate the grace of God.

But do not get the idea that grace is God's only attribute or that it is license to sin. God is still righteous, and He demands righteousness. And His grace teaches us that, "denying ungodliness and worldly lusts, we should live soberly, righteously, and godly" (Titus 2:12). It is a serious sin to take God's grace for granted or to do "despite unto the Spirit of grace" (Hebrews 10:29).

A little-understood attribute of God is that He is *longsuffering*. Unbelievers often mistake God's longsuffering for His silence. *Longsuffering* means that God frequently bears with sinners in spite of their continued disobedience. He does not often punish immediately. He is perfect in His patience, "slow to anger." God's patience does not mean God's approval. Romans 2:4 says that God's longsuffering forbearance is a tool designed to lead a sinner to repentance. God's patience and even God's goodness may be extended for a time to one who persists in sin, in an attempt to win him to repentance.

But God's longsuffering is not forever, and Romans 2:5 indicates that those who persist in sin are treasuring up wrath and judgment for that day when God's longsuffering gives way to perfect justice. "Be not deceived; God is not mocked: for whatsoever a man soweth, that shall he also reap" (Galatians 6:7).

Finally, *God is loving.* In fact, 1 John 4:8 says, "God is love." Some doubt the love of God. But let me remind you that God not only says He loves us; He has given supreme and final proof as well. Paul reminds us of that fact in Romans 5:8: "But God commendeth his love toward us, in that, while we were yet sinners, Christ died for us." God does not simply talk—He acts. The eternal memorial of His love is a blood-stained cross and an empty tomb.

Have you allowed God's love to grip your heart? John wrote, "He that loveth not knoweth not God" (1 John 4:8). Is your life filled with the love of God?

God loves us, you see, not because there is anything in us that makes us worthy of His love. He loves us because love is His nature. His love is an unconditional love. He loves us in spite of our sin.

Down through the years God's love has shined through misery, tears, and sin like a shaft of sunlight on a dark day. We see God's love in His revelation, in His mercy, in His patience, and in His redemption. We see the love of God as the infinite one becomes an infant in Bethlehem's manger. We see it in His life and ministry. And most of all we see it as as He hangs on the cross, dying for our sins.

Yes, the evidence of God's love is overwhelming. His forgiveness and mercy were purchased at great personal cost. Salavation is not cheap. But it is offered freely to all who believe.

God must be worshiped in spirit and in truth, because He is spirit, and He is truth. Do you know the God of the Bible? I do not ask if you know about Him or if you know what He is like. Do you know Him personally? Are you daily walking in His fellowship, seeing His attributes reflected in your life?

He is holy. He is just. He is faithful. He is gracious. He is longsuffering. But above all He is loving. He loves you. Let God's love speak to your life today. Respond in faith.

NOTES

1. A. W. Tozer, *The Knowledge of the Holy* (New York: Harper & Row, 1961), p. 9.

THREE

The Proof of Christ's Deity

Throughout our world we are witnessing an unparalleled interest in the Person of Jesus Christ. Books, motion pictures, popular songs, documentaries, and plays are being written about Him. Newspaper and magazine articles deal with the quest for the "historical Jesus." Recent interest in the shroud of Turin has stirred new speculation as to its authenticity and, along with it, new interest in the Man whose image it is thought by some to bear.

But despite all the media coverage, there are still millions of men and women worldwide who know nothing about Jesus Christ of Nazareth. And as sad as that fact is, more shameful is the truth that even those who have the greatest access to biblical truth, people right here in our country, know very little about the Lord Jesus.

Once while Jesus was ministering along the coast of Caesarea, He asked His disciples, "Whom do men say that I, the Son of Man am?" Matthew tells us that His disciples answered Him and said, "Some say that thou art John the Baptist: some, Elias; and others, Jeremias, or one of the prophets" (Matthew 16:14).

Jesus asked, "Whom say ye that I am?" (v. 15).

That question of our Lord's has been declared to be life's most important question. How do you answer it? Who is Jesus?

The Muslim would say, "Jesus was a prophet of Allah, but nothing more." A Jehovah's Witness would tell you that He is a created angel. Some say He was a good man, a great teacher, or a wise philosopher. Some say He was a son of God—a man with a spark of divinity. What do you say?

Who is Jesus? What do we know about Him? Throughout the centuries many have attempted to answer that most important of questions. Jesus was "a great teacher of morality and an artist in parable," said Joseph Klausner. He was "an inexhaustible principle of moral regeneration," said Ernest Renan. "The most scientific man that ever walked the globe," was Mary Baker Eddy's reply.

Although there is an element of truth in each of those answers, they all are inadequate, for they all fail to recognize the deity of the Man Jesus Christ.

Jesus is God, and it is that fact that gives His teachings their authority. It is that fact that makes obedience to His commandments imperative. It is that fact that makes faith in Him mandatory.

Some would declare that it really does not matter who Christ is as long as we receive help from His teachings. Nothing could be further from the truth! It makes all the difference in the world who Jesus is. Some years ago a well-known author made the statement that it really did not make any difference whether Jesus even lived as long as He had the teaching of the Bible attributed to Him.

But wait a minute. It is deadly error to try to dispense with Jesus' deity as quickly as that. If He indeed is God, He deserves our reverence and our unquestioning obedience. If He is not God, He was either a madman or a fraud. If you are not totally convinced of His deity, you must settle the issue.

The Bible teaches that Jesus is God. He exercises the prerogatives of deity. He has the attributes of deity. He bears the titles of deity. And His commandments are the commandments of deity. The Bible gives evidence of Jesus' deity from at least three sources.

THE TESTIMONY OF THE PROPHETS

First, *there is the record of the prophets*. Although the prophets did not fully understand many of the things God led them to write, they revealed repeatedly that the coming Messiah would be God in the flesh.

For example, Isaiah 9:6 prophesied centuries before Jesus' birth that a child would be born and a son would be given. Whose Son was He to be ? God's Son. And as if to make sure that no honest searcher could miss the point, Isaiah added, "And his name shall be called Wonderful, Counsellor, The mighty God, The everlasting Father, The Prince of Peace." Those are names reserved for God. Isaiah was saying in the plainest possible language that the Messiah would be the very incarnation of God.

Other prophets did the same. Micah made an amazing prophecy about the place of Jesus' birth. Micah 5:2 says not only that Jesus' birth would be in Bethlehem, but also that He was to be one "whose goings forth have been from of old, from everlasting."

Whom but God could that phrase describe? Micah was saying plainly that the One who was to be born in Bethlehem was to be God in the flesh.

Many of the prophetic Psalms ascribe to Jesus the names and attributes of deity. Psalm 45:6, quoted in Hebrews 1:8 as being spoken by God the Father to His Son, says, "Thy throne, O God, is for ever and ever: the sceptre of thy kingdom is a right sceptre." There Jesus is addressed by His Father as "God."

Psalm 110:1 was spoken of by Jesus Himself as being

prophetic of Him (Matthew 22:41-44). Paul also referred to the same psalm in 1 Corinthians 15:25-26, and he indicated that it spoke of the Lord Jesus. In that psalm, God the Father again speaks to God the Son, "The LORD said unto my Lord, sit thou at my right hand, until I make thine enemies thy footstool" (v. 1). Jesus, in quoting that verse to the Pharisees, posed the question how David could call One who was to be the Son of David "Lord."

The answer, simply, is that Jesus is God. David knew it, Micah prophesied it, and Isaiah spoke of it too. The prophets all bear testimony to it.

THE TESTIMONY OF JESUS' CONTEMPORARIES

A second source of evidence that Jesus is God is the testimony of Jesus' contemporaries. His closest associates, interested observers, and even His enemies bore witness to the fact that He was God in the flesh. What those associated with Jesus said and believed concerning Him can hardly be ignored. Reporters of important events always seek eyewitnesses — people who were on hand and saw things for themselves. The honest seeker of the truth about Jesus cannot neglect the testimony of His contemporaries.

Nathaniel, one of Jesus' apostles, by some insight not fully explained, recognized Jesus' deity at their first meeting. "Rabbi," he said in amazement, "thou art the Son of God; thou art the King of Israel" (John 1:49). His calling the Lord Jesus "the Son" by no means was meant to imply that He was somehow less than God the Father. Even the Pharisees understood that Jesus' claim to sonship was a claim to equality. In John 5:18 we are told that "the Jews sought the more to kill him, because he not only had broken the sabbath, but said also that God was his Father, *making himself equal with God"* (italics added).

Peter's confession in answer to Jesus' question concerning His own identity is well known. Matthew 16:16 tells us that he said: "Thou art the Christ, the Son of the living God." Imagine that! The other disciples must have held their breath. Would Jesus rebuke Peter for such an answer? But Jesus endorsed it, assuring Peter that His deity was a truth not taught to him by flesh and blood but revealed to him by revelation from the heavenly Father.

John the Baptist acknowledged Jesus' deity, saying that Christ was such a One whose shoes he was not worthy to stoop and unloose. After he had baptized Christ, he said, "I saw, and bare record that this is the Son of God" (John 1:34).

The apostle John wrote unmistakably in the first verse of his gospel that Jesus is God. "In the beginning was the Word, and the Word was with God, and the Word was God" (John 1:1). His gospel is filled with statements demonstrating the deity of this One whom John called "the Word," who "was made flesh, and dwelt among us" (John 1:14). John further declares Him to be the Creator. "All things were made by him," he wrote in John 1:3, "and without him was not anything made that was made."

Even Thomas, the apostle who doubted the truth of Christ's resurrection, confessed His deity when he saw the Lord risen from the dead. "My Lord and my God," he said (John 20:28).

A Roman centurion, by no means sympathetic to Jesus, had to exclaim as he watched Him die, "Truly this man was the Son of God" (Mark 15:39). His testimony stands as additional proof that Jesus' contemporaries recognized His deity. His friends, his enemies, and even the demons had to acknowledge that He was indeed the Son of God.

From the time of Jesus' birth, when wise men from the East came to pay homage to Him, to the years after His ascension into heaven when His apostles continued to write of Him, the testimony of His contemporaries was that He is "equal with God" (Philippians 2:6).

A third source of evidence about Jesus' deity is the testimony of the Lord Himself. Here the evidence of His deity is over-whelming. His life, teachings, and miracles speak insis-tently of who He is. He demonstrated power over every form of sickness and disease. He fed multitudes, stilled storms, and walked upon water. He taught with clarity and pro-found authority concerning the deepest and most basic is-sues of life. In spite of the constant opposition He received, He demonstrated command of every situation. No question was ever too hard, no issue too involved or sensitive, and no situation ever too difficult for Him to deal with.

He predicted His own death and resurrection. During His ordeal He calmly faced malicious accusers, accepted outrageous abuse, submitted to trials that made a mockery of justice, and without any protest went on to a slow and agonizing death.

He rose from the dead, appearing repeatedly to friends who were convinced He was dead and, in at least one case, who were unwilling to be convinced otherwise. And at the end of His earthly life, He was observed by several witnesses as He ascended into heaven.

In all His lifetime, in the midst of controversy and oppo-sition, despite misunderstanding and unjust treatment, He never swerved from doing right. In the end the greatest frustration of His enemies was that they could find no valid accusations to bring against Him.

Historian Philip Schaff sums up the life of Christ with this discerning comment:

> His zeal never degenerated into passion, nor His constancy into obstinacy, nor His benevolence into weakness, nor His tenderness into sentimentality. His unworldliness was free from indifference and unsociability, His dignity from pride and presumption, His affectability from undue familiarity,

His self-denial from moroseness, His temperance from austerity. He combined child-like innocency with manly strength, absorbing devotion to God with untiring interest in the welfare of man, tender love to the sinner with uncompromising severity against sin, commanding dignity with winning humility, fearless courage with wise caution, unyielding firmness with sweet gentleness![1]

Everything about Christ's demeanor and attitudes reflected the fact that He was God. It showed in His life. It showed in the fact that He accepted worship and allowed people to address Him in the loftiest terms. He received praise that is reserved exclusively for deity. But more than that, he claimed to be God. He did that directly as well as by implication.

At the age of twelve, He consulted with the scribes in the Temple. When His parents found him talking with the scholars, He asked, "Know ye not that I must be about my Father's business?" (Luke 2:49). Later, in His adult ministry, when He cleansed the Temple, He spoke of it as "my Father's house."

Clearly, Jesus claimed that God was His father in a special way that no one before or since could legitimately claim. He spoke of His Father in such a way that no one else would dare to speak. "I and my Father are one," He said (John 10:30).

He taught that to know Him is to know God, to see Him is to see God, to believe Him is to believe God, to obey Him is to obey God, to honor Him is to honor God, and to hate Him is to hate God. "He that hath seen me hath seen the Father," He said in John 14:9. He could not have spoken more clearly.

At the close of His life He made a final statement under oath before the Sanhedrin, the Jewish council. The episode is described in Matthew 26:63-66.

"I adjure thee by the living God [said the high priest,

473

v. 63] that thou tell us whether thou be the Christ, the Son of God. Jesus saith unto him, Thou hast said." In other words, "That's right. You are correct about who I am." And He went on. "Nevertheless I say unto you, Hereafter shall ye see the Son of man sitting on the right hand of power, and coming in the clouds of heaven" (v. 64).

For that statement He was condemned to death. Why? Because it was a claim to deity, and they correctly understood it. They would not acknowledge His deity, so they declared Him worthy of death (v. 66).

But the darkness and earthquake at His crucifixion, the rending of the Temple veil, and the empty tomb all gave proof that His claim was true. He was indeed God in the flesh.

Why is this such an important truth? John made it a test of fellowship (2 John 7-10). It is vital to all Christian doctrine because the Lord Jesus is the object of our faith. He invited and even commanded that we place our faith in Him. If He were not God, He would not be a proper object for faith. He could not have purchased our salvation. If He were a mere man, or even another created being such as an angel, He could not have purchased redemption for mankind. But because He is God, the Father has accepted His finished work on behalf of us, and our salvation is accomplished. It is perfect. There is nothing that we can add to it. We must simply trust Him.

Have you trusted Christ? Is your salvation sure? How do you answer the question, Who is Jesus? Is He a mere man to you? Or is He your Savior, your Lord, your God? I challenge you to put your faith in Him.

NOTES

1. Philip Schaff, cited in Bernard L. Ramm, *Protestant Christian Evidences* (Chicago: Moody, 1953), p. 177.

FOUR

The Reality of the Virgin Birth

Perhaps no theological issue is as hotly contested as the virgin birth of Christ. The Bible teaches that He was born without a human father. Mary, His mother, was a virgin.

Some people are troubled by miracles, and the supernatural birth of Jesus is a case in point. Either it is true or it is not, and there are some very serious implications either way. The question of the virgin birth is not one to be lightly brushed off.

One of our Moody Bible Institute staff spent his early years in a church where the gospel was not preached and the Bible was not believed to be God's Word. He told me of an incident that happened one Sunday morning when a Sunday school student asked about the virgin birth of Jesus Christ. "Do you really expect us to swallow a story like that?" the student asked the teacher.

Immediately there was a burst of comment. Some, incredibly, were not even aware that the Bible spoke of a virgin birth. Others had heard of it but considered the story a myth. A few were not sure.

The teacher was taken off guard. "That's not the point of the lesson," he tried to say. "the real point is—" But he could not finish. Either he was not sure himself if the virgin birth was a fact, or he did not understand the real point of the story at all.

My guess is that both things are true. The fact is that "the real point of the story" cannot be separated from the truth of the virgin birth. Infidels may try to deny it—and they have consistently tried to deny it through the centuries. But the fact remains that all the truth of Christian doctrine is related to the fact of the virgin birth.

I would like to suggest to you four reasons I consider faith in the virgin birth essential to Christianity.

IT IS ESSENTIAL TO MARY'S PURITY

First of all, *it is essential to Mary's purity.* The Bible teaches that the mother of Jesus was pure and chaste. Critics often have aimed their attack at Mary, and a denial of the virgin birth naturally impugns her character.

"There was nothing peculiar about the birth of Jesus," Hugh Schonfield writes. "He was not God incarnate and no Virgin Mother bore him. The Church in its ancient zeal fathered a myth and became bound to it as a dogma."[1] More blatantly still, Nels Ferre, in his notorious volume *The Christian Understanding of God* has claimed that if Jesus was not the natural son of Joseph then He had to be the illegitimate child of a German soldier.[2]

Such a flippant statement must be examined in the light of what the Bible has to say about Mary. Mary was not sinless, and the Bible does not teach that she was. But she was holy, blessed of the Lord for her purity and character. She knew the Word of God intimately, as we see in the *Magnificat* in Luke 1:46-55.

"My soul doth magnify the Lord, And my spirit hath rejoiced in God my Saviour. For he hath regarded the low estate of his handmaiden: for, behold, from henceforth all generations shall call me blessed" (vv. 46-48). Those are the words of one who knows the Word of God and who knows the Lord God intimately. They are not the words of a hypocrite.

To deny the virgin birth is to reject the character of Mary as revealed in Scripture. It is highly improbable that if the story of Christ's miraculous birth were a myth, no one in the first century would have challenged it on the basis of some flaw in Mary's character. But there is no record that anyone closely associated with her ever doubted the account.

It Is Essential to the Bible's Authority

Far more important than any consideration of Mary's character is the fact that *the truth of the virgin birth is essential to the authority of the Word of God.* To deny the virgin birth is to deny the Word of God, for the Bible teaches in the clearest terms that Jesus was virgin born.

The Bible is a factual record, not an apologetic argument or a refutation of criticism. Attacks on it through the years have only confirmed the accuracy of its account.

No statement of the Bible stands alone. Each portion of the Word of God has its place in the tapestry of the whole, woven and inscribed with meaning through the centuries.

The virgin birth was first intimated in the opening book of the Bible, Genesis. Genesis 3:15 makes reference to the seed of the woman, who would overcome the enemy, Satan. "Seed" is an interesting expression to describe the offspring of the woman. It seems to be a clear reference to the virgin birth.

Many centuries later God confirmed His purpose in Isaiah 7:14. A little less than a thousand years prior to the birth of Christ, He led the prophet to write, "Therefore the Lord himself shall give you a sign; Behold, a virgin shall conceive, and bear a son, and shall call his name Immanuel." Clearly, this would be no ordinary birth. A child was to be born of a virgin, and His name would be Immanuel, which means "God with us."

The Angel of the Lord confirmed to Joseph in a dream that he would see the fulfillment of Isaiah's prophecy (Matthew 1:20-23). And Luke records Mary's reaction to the news that she was to be the one who would bring forth the child who was to be the Deliverer. Astonished, she asked, "How shall this be, seeing I know not a man?" (Luke 1:34).

Look at the angel's response to her. "The Holy Ghost shall come upon thee, and the power of the Highest shall overshadow thee: therefore also that holy thing which shall be born of thee shall be called the Son of God" (v. 35). And in verse 37 he added, "For with God nothing shall be impossible."

Some have suggested that we cannot trust the accounts of Matthew and Luke because they are the only gospels that record the virgin birth. But the fact is that they are the only two gospels that even deal with the birth of Jesus at all. And the overall teaching of the Bible is clear. Wherever the issue is mentioned, the virgin birth is taught.

Paul made reference to the birth of Christ in his epistle to the Galatians. There he wrote, "But when the fulness of the time was come, God sent forth his Son, made of a woman, made under the law" (Galatians 4:4). Even as early as the first century, the belief of the church was that Jesus was "made of a woman"; He was virgin born.

To doubt that truth is to doubt the Word of God. To challenge it is to challenge the authority of the Scriptures. To reject it is to reject the truth of revelation.

It Is Essential to Jesus' Deity

But the truth of the virgin birth is vital for another reason. It is essential to Jesus' Deity. Jesus is God. He claimed to be God. The Bible teaches that He is God. That is why we call Him the *Lord* Jesus.

Remember Isaiah's prophecy that a virgin would bear a son and call his name Immanuel? *Immanuel* means "God with us." The child who was to be born of a virgin would be God in the flesh. Isaiah prophesied further about the child: "For unto us a child is born, unto us a child is given: and the government shall be upon his shoulder: and his name shall be called Wonderful, Counsellor, The mighty God, The everlasting Father, The Prince of Peace" (Isaiah 9:6).

Truly, that was no ordinary child. He would take the government upon his shoulder, and as verse 7 says, there would be no end to its increase, as He established the throne with "judgment and with justice from henceforth even for ever." Clearly, He was not to be mere man.

His names were to be the names of deity. Look again at the list of names. "Wonderful, Counsellor, The mighty God, The everlasting Father, The Prince of Peace." Isaiah could not say it more clearly. That child was to be God in the flesh.

Jesus Himself claimed to be God in the flesh. He said in John 14:9: "He that hath seen me hath seen the Father," and in John 10:30: "I and my Father are one." He consistently spoke of God as His father, which His contemporaries correctly understood to be a claim to deity (John 5:18).

His miracles and His teaching both proved that His claim to be God was true. He demonstrated power over evil spirits and every disease. His teaching was with great authority. Undisputably, He was God in the flesh.

Why is the virgin birth so crucial to Jesus' deity? Simply because an unalterable principle from the beginning of creation is that creatures bring forth offspring after their own kind. Like begets like. Cats beget cats. Cows beget cows. Fish beget fish. Amoeba beget amoeba.

We beget our children in our own likeness. Sinful fathers can beget only sinful children. Man could never break the chain of sin. No generation in the history of mankind has ever been able to rise above the sin pollution of the past.

It began with Adam. Romans 5:12 says, "By one man sin

entered into the world, and death by sin; and so death passed upon all men." First Corinthians 15:22 suggests the same truth: "In Adam all die."

You see, we have inherited an inclination to sin from our fathers. And they inherited it from their fathers, and so on all the way back to Adam. His sin and the death that results was passed on to every member of the race. In all man's generations, not one descendant of human parents was ever free from sin. Each went to death condemned by his own sin.

God is sinless, and if He would become man, He must do it in such a way that He remains untainted by human sin. The way God designed to do that was by the virgin birth. If Jesus had had a human father, He would have inherited human sin. But through the virgin birth, the Holy Son of God became a man in a perfect human body untainted by sin.

To deny the virgin birth is to say that the Lord Jesus inherited human sin. And to say that He had sin is to say that He was not God. A denial of the virgin birth is a denial of His deity.

It Is Essential to Salvation's Finality

The virgin birth is essential to salvation's finality. Without a sinless being, God in the flesh, our salvation could never have been accomplished. God's method of redemption always has been by subsitutionary atonement. In the Old Testament, under Moses' law, God required that a spotless lamb be sacrificed for sin. As the sacrifice was made, just before the lamb was killed, the one offering the lamb would place his hand on it to show his identification with the lamb who would die to make atonement for his sins. Then the blood of the lamb would be shed, for no atonement could be made without shedding of blood (Hebrews 9:22).

Hebrews 10:4 tells us, however, that "it is not possible

that the blood of bulls and goats should take away sins." The Mosaic sacrifices were symbolic; they pictured a greater sacrifice that would take place when a sinless human being shed His blood to pay for the sins of others.

But the One who was to shed His blood had to be spotless, sinless. It was to be the Son of God, the virgin-born Savior, who would shed His blood to make atonement.

John the Baptist was the first to recognize Jesus publicly as the Savior. He said, "Behold the Lamb of God, which taketh away the sin of the world" (John 1:29). By some special revelation he realized that the Lord Jesus would be the one to make atonement for the sin of man.

And Jesus did just that on the cross. At His death He cried, "It is finished," meaning that the work of salvation was complete. There was nothing left for man to do but trust Him. Salvation could be offered freely to those who believe.

But what if Jesus had not been born of a virgin? He would not have been sinless, so He could not have qualified to pay for the sins of man. He would not have been God in the flesh, so He could not have borne the sin of the world.

Without the virgin birth, very little of the Christian faith remains intact. The virgin birth is proof of the love of God. Hebrews 2:14 says, "Forasmuch then as the children are partakers of flesh and blood, he also himself [that is, Jesus Christ] likewise took part of the same; that through death he might destroy him that had the power of death, that is, the devil."

What a glorious, incredible act! God became man to demonstrate His love by freeing us from the grip of the devil. And He could not have done it without the virgin birth.

Shall we scrap our faith in the virgin birth? Does it really matter? Of course it does. Do you have difficulty believing it? Listen again to Isaiah:

"For my thoughts are not your thoughts, neither are your ways my ways, saith the LORD. For as the heavens are higher than the earth, so are my ways higher than your ways, and my thoughts than your thoughts" (Isaiah 55:8-9). It should not be difficult for us to accept a God who does miraculous things. In fact, I would find it hard to believe if He did not do supernatural things. He is God, and we are but men.

Have you put your faith in Him? Have you trusted the Lamb of God who died to take away your sins? It may be later than you think. Will you trust Him today? He is God in human form. Look to Him now as your Savior and Lord.

NOTES

1. Hugh Schonfield, *The Passover Plot* (New York: Bantam, 1967), p. 42.
2. Nels Ferre, *The Christian Understanding of God* (New York: Harper, 1951), p. 191.

FIVE

The Truth About the Holy Spirit

There is much talk today of the Holy Spirit. Charismatics, noncharismatics, cultists, and members of mainline denominations have demonstrated a renewed interest in His person and work. Tune your television or radio to a religious broadcast, and chances are you will hear mention of the Holy Spirit.

Until relatively recently it seemed that the Holy Spirit was the forgotten member of the Trinity. He was rarely mentioned and little understood. His ministry has been unknown or ignored, and His power has been unused. There is now more talk than ever before about the Holy Spirit, but unfortunately, much of what we hear about Him is error.

Who is the Holy Spirit? What does He do? What does the Bible really teach about Him? Why is He so misunderstood? What does it mean to be Spirit-filled?

There are three areas of misunderstanding about the Holy Spirit, and I would like to look at what the Bible teaches about each of them. God's Word will shed some light on all our questions.

His Personality

The first great area of misunderstanding about the Holy Spirit is in regard to His personality. Perhaps some of the misunderstanding about the Holy Spirit's personality comes from our King James translation of the Bible. There the pronoun sometimes used to describe the Holy Spirit is "it." But the Holy Spirit is not an inanimate or impersonal "it." He is a person.

The King James Version also speaks of Him as the "Holy Ghost." But He is not a ghost. He is a spirit being, but not a "spook" or goblin. The Holy Spirit is a person, not a force or an influence. And the Bible says he possesses all the attributes of personality—intellect, emotions, and will.

The Holy Spirit has *intelligence.* Before His crucifixion Jesus predicted that He would go away to the Father, but He promised to send One whom He called the "Comforter." "The Comforter, which is the Holy Ghost, whom the Father will send in my name, he shall teach you all things, and bring all things to your remembrance, whatsoever I have said unto you" (John 14:26). Only a being with intellect could teach.

Again Jesus, still speaking of the Holy Spirit, told His disciples, "But when the Comforter is come, whom I will send unto you from the Father, even the Spirit of truth, which proceedeth from the Father, he shall testify of me" (John 15:26). That is descriptive of an activity that can be carried out only by a personal being with an intellect.

Romans 8:16 and 26 say that the Holy Spirit bears witness with the spirits of the saved to give assurance of salvation, and that He makes intercession for those who are saved. Those verses imply personality in that they describe acts of the intellect—things that no mere force or influence can do.

The Bible indicates also that the Holy Spirit has *emotions.* He can be grieved, according to Ephesians 4:30; and He can be vexed, according to Isaiah 63:10. Those terms certainly imply emotional responses.

488

Romans 8:26 indicates that He is capable of expressing prayers on our behalf with "groanings which cannot be uttered." That speaks of his intercession for us in terms of a means of expression possible only to a being with emotions.

The Holy Spirit has a *will*. First Corinthians 12:11 says that His distribution of spiritual gifts to believers is according to His own will. Acts 16:7 indicates that He would not allow Paul to go into Bithynia. He leads, He directs. He has a will.

The actions of the Holy Spirit are the actions of a person. He intercedes, He searches, He speaks, He commands, He moves, and He strives. He strengthens us, witnesses within us, and convicts us of sin.

The words the Lord Jesus used when He promised to send the Holy Spirit leave no room for the idea that He is merely a force or an impersonal influence. Jesus said, "I will pray the Father, and he shall give you another Comforter" (John 14:16). The word *another* in the Greek means "one the same as." The Holy Spirit is the same as Christ; He is a person. The word *comforter* is from the Greek word *paraklete,* which means "one called alongside." It is the same word translated "advocate" in 1 John 2:1. It is a word that only makes sense if it is applied to a personal being. The Holy Spirit is our Paraclete. He is one called to aid us, to instruct us, to intercede for us. He is a person.

HIS DEITY

Another area of misunderstanding about the Holy Spirit concerns His Deity. He is God, an eternal member of the Trinity. How do we know that He is God?

First, He is called God. Acts 5 records the sin of Ananias and Sapphira, who claimed that they were giving to the apostles the full price of a piece of land they had sold. They had in reality kept back part of the price for themselves. The Scriptures tell us that Peter said, "Ananias, why hath Satan filled thine heart to lie to the Holy Ghost?" (v. 3). The following verse follows that question with a very revealing statement. Peter said to Ananias, "Thou hast not lied unto men, but unto God" (v. 4). The Holy Spirit is God.

First Corinthians 3:16 also says that the Holy Spirit is God. "Know ye not that ye are the temple of God, and that the Spirit of God dwelleth in you?" it asks. Think of it! The Holy Spirit is God, and His dwelling place is in the believer.

Second Peter 1:21 informs us that the Holy Spirit oversaw the writing of the Word of God. That implies that He is God, because 2 Timothy 3:16 tells us that "all scripture is given by inspiration of God."

We know that the Holy Spirit is God further because He has the attributes of God. *He is omnipresent.* Psalm 139 says, "Whither shall I go from thy spirit? or whither shall I flee from thy presence? If I ascend up into heaven, thou art there: if I make my bed in hell, behold, thou art there. If I take the wings of the morning, and dwell in the uttermost parts of the sea; Even there shall thy hand lead me, and thy right hand shall hold me" (v. 7-10).

He is omniscient. Isaiah was led to write in His prophecy, "Who hath directed the Spirit of the LORD, or being his counselor hath taught him? With whom took he counsel, and who instructed him, and taught him in the path of [justice], and taught him knowledge, and showed him the way of understanding?" (Isaiah 40:13-14, NSRB). The obvious answer is that no one taught Him. He is God, and He is omniscient.

He has power that indicates *He is omnipotent.* Luke 1:35 indicates that in Him resides the power of God, and Romans 15:19 indicates that it is the power of the Holy Spirit that works miracles.

The Holy Spirit can be blasphemed. Look at Jesus' warning in Matthew 12:31. "All manner of sin and blasphemy shall be forgiven unto men: but the blasphemy against the Holy Ghost shall not be forgiven unto men." Jesus taught that blasphemy against the Holy Spirit is such a serious sin that it will never be forgiven. Surely none can deny the deity of the Holy Spirit.

HIS ACTIVITY

A third area of misunderstanding about the Holy Spirit is His activity in the present age. What is the Holy Spirit doing today? There are those who claim that He is engaged in an outpouring of miracles such as man has never seen. Others give Him credit for everything from the outcomes of political elections to the progress of the ecumenical movement.

But what did Jesus say would be the work of the Holy Spirit in this age? Look at a key phrase of the Lord's in John 15:26. He said that when the Holy Spirit would come, "he shall testify of me." That is the main work of the Holy Spirit today, and everything He does corresponds to that activity. He testifies of Christ.

He is a teacher (John 14:26), but what does He teach? He teaches truth about the Lord Jesus Christ, and He guides men into truth concerning Him. His special ministry to the apostles was to bring to their memories all the things that the Lord Jesus had spoken to them.

Another ministry of the Holy Spirit is to convict unbelievers, and even that ministry involves testifying the truth about Christ. Jesus' words about that ministry of the Holy Spirit are often misunderstood.

In John 16:8 Jesus said that when the Holy Spirit came, He would reprove the world of sin, righteousness, and judgment. His special ministry to the unsaved is to convict in those three areas.

Look closely at the verses that follow. In verse 9, Jesus says that the Holy Spirit will convict the world "of sin, because they believe not on me." The greatest sin any man or woman can commit is the sin of unbelief. And the worst kind of unbelief is to reject the Lord Jesus Christ. It is that kind of unbelief of which the Holy Spirit convicts the unsaved. Why? Because all His ministries are Christ-centered. He convicts the world of sin, but the sin that He primarily convicts is not the sin of covetousness, or murder, or adultery, or hatred. It is the sin of unbelief in regard to the Lord Jesus Christ.

In verse 10 Jesus says that the Holy Spirit will convict "of righteousness, because I go to my Father, and ye see me no more." The Lord Jesus is God's standard of perfect righteousness. He alone is perfectly sinless, wholly righteous. And while He was here on earth, He was a visible example to men of true righteousness. Since His ascension into heaven, however, it has been the work of the Holy Spirit to convict men of that righteousness. He does it primarily by pointing men to Christ.

In verse 11, the Lord says that the Holy Spirit convicts men "of judgment, because the prince of this world is judged." Judgment is near. Satan is already judged. And the Father has committed all judgment to the Son (John 5:22). The Lord Jesus is the Judge, and judgment is coming. The Holy Spirit convicts the unsaved of those truths.

So the Holy Spirit convicts men of the necessity of faith in Christ, of true righteousness as revealed in Christ, and of judgment to be carried out by Christ. His ministry is Christ-centered in every way. When He teaches, He teaches about Christ; when He convicts, He convicts about Christ; and when He testifies, He testifies about Christ. He always points to Christ.

The Holy Spirit's ministry to the believer is multifaceted. He seals him, baptizes him, indwells him, gives him gifts, and fills him. But even those ministries are Christ-centered and serve to make Christ the focus of the believer's attention. The Holy Spirit testifies not of Himself, but of Christ.

And that is just the issue that has caused so much confusion. There are those who teach that the Holy Spirit is mainly involved in a ministry of miracles. Others claim that His main work in this age is to give personal guidance to Christians. But although the Holy Spirit may do miracles and He certainly does guide believers, those are not His main ministries. His main work is to point to Christ. And He will never direct a person to do or believe or say something contrary to the Word of God.

Watch out for any ministry or person who claims to be led by the Holy Spirit but acts contrary to the Word of God. And beware of any movement or group whose focus is the Holy Spirit. The Holy Spirit points not to Himself but to the Lord Jesus.

Yes, the work of the Holy Spirit is Christ-centered. And for the Christian His work is continuous. He never departs from the believer.

That has not always been true. The Old Testament contains eighty-eight references to the Holy Spirit. Each reference seems to indicate that in those days the Holy Spirit would come upon a person for a specific task and then leave when that task was complete. David had to pray, "Take not thy holy Spirit from me" (Psalm 51:11, NSRB).

No believer today ever needs to pray that prayer. In John 14:16 we have the Lord Jesus' promise that the Holy Spirit would abide with us forever. Acts 2 records His coming. He has been with the church, the Body of Christ, ever since. We may fail to obey Him. We may grieve or vex Him. But He is never absent.

The Bible plainly teaches that each believer is the dwelling place of the Spirit of God. That is a staggering truth. Think of it—God Himself lives in every Christian. The Apostle Paul wrote to the church at Corinth, "Know ye not that ye are the temple of God, and that the Spirit of God dwelleth in you?" (1 Corinthians 3:16). The word *dwell* is a beautiful word. It means "to inhabit, to live in." The Holy Spirit is a permanent, personal inhabitant within every believer. He indwells all believers all the time.

As a resident, the Holy Spirit gives strength for our weaknesses. He guides us in understanding God's Word and will. He helps us to pray. He empowers us to serve. He comforts us in our sorrow. And He does it all by pointing us to Christ.

In Ephesians 5:18 there is a powerful admonition to every believer. "Be not drunk with wine, wherein is exess; but be filled with the Spirit." Being drunk with wine means being given over to its influence. Paul is drawing a parallel. Being filled with the Spirit means being given over to His influence. A person who is filled with the Holy Spirit does not have more of the Holy Spirit than a person who is not filled. Remember that the Holy Spirit is a person; He is not given in measure. But the Holy Spirit has more influence over a person who is filled, and that person has more of the Holy Spirit's blessings.

Look at what is to characterize the life of the person who is Spirit-filled. He is a *singing* Christian, according to Ephesians 5:19. He speaks in psalms and hymns and spiritual songs, and his heart is filled with melody and singing. He is filled with the joy of the Lord.

He is a *satisfied* Christian, according to verse 20. He is always to give thanks, grateful to the Lord for His blessings, even in the adverse circumstances of life.

And he is a *submissive* Christian, yielded to the Lord as well as to his fellow Christians, according to verse 21. He is concerned for the needs and desires of others more than his own. He is not self-centered.

D. L. Moody was a Spirit-filled man. His life was a wonderful example of what God can do with a man fully yielded to His Spirit. The power of God flowed through his life, and everywhere he went, people's lives were touched and permanently transformed. When he was at the height of his ministry, a group of pastors met in Philadelphia to discuss plans for a city-wide effort. Among other decisions to be made, they had to select an evangelist. Quite a number of men were solidly in favor of inviting Moody, and they kept talking of the wonderful things God was doing through him.

One of the opposition spoke up and somewhat sarcastically said, "To hear you talk, one would think that D. L. Moody has a monopoly on the Holy Spirit."

"No," said one pastor wisely. "We did not intend to create that impression. But I am convinced that the Holy Spirit has a monopoly on D. L. Moody."

That is what we need—for the Holy Spirit to have a monopoly on us. Let the Holy Spirit exercise unchallenged influence on your life.

Notice three important facts about Ephesians 5:18. First, it is in the imperative mood. It is not a suggestion or an appeal, but a command. Anything less than the fullness of the Spirit is disobedience to the Word of God.

Second, it is a present tense verb. We are to be filled with the Holy Spirit now. And it is a continuous action verb. It could be translated, "Be being filled with the Spirit." We must be filled daily, constantly, moment by moment. Yesterday's blessings are not sufficient for today or tomorrow.

Third, it is a passive verb. That means that being filled with the Spirit is not something we do, but something that is done for us. We must be yielded. We must be willing. We must be believing. But God does the filling. We simply receive it by faith.

The Bible is quite clear in its warnings to those who resist the workings of the Holy Spirit. Ephesians 4:30 warns believers not to grieve the Holy Spirit. First Thessalonians 5:19 cautions us not to quench His ministry. *Quench* means to "cool down" or "subdue" or "extinguish."

Have you been trying to ignore the voice of the Holy Spirit? Have you been rejecting His leading in your life? Are you guilty of grieving Him or quenching Him?

Won't you open every area of your life today to the Holy Spirit? Listen to the call of God. "Be filled with the Spirit."

SIX

What Is Man?

A recent article carried by United Press International reported the finding of stone tools near the city of Hadar in eastern Ethiopia. The article suggested that the tools, which it said were at least 2.5 million years old, represented the earliest known evidence of human technology. Such evidence, it said, would push back the date considered by evolutionists to be the dawn of human culture at least a half million years.

Such discoveries seem to be popping up with increasing frequency. Several years ago a cover article in *Time* magazine devoted several pages to an analysis of recent trends in thinking concerning the theory of evolution. "As recently as [the 1960s,]" the article declared, "scientists talked about a direct, unbranching line of descent. . . . Now all that has changed. We would think rather of multiple strands, forming a network of evolving populations."[1]

Since 1859, when Charles Darwin first voiced his theories, many such changes in evolutionary hypotheses have been first applauded and then quietly laid to rest. What *Time* referred to as "radical revision"[2] is in reality a way of life for those pursuing proof that man's origin came about by chance.

It is interesting to note, however, the intensity with

which man searches for his roots. The *Time* article made this interesting observation: "As the patient searchers discern more and more about early man and his predecessors, they also may gain an ever-widening insight about modern man, his nature, his failings, and his future."[3]

Yes, man is intensely concerned about his origin, his nature, and his destiny. And rightly so. We want to know who we are, where we are going, and why. Answers to those questions are crucial to each of us, because we have only one life. We are here on this earth for only a few short years, while time and eternity pass on.

The wood of man's cradle rubs against the marble of his tomb. If he is fortunate enough to live seventy years, he is still subject to sorrow and disease, flood, drouth, and famine. If an earthquake shakes his land, his cities crumble. If a tornado dips too close, his countryside is stripped. Let an epidemic cross his path, and chances are he will fall victim. He is dwarfed by space and intimidated by his environment. He cannot endure extremes of heat, or cold, or elevation.

No wonder we ask, "Who am I? Where am I going?"

Fortunately the Word of God gives us some answers. The view it gives is quite different from the view presented by evolutionists, humanists, and secular philosophers, who see man merely as a highly developed animal. But since the Bible claims to be God's message to man, no individual should fail to consider what it has to say concerning the origin, nature, and destiny of the human race.

The Bible gives three insights concerning man. They are so basic that no man or woman can let them grip his consciousness and ever be the same.

MAN WAS CREATED BY GOD

First is the truth that *man is a special creation of a sovereign, loving, and all-wise God.* Man, according to the Bible, is not merely an accident of time and space. He is a crucial part of the eternal plan and purpose of an all-wise Creator. And furthermore, God made man in His own image.

Genesis 1:26 says, "Let us make man in our image, after our likeness." God made us not like the animals, but in His own likeness and image. What makes that unique? Physical appearance? Probably not. God is a Spirit, according to Jesus' own words in John 4:24. The thing that constitutes God's image in man is precisely what makes him distinct from the animals—the ability to make moral judgments and the desire to have fellowship with God. In short, Paul describes it as the "spirit of man" in 1 Corinthians 2:11. Our spirit is patterned after God's Spirit. We have the ability to think, to reason, to establish relationships. We have emotions, will, and intellect. We are morally responsible for our actions. We are in the image of God.

Only as we understand our relationship to God can we understand who we are and why we are here. Man is not God. He is not a supreme being with the highest intelligence in the universe. He is a creation of God, endued with God-given powers and responsibilities.

God made man for a special purpose. In the opening chapters of the Bible we are told that man was to have dominion over the earth. He was to subdue it and control it. He was to walk and talk with God. He was God's representative in charge of God's creation.

In Psalm 8 David marvels at the high position God gave to man. "When I consider thy heavens," he writes, "the work of thy fingers, the moon and the stars, which thou hast ordained; What is man, that thou art mindful of him? and the son of man, that thou visitest him? For thou hast made him a little lower than the angels, and hast crowned him with glory and honour. Thou madest him to have dominion over the works of thy hands; thou hast put all things under his feet" (vv. 3-6).

Do not sell yourself short as an individual. You are of great worth in God's sight. You are unique. You are in God's image. God has a plan for you. You are special to Him.

You see, we did not just happen. The Bible tells us that man was created in a special way. God "formed man of the dust of the ground, and breathed into his nostrils the breath of life; and man became a living soul" (Genesis 2:7).

In our age of so-called sophisticated thinking, it is not popular to believe in creation. Prominent scientist Carl Sagan recently made headlines by asserting on public television that the evidence for evolution had sufficiently advanced it beyond the status of a theory. Evolution, he claimed, is now an accepted scientific fact, like the law of gravity or the principles of aerodynamics.

Can such a statement be substantiated, or is it merely the wishful thinking of an overzealous evolutionist? To be sure, many scientists and science textbooks have long treated the theory of evolution as if it were fact. But there is a growing number of highly qualified scientists who believe that the evidence to support evolution is lacking.

The Institute for Creation Research in San Diego, California, is an organization of scientists from all over the United States who are creationists and who repudiate any form of evolution in their analysis and use of scientific data. They point out that acceptance of the theory of evolution says more about a person's social philosophy than it does about his awareness of scientific facts. Many of these men and women hold doctorates in their fields and are professors in some of our country's finest institutions of higher learning. They are not eccentric or ignorant. They have studied the fossil evidence, the genetic evidence, and the other scientific data, and they do not believe that evidence allows for the theory of evolution.

Evolution is, in fact, a kind of religion. Accepting evolution requires just as much faith as accepting creation—and perhaps a little credulity. It is a system of belief based not on observable phenomena but rather on assumptions, guesses, and speculation. It is constantly changing in its hypotheses, and there really is no single uniform theory of evolution. The theory differs from scientist to scientist.

We believe the biblical account of creation. Man did not evolve. He was created in God's image by a special, direct act of creation. He is not an animal.

MAN WAS CORRUPTED BY SIN

A second great insight given to us in the Scriptures about man's nature is also found in the early chapters of Genesis. There is recorded for us the sad account of man's fall. *Man sinned against God,* and because of his disobedience he was plunged into a fallen state of darkness. *Man became a fallen and corrupted creature.* Although created in the image of God, he was warped and twisted. The image was marred.

God did not make man to be a robot. He had the power to choose. He had a free will. He was obedient or disobedient by his own choice, and man chose to disobey.

God had placed man in a perfect environment. He was in a garden, and God gave him permission to eat freely from every tree but one: the tree of the knowledge of good and evil. The Lord said, "But of the tree of the knowledge of good and evil, thou shalt not eat of it: for in the day that thou eatest thereof thou shalt surely die" (Genesis 2:17).

But Satan came to them in the form of a serpent and told a lie. "Ye shall not surely die," he said to the woman (Genesis 3:4). He implied that God was holding back the best from them. "God doth know that in the day ye eat thereof, then your eyes shall be opened, and ye shall be as gods, knowing good and evil" (v. 5).

Goaded by Satan and driven by her own lust and self-seeking, Eve chose to follow Satan, and Adam followed her.

The results, the Bible tells us, were catastrophic—not only for Adam and Eve, but also for the race they established. What they became was passed on to their children and their children's children.

Adam and Eve did indeed experience death that day. They died spiritually, and as a result were separated from Almighty God. They knew fear, shame, and guilt. Their bodies became subject to pain and sickness and ultimately death. They became spiritual subjects of Satan. They began to sense continuously the pull and tug of temptation and the deadly urge to sin.

All those effects passed into the lifestream of the human race. The effects became visible immediately. The first child became the first murderer. Early civilizations were filled with corruption and sin, and in just a few generations God judged the earth with a flood.

You see, a principle of God's creation is that life reproduces after its kind. Trees, plants, and animals produce offspring that are similar in appearance, nature, and characteristics. Read again the first chapter of Genesis and notice how many times the expression "after his kind" appears. Forms of life do not come one from another. That is a law of genetics, and it is a principle by which all forms of life are governed.

Paul wrote in Romans 5:12, "Wherefore as by one man sin entered into the world, and death by sin; and so death passed upon all men, for that all have sinned." So sin is inborn in every man, and every man sins by choice as well. None of us can claim to be free from the power and influence of sin.

Some people react against the idea of sin. Some have even tried to deny that sin exists at all. But the Bible, as well as personal experience, assures us that sin is real and deadly. Every parent observes the working of sin in his own children. We do not have to teach our children to lie or be

504

selfish or lose their tempers. Those things are inborn in them.

To be sure, sin does not manifest itself in every man to the same degree or in the same manner. Not all are violent or lascivious or habitual thieves. Not all commit murder, or adultery, or such sins. But there is not a person who is not tainted in some way by sin. Romans 3:10 charges, "There is none righteous, no, not one." And verse 23 adds, "For all have sinned, and come short of the glory of God."

Each of us must reckon with the fact of personal sin. We have invited God's judgment in countless ways. We have violated His holy nature repeatedly, and we have rendered ourselves unfit for the role and future for which we were created. Our sin has separated us from a righteous God. Man is a tragic figure—the highest of God's earthly creations, yet marred and in bondage because of sin.

No man can understand himself or the world in which he lives apart from the knowledge that he is corrupted by sin. And apart from accepting that fact, no man will be in any position to change his future. To reject the truth of personal sin is to reject the possibility of redemption.

Man Was Completed by Christ

But there is good news. Redemption has been purchased for man. *Man,* who was created by God and corrupted by sin, *has been completed by Christ.* Colossians 2:10 says, "Ye are complete in him [Christ], which is the head of all principality and power." The image of God, which was marred in Adam, is restored in Christ.

That is the good news of the gospel. God intervened because He loves man. The door stands open to every man or woman who so desires to take the way that leads to forgiveness and restoration.

The way, of course, is Jesus Christ. He said, "I am the way, the truth, and the life: no man cometh unto the Father, but by me" (John 14:6). For every person, there is now not just one choice, but two.

First Corinthians 15:22 speaks of two choices. "For as in Adam all die, even so in Christ shall all be made alive." The opportunity for spiritual life is open to all men in Christ. As the head of his race, Adam led all men into sin and death. But as the head of a new race, the Lord Jesus Christ leads His saints into righteousness and eternal life.

You see, the Lord Jesus was without sin. He was the son of God, not of Adam. And since He was without sin, He did not deserve to die. But the Bible tells us that "God commendeth his love toward us, in that, while we were yet sinners, Christ died for us" (Romans 5:8). His death paid the penalty for sin for us. All we must do to appropriate this payment is receive Him by faith.

John 1:12 says, "As many as received him, to them gave he power to become the sons of God, even to them that believe on his name." In other words, those who receive the Lord Jesus by faith are no longer sons of Adam's race. They are sons of God. God's image in them can be restored.

Second Peter 1:3 says that God has in Christ "given unto us all things that pertain unto life and godliness." Truly man is completed in Christ.

Have you believed? Have you received the Lord Jesus Christ as your personal Savior?

God gives many invitations to man in the Scriptures. But the very last one is in Revelation 22:17. Look at it closely. "And the Spirit and the bride say, Come. And let him that heareth say, Come. And let him that is athirst come. And whosoever will, let him take the water of life freely."

God loves you. You cannot let his invitation go unanswered. He has a plan and purpose for your life. He has paid the price to make you His own and to restore His image in you. Will you respond to Him in faith today?

NOTES

1. *Time,* 7 November 1977, p. 67.
2. Ibid.
3. Ibid., p. 78.

SEVEN

Satan Is No Joke

The devil is no laughing matter. Although people tell jokes about him and try to deny his existence, there is no question that he is alive and working in the lives of individuals. What does he do? How does he affect us? How far does his power extend? What kind of authority does he have?

Have you ever wondered about Satan? Perhaps at one time or another you have been certain of his evil power working against you. But what do you know about him?

God wants us to be alert to Satan and his evil tactics. We are told in James 4:7, "Resist the devil, and he will flee from you." And in Ephesians 6:11 we are urged to "put on the whole armour of God, that [we] may be able to stand against the wiles of the devil." Clearly, God's Word teaches that there is a devil and we are to resist him. And the more we know about his evil schemes the better equipped we will be to resist them.

Paul wrote to the Corinthians that they ought to practice forgiveness for each other, "Lest Satan should get an advantage of us: for we are not ignorant of his devices" (2 Corinthians 2:11). Ignorance of Satan's devices places a Christian

508

in a most dangerous position.

I would like to suggest three evil devices that make up most of Satan's repertoire.

OPPOSITION

The first is opposition. The very name *Satan* means opposer, and he has opposed the work of God from the day he fell. To the Christian he is the chief adversary. First Peter 5:8 says, "Be sober, be vigilant; because your adversary the devil, as a roaring lion, walketh about, seeking whom he may devour."

Satan began his career of opposition to God when He decided to exalt himself against God. To understand his power and influence it is important to understand how he got to be an enemy of God. He was not created evil. He was created to be an archangel, and was the most beautiful and intelligent of all God's creatures.

Ezekiel 28 describes him in his original state. That chapter is Ezekiel's prophecy against the wicked king of Tyre, but most Bible students believe that the message there goes beyond the king of Tyre to Satan, who was the one behind the king's evil activities. The words of Ezekiel 28 cannot apply to a mere man; they must describe Satan in his original state.

"Thou sealest up the sum," wrote Ezekiel, "full of wisdom, and perfect in beauty. Thou hast been in Eden the garden of God. . . . Thou art the anointed cherub that covereth; and I have set thee so. . . . Thou wast perfect in thy ways from the day that thou wast created, till iniquity was found in thee" (vv. 12-15).

Isaiah 14 gives us some insight into what that iniquity was. "How art thou fallen from heaven, O Lucifer, son of the morning! how art thou cut down to the ground, which didst weaken the nations! For thou hast said in thine heart, I will ascend into heaven, I will exalt my throne above the stars of God: I will sit also upon the mount of the congregation, in the sides of the north: I will ascend above the heights of the clouds; I will be like the most High" (vv. 12-14).

Satan's original sin was the sin of pride, of wanting to be like God. His exalting himself was a direct challenge to the authority of God. No wonder he is called the opposer.

Satan opposes God's authority, His Word, His work, His people, His glory, and His will. Satan has always opposed the plan of God. He tempted the Lord Jesus in the wilderness (Matthew 4), and his temptations were designed to thwart God's plan of redemption. He takes away the Word of God from the hearts of those who hear it (Matthew 13:19); and he sows seeds of falsehood (v. 3-8).

It was Satan who put in the heart of Judas Iscariot the thought to betray the Lord Jesus (John 13:2). He blinds the minds of unbelievers so that they cannot see the light of the gospel (2 Corinthians 4:4). He sows the seeds of hatred, dishonesty, misunderstanding, error, and sin among God's people. He is in opposition to God in every sense.

IMITATION

Another of Satan's devices is imitation. Often he is more successful at imitation than he could be with blatant opposition. Satan has always imitated God. It was his desire to be like God that led to his fall in the first place.

Whatever God does, Satan is sure to substitute his own imitation. When Moses demonstrated the power of God to Pharaoh with miracles, Satan enabled Pharaoh's magicians to imitate those miracles. Throughout the Old Testament when God raised up His prophets, Satan countered by raising up false prophets.

Satan specializes in religion—false religion. He is subtle. And it is just that subtlety that makes him so deadly. Although most people think of the devil as something ugly and horribly evil, he is not always like that. He is not a little red man with a trident and a tail.

Paul warned the Corinthians of the subtlety of Satan. "For Satan himself is transformed into an angel of light," he wrote. "Therefore it is no great thing if his ministers also be transformed as the ministers of righteousness" (2 Corinthians 11:14-15).

Satan is a master at making himself and his demons look like something good—ministers of light. And many of Satan's most effective gimmicks are his counterfeits. He has counterfeit religions, counterfeit ministers, counterfeit churches, a counterfeit righteousness, and even a counterfeit gospel.

Paul wrote to the Galatians, "I marvel that ye are so soon removed from him that called you into the grace of Christ unto another gospel" (Galatians 1:6). They had accepted a counterfeit gospel, a gospel of works and law. Paul went on to write, "But though we, or an angel from heaven, preach any other gospel unto you than that which we have preached unto you, let him be accursed" (v. 8).

Paul was saying that the subtlety of Satan is such that we cannot trust our own experience—the things we can see, or touch, or know with the senses. Satan can create a counterfeit experience, a false feeling. The only sure guide for the Christian is the Word of God.

Satan's ultimate imitation will take place in the Tribulation. He has always had false christs, but his crowning imitation will be the Antichrist, whom Paul describes in 2 Thessalonians 2:3 as "that man of sin . . . the son of perdition." This evil being will set himself up as the world ruler and demand worship from all men. Paul describes him as one "who opposeth and exalteth himself above all that is called God, or that is worshipped; so that he as God sitteth in the temple of God, shewing himself that he is God" (2 Thessalonians 2:4).

How can a believer avoid being tricked by Satan's lies and deceit and imitation? Know the Word of God. A love of the truth is the surest way to avoid being taken in by error. Second Thessalonians 2:11 talks about those who are judged with a "strong delusion, that they should believe a lie." Why? "Because they received not the love of the truth" (v. 10). Satan cannot easily deceive a believer unless he is willing to be deceived.

Our Lord Himself talked about "false Christs, and false prophets, and . . . great signs and wonders" so convincing and so real that "if it were possible, they shall deceive the very elect" (Matthew 24:24). That implies, of course, that Satan's powers of deception are limited against believers. But we must be alert to his tactics.

ACCUSATION

A third device of Satan is accusation. He is called the "accuser of our brethren" in Revelation 12:10. That same verse says that Satan accuses believers before God day and night. It is the picture of one pointing his finger at others, accusing of wrongdoing, shortcoming, false motives, and sin.

When Satan cannot openly oppose, he imitates. When he cannot deceive through imitation, he accuses. How can Satan accuse a Christian before God?

The book of Job gives us an unusual look into the activities of Satan before God. "There was a day when the sons of God came to present themselves before the LORD, and Satan came also among them. And the LORD said unto Satan, Whence comest thou? Then Satan answered the LORD, and said, From going to and fro in the earth, and from walking up and down in it" (Job 1:6-7).

It would be good to point out that Satan is not omnipresent; he cannot be in more than one place at a time. Some people mistakenly have the idea that Satan is like God in that he can be everywhere at once. Of course, he cannot. But such is his network of evil spirits that he can make his influence felt in more than one place at once. And as a spirit,

512

he is not hindered by distance in traveling from place to place rapidly. So while it may seem that he is everywhere at once, he is not.

Job tells us that Satan accused him before God of serving the Lord with false motives. Satan implied that Job served God just for what was in it for him in the way of material benefits. Satan challenged God, "Put forth thine hand now, and touch all that he hath, and he will curse thee to thy face" (v. 11).

What follows shows us something of how Satan works. He stripped Job of all his possessions, his children, and ultimately his health. He had such awesome power that all he had to do was speak the word, and Job's world was destroyed.

But do not get the idea that Satan is omnipotent. His power has its limits, and God controls them. Until God gave permission, Satan could not touch Job. Satan's words to the Lord were, "Hast thou not made an hedge about him, and about his house, and about all that he hath on every side?" (v. 10).

Satan could not use his awesome power unless God permitted. And the same thing is true for the Christian living in today's world. First Corinthians 10:13 says, "There hath no temptation taken you but such as is common to man: but God is faithful, who will not suffer you to be tempted above that ye are able; but will with the temptation also make a way of escape, that ye may be able to bear it."

And God did make a way for Job to escape. In the end Job was victorious, and Satan was defeated. His accusation against Job was to no avail. Job was justified.

But what if Satan has a legitimate accusation against us? What if I commit a sin and Satan accuses me to God? Can Satan destroy me?

Satan can never destroy a believer because of sin. That is why Christ died. David was a believer involved in terrible sin. He committed adultery and murder. Yet he wrote, "Blessed is he whose transgression is forgiven, and whose sin is covered. Blessed is the man unto whom the Lord imputeth not iniquity" (Psalm 32:1-2). David repented, his sin was forgiven, and he was restored.

Christ died to pay for our sins. Satan cannot use those same sins, for which Christ has died, as a means to destroy a believer. Paul wrote to the Romans concerning that truth. "Who shall lay any thing to the charge of God's elect? It is God that justifieth. Who is he that condemneth? It is Christ that died, yea rather, that is risen again, who is even at the right hand of God, who also maketh intercession for us" (Romans 8:33-34).

No one, including Satan, can lay anything to the charge of God's elect, because God justifies them, meaning He declares them to be righteous in Christ. And no one, including Satan, can condemn the believer, because Christ has died and is risen and is even now making intercession for the saints.

Satan can oppose the believer, he can attempt to deceive him, and he can accuse him before God. But he is powerless to separate any believer from the love of God. "For I am persuaded," wrote Paul, "that neither death, nor life, nor angels, nor principalities, nor powers, nor things present, nor things to come, nor height, nor depth, nor any other creature, shall be able to separate us from the love of God, which is in Christ Jesus our Lord" (Romans 8:38-39).

As I see it, there are two possible mistakes to be made. One is to overestimate the power of Satan, and the other is to underestimate it.

A believer who overestimates Satan's power can live an entire lifetime in fear, always terrified of what Satan might do. Satan likes nothing better than to stir up that kind of fear in a believer, because it destroys his effectiveness for the Lord.

On the other hand, a person who underestimates the power and cunning of Satan may become unconcerned with Satan's activity and be lulled into complacency. That is where Satan can do his most damaging work.

God would have us to be alert to Satan's maneuvers, aware and ready to resist his evil works. But He would also have us be confident in His power to destroy the works of the enemy.

You see, God does not ask us to fight Satan with our own power and abilities. We could never do that. But He has promised victory and purchased it with the blood of Christ, and that is our refuge against Satan and his wiles. Revelation 12:11 talks about those who were ultimately victorious over the devil: "And they overcame him by the blood of the Lamb, and by the word of their testimony."

There is the victory over Satan—in the blood of Christ and the testimony of His power working in our lives. And those are two things that Satan can never destroy. We in ourselves are no match for the devil. But "we are more than conquerors through him that loved us" (Romans 8:37) and shed His blood that we might be redeemed from Satan's power. Remember, Christian, "Greater is he that is in you, than he that is in the world" (1 John 4:4).

Perhaps you cannot claim that verse for yourself. Perhaps you have never trusted Christ as your Savior and been freed from the powers of evil. If not, I urge you to yield your life to Jesus Christ today and experience His transforming power in your life.

EIGHT

Sin—The Bad News and the Good

The great scourge of the human race is not cancer, not crime, not even war, but an unseen enemy called sin. Few people realize the power of sin or their helplessness before it. Through the centuries sin has claimed its victims by the millions, yet many mock sin. Some even try to deny its existence. And few truly understand its seriousness.

Everyone can see the effects of sin. Most people in business have heard of Murphy's law. It is the principle that if anything can go wrong, it will. Such an observation is made, of course, with tongue in cheek, but most people will testify of firsthand experience that seems to authenticate Murphy's law.

Why is it that things seem so often to go wrong?

Life certainly is not easy. Disease, misery, poverty, death, crime, heartache, and war touch all our lives at one time or another. Everybody has problems. And it has always been that way. Since the Fall, there never really has been a time that was free from problems. The "good old days" are always in the past, and as we look at them objectively, we have to admit that they were not without their share of troubles.

All the technical progress man has been able to make in

the past century has done little to combat racial prejudice, fear, war, lust, hatred, pride, or anger. Man has reached out for happiness only to find that the perfect life he hopes for slips ever farther from his grasp.

Sin is the problem at the root of all of man's troubles. It is the one thing through the centuries that has made man stumble. It has always cursed his world and made his hopes come crashing to the ground. It is inbred in man, in his heart, desperately wrong but hopelessly ingrained in the fabric of his being.

Jeremiah 17:9 points out the problem. "The heart is deceitful above all things, and desperately wicked: who can know it?" Man's heart is corrupted and deceived by sin. His own heart is the source of evil desire, hatred, deceit, and pride. It has been that way since Adam sinned.

Peculiar as it may seem, we will go to almost any length to keep from recognizing sin. We pretend it really is not there. We laugh or scoff at it. We excuse it or brush it off as merely human failure. We minimize it by trying to persuade ourselves that since sin is so common, it really does not matter.

How wrong we are! Sin has made our world a place of chaos, pain, and sorrow. It has spawned wars, violence, family problems, sadness, and frustration. It is man's fatal flaw, the destroyer of his dreams and hopes, the enemy of his happiness. Yet so few of us know anything about the real character of sin.

I would like to look at the question of sin from three viewpoints—what sin is, what sin does, and what sin cannot do.

WHAT SIN IS

The dictionary provides a weak and limited definition of sin. *"Sin,"* it says, *"is an offense against God, a misdeed or fault, a transgression of the law of God."* The Encyclopaedia

517

Britannica gives twenty-two pages to the subject of anthropology but little more than half a column to sin.

For the most part, the world would like to take the subject of sin and sweep it under the rug, forgetting it forever. Many people really do not care what sin is. They usually think of sin as a technicality, an incidental infringement of a petty rule or regulation.

Some assume that God has arbitrarily set some hard-to-follow guidelines that they may choose to keep or not. If they break them, that is sin.

Others think that sin is only the most digusting kind of behavior. Skid-row derelicts are sinners in their eyes as well as murderers, child molesters, and criminals, but not average, "respectable" people.

Both views are wrong. Sin is a deliberate decision to do or say or think my own way rather than God's. It is a departure from the will of God. It is an expression of a rebellious attitude toward God.

Sin says, "I reject God's right to tell me what to do. I'll choose my own way. I'll act the way I want to act."

Sin began with a revolt in heaven. Lucifer, a being God had created without sin, determined that he would exalt himself above the Lord God. Speaking of him, Isaiah 14:13-14 says, "Thou hast said in thine heart, I will ascend into heaven, I will exalt my throne above the stars of God: I will sit also upon the mount of the congregation, in the sides of the north: I will ascend above the heights of the clouds; I will be like the most High."

Notice two things that first act of sin teaches us about all sin. First, *sin is an assertion of self-will.* Look at the number of times Lucifer used the phrase "I will." "I will exalt"; "I will sit"; "I will ascend"; "I will be." His sin was a deliberate assertion of his own will over the will of God, and that is the essence of all sin.

Second, *sin is an assumption of divine rights.* Lucifer's state-

518

ment "I will be like the most High" reveals what was truly in his heart. He wanted to be his own god. He did not want to obey God, worship God, or give God glory. He wanted the glory for himself, and that, too, is at the root of all sin.

Jesus exemplified the exact opposite of both of those attitudes. He sought not His own will, but the will of the Father. "I came down from heaven," He said, "not to do mine own will, but the will of him that sent me" (John 6:38). He said, "I can of mine own self do nothing: as I hear, I judge: and my judgment is just; because I seek not mine own will, but the will of the Father which hath sent me" (John 5:30). Everything He did was done not because it was the will of the Lord Jesus, but because it was the will of the Father. He never asserted His own will. When He prayed, He prayed, "Not my will, but thine be done."

And He gave up the rights that were His as God. Paul wrote in Philippians 2:5-7, "Let this mind be in you, which was also in Christ Jesus: who, being in the form of God, thought it not robbery [a thing to be grasped] to be equal with God: but made himself of no reputation, and took upon him the form of a servant."

Think of it! He was God from eternity past, but rather than asserting His own will and demanding the divine rights that were His, He chose to make Himself a servant.

What is sin? It is that in every man that makes him want to have his own way. It is the desire that makes us respond to Satan's temptation, "Ye shall be as gods" (Genesis 3:5).

That is why sin is such a serious issue. It is not a mere breaking of an arbitrary rule, but a direct challenge to the authority of God.

Perhaps you are like a man who said, "I don't understand why Adam and Eve's tasting the fruit was such a serious thing. It doesn't seem like a transgression worthy of death."

What made Adam and Eve's sin so serious was that it was a sin exactly like Satan's original sin. It was an assertion of their wills over the will of God. God had said, "Don't." They did it anyway. And even worse, it was an assumption of rights that belonged only to God. They responded to Satan's suggestion that they would be like gods.

Their sin was not a simple mistake or an oversight. It was a deliberate attempt to usurp God and His authority. It was no minor matter.

And all sin is like that. No matter how small it may seem to us, it constitutes outright rebellion against God and His will. And none of us can honestly claim to be innocent of it. "All we like sheep have gone astray; we have turned every one to his own way" (Isaiah 53:6).

What Sin Does

What are some of the effects of sin? *Sin makes the body subject to sickness, pain, aging, and ultimately, death.* It is universal in those effects.

From the beginning God had made clear that sin would have disastrous effects. "Thou shalt not eat of it: for in the day that thou eatest thereof thou shalt surely die" (Genesis 2:17).

Satan's response was to deny the effect of sin. "Ye shall not surely die," he said (Genesis 3:4). He was saying, in effect, "You can sin with impugnity. Nothing will happen if you sin. You can get away with it."

But it was a lie. The man did indeed die that day—not physically, but spiritually. His body started going through a process of aging, susceptibility to sickness, and deterioration that would lead eventually to physical death.

What were the results of sin? The man was cursed, the race was cursed, and all of nature was cursed. God said to Adam, "Cursed is the ground for thy sake; in sorrow shalt thou eat of it all the days of thy life; thorns also and thistles shall it bring forth to thee; and thou shalt eat the herb of the field; In the sweat of thy face shalt thou eat bread, till thou return unto the ground; for out of it wast thou taken: for dust thou art, and unto dust shalt thou return" (Genesis 3:17-19).

Paul wrote in Romans 8:22-23, "For we know that the whole creation groaneth and travaileth in pain together until now."

Those were the results of sin: sweat, toil, pain, groaning, death, sickness, disease, and trouble for all of creation. The perfect environment that God made for the man was marred. Instead of bearing fruit naturally, the ground would have to be cultivated. Weeds would grow instead of fruit. Man's diet would be changed to include leafy plants as well as fruits and vegetables and grain. Man would have to work and sweat, he would grow old and die, and his body would deteriorate and turn to dust again.

There were other effects. Sin would beget more sin, more death, and more heartache. The first child born would become the first murderer. Sin would be passed on through the race and infect every child born of a human father. "Wherefore, as by one man sin entered into the world, and death by sin; and so death passed upon all men, for that all have sinned" (Romans 5:12).

Death is the ultimate result of sin, and every man experiences it. We all grow old and die. Worse still, we all experience spiritual death, that same separation from God that Adam knew the day he tasted the forbidden fruit.

What does it mean to be spiritually dead? Ephesians 2:1 says that every unsaved person is "dead in trespasses and sins." He has his "understanding darkened . . . alienated from the life of God . . . because of the blindness of [his] heart" (Ephesians 4:18). That is spiritual death.

The spiritually dead person cannot stand the presence of God. Adam and Eve sinned and then hid from God. Cain killed Abel and went out from the presence of the Lord. The prodigal son journeyed into a far country. Judas betrayed the

Lord Jesus and then went and hanged himself. Sin is a destroyer. It creates fear, breeds confusion, and gives way to defeat and sadness. It drains us of our vitality; it dims our sensitivity; it dulls our spiritual senses. It defiles us, robs us of our joy, and drives us away from God.

WHAT SIN CANNOT DO

But the sin situation is not hopeless, thanks to Jesus Christ. He intervened in the course of human history to offer "one sacrifice for sins for ever" (Hebrews 10:12). He came "to put away sin by the sacrifice of himself" (Hebrews 9:26).

You see, Jesus never sinned. First Peter 2:22 says He "did no sin, neither was guile found in his mouth." And since death is the wages of sin, He did not deserve to die. But He chose to die, and to die for the sins of the world. His death was a sacrifice to pay the price of sin.

Now He offers eternal life and peace and salvation from sin to those who accept Him by faith. "For by grace are ye saved through faith; and that not of yourselves: it is the gift of God: not of works, lest any man should boast" (Ephesians 2:8-9). We cannot save ourselves from sin, but by God's grace we can receive salvation by faith in what Christ has accomplished for us on the cross.

So the grip of sin is broken. If you trust Christ, *sin cannot claim you*. Christ has put away sin forever by the sacrifice of Himself. That is the good news about sin. Here is more.

Sin cannot hold you. You can never on your own overcome the power of sin in your life. None of us can work our way out of its grip. We cannot rise above it simply by trying harder. No amount of effort, no mass of good intentions will avail. But the moment a man trusts Christ as his personal Savior, he is reckoned by God to be dead to sin. Paul asks, "How shall we, that are dead to sin, live any longer therein? Know ye not, that so many of us as were baptized into Jesus

Christ were baptized into his death?" (Romans 6:2-3).

You see, Jesus' death did more than just deal with the penalty of sin. It dealt with sin's power as well. God sees each Christian as "crucified with Christ" (Galatians 2:20), and therefore dead to the power of sin. Sin has no power over a dead person, and it has no legitimate claim to power over a believer in Christ. "For he that is dead is freed from sin" (Romans 6:7).

In addition, *sin need not control you.* Not only are we counted dead with Christ, but we are counted risen with Him as well. Romans 6:8 says, "Now if we be dead with Christ, we believe that we shall also live with him." We are raised up from the dead in Him that we "should walk in newness of life" (v. 4).

Only the Christian has the power of Christ's resurrection to enable him to live above the dominion of sin. And that resurrection power, working in his life, is what enables him to be free from the practice of habitual sin. "Sin shall not have dominion over [him]" (Romans 6:14).

Finally, if you are a believer in Christ, *sin cannot condemn you.* Jesus Himself said, "He that believeth on him [Jesus] is not condemned" (John 3:18). Why? Because he is "passed from death unto life" (John 5:24).

Sin can never separate the believer from the love of God. It can never threaten him with condemnation. It can never exact the supreme penalty of eternal death. Jesus has paid the price. The wages of sin have been paid, and the gift of life is freely offered. Have you received it? If not, will you receive it today?

NINE

The Cross—The Pivot Point of History

It is not always easy to recognize history in the making. Sometimes our closeness to events causes us to underestimate or overestimate their relative significance. Sometimes major crises in history pass relatively unnoticed, and only a later generation fully appreciates their importance. Other times, events fairly scream with historical importance. Such was the case on a recent day in our nation's history when a president was inaugurated and fifty-two hostages were released from a long period of captivity all in one day.

But the most crucial event of all history, the one crisis that forms a watershed by which we number our years, write all our history, and reckon our relationship with God—the crucifixion of Christ—was one of those events that passed without much notice. Yet it is the cross of Christ to which all previous history looked forward and to which all history since looks back. It is the crucifixion that gives meaning to the flow of human history. It is Christ's death that makes sense of the pattern of events from the beginning of history.

Yes, the cross is the hinge of history. The great events that were compressed into the four days surrounding

Christ's death touch the lives and hopes of everyone.

How, you might wonder, can an event so far in the distant past—an event that occurred close to two thousand years ago—be of any significance in today's world and especially in your life? To understand the answer to that question, let us look at three aspects of the cross of the Lord Jesus.

The Place of the Cross

First, *look at the place of the cross.* Matthew 27:33 says, "And when they were come unto a place called Golgotha, that is to say, a place of a skull," they crucified him. Golgotha—what a frightful name! *Golgotha* means "a skull," and *calvary,* the name by which most of us know it, is the Latin word that also means "a skull."

The hill was located just outside the city of Jerusalem, and that itself is significant. It was unprotected by the city walls; it was a place of death. It was a playground for jackals and hyenas and vultures. But, more important, it was the place of the sin offering.

According to Moses' law, certain offerings could be made only outside the camp of the Israelites. Many of the offerings took place in the Tabernacle at the altar, and they were burned there at the altar, but the sin offerings had to be burned outside the camp.

The writer to the Hebrews recognized that fact and the way it was fulfilled in Christ. In Hebrews 13:12-13 he wrote, "Wherefore Jesus also, that he might sanctify the people with his own blood, suffered without the gate. Let us go forth therefore unto him without the camp, bearing his reproach."

The place of the crucifixion was a place of reproach. It was a place of shame and horrible suffering. That is the meaning of the cross itself.

Perhaps it does not strike you as unusual that we sing songs about the cross, wear replicas of it for jewelry, and erect large images of it in our church buildings. But it would if you lived in a first-century Roman culture. There the cross was an instrument of capital punishment, an executioner's device, like the electric chair or a hangman's noose. Imagine singing a song about the guillotine or wearing a little gold gallows on one's lapel.

The cross is revered because of the One who died on it. But originally it had a stigma attached to it. It was the lowest form of execution under Roman law. It was a slow, agonizing, humiliating form of death, and the cross itself was a symbol of that kind of reproach.

Put to death on the cross were the lowest of criminals — the thieves, the murderers, the rapists, the scum of the earth. It was anything but a noble death. Victims were often chained to a pillar, whipped, spit upon, and insulted by rude, barbarous men who were attracted to the executions like flies.

The victim would be stripped and scourged with an instrument made of thin strips of rawhide having pieces of bone and metal attached to the ends. The lashing would continue until the arms of the scourgers grew weary. Then new recruits would take their places until the back of the victim was one massive wound.

It was not a pretty scene. The victim would be beaten into helplessness, and then further mocked. Matthew 27:28-31 describes this stage of Jesus' crucifixion. "And they stripped him, and put on him a scarlet robe. And when they had platted a crown of thorns, they put it upon his head, and a reed in his right hand: and they bowed the knee before him, and mocked him, saying, Hail, King of the Jews! And they spit upon him, and took the reed, and smote him on the head. And after that they had mocked him, they took the robe off from him, and put his own raiment on him, and led him away to crucify him."

You know the method used. Cruel nails were driven through His hands and feet to hold Him on the cross while he was subjected to public ridicule and scorn. Psalm 22:7 describes some of the humilation Jesus faced. "All they that see me laugh me to scorn: they shoot out the lip, they shake the head."

Yes, the place of the cross was a place of humiliation, shame, scorn, and reproach. It was a horrible place, a place of darkness. It was a place of rejection and torture and pain. It was a place of judgment and death.

THE PERSON OF THE CROSS

All this is more awesome when we remember the person of the cross. If He had been a mere thief or criminal or blasphemer, that day in history would not be remembered today. But this was no common criminal; He was the Lamb of God, come to take away the sin of the world.

Jesus made His appearance on earth as a baby in a manger. But that was not where He really began. He had no beginning. He was the beginning. He existed from eternity past. He was God. John opens his gospel with these words: "In the beginning was the Word, and the Word was with God, and the Word was God. . . . And the Word was made flesh, and dwelt among us (and we beheld his glory, the glory as of the only begotten of the Father,) full of grace and truth" (John 1:1, 14).

Yes, Jesus was God in human form. Permeating His very being were grace and truth and glory. He was no mere man. He was the virgin-born Son of Almighty God.

A realization of that fact makes the crucifixion seem more heinous than ever. Jesus himself told a parable recorded for us in Matthew 21:33-44 about a householder who hired some husbandmen to keep his vineyard while he was away. He sent servants to check on the husbandmen, and they beat one, killed another, and stoned yet another. He sent his own son, thinking that the men would reverence his son. But they killed him too.

The son in that parable represents the Lord Jesus, sent by God as an expression of His love and longsuffering. But He was killed, and all mankind stands guilty of His death, because it was the sins of all of us that sent Him to the cross.

Do you see the Person of the cross? He is the sinless one, the only man ever of whom it could accurately be said, "[He] did no sin, neither was guile found in his mouth" (1 Peter 2:22). He was "in all points tempted like as we are, yet without sin" (Hebrews 4:15). He was "holy, harmless, undefiled, separate from sinners" (Hebrews 7:26).

He was perfectly righteous, perfectly holy, and sinless; yet He died willingly for our sin. First Peter 2:23-24 tells us, "When he was reviled, [he] reviled not again; when he suffered, he threatened not; but committed himself to him that judgeth righteously: Who his own self bare our sins in his own body on the tree, that we, being dead to sins, should live unto righteousness."

Isaiah had prophesied the crucifixion centuries before. Speaking of the Person of the cross, he had written, "He was oppressed, and he was afflicted, yet he opened not his mouth: he is brought as a lamb to the slaughter, and as a sheep before her shearers is dumb, so he openeth not his mouth" (Isaiah 53:7).

No wonder the earth rocked and reeled in protest. No wonder all the people came together to that sight, beheld the things that were done, smote their breasts, and returned. No wonder the rocks broke and the sky darkened in view of such atrocity.

Here was pure love—God's love poured out in the person of His Son, dying for the sins of ungrateful man—and mankind met that love with contempt.

Why would God allow such a thing to happen? *What was the purpose of the cross? God was obtaining salvation for sinful men.*

In fact, the cross of Christ is the heart of the gospel. Paul wrote to the Corinthians, "For I delivered unto you first of all that which I also received, how that Christ died for our sins according to the scriptures; and that he was buried, and that he rose again the third day according to the scriptures" (1 Corinthians 15:3-4).

"Christ died for our sins." That is a phrase that appears on gospel tracts, billboards, church buildings, and in newspaper advertisements. What does it mean? Perhaps you find it difficult to understand the connection between our sins and Christ's death, as did a young man who confided that he had difficulty seeing how he could be held responsible for the sins of a relatively few men in first-century Palestine.

No one, that student said, had ever explained to him that Jesus' death on the cross was a sacrifice—a payment of the penalty of sin. The Bible uses the word *propitiation*. It means "to appease," or "to make favorable."

First John 2:2 says of Jesus, "And he is the propitiation for our sins: and not for ours only, but also for the sins of the whole world." His death made propitiation for our sins; that is, it satisfied the justice of God.

You see, God could not simply overlook our sin without compromising His own righteousness. His perfect justice demands that all sin be punished, and the wages of sin is death.

You and I cannot begin to grasp the seriousness of sin to a holy God. Each act of sin is a challenge to His holy will and purpose. Every transgression, no matter how small it may seem to human reason, is a direct affront to God's holiness. And sin demands a payment of death.

That brought about a monumental conflict. God in His righteousness must punish sin. But God in His love does not want sinners to perish. Only God Himself could solve the dilemma, and He did it by personally paying the penalty for man's sin.

But you ask, "How could He possibly make such a payment?"

The answer lies in an understanding of who Christ was. Remember, He was eternal God in the flesh, and He was perfectly without sin. He alone in all the history of mankind did not deserve to die.

But He chose to die for us. "I am the good shepherd," He said in John 10:14, "and know my sheep. . . . I lay down my life for the sheep. . . . No man taketh it from me, but I lay it down of myself. I have power to lay it down, and I have power to take it again" (v. 15, 18).

How can one man's death pay for the sins of so many? Think of all your sins and all the sins of the world laid on one side of a balance scale. Think of Christ's righteousness laid on the other side. The righteousness of Christ is so full, so perfect, so complete, that it more than outweighs the sins of the world. Christ's death was more than sufficient to pay for them.

Paul assures us in Romans 8:1, "There is therefore now no condemnation to them which are in Christ Jesus." If you are trusting Christ, your sins are forgiven. You have been washed and cleansed forever. Jesus Christ has paid the price of your sin. You need not fear condemnation.

The Bible is full of such promises. Isaiah 1:18 says, "Though your sins be as scarlet, they shall be as white as snow; though they be red like crimson, they shall be as wool."

Isaiah 53:6 says, "All we like sheep have gone astray; we have turned every one to his own way; and the LORD hath laid on him the iniquity of us all."

And perhaps the best-known verse in all the Bible, John 3:16, says, "For God so loved the world, that he gave his only begotten Son, that whosoever believeth in him should not perish, but have everlasting life."

But paying the penalty of man's sin is not all that Christ accomplished at the cross. In addition, He reconciled men to God.

Christ's work of reconciliation was all the more amazing because He did it for unwilling men. Paul wrote in Romans 5:6-8, "For when we were yet without strength, in due time Christ died for the ungodly. For scarcely for a righteous man will one die: yet peradventure for a good man some would even dare to die. But God commendeth his love toward us, in that, while we were yet sinners, Christ died for us."

It is not as if sinful man wanted to come to God but could not. Clearly, man in his sin was voluntarily at enmity with God, not desiring to be reconciled. But God's love reached beyond man's sin, and in the cross, He brought us to Himself in love and mercy.

C. I. Scofield once wrote, "God was not changed, for He had always loved the world; nor was the world changed, for it continued in sinful rebellion against God. But by the death of Christ the relationship between God and the world was changed." God took away the wall between Himself and man the day Christ died.

For centuries a curtain had hung first in the Tabernacle and later in the Temple to separate the middle court from the Holy of Holies. That veil symbolized the limited access man had to God. No one was allowed to enter that room beyond the veil except the high priest on the Day of Atonement. But on the day Christ died, Matthew tells us, "The vail of the temple was rent in twain from the top to the bottom" (Matthew 27:51). The way it was torn signifies that the rending was an act of God, not man.

Truly, Christ died for our sins according to the Scriptures.

Have you been reconciled to God? Have you put your faith in Christ and His work on the cross for you? He offers you the gift of eternal life. You cannot earn it yourself. But Christ has already purchased it for you on the cross. Will you trust Him and receive His gift?

TEN

The Three Rs of the Atonement

Educators have long disagreed about whether education ought to concentrate on the fundamentals—the "three Rs," reading, 'riting, and 'rithmetic, as they are often referred to—or on less basic subjects with the hope that the fundamentals would be assimilated on the way. For the past decade or two, those who deemphasize the fundamentals have by and large had their way in public education. The test scores of children indicate that they have not assimilated the ability to read and write and figure mathematical problems. Students are having trouble with the "three Rs," and educators now seem to be swinging back to the practice of teaching the basics.

Spiritually too, we have deemphasized the basics in the past few years, and the average churchgoer shows it in his lack of understanding of important spiritual issues. Words like *propitiation, sanctification, inspiration,* and *perdition* are misunderstood by or meaningless to many church members.

Even a crucial issue like atonement is vastly misunderstood, and few people, if pressed, could give an adequate definition of the term. I would like to examine the three Rs of the atonement—three significant benefits man receives from Christ's work for us on the cross.

The first is redemption. Redemption comes from a Greek word that is sometimes translated "ransom." It means "a payment." To a first-century Greek, the term *redemption* suggested a payment to free a slave. If a slave could obtain enough money to buy his freedom, that was called "redemption."

Did you know that Jesus' death on the cross was actually a payment of ransom? When He died for us, He paid the price to free us from the slavery of sin. Romans 6:23 says, "The wages of sin is death." Verse 7 of that same chapter says, "For he that is dead is freed from sin."

Death is the only price that can free a man from sin, and the Lord Jesus paid that price for us all. He paid the ransom for us. Jesus said, "The Son of man came . . . to give his life a ransom for many" (Mark 10:45). First Timothy 2:6 says that Christ "gave himself a ransom for all."

Notice that Christ's redemption is for all. No one is excluded from the redemption that Christ obtained in His death. The invitation for salvation is open to anyone. "Whosoever will" can drink of the water of life freely (Revelation 22:17). There are no restrictions based on race, sex, age, intelligence, health, or any other qualifications.

How can one man's death be a ransom for so many? The answer to that lies in an understanding of who Jesus is. Notice that Jesus said, "The Son of man *came.*" Where did He come from? In John 6:38 He says, "I came down from heaven."

Neither you nor I can claim to have come down from heaven. We were born, and that was the beginning of our independent existence. But not Jesus. He existed before He was born. In what form? In the form of God. Philippians 2:6 says that He was in the form of God but that He considered equality with God not a thing to be grasped.

Yes, Jesus is God. And Philippians 2:7 goes on to tell us

that He "took upon him the form of a servant, and was made in the likeness of men." He was born as a baby here on earth, born of a virgin mother in a small town and into a poor family. And He lived His entire life without any sin whatsoever. Near the end of His life He was able to ask, "Which of you convinceth me of sin?" (John 8:46), and no one could answer. He said, "The prince of this world [Satan] cometh, and hath nothing in me" (John 14:30).

One of His closest associates said about him, "[He] did no sin, neither was guile found in his mouth" (1 Peter 2:22). He was "holy, harmless, undefiled, separate from sinners" (Hebrews 7:26). His righteousness was pure righteousness, and He never once committed even the smallest sin.

The death of this sinless One, who was God in the flesh, was more than sufficient to pay for the sins of all men. His righteousness more than outweighed the sins of man from the beginning of the world through eternity future. He alone could have made the sacrifice, and in His perfect love He did.

Nothing is left for man to do but believe. "For by grace are ye saved through faith; and that not of yourselves: it is the gift of God: not of works, lest any man should boast" (Ephesians 2:8-9). Anything that we could try to add to the work of Christ's redemption would be sin. We can only receive by faith the gift of salvation that Christ's redemption made available to every man.

But to whom was the ransom paid? To God. There are those who think that the ransom for our sins was paid by Christ to Satan. But the Bible does not teach that Christ ever paid anything to Satan. Satan did not demand a payment for sin.

God did. Why? If God loved sinners and wanted them to have eternal life, why could He not simply pardon them? Why could He not just overlook their sin and accept them into His fellowship in spite of it? Because God is perfectly holy, and He cannot tolerate sin. Because He is perfectly just, He must demand a payment for sin.

He elected to make the payment for sin Himself in the person of His Son, the Lord Jesus. It is as if a judge assessed a fine in passing sentence on a crime and then stepped down from the bench and paid the fine himself. It is as if a landlord paid the rent for all his tenants. But it is even more wonderful than that. Almighty God has paid the ransom to redeem us from sin.

You might ask, "In what sense are we free from sin? Does this mean that a believer never sins?" No, but every believer is freed from the slavery of sin in four ways.

First, he is free from the *penalty* of sin, which is death. "Verily, verily, I say unto you," says Jesus in John 5:24, "He that heareth my word, and believeth on him that sent me, hath everlasting life, and shall not come into condemnation; but is passed from death unto life."

Second, he is free from the *power* of sin. "For sin shall not have dominion over you: for ye are not under the law, but under grace." says Romans 6:14. No Christian has to be bound to any habitual sin, sinful attitude, or evil activity.

Third, he can be free from the *practice* of sin in his daily life. As the Christian grows spiritually he becomes more and more like the Lord Jesus. He becomes more sensitive to sin in his life and less inclined to do the sinful things he loved to do before.

Finally, he will be free from the *presence* of sin. First John 3:2 says, "Beloved, now are we the sons of God, and it doth not yet appear what we shall be: but we know that, when he shall appear, we shall be like him; for we shall see him as he is." First Thessalonians 4:17 speaks of the same event: "And so shall we ever be with the Lord." Each Christian has the promise that one day he will see the Lord Jesus and be transformed to be like Him and with Him throughout eternity, free from the presence of sin.

And that is when our redemption reaches its fruition. Paul wrote to the Romans, "Even we ourselves groan within ourselves, waiting for the adoption, to wit, the redemption of our body" (Romans 8:23). Even our bodies are redeemed, freed from the curse of sin.

RECONCILIATION

The second R of the atonement is reconciliation. When we think of reconciliation we usually think in terms of two marriage partners who have separated but are getting back together. *Reconciliation* means, "a settling of differences, a bringing together of two conflicting sides."

Man's sin built a wall of separation between him and God. God, a holy and perfectly righteous being, cannot tolerate the presence of sin. Sin is contrary to His nature. Man's decision to sin was a decision to be at enmity with God. Man had declared war.

But that did not change God's love for man. Although God in His perfect righteousness could not tolerate sin, He was not willing to stay at enmity with man. He could not simply overlook sin, so He paid for it Himself in the Person of the Lord Jesus. In that way He was able to declare man righteous without sacrificing His own righteousness.

As a sinless being the Lord Jesus would not have had to suffer the penalty and punishment for sin. But since He did, and He was "made . . . to be sin for us, who knew no sin," we can "be made the righteousness of God in him" (2 Corinthians 5:21). And now God can be "just, and the justifier of him which believeth in Jesus" (Romans 3:26).

Romans 5:1 says, "Therefore being justified by faith, we have peace with God through our Lord Jesus Christ." God made a way for peace instead of enmity, and He did it for unwilling man. "When we were enemies, we were reconciled to God through the death of his Son," says Romans 5:10.

Do you sense the love and mercy of God? Despite man's sin, despite his hatred for God, and despite his unwilling-ness to be reconciled, God poured out mercy instead of wrath, love instead of enmity, and peace instead of judg-ment. God has made reconciliation possible.

But the key to reconciliation is each individual's response to the Lord Jesus Christ. God has done His part. He has paid the ransom, and He has made reconciliation possible. But each individual must respond to Christ in faith. To each Christian is given the responsibility to witness, to be an ambassador of God's message of reconciliation.

Second Corinthians 5:18-20 says, "All things are of God, who hath reconciled us to himself by Jesus Christ, and hath given to us the ministry of reconciliation; to wit, that God was in Christ, reconciling the world unto himself . . . and hath committed unto us the word of reconciliation. Now then we are ambassadors for Christ, as though God did beseech you by us: we pray you in Christ's stead, be ye reconciled to God."

That means that when a believer declares the gospel, he is speaking for God. He is involved in the ministry of recon-ciliation.

RESURRECTION

The third R of the atonement is resurrection. Without the resurrection there is no meaning to the atonement. Paul wrote in 1 Corinthians 15:17, "If Christ be not raised, your faith is vain; ye are yet in your sins."

The resurrection is the heart of the gospel. "That he rose again the third day according to the scriptures" (1 Corinthi-ans 15:4) was central in the apostles' preaching—and with good reason.

It is the resurrection of Christ that gives us the assurance that the atonement was accepted by God. The resurrection was the Holy Spirit's seal of approval on the work of Christ. Paul wrote to the Romans that Christ was "declared to be the son of God with power, according to the spirit of holiness, by the resurrection of the dead" (Romans 1:4).

And it is the resurrection of Christ that gives us the assurance of eternal life. "If in this life only we have hope in Christ," wrote Paul in 1 Corinthians 15:19-21, "we are of all men most miserable. But now is Christ risen from the dead, and become the firstfruits of them that slept. For since by man came death, by man came also the resurrection of the dead."

Christ's resurrection is the proof that all believers will rise from the dead. It is the source of hope and great confidence for those who have lost loved ones in the Lord. But even more important, it is the power for a transformed life.

The apostle Paul wrote to the Philippians that his great desire was "That I may know him, and the power of his resurrection" (Philippians 3:10). Why? Because Paul understood that resurrection power is the key to a transformed life. It is the life of the resurrected Christ in an individual that enables him to fulfill God's righteousness.

In Galatians 2:20 Paul wrote, "I am crucified with Christ: nevertheless I live; yet not I, but Christ liveth in me: and the life which I now live in the flesh I live by the faith of the Son of God." The resurrected Christ was the source of his power for living.

In his epistle to the Romans, Paul stressed the same truth. "As Christ was raised up from the dead by the glory of the Father, even so we also should walk in newness of life" (Romans 6:4).

Let me ask you personally, Is that power at work in your life? Are you walking in newness of life, experiencing the three Rs of the atonement?

Unfortunately most people miss the entire point of the

atonement. Christ's death on the cross was a substitutionary atonement, a vicarious payment of the price of redemption on our behalf. There is nothing we can do to add to His work. No good work, no religious ceremony we can perform can add one iota to our salvation. We can not atone for our own sin. Christ has done it already.

But the average person feels he must do something to earn his salvation. Most people will say that they are hoping for God's favor because of the moral principles they have followed, such as the Ten Commandments or the Sermon on the Mount. Or they will say that they believe their religion makes them acceptable with God. But all those things fall short of what Christ has done for us already.

He has redeemed us. He has reconciled us to God. He has assured our resurrection from the dead. Those are the three Rs of the atonement, and no man can add to them or take away from them in any way.

Have you been reconciled to God? Have you received His gift of eternal life and redemption in Christ? Are you walking in the power of His resurrection? If not, you need to come to Him in faith.

ELEVEN

The Real Meaning
of the Resurrection

A broken man sat in the ruins of his home. His earthly possessions had been destroyed, the lives of his children had been snuffed out by tragedy, and his body was wracked with pain. As he viewed the remains of his once happy home, he pondered the question, "If a man die, shall he live again?" (Job 14:14). The man was Job, and his question has been asked by people throughout the centuries.

Death is inescapable. It comes to us from the battlefields of the world, from our streets and highways, and even from our own neighborhoods. Death is a fact of life. It touches all our families and eventually claims us all.

Despite that fact, death is a subject about which many of us feel uncomfortable. Our society reflects a widespread fear of death. People cannot face the fact that death is a reality.

The Bible has much to say about death. "It is appointed unto men once to die," says Hebrews 9:27. First Peter 1:24 says, "For all flesh is as grass, and all the glory of man as the flower of grass. The grass withereth, and the flower thereof falleth away."

Not everything the Bible has to say about the subject of death is grim. The Bible tells the story of how death is conquered. Jesus said, "I am the resurrection, and the life: he that believeth in me, though he were dead, yet shall he live: and whosoever liveth and believeth in me shall never die" (John 11:25-26).

The resurrection was the heart of the apostles' preaching. Belief in the resurrection of the human body was unusual in the first century; the Greeks accepted the immortality of the soul but not the idea of bodily resurrection, and even the Sadducees, a sect of the Jews, bitterly opposed the idea of resurrection. But whenever the apostles preached, their message was that Christ was risen from the dead.

Acts 17 tells of Paul's ministry in the city of Athens. He preached to the intellectuals of the city at Mars' hill. Verses 32-34 tell us of three dramatically different responses he received from those who heard him. "And when they heard of the resurrection of the dead, some mocked: and others said, We will hear thee again of this matter. So Paul departed from among them. Howbeit certain men clave unto him, and believed."

Those three responses—mocking, procrastination, and belief—are common attitudes toward the resurrection today. But it is my conviction that the only reasonable response to the Bible's teaching of the resurrection is the latter—absolute faith. There are three ways a believer can look at the resurrection of Jesus Christ.

THE OBJECT OF FAITH

First, *it is the object of his faith.* In fact, without the resurrection faith is meaningless. Paul says in 1 Corinthians 15:14, "If Christ be not risen, then is our preaching vain, and your faith is also vain."

That Jesus was raised from the dead is the basic message of the gospel, as Paul wrote in 1 Corinthians 15:3-4. "For I delivered unto you first of all that which I also received, how that Christ died for our sins according to the scriptures; and that he was buried, and that he rose again the third day according to the scriptures."

These are facts, not suppositions. The details surrounding the resurrection of Jesus Christ are among the best attested to in all history. Paul goes on to name several eyewitnesses to the resurrection. "He was seen of Cephas, then of the twelve: after that, he was seen of above five hundred brethren at once. . . . After that, he was seen of James; then of all the apostles" (vv. 4-7).

Christ had been laid in a sealed tomb with a Roman military guard placed outside. His body simply could not have been stolen, as some have suggested. It would have taken several men to move the stone, and anyone doing that would be committing a capital crime against the Roman government. Pilate himself had ordered the guard because he had been told Christ's words that He would rise from the dead (Matthew 27:63-65).

In fact, the soldiers themselves disseminated the story that they had been asleep and the disciples had stolen the body (Matthew 28:13). If they had truly been asleep, they could not have known what had happened. Their lie was a cover-up that they could have paid for with their lives if it were not for the collaboration of some of the chief priests (Matthew 28:14). No, there is no good way to explain the empty tomb apart from the fact that Jesus truly rose from the dead.

The eyewitness testimony is even more difficult to explain. How could all those people have been deceived? The character of the witnesses to Jesus' resurrection is well-known. The apostles had the highest moral standards and were not the kind of men who would or could conspire together to perpetuate such an incredible lie.

And they were not the only witnesses to Jesus' resurrection. He was seen, Paul tells us, by more than five hundred people at once on at least one occasion. He was seen by

Thomas, a man who was unwilling to believe the accounts of the other apostles. He was seen on scores of occasions by scores of different people under circumstances that varied and in situations that were inadequately explained by trickery, hallucination, or hysteria. He appeared to people for extended lengths of time, held conversations with them, ate with them, walked distances with them, and encouraged them to touch Him to test His reality. In each case the conclusion of the eyewitnesses was the same: Jesus was alive from the dead.

And what of the other evidence of the resurrection? I am speaking of the transformed lives of those who saw Him. Men such as Peter, who a short time before was cowering in fear, saw the risen Christ and preached a magnificently courageous sermon on the Day of Pentecost. Those men had only days before been crushed, defeated, discouraged, and afraid. Now they were totally changed. In the face of almost certain death they went out and boldly preached Christ's resurrection everywhere. The only explanation for their actions is that they knew Jesus was indeed alive.

Saul of Tarsus was completely transformed by a vision of the resurrected Christ. Previously he had been a persecutor, and his personal goal was to stamp out Christianity wherever he could find it. Now he was the main evangelist and missionary to the Gentile world, establishing churches and writing epistles that speak to us with power today.

Yes, the resurrection of Jesus Christ stands as a solid object for the believer's faith. The famous Greek scholar Bishop Westcott said, "Taking all the evidence together, it is not too much to say that there is no single historic incident better or more variously supported than the resurrection of Jesus Christ."

THE SOURCE OF HOPE

The believer also sees the resurrection of Jesus Christ as the source of his hope. Paul wrote, "If in this life only we have hope in Christ, we are of all men most miserable. But now is Christ risen from the dead, and become the firstfruits of them that slept" (1 Corinthians 15:20).

Christ's resurrection is the believer's assurance that he too will one day live in a resurrection body. It is a source of comfort in the knowledge that those who have died in Christ will one day be raised in Him. It is the basis for our confidence that the last enemy—death—will be destroyed.

For the child of God, death is not the end. Death is not a black, blank nothingness. Jesus promised His disciples, "Because I live, ye shall live also" (John 14:19). Only the believer in Christ can face the ultimate future with certainty and with a spirit of optimism. Christ's resurrection has assured our resurrection. The broken seal on the tomb established the seal on God's promise of eternal life.

And that is why the resurrection is so inseparably linked with the gospel. Paul wrote in 1 Corinthians 15:17-18, "And if Christ be not raised, your faith is vain; ye are yet in your sins. Then they also which are fallen asleep in Christ are perished." There is no hope without the fact of the resurrection.

Germany's Count Bismarck is said to have remarked, "Without the hope of eternal life, this life is not worth the effort of getting dressed in the morning." There is a great deal of truth in that statement. "For what is your life?" asks James, "It is even a vapour, that appeareth for a little time, and then vanisheth away" (James 4:14).

Job knew something of the brevity and futility of life. "My days are swifter than a weaver's shuttle," he said, "and are spent without hope" (Job 7:6). "Man that is born of a woman is of few days, and full of trouble. He cometh forth like a flower, and is cut down: he fleeth also as a shadow, and continueth not" (Job 14:1-2).

Isaiah wrote, "All flesh is grass, and all the goodliness

549

thereof is as the flower of the field: the grass withereth, the flower fadeth" (Isaiah 40:6-7).

Yes, this life is brief and full of sorrows. And if our existence ends with the grave, what is the use? That is what Paul meant when he wrote in 1 Corinthians 15:19, "If in this life only we have hope in Christ, we are of all men most miserable." But the hope that Jesus gives goes beyond the grave, and His resurrection is the proof of it.

Paul goes on to say, "But now is Christ risen from the dead, and become the firstfruits of them that slept" (v. 20). He is the firstfruits. The harvest is yet to come. All who put their trust in Him will be a part of that great harvest of souls that will rise from the dead.

In Glendale, California, at Forest Lawn Cemetery hundreds of people each year stand before two huge paintings. One pictures the crucifixion of Christ. The other depicts His resurrection. In the second painting the artist has pictured an empty tomb with an angel near the entrance. In the foreground stands the figure of the risen Christ. But the striking feature of that huge canvas is a vast throng of people, back in the misty background, stretching into the distance and out of sight, suggesting the multitude who will be raised from the dead because Jesus first died and rose for them.

Yes, there is hope. Jesus has died and risen again, and He offers eternal life to those who trust Him. His resurrection is the source of the believer's hope.

THE PROOF OF LOVE

Finally, *the believer sees the resurrection of Jesus Christ as the ultimate proof of God's love.* John 3:16 is perhaps the most familiar verse in all the Bible. "For God so loved the world, that he gave his only begotten Son, that whosoever believeth in him should not perish, but have everlasting life."

Christ died for us as a sacrifice to pay the price of our sin. And the resurrection was God's loving stamp of approval on Christ's redemptive work. "For since by man came death, by man came also the resurrection of the dead. For as in Adam all die, even so in Christ shall all be made alive" (1 Corinthians 15:21-22).

Through the resurrection of Christ, God made it possible for all men to share eternal life with Him. He said, "Because I live, ye shall live also" (John 14:19).

Jesus' love for Lazarus was visible even to the doubters. The shortest verse in our Bible, John 11:35, says, "Jesus wept." He was weeping at Lazarus's death. "Behold how he loved him!" said the Jews that were there (v. 36). But the ultimate proof of His love for Lazarus was not in His tears. It was in what He did for Lazarus. He raised him from the dead.

"I am the resurrection and the life," He said on that occasion (v. 25-26). "He that believeth in me, though he were dead, yet shall he live: and whosoever liveth and believeth in me shall never die."

Yes, God loves you. He sent his Son to die on the cross for you. And He confirmed His love for you by raising Christ from the dead. Now He offers to you eternal life. Will you accept it by faith?

First Corinthians 13:13 tells us that there are three great issues in the Christian life: faith, hope, and love. The resurrecton is the foundation of each of those three issues. It is the object of our faith. It is the source of our hope. And it is the proof of God's love to us.

What is your attitude to the resurrection? Do you doubt it? Or do you believe it with all your heart?

You must have Christ! No power within you can overcome the bonds of death. But Jesus already has, and He promises you the gift of eternal life. Will you put your trust in Him today?

TWELVE

God Loves the Church

What is wrong with the church today? Why is it not making a greater impact upon our world? Is the church dying?

Those questions are being asked repeatedly as clergy and laymen view the sagging conditions of organized religion. Critics suggest that the church is outdated, a played-out institution, and although recent attendance figures might be used to refute that claim it would have to be conceded that the church does not seem to be doing the job it should be doing.

Friends and foes alike have suggested that the church is failing to meet the spiritual needs of the nation. Parachurch organizations have flourished in the past two decades, and many of those organizations publish their own magazines, do missionary work, evangelize, and baptize believers. "The electronic church" is a term coined to describe the multitude of religious broadcasts on radio and television, and the evidence suggests that many people are staying home from their local churches to worship via the airwaves.

Why is it that many churches seem to be failing? Many churches have confused theology and a lack of commitment to biblical truth. In the midst of an increasingly secular society, those churches have lost their identity and their voice. They have indeed failed to meet the spiritual needs of an amoral age. But I would like to suggest that such churches are not really churches at all.

What is a church, anyway? It is not the building, although we often refer to the building where a church meets as the church. A *church* is a group of believers organized with leaders in the biblical offices of elders and deacons, committed together to the ministry of the Word of God.

We often refer to such an organization as a "local church" to distinguish it from the universal church, which is the group of all believers since Pentecost. But by and large, whenever the word *church* is used in the New Testament, it refers to a specific local church. It is my conviction that the local church is God's main instrument for accomplishing His work in this age.

The local church should be seen as part of the universal church, not distinct from it. The first epistle to the Corinthians begins with these words: "Unto the church of God which is at Corinth, to them that are sanctified in Christ Jesus, called to be saints, with all that in every place call upon the name of Jesus Christ our Lord" (1 Corinthians 1:2). The first half of that verse describes the local church at Corinth, and the second half describes the universal church.

P. T. Forsythe spoke of the local church as "the outcrop of the church universal." The local church is the only church that can send out missionaries, observe the Lord's Supper, baptize believers, and gather together for worship. Those who suggest that they can be "good Christians" without being a part of a local church are wrong. God's plan for the believer in this age includes the local church.

Christ died for the church. God loves the church. The Bible gives us three separate pictures of the church that demonstrate God's love for it as an institution.

A BUILDING

First, *the church is a building.* Christ said in Matthew 16:18, "Upon this rock I will build my church; and the gates of hell shall not prevail against it." Do not misunderstand. The church is not the building where believers meet to worship. It is a spiritual building—a temple—made up of the saints, with the Lord Jesus Himself the chief cornerstone.

Ephesians 2:19-22 says, "Now therefore ye are no more strangers and foreigners, but fellowcitizens with the saints, and of the household of God; and are built upon the foundation of the apostles and prophets, Jesus Christ himself being the chief corner stone; in whom all the building fitly framed together groweth unto an holy temple in the Lord: in whom ye also are builded together for an habitation of God through the Spirit."

So the church itself is the temple of God. It is the dwelling place of His Spirit. First Corinthians 3:16 says, "Know ye not that ye are the temple of God, and that the Spirit of God dwelleth in you?"

The Israelites in the wilderness were instructed by God to build the Tabernacle, a movable place of worship. When it was completed according to God's instructions, God Himself moved in. His visible glory, known as the *Shekinah,* was there as a manifestation of His presence. All worship and sacrifices were made at the Tabernacle, for that was the place of the presence of God.

Later a permanent place of worship, the Temple, was built. At its opening it too was filled with the visible manifestation of the presence of God. His glory filled the place, again signifying that it was the dwelling place of God.

But in the New Testament age, there is no man-made building where God dwells. Paul said in Acts 17:24, "God . . . dwelleth not in temples made with hands." His temple is the church, a new kind of building made without human hands. Paul described its construction in 1 Corinthians 3:10-11. "I have laid the foundation. . . ." he said. "But let every man take heed how he buildeth thereupon. For other foundation can no man lay than that is laid, which is Jesus Christ."

The first Temple, the Tabernacle, was made of cloth and animal skins. The second was made of stones and cedar. But God's present temple, the church, is made of people. And it too should be a visible manifestation of the glory and presence of God. Unbelievers ought to be able to look at Christians and see in them a display of the *Shekinah*.

A BODY

The church is also pictured in the New Testament as a body, the Body of Christ. Colossians 1:18 says that Christ is "the head of the body, the church." As the body of which He is the head, the church looks to Christ for leadership, nourishment, protection, and a sense of unity of purpose.

The word *church* in our Bible is translated from the Greek word *ekklesia,* which is a compound of two words meaning "to call out." The church is a body of believers called out from the world to be members of His Body. In that sense, the church is an organism, not merely an organization. It is a living, growing, working body, and Christ is its head.

Just as our heads cannot be separated from our bodies without destroying the life, so it is with the church and Christ. The Head is inseparable from the Body. They are partakers of the same life. They work together as a unit. They are vitally connected.

Like the physical body, its members are different but all necessary—functionally separate but interdependent. Each church member has an individual function, a gift that is unique to him, abilities that other Christians may not possess. But he is no less or more a member of the Body than any other believer in Christ.

Do you see that? There is room for individuality in the body of Christ, but we are all working toward the same goal. There are many differing kinds of ministries, but ultimately we all are of one mind.

Paul instructed the Corinthians in the use of spiritual gifts. He pointed out that the Holy Spirit gives a multitude of gifts, "dividing to every man severally as he will. For as the body is one, and hath many members, and all the members of that one body, being many, are one body: so also is Christ" (1 Corinthians 12:11-12).

Paul uses the illustration to exhort the Corinthians to unity. "That there should be no schism in the body; but that the members should have the same care one for another. And whether one member suffer, all the members suffer with it; or one member be honoured, all the members rejoice with it" (vv. 25-26).

The responsibility of every church member is the same. We are to be united in purpose, in mind, in heart, in goals, and in care for one another. There is no room for pride or arrogance, and there is no room for inferiority complexes. "For the body is not one member, but many. If the foot shall say, Because I am not the hand, I am not of the body; is it therefore not of the body? And if the ear shall say, Because I am not the eye, I am not of the body; is it therefore not of the body? If the whole body were an eye, where were the hearing? If the whole were hearing, where were the smelling? But now hath God set the members every one of them in the body, as it hath pleased him. And if they were all one member, where were the body? But now are they many members, yet but one body. And the eye cannot say unto the hand, I have no need of thee: nor again the head to the feet, I have no need of you" (v. 14-21).

Each member of the Body of Christ has unique gifts and

ministries, because that is the way the body functions best. The diversity lends itself to unity. No member is less necessary than any other.

Members of the Body of Christ, are you performing your function in harmony with the rest of the body? Do not try to be like someone else. Do not try to imitate the gifts of another member of the Body. And do not fight against those who may differ slightly in function from you as long as they are united in purpose. Remember, diversity of function is just as important as unity of purpose.

Perhaps you are not a member of the Body. You are not "in Christ," as Paul says. "Therefore if any man be in Christ, he is a new creature: old things are passed away; behold, all things are become new" (2 Corinthians 5:17). I urge you to trust Christ this moment and become a new creation, a member of His Body, the church.

A BRIDE

A third picture of the church in the Scriptures is that of a bride. The church is the Bride of Christ. In Ephesians 5 Paul deals with the correct relationship of a husband and wife. In verse 32 he ends his discussion by saying, "This is a great mystery: but I speak concerning Christ and the church."

Throughout the New Testament the church is portrayed as pure, like a bride arrayed in white—obedient, submissive, responsive to the love and leadership of Christ.

The marriage relationship is holy, partly for that precise reason; it is a picture of the relationship between Christ and His church. It is a permanent relationship, a relationship based on love and trust and mutual sacrifice. It is a relationship of unity based on common goals and a shared commitment. And most of all, it is a relationship of purity.

As a building, the church is the dwelling place of God, and that speaks of the importance of holiness. As a body, the church is an organism of which Christ is head, and that speaks of the importance of unity. And as a bride, the church is married to Christ, and that speaks of the importance of purity.

Holiness, unity, and purity—those are the qualities emphasized in these three great pictures of the church. And if the church is indeed failing in her mission today, it is precisely in those areas that she is failing.

Holiness means separation from all that is evil or worldly or ungodly. And as God's temple, the church must be holy. Paul wrote in 2 Corinthians 6:16-17, "And what agreement hath the temple of God with idols? for ye are the temple of the living God; as God hath said, I will dwell in them, and walk in them; and I will be their God, and they shall be my people. Wherefore come out from among them and be ye separate, saith the Lord, and touch not the unclean thing; and I will receive you."

What a timely exhortation that is for today's churches! It is a call to separation, to holiness. It is a rebuke for our worldliness and compromise.

Many people today see the church as a center for social activities or as an organization to promote community welfare. But while the church may be legitimately engaged in those activities, it is first of all the temple of God. Worship should come before welfare, and holiness before activity. We are God's temple, and we must be holy.

Unity is yet another quality lacking in many of today's churches. Paul wrote to the Philippians, "Fulfil ye my joy, that ye be likeminded, having the same love, being of one accord, of one mind" (Philippians 2:2). We are one body, and a body can function properly only with a unified mind.

Disunity kills more churches than anything else. Churches divide over minor issues, doctrinal disputes, and personality conflicts. Occasionally church splits are necessary and justifiable. Most often they are not. If church members saw clearly the biblical concept that the church is a body, perhaps there would be more harmony in our churches. It is certain that a church that functions harmoniously as a body is a better testimony and can better fulfill its mission than a church where there is division.

Purity or the lack of it is the ultimate determiner of a church's effectiveness, validity, and usefulness to the Lord. I am speaking primarily of doctrinal purity. Doctrinal purity is as important to a church as chastity is to a bride. The church is the Bride of Christ, and its doctrinal purity is indispensable. When a church lets down its doctrinal standards, it begins to suffer in other areas as well. Missionary zeal wanes, the church's effectiveness in its community is diminished, and it is beset by defeat and failure in every area of ministry.

Why is the church failing? Perhaps we have lost sight of what the church really is. It is Christ's building. It is His Body. It is His Bride. It must then be holy, united, and pure.

Is the church dying? I am convinced that it is not. God loves the church. Christ gave His life for the church. The Holy Spirit will not leave His dwelling place, which is the church.

Some churches may die. Some denominations may fade as others gain prominence. But God always has His church, and there are churches that remain faithful to His Word and thrive.

Are you a member of the true church? I am not asking if your name is on a church roll. Are you a believer in Christ? Have you been baptized by the Holy Spirit into His Body? If not, I invite you to trust Him today. You may not feel anything, but the moment you put your faith in Christ, the Holy Spirit makes you a member of His Body, the church.

Perhaps you are a believer but have never been active in a local church. I urge you to be obedient to God in this matter. God has ordained the local church. It is His means of doing His work in this age. You should be active in a church that believes and obeys the Bible. You should be investing your time, your money, and your life in a sound, local church. Will you today purpose to be that kind of Christian? Jesus Christ gave Himself for the church. What will you do for the church?

THIRTEEN

The Promise of His Coming

The future is big business these days. Playwrights, scientists, historians, and politicians are making predictions about the future. *Time* magazine reported more than ten years ago that in excess of 1,200 daily newspapers in the United States were carrying astrology columns. The interest in astrology has mushroomed since then. At the beginning of every year newsstands are inundated with printed predictions of scores of popular psychics. People buy them and devour them to learn what the seers have to say about everything from national elections to the future of a favorite television series.

But interest in the future is not a new phenomenon. From the beginning of time people have had an obsession to know about the future. In the past, magicians, astrologers, seers, and witches were consulted to interpret dreams or discern the signs in the heavens. No less a leader than Julius Caesar placed great confidence in astrology as he ruled the Roman empire. In fact most rulers in ancient times depended on astrologers to counsel them.

It is my conviction that the only source of authoritative prophecy is the Bible. And almost one-third of the Bible is predictive prophecy, dealing with future events. The focus of all biblical prophecy is the return of the Lord Jesus Christ.

The fact that the Bible deals so much with predictive prophecy tells us plainly that God intends and expects His children to be informed about the future. Yet in spite of that, there really is a dearth of genuine interest in Bible prophecy. There are hobbyists who like to study and discuss and speculate about Bible prophecy, but I am apalled at the lack of sincere interest in Christ's coming, motivated by concern rather than by mere curiosity.

You see, the Lord's return and the Bible's prophecies of the end times are meant to be an encouragement to us. Jesus' second coming should motivate us to a deeper commitment and a greater obedience. That is the way it was in the early church.

Dr. James Denny said, "The bloom of beauty on apostolic Christianity was created by the upward look." The early Christians lived in the atmosphere and glow of expectation of the imminent return of Christ. Their whole life-style was that of enthusiastic witness and holy anticipation.

The Christian who truly looks for the return of the Lord will live a transformed life. He will have no time for the trivial diversions that waste so much of the valuable time of most people. His life will be different in at least four ways.

HIS WORSHIP

First, *his worship will be different.* The believer that looks for Christ's return will be faithful in meeting with fellow believers for worship. The writer of the book of Hebrews called for faithfulness in the light of Christ's return. "Not forsaking the assembling of ourselves together, as the manner of some is; but exhorting one another: and so much the more, as ye see the day approaching" (Hebrews 10:25).

What approaching day is he speaking of that should

motivate us to be more diligent in our worship? The Day of the Lord. Most Bible students understand that to mean the period of time that begins with Christ's return for His saints.

Why should the approaching of the Day of the Lord make a believer want to be more faithful in assembling together with the saints for worship? First, as we approach the end of this age, the world is becoming increasingly hostile to believers and their values. Christians need fellowship with each other and with the Lord. We as believers must have that sense of unity and fellowship that only mutual worship can bring.

In addition, the certainty of the Lord's return makes the believer more aware that this age and its values are not lasting and not fulfilling. He has priorities that differ from those of the world, and worship with fellow believers is one of his priorities.

I am not suggesting that church attendance is a requirement for salvation. It is possible—technically—to be a Christian without attending church. Many of the finest Christians I know about are shut-ins and cannot attend church. But I am convinced that God's plan for believers includes fellowship in a local church, if they are at all able to attend.

Much has been written and said about what is called "the electronic church," referring to the large numbers of religious radio and television broadcasts. The name itself is misleading. It implies that watching a church service on television or listening to a broadcast on the radio is a substitute for attending in person. But the electronic church is really no church at all. You cannot have real fellowship through a television screen. You cannot be visited in the hospital by a pastor who is hundreds of miles away. You cannot support such a work by teaching Sunday school, helping in the nursery, or participating in a work day.

Do not misunderstand. Christian broadcasting has its value. I have been involved for many years in Christian radio, and I am convinced that it is one of the most effective ways we have of spreading the gospel of Christ. But it is an auxiliary of the local church, not a substitute.

His Work

Second, *the work of the believer who is looking for the return of Christ will be different.* He is looking to the future, and he knows that his labor for the Lord will be rewarded. Paul wrote to the Corinthians, "Therefore, my beloved brethren, be ye stedfast, unmoveable, always abounding in the work of the Lord, forasmuch as ye know that your labour is not in vain in the Lord" (1 Corinthians 15:58).

Yes, we know that our labor in the Lord and for Him is not in vain. It is bearing fruit now, and it will be rewarded at the judgment. In that same epistle Paul wrote about the judgment of believers' works. "Every man's work shall be made manifest: for the day shall declare it, because it shall be revealed by fire; and the fire shall try every man's work of what sort it is. If any man's work abide which he hath built thereupon, he shall receive a reward" (1 Corinthians 3:13-14). The "day" in that passage again refers to the Day of the Lord, which shall immediately follow Christ's return for His church.

James also ties together the coming of the Lord and judgment for believers. In James 5:8 he says, "Be ye also patient . . . for the coming of the Lord draweth nigh." In verse 9, he writes, "Behold, the judge standeth before the door."

Yes, there is coming a day of reckoning, and God wants us to be encouraged by that fact. We are going to be rewarded for our labor in the Lord. Is that not a powerful motivation to work more for Him, to work harder for Him, and to work more consistently for Him?

There is another fact that motivates to work the believer who looks for Christ's return, and that is the realization that there is not much time. Jesus said, "I must work the works of him that sent me, while it is day: the night cometh, when no man can work" (John 9:4). Of course Jesus was speaking of the fact that His time of ministry was limited. He knew that He was going to be crucified. But the same principle holds true for the Christian who is looking for the return of Christ. In fact, we sing a gospel song entitled "Work, for the Night Is Coming," which speaks of the same truth. Our time is limited. Jesus is coming. The time to work for Him is now.

HIS WITNESS

A third difference in the believer who looks for Christ is closely related to that of his work. *His witness will be different* as well. Because he knows there is not much time, his witnessing for Christ will be marked by a sense of urgency. His appeal will be an urgent one. His concern will be for those who may be left behind when Christ returns for His saints.

The next event on God's prophetic calendar is what Bible students refer to as the rapture. That is the return of Jesus Christ to meet His saints in the air. Paul describes it in 1 Thessalonians 4:16-17: "For the Lord himself shall descend from heaven with a shout, with the voice of the archangel, and with the trump of God: and the dead in Christ shall rise first: then we which are alive and remain shall be caught up together with them in the clouds to meet the Lord in the air: and so shall we ever be with the Lord."

We who trust Christ will go to dwell in His presence forever, but those who do not know Him will be left behind. Most of us have loved ones who are unsaved. Do we understand the urgency of bringing them the message of salvation? Christ is coming. There is not much time.

Finally, *the believer's walk is different when he realizes the truth of the Lord's imminent return.* I am speaking of the way he conducts his life, the way he confronts his spiritual responsibilities.

Paul wrote of the believer's walk in the light of Christ's return in Philippians 3:18-20. "For many walk, of whom I have told you often, and now tell you even weeping, that they are the enemies of the cross of Christ: whose end is destruction, whose God is their belly, and whose glory is in their shame, who mind earthly things. [But our citizenship] is in heaven; from whence also we look for the Saviour, the Lord Jesus Christ."

Paul was saying to the Philippians that they were preparing to meet the Lord face to face. Salvation had given them a new citizenship in heaven, and they were to be living the manner of life that represented heaven. Meanwhile they were to be looking for Christ's return.

These are not easy times. We live in a very confusing world. Things that once were almost universally viewed as wrong are now called "alternate life-styles" and widely accepted by society. Sin is a forgotten concept. Society is corrupt. But believers are members of a different society. They are citizens of heaven. And Christ's return is now closer than when Paul told the Philippians to look for it. His words are more relevant today than they ever have been. It is more important than ever that Christians live holy lives.

Some have taught that since this is the age of grace, believers are free to do as they wish. They wrongly assume that since we are not under the law we are not accountable for our behavior. But did you know that the teaching of grace is just the opposite?

Titus 2:11-13 says, "For the grace of God that bringeth salvation hath appeared to all men, teaching us that, denying ungodliness and worldly lusts, we should live soberly, righteously, and godly in this present world; looking for that blessed hope, and the glorious appearing of the great God and our Saviour Jesus Christ." Paul says that the teaching of grace is that we should live holy lives in the light of Christ's return.

What is it about the return of Christ that should motivate us to live "soberly, righteously, and godly in this present world?" We are preparing to meet Christ.

The apostle John indicates that the Christian life is a process of becoming more and more like Jesus Christ. "Beloved, now are we the sons of God, and it doth not yet appear what we shall be: but we know that, when he shall appear, we shall be like him; for we shall see him as he is" (1 John 3:2). John is saying that although none of us has yet attained the goal, we are progressing toward it, and we have the promise that when He comes, we will finally reach that goal of being like Him in character and in holiness.

And John goes on to write, "And every man that hath this hope in him purifieth himself, even as he is pure" (v. 3). He is saying that the greatest single motivation to purity is the knowledge that Christ, who alone is totally pure, is returning soon to receive His saints.

How soon will the Lord return? No one knows. Jesus said, "But of that day and hour knoweth no man, no, not the angels of heaven, but my Father only" (Matthew 24:36). But there are signs that His coming may be very near.

Are you ready for the return of the Lord? Have you received Him as Savior? If He should come today, will you be ready to meet Him?

Christian, is your life being transformed by the knowledge that Christ could return at any moment? Does it affect your worship? Your work? Your witness? Your walk?

The Bible hints that some believers will be ashamed at the Lord's return. There are those who, because they do not

569

really believe that the Lord's return is imminent, will not be ready to meet Him. "Be ye therefore ready also: for the Son of man cometh at an hour when ye think not" (Luke 12:40).

Watch, "Lest coming suddenly he find you sleeping" (Mark 13:36).

FOURTEEN

The Hope of Judgment

One of the famous tourist attractions of Europe was already a source of worry to its city fathers when Columbus set sail for America. I refer to the leaning tower of Pisa. The well-known tower was built with too shallow a foundation. Even before it was completed in 1350, it had already begun to tip.

Today the tower, which is 185 feet tall, leans some fifteen feet out of perpendicular, and its tilt is increasing at the rate of one-sixteenth of an inch each year.

A few years ago a government commission offered a prize for a usable plan to save the endangered structure. More than four thousand entries were offered. After sifting through them all, the commission announced that none of the suggestions could possibly be made to work. And so each day engineers measure the tilt, and unless the tilting stops, the tower will eventually fall, smashing to bits.

Many thoughtful people are convinced that the modern world is very much like the leaning tower. Civilization, they believe, is tipping more and more under the weight of moral decline, decadence, and world problems. And indeed, the evidence seems to support such a conclusion. Pollution, the population explosion, political conflicts, the energy crisis, unemployment, and perhaps a dozen other major problems threaten our very existence as a society.

It is easy to be a pessimist in a world like ours. Why is our world so dark? Why do we seem unable to rise above circumstances?

The Bible has the answers, and its outlook is not pessimistic, although it is realistic. The heart of the problem in our world is the problem of sin in the human heart. And man can rise above his sin through the Lord Jesus. He has died to redeem us from our sin. But we must trust Him in order to be saved. That is the gospel. It is truth. And a day is coming when every man will be judged on his response to the truth.

There are those who ask how an all-powerful and loving God could allow so much suffering and pain and heartache. They suggest that if there really was a righteous, omnipotent God, He would be morally obligated to stamp out such evil.

There is a God, and He is righteous and omnipotent; a day of reckoning is coming. In that day God will wipe out all evil forever. He delays that judgment now because of His love. He is dealing with mankind in grace and mercy in this age, bringing men to faith in Christ in order that they may be redeemed from their sin.

The knowledge that a day of judgment is coming is frightening to some, but it does not have to be. The promise of judgment is God's promise that this world will not have to go through misery and pain and suffering indefinitely. His judgment has already begun, and He will complete what He has started. Here is our ground for hope: God's judgment.

Let me suggest three facts about God's judgment that give believers great hope.

First, *judgment is certain.* Genuine certainties are rare in today's world. Possibilities abound, but certainties are few. But God's Word shows that a day of judgment is coming, and it is a certainty.

Why is judgment certain? Because of who and what God is. He is a holy God. The psalmist writes in Psalm 7:11, "God is angry with the wicked every day." In modern terminology, God never makes détente with sin.

Some sins are judged immediately. Others are judged later. But the great and final judgment is yet to come.

Paul wrote to the Galatians about the certainty of judgment. "Be not deceived; God is not mocked: for whatsoever a man soweth, that shall he also reap. For he that soweth to his flesh shall of the flesh reap corruption; but he that soweth to the Spirit shall of the Spirit reap life everlasting" (Galatians 6:7-8).

Do you see it? Sin and judgment are like sowing and reaping. The sin itself determines the judgment, just like the seed that is sown determines what is harvested. Sowing to the flesh, Paul says, is asking for a harvest of corruption. God may delay the judgment, but He will not be mocked. Judgment is coming for sure.

Satan has always tried to deny the certainty of judgment. God told Adam, "But of the tree of the knowledge of good and evil, thou shalt not eat of it: for in the day that thou eatest thereof thou shalt surely die" (Genesis 2:17). But Satan told Eve, "Ye shall not surely die: for God doth know that in the day ye eat thereof, then your eyes shall be opened, and ye shall be as gods, knowing good and evil" (Genesis 3:4-5).

Adam and Eve disobeyed, and they died spiritually that very day. Satan had lied. God's judgment was certain. The man and his wife had sown to the flesh, and they began to reap corruption. From that very day their bodies began to die. They were subject to sickness, aging, and, ultimately, death.

Yes, God's judgment is sure. And the assurance that judgment is coming is that Jesus Christ rose from the dead. Acts 17:31 says, "He hath appointed a day, in the which he will judge the world in righteousness by that man whom he hath ordained; whereof he hath given assurance unto all men, in that he hath raised him from the dead." Judgment is as certain as the resurrection of Jesus Christ.

You see, Jesus is the judge. He said, "The Father judgeth no man, but hath committed all judgment unto the Son" (John 5:22). And His resurrection from the dead is the proof that judgment is coming, because the resurrection signified victory over sin. His crucifixion was the decisive battle with sin and death and Satan, and His resurrection was the proof of victory. As the victor, He becomes the judge.

How certain is judgment? It is as certain as God's Word, and God's Word cannot be broken (John 10:35).

JUDGMENT IS NEAR

A second fact about the judgment that makes it an encouragement to believers is that it is near. Jesus told His disciples that when the Holy Spirit would come, He would convict the world "of judgment, because the prince of this world is judged" (John 16:11). He was saying that judgment has already begun. Satan himself has been judged. He was judged and defeated at the cross of Christ.

How near is judgment? Of course no one knows. But several warnings in the Scriptures advise us to regard it as very near. The last chapter in the Bible includes this warning: "The time is at hand. He that is unjust, let him be unjust still: and he which is filthy, let him be filthy still: and he that is righteous, let him be righteous still: and he that is holy, let him be holy still" (Revelation 22:10-11). The apostle John is saying that judgment will not alter a person's character. If he is filthy, he will remain filthy; if he is holy, he will remain holy. And the judgment is at hand.

Peter wrote to the saints about the judgment. His message to believers was, "But the end of all things is at hand: be ye therefore sober, and watch unto prayer" (1 Peter 4:7). We must be alert and sober in light of the coming judgment.

James shared Peter's conviction that judgment was coming soon. In James 5:9 he wrote, "Behold, the judge standeth before the door."

Judgment is as close as the return of the Lord Jesus. Paul wrote to Timothy that the Lord Jesus Christ "shall judge the quick and the dead at his appearing and his kingdom" (2 Timothy 4:1). Jesus said, "Watch therefore, for ye know neither the day nor the hour wherein the Son of man cometh" (Matthew 25:13).

We are to be prepared for the judgment. It could be at any time. Why is that an encouragement to believers? Because we are looking for the return of the Lord Jesus. We are citizens of heaven, not of this world. And we have His promise that we will not come into condemnation (John 5:24). The judgment is not a fearful thing but a blessed hope.

JUDGMENT IS GOOD

Yes, judgment is certain. It is near. But consider a third fact. *Judgment is good.*

Most people think of God's judgment as a negative thing. Sermons on judgment are not popular. But God wants us to be encouraged by the knowledge that His judgment is good.

Believers do not need to fear condemnation. Jesus said, "He that believeth on him is not condemned" (John 3:18), and, "Verily verily, I say unto you, He that heareth my word, and believeth on him that sent me, hath everlasting life, and shall not come into condemnation; but is passed from death unto life" (John 5:24).

The Christian will not be judged to see if he is going to heaven or hell. His place in eternity is already determined. Christ bore his sins and his judgment on the cross, and his place in heaven is secure. He has already passed from death unto life. He will not come into condemnation.

But his works will be judged. They will be tested by fire at the judgment seat of Christ. Paul described that judgment in 1 Corinthians 3:13-15. "Every man's work shall be made manifest: for the day shall declare it, because it shall be revealed by fire; and the fire shall try every man's work of what sort it is. If any man's work abide which he hath built thereupon, he shall receive a reward. If any man's work shall be burned, he shall suffer loss: but he himself shall be saved; yet so as by fire."

Even the believer whose works are judged unworthy has the promise of no condemnation. ("He himself shall be saved; yet so as by fire.") For the believer whose works withstand the test of fire is the promise of rewards. Salvation, rewards—those are the results of God's judgment of believers.

But what about unbelievers? They are not judged at the judgment seat of Christ with believers. They will be judged at a judgment known as the great white throne judgment, described in Revelation 20:11-15. For them the results of judgment are different.

They too are judged according to their works, and when their names are not found in the book of life, they are cast into the lake of fire, a place of eternal punishment.

That is not a pleasant picture. But it does not alter the fact that God's judgment is good. Paul gives us several principles in Romans 2 that demonstrate why God's judgment is always good.

First, *God's judgment is according to truth.* Paul begins Romans 2 with a description of man's judgment. "Thou art inexcusable, O man . . . for thou that judgest doest the same things" (v. 1). Then he contrasts man's judgment with God's: "But we are sure that the judgment of God is according to truth against them which commit such things" (v. 2).

There is no hypocrisy, no inaccuracy, no falsehood in God's judgment. His judgment is righteous. His standards are perfect. He makes no mistakes. No one can claim unfairness at the judgment of God. His judgment is according to truth.

Second, *God's judgment is preceded by mercy.* Paul asks the question of every hypocrite, "Thinkest thou this, O man, that judgest them which do such things, and doest the same, that thou shalt escape the judgment of God? Or despisest thou the riches of his goodness and forbearance and longsuffering; not knowing that the goodness of God leadeth thee to repentance?" (v. 3-4).

God never judges but that He first shows mercy. Before God destroyed the world with a flood, He warned the people through Noah of the impending destruction. He was willing to spare Sodom and Gommorah for the sake of ten righteous men. And He will save anyone who turns to Christ in simple faith.

Do not misinterpret the goodness of God. It does not always signify His blessing. Some people allow themselves to be lulled into a false sense of security by thinking that God's goodness to them is His sign of approval and blessing on their lives. But Paul says that often the purpose of God's goodness is to lead a person to repentance.

Finally, *God's judgment is based on our works.* Do not be

fooled by those who tell you that works are unimportant. In every judgment the Bible describes, the criteria for judgment is the individuals' works. Believers are judged at the judgment seat of Christ for the quality of their works. Unbelievers are condemned at the great white throne judgment "according to their works" (Revelation 20:12).

In Romans 2 Paul says that God "will render to every man according to his deeds" (v. 6).

You ask, Doesn't the Bible say that a man cannot be saved by his works? Yes, it does. Titus 3:5 says, "Not by works of righteousness which we have done, but according to his mercy he saved us." Ephesians 2:8-9 says, "For by grace are ye saved through faith; and that not of yourselves: it is the gift of God: Not of works, lest any man should boast." Second Timothy 1:9 says that God has saved us and called us "not according to our works." Romans 4:5 says, "But to him that worketh not, but believeth on him that justifieth the ungodly, his faith is counted for righteousness."

This is God's principle: judgment is according to works, but justification is according to faith. The one who trusts Christ for salvation has his sins forgiven, and God has promised to remember them no more. He cannot be judged for his sins, because Christ has paid for them. They have been dealt with. They are under the blood of Chirst. They are as far from the believer as the east is from the west. He has been washed whiter than snow. He cannot be judged for them.

For what then is the believer judged? For his good works. They are judged not to determine if they are good works or bad works but to determine their quality. It is possible to do a good thing in the power of the flesh. And such a good work is like wood, hay, or stubble. It will not stand the test of fire.

But perhaps you are not a believer. Perhaps you believe

that if you can do enough good works, you will be judged worthy of eternal life. Look at what God says in Isaiah 64:6. "But we are all as an unclean thing, and all our righteousnesses are as filthy rags." That means that even the good things we try to do to earn favor with God are defiled in His eyes. It is not possible to earn salvation by works. It is not possible to please God with religious exercise and ceremonies and rituals. The only way for a man to be truly righteous is to receive God's righteousness by faith.

Have you been saved? Have you trusted Christ and had your sins forgiven? If you have not, you will be judged for them. You cannot atone for them yourself. You cannot do enough good to make up for them. "The wages of sin is death," says Romans 6:23.

But there is another side to that verse. "The gift of God is eternal life through Jesus Christ our Lord." God's judgment is always preceded by His mercy. And He is reaching out to you in loving mercy right now. Is God's judgment a fearful thing to you? Romans 8:1 says, "There is therefore now no condemnation to them which are in Christ Jesus." Trust Him and receive His gift of life right now.

Book 5

SPECIAL SERMONS
FOR
EVANGELISM

Special gratitude is extended to Phil Johnson, who has assisted me in research and editing.

ONE

What Must I Do to Be Saved?

No one gets to heaven by accident! Although salvation is a gift, it is not something we simply acquire along life's way. No one ever drifted to heaven.

Jesus said, "Except a man be born again, he cannot see the kingdom of God" (John 3:3). What did He mean? Simply that unless each individual undergoes a life-transforming experience of salvation, he will not get to heaven. Salvation is a prerequisite to heaven.

Perhaps you are wondering, How can a person be saved? It is not a new question, but it is a question more relevant and more important to modern man than perhaps any other question. It was first asked on a dark night in a jail in ancient Greece, but it comes to us through the ages with the same ringing urgency.

In Acts 16 we read the account of the apostle Paul's ministry to the city of Philippi. Paul and Silas were conducting a series of meetings in that town. A young girl who was demon-possessed and had an ugly reputation followed Paul and his group around, calling out, "These men are the servants of the most high God, which shew unto us the way of salvation" (Acts 16:17).

Because this girl sanctioned the ministry and message of Paul, the people turned away in disgust. Paul knew that something had to be done, and it had to be done right away. So in the name of Jesus, he turned to the girl and commanded the unclean spirit to come out of her. Immediately she was set free.

But there was a group of men who made money from the girl because the demon gave her the ability to tell fortunes. When the demon left the girl, their business was destroyed. The men stirred up the multitudes against Paul and Silas, dragged them to the magistrates, and falsely accused them. Paul and Silas were severely beaten and cast into the inner dungeon in the Philippian jail.

Acts 16:25 tells us that Paul and Silas sang at midnight. They "prayed, and sang praises unto God: and the prisoners heard them." It was midnight, not normally the hour of prayer, but they prayed. It was a dungeon, not the normal place of prayer, but they prayed. They had been severely beaten, and you would think they wouldn't have felt much like singing, but they sang praises unto God. It was a dark, dismal dungeon, with no choir or musical accompaniment, but they sang praises unto God.

Prayer is always in order. Praising God is also appropriate. And the prayers and praises of Paul and Silas reached to heaven. God heard and answered their prayers. Their singing pleased Him, and He seemed to say Amen.

The Scripture says that there was an earthquake. The ground started to shake, and the doors were sprung. The bars were twisted, the chains fell off, and Paul and Silas were free.

The jailer awoke. He drew his sword and was about to commit suicide, knowing that he would have to pay with his life anyway at the hands of brutal authorities if the prisoners had escaped. But Paul and Silas were still there; and Paul, led by the Spirit of God, said, "Do thyself no harm, for we are all here" (v. 28).

Touched by the testimony of the power of their God and the reality of their compassion, the jailer "came trembling, and fell down before Paul and Silas, and brought them out, and said, Sirs, what must I do to be saved?" (vv. 29-30).

Now let's consider that question for a minute. Let us examine it from three different perspectives.

A PERSONAL QUESTION

First of all, the jailer's question was a personal question. "What must I do?" (v. 29). He correctly perceived salvation as a personal matter. God deals with us on a personal basis. He deals with us primarily as individuals, not as races, or as nations, or as families.

You may be a number in the eyes of the government or your employer, but you are a much-loved individual in the sight of God. He created you as an individual, He gave His Son to die for you as an individual, and He loves you as an individual.

Notice how God opened the jailer's eyes to his spiritual need. He was in an earthquake, his prison was damaged, and his life seemed in jeopardy. He was at the end of himself. He was ready to take his own life.

God often uses such circumstances to speak to a heart. Man's extremity is God's opportunity. And man's extremity is also man's opportunity. I have lived long enough to discover that moments of catastrophe and calamity often mark the beginning of a brand-new start.

Some time ago a soldier in a wheelchair came up to me. He said, "Dr. Sweeting, I was stricken with polio while in the military."

Naturally, I responded with, "I'm sorry."

"Oh," he said, "you don't have to be sorry. I'm glad God permitted me to be afflicted because it was in my despair that a fellow soldier related the claims of Christ. I heard the knocking of God through my affliction. I opened my life to

Jesus Christ. If I had never been stricken, I would not have sensed my need."

My friend, that is too often how it must happen. God must allow us to be stricken before we can see our need. Many people never see that salvation is a personal, individual issue that must be considered personally, individually by each one of us.

The Philippian jailer had to come to the point where his very life was in danger before he asked the question, "What must *I* do to be saved?"

But saying that salvation is a personal issue does not mean that it is a private one. The keeper of the prison certainly did not have the attitude that the state of his soul was no one else's business.

D. L. Moody once stopped a man on the street to ask if he had trusted the Lord Jesus as his personal Savior.

"That is none of your business!" answered the man.

"Oh, but it is my business," replied Mr. Moody.

"Then you must be D. L. Moody," the man said.

Yes, salvation is a personal matter, but not a private one. If you are a Christian, make it your business to lovingly confront men and women with the claims of the Lord Jesus Christ. Many people will never see the need for personal salvation unless we tell them.

Have you responded personally to the claims of the gospel? Have you personally put your faith in the Lord Jesus as the One who died for you, personally, on the cross? Salvation is not just for the down and out. It is for the up and in, the in and around, the good, the bad, the religious, the indifferent, the poor, the wealthy. It is for everyone. No matter who you are, you must be born again.

An Urgent Question

But also notice that the jailer's question was an urgent one. The question of salvation always is.

I notice that the apostle Paul did not say, "Let's talk about it when the excitement is over." Can you sense the urgency of the situation? A massive earthquake, widespread confusion, a suicide attempt, and an opportunity to escape the prison all contributed to the excitement. But the only thing crucial in the mind of the apostle Paul was the salvation of the jailer.

Some time ago a man spoke to me about receiving Christ as Savior. I had just concluded an evangelistic service, in which I had emphasized the urgency of the Bible's invitation to sinners to trust Christ. The man told me that he knew that he should receive Christ as Savior, but, he said, he did not feel quite ready.

I spoke with him kindly and lovingly and sought to challenge him to trust Christ then and there, but he repeatedly told me that although he was sure that what I was saying was right, he simply was not ready to receive Christ. He left without changing his mind.

But that man who was in no hurry to trust Christ was in too much of a hurry to get to where he was going. That same night, while driving at an excessive speed, he lost control of his car on a treacherous road. The car turned over and burst into flames, and that man perished that night. Earlier in the evening, he had told me that he was not ready to trust Christ. All I could think about upon hearing of his death was that he was not ready to die, either.

How I wish that I had talked to him a little bit longer! How I wish that I had pressed on him the claims of Christ just a bit further! But I learned one important thing from that incident, and I have never forgotten it. The message of the gospel is urgent!

I do not preach but that I think that there may be someone present who will never again have an opportunity to respond to the invitation of Christ. I do not share the gospel personally with a person but that I recognize the very real possibility that he may never again be confronted with the gospel.

D. L. Moody preached in a Chicago assembly hall on October 8, 1871. His message, as always, had an evangelistic theme, and he closed it by saying, "I want you to take home the question 'What shall I do with Jesus?' and come back next week with your answer."

Even as the service was closing, a commotion could be heard outside the building. People were shouting, and fire engines were moving through the street. The fire that was to destroy the city of Chicago was beginning to spread.

Many of the people in the service that night perished in the fire. There never was another meeting in that hall, and D. L. Moody learned one of the greatest lessons of his life. Never again did he close a message without pressing the congregation with the urgency of the gospel's claims. He never forgot that night of the fire when he had sent the people home to think about the gospel without giving an invitation for them to trust Christ then and there. And from that time on, his preaching was characterized by a sense of urgency that gave emphasis to everything he said.

My dear friend, delay can be dangerous. The road marked *tomorrow* leads to the town of *never*. Tomorrow is not God's time, it is the adversary's time.

The jailer in Philippi had no desire to wait. Delay was the farthest thing from his mind. "What must I do to be saved?" he asked, trembling. He was anxious to be saved. He had just been through an earthquake that might have killed him; he might have been killed for allowing prisoners to escape; and if Paul had not stopped him, he would have killed himself. He had perfect understanding that there is no guarantee of tomorrow. The only time that is certain is right now. His question was an urgent one.

But the question "What must I do to be saved?" is also a vital one. There is no hope for any man apart from salvation through the Lord Jesus Christ. The Philippian jailer was a man who had absolutely run out of hope. He was on the verge of suicide. He saw nothing to live for, and was prepared to end it all right there.

You may not be on the verge of suicide, but if you have never trusted the Lord Jesus and been saved, you know something of the hopelessness of life. No man can save himself. Human works are futile to produce genuine righteousness, "for there is none other name under heaven given among men, whereby we must be saved" (Acts 4:12).

Notice Paul's answer to the jailer's question. He did not say, "You are going to have to change your environment. You will have to get out of this jail and start going to church."

He did not say, "You are going to have to try to make yourself better. You must clean yourself up, change your image."

No, Paul simply pointed the man to the Lord Jesus Christ. "Believe on the Lord Jesus Christ, and thou shalt be saved" (Acts 16:31).

There are two ingredients in salvation: repentance and faith. The jailer had repented. His attitude and question to Paul were proof of that. He came as a broken, trembling, repentant man and asked the way of salvation. He was turning from his sin and selfishness and wanted to know where to turn. That is repentance.

Paul directed him to turn toward the Lord Jesus. That is faith. Faith is committing yourself to the Lord Jesus. It is trusting Him, casting yourself completely on Him.

That is vastly different from a mere academic faith. Paul did not tell the jailer to believe the truth *about* Jesus. Demons have that kind of faith, and that kind of faith alone cannot save.

Paul spoke of the kind of faith that believes *"on* the Lord Jesus Christ." That is faith that abandons itself completely to the object.

A minister was trying to lead an elderly Scottish woman to Christ. Try as he might, he could not seem to communicate to her the meaning of believing.

Leaving the woman's house he had to cross a small brook that flowed in front of the house. He paused at the rickety looking bridge and then gingerly touched it with a toe. The woman, sensing his hesitation, called out, "Can ye nay lippen the bridge?" which, translated from the Scottish dialect, means, "Can't you put your full weight on the bridge?"

He had just the expression he needed. Immediately he went back to the woman. "Can ye nay lippen Jesus?" he asked. Can't you cast your full weight upon Jesus? Can't you trust Him? Can't you commit yourself to Him?

With that expression the woman understood what it meant to believe. She trusted the Lord Jesus, and her life was changed.

My friend, God calls, but you must answer. There is something you must do to be saved, and that is to believe.

I asked a man the simple question, "Are you a Christian?"

"No," he said, "I'm waiting for God to do something."

"God loves you," I replied. "Christ came into this world and died for your sins. When the Lord Jesus left this world, He sent the Holy Spirit, and He has called you and convicted you of your sins. God has done all that He is going to do. If you are ever to know God's salvation, You must respond. You must believe on the Lord Jesus Christ."

"What must I do to be saved?" Perhaps you are asking that question. The answer is the same for you as it was for the jailer at Philippi. You must believe on the Lord Jesus Christ. Will you do it today? You will never make a more important decision.

TWO

You Must Be Born Again

Yesterday a twenty-seven-year-old man sat in my office and said to me, "I am confused and mixed up. I have broken God's laws. I have lived contrary to His commandments. I thought I could get along without God. I made up my own rules, lived life my own way. But I failed. I would give anything to be able to go back, to start all over—to be born again."

I had the thrill of opening the Bible and sharing with him from God's Word about how he could indeed be born again.

According to John 3, the early ministry of Jesus attracted sensational attention, so much so that the Bible says, "Many believed in his name, when they saw the miracles which he did" (John 2:23). Nicodemus was one of those who had heard of the marvelous miracles the Lord was doing. He was a leader of the Jews, a respected teacher in Israel, and he came to the Lord Jesus at night, possibly to avoid detection.

Nicodemus began his conversation with a compliment and an especially wise observation. "Rabbi, we know that thou art a teacher come from God: for no man can do these miracles that thou doest, except God be with him" (John 3:2).

Nicodemus was very much like many people today who recognize Jesus as a great moral teacher, but do not see beyond that. The historian Klausner called Jesus the greatest moral teacher who ever lived, but nothing more! Others see him as a great religious leader, or as a teacher whose teaching methods were far ahead of His time.

But that is not enough. It is not enough to admire the Lord Jesus, or even to imitate Him. We must recognize that He is God and has authority to demand the right to be Lord of our lives. He is not simply a man, or even a great man. He is the God-man.

Jesus answered Nicodemus with a sledgehammer blow. "Verily, verily, I say unto thee, Except a man be born again, he cannot see the kingdom of God" (v. 3).

Born again? Perhaps your reaction is the same as Nicodemus's. He wondered how it was possible for a man to be reborn. Certainly it was not possible for a grown man to be born again in a physical sense. His mind was filled with questions.

Perhaps you have questions of your own about the new birth. I would like to examine four questions that people are asking today about the new birth.

WHAT IS THE NEW BIRTH?

What is the new birth? Look at Jesus' answer to Nicodemus. "That which is born of the flesh is flesh; and that which is born of the Spirit is spirit" (v. 6). The new birth is *a spiritual birth.* It has to do with a man's spirit, not his physical being. It is not a thing that can be observed with the eyes. Jesus said, "The wind bloweth where it listeth, and thou hearest the sound thereof, but canst not tell whence it cometh, and whither it goeth: so is everyone that is born of the Spirit" (v. 8).

The Lord was saying that the new birth is like the wind.

It cannot be seen or touched, but its effects are easily visible. That is because the new birth is *a new creating.* The apostle Paul put it this way, "Therefore if any man be in Christ, he is a new creature: old things are passed away; behold, all things are become new" (2 Corinthians 5:17).

And the apostle Paul knew all about it. Look at what we know of his life from the books of Acts. In 7:58 we see him as Saul of Tarsus, holding the coats of those who were stoning Stephen for his faith. In Acts 8:1-3, he is leading an attack against the church at Jerusalem. In Acts 9, he is on his way to Damascus when he is arrested by the Lord.

Saul became a believer, and his life was transformed. He was born again. He had a new allegiance and a new purpose. Instead of the greatest persecutor of the early church, he became its greatest missionary. His name was changed from Saul to Paul. Truly, all things became new; that is the essence of the new birth.

What is the new birth? It is *a passing from death to life.* Ephesians 2:1 says, "And you hath he quickened, who were dead in trespasses and sins." John 5:24 says, "He that heareth my word, and believeth on him that sent me, hath everlasting life, and shall not come into condemnation; but is passed from death unto life."

Sin kills. "For the wages of sin is death" (Romans 6:23). And every person is dead in his trespasses and sins until he is born again. The new birth brings life where there was death.

What is the new birth? It is *a calling out of darkness into God's light.* A few days ago I had the joy of leading a student to Jesus Christ. He said, "Dr. Sweeting, when I took the first step of faith in Jesus Christ, it was like a flood of light welling up in my life. My past was dark and foggy. Nothing was certain. Nothing was secure. But now I see. Things are clear. It is as if all the darkness in my life has been swept away by a spectacular light."

601

The apostle Peter wrote, "But ye are a chosen generation, a royal priesthood, an holy nation, a peculiar people; that ye should shew forth the praises of him who hath called you out of darkness into his marvellous light" (1 Peter 2:9).

The new birth, then, is a spiritual birth, a new creating, a passing from death to life, a calling out of darkness into God's light. The theological word for the new birth is *regeneration*. It all has a wonderful ring of newness about it, doesn't it? And that is what the Lord Jesus was saying to Nicodemus. All our old sins, the darkness of our hearts, the drudgery of our lives are replaced by a new, living, vibrant freshness. That is the new birth. It is a fresh start, a new beginning, a rebirth. Have you experienced that?

Why Do We Need the New Birth?

A second question you may be asking is, "Why do we need the new birth?" The Lord Jesus told Nicodemus that apart from the new birth a man will never see the kingdom of God. You see, there is something wrong with every man, something that can be supplied only by the new birth.

When a new baby is born, the doctors examine it very carefully and give each newborn a rating that is known as the Apgar score. Based on a scale of one to ten, the Apgar score rates an infant in regard to heart rate, respiration, reflex sensitivity, muscle tone, and color. A perfect score of ten is relatively rare, but it is not unheard of. But even those babies that receive a perfect Apgar rating have a defect that the Apgar score does not test for—a sinful nature.

The Bible is clear on the truth that all have sinned. Romans 3:10 says, "There is none righteous, no, not one." Verse 23 of that same chapter says, "For all have sinned, and come short of the glory of God." Isaiah wrote, "All we like sheep have gone astray; we have turned every one to his own way" (Isaiah 53:6).

Someone said concerning mankind, "Man has made great strides. He can swim like the fish and fly like the birds. Now he needs to learn to live like man." You see, all the greatest accomplishments of man—his art, music, philosophy; his great intellect; his scientific and medical discoveries; his laws and institutions; his architecture and engineering accomplishments; his religious and moral systems—all that combined has done nothing to lessen or eradicate the effects of sin.

Even the great Swiss psychologist Carl Jung said, "All the old primitive sins are not dead but just crouching in the dark corners of our modern hearts—still there, and still as ghastly as ever."

Look at any updated crime statistics and you will see that what Dr. Jung said is truer than ever today. Murder, rape, child abuse, incest, and even more hideous crimes are on the increase in our nation at alarming rates. Something is desperately wrong with mankind!

Political analyst Walter Lippmann commented several years ago, "We ourselves were sure that at long last a generation had arisen keen and eager to put this disorderly earth to right—and fit to do it. We meant so well, we tried so hard, and look what we have made of it. We can only muddle in the muddle. What is required is a new kind of man."

Man has always tried to improve himself, but to no avail. What we need is indeed a new kind of man. And only the new birth can bring that about.

The Lord Jesus did not recognize class distinctions. He divided all the world into two groups: converted and unconverted—once-born and twice-born. *No* other divisions really matter. This is the decisive division; it is the division that runs through time and lasts for eternity. Into which division do you fit?

A third question commonly asked about the new birth is, "What will the new birth do for me?"

The new birth will *make you a member of God's family.* When you were born as an infant, you were born into a family. And unless you were adopted into another family, you took your name, your looks, and many of your characteristics from your mother and father. The same principles apply in the spiritual realm. When a person is born again, he is born into God's family. God is his Father, and he assumes the position and characteristics of a child of God. At first, he is a spiritual baby, but as he grows, he grows more and more into the likeness of his Father.

The only way into God's family is by birth. We do not become members of God's family by creation; it is a fallacy to say that all men are God's children. The apostle Paul, writing to the Christians at Ephesus, reminded them that, prior to their new births, they "were by nature the children of wrath, even as others" (Ephesians 2:3). He was saying that they were children of wrath, not children of God, until they were born into God's family; that is true of every man.

What will the new birth do for you? The new birth is a fresh start, a renewal. It will *renew your intellect and moral nature.* Colossians 3:10 reads, "And [you] have put on the new man, which is renewed in knowledge after the image of him that created him." In Ephesians 4:23-24 Paul wrote, "And be renewed in the spirit of your mind; And . . . put on the new man, which after God is created in righteousness and true holiness." A person who is born into God's family begins to assume the nature and mental and moral characteristics of God, his Father.

The new birth gives us a sensitivity to the things of God. The man who is born again seeks that which is pure (those things which are above—spiritual things). His affections undergo a transformation. He begins to love the things of

God—God's people, God's Word, and God's righteousness. His determination is different. His motives are changed, his desires are changed, his whole life is changed.

What will the new birth do for you? It will *make you the abiding place of God's Spirit.* When a man is born again, the Spirit of God takes up permanent residence in his body. Paul wrote to the Corinthian believers, "Know ye not that ye are the temple of God, and that the Spirit of God dwelleth in you?" (1 Corinthians 3:16).

Nothing can so transform a life as the complete surrender to the power of the indwelling Holy Spirit. Immediately there is a new authority in the life. The human will is conformed to the will of God. There is a new desire to do the will of God. The whole being is transformed.

HOW CAN I BE BORN AGAIN?

You may be asking, "How can I be born again?" The answer is surprisingly simple. "Believe on the Lord Jesus Christ, and thou shalt be saved" (Acts 16:31). Put your faith in Christ, trust Him completely, and you will be born again. There is nothing you can do to earn God's favor. Your works of righteousness are powerless to save you; they are like filthy rags in God's eyes (see Isaiah 64:6). You can no more obtain the new birth by your own efforts than an infant could be conceived and born through its own efforts.

"For by grace are ye saved through faith; and that not of yourselves: it is the gift of God: not of works, lest any man should boast" (Ephesians 2:8-9). Titus 3:5 says that it is "Not by works of righteousness which we have done, but according to his mercy he saved us, by the washing of regeneration [the new birth], and renewing of the Holy Ghost."

The new birth is a work of God. All we must do is trust Him completely. We must believe Him implicitly. We must put our faith in Him absolutely. Peter wrote that we are "born again, not of corruptible seed, but of incorruptible, by the word of God, which liveth and abideth forever" (1 Peter 1:23).

Has the seed of God's Word been placed in your heart? Do you see your need before God as a sinner? Do you long for a fresh start, a new birth, a regeneration?

The Lord Jesus died on the cross to make it possible for you to experience the new birth. He had never sinned; He did not deserve to die. But the Bible says, "For he hath made him to be sin for us, who knew no sin; that we might be made the righteousness of God in him" (2 Corinthians 5:21).

Christ's death on the cross was a payment for your sins. He paid the wages of sin—death—to make it possible for you to experience the abundant life He offered. But you must be born again. Will you trust Him today and experience that new birth?

THREE

Three Unpopular Sermon Topics

Not every subject in the Bible is pleasant. And one of the things that makes preaching the gospel such a challenging task is the responsibility in preaching the complete Word of God to deal with those topics that are not easy to preach about.

And yet the glorious truth is that for every negative there is a positive. For every unpleasant subject there is a victorious side—God has provided an answer to every problem mankind faces.

Today it is my task to speak on three sermon topics that are not popular. In recent years they have been neglected in many pulpits, yet they are vital in God's overall revelation to man. I would like here to examine what God's Word has to say about the subjects of sin, death, and hell.

SIN

Sin is virtually a forgotten word in the vocabulary of modern man. We talk about "personality disorders," "new morality," and "alternate life-styles," in our attempts to redefine what God's Word calls sin. We treat certain sins as sicknesses, without much success at finding a cure. Biblical standards are widely viewed as archaic, passé, and out-dated. Modern man has his own ideas, and they make no room for such a narrow concept as sin.

And yet there is no denying that the Bible teaches that sin is the real root of all of this world's problems. Denying the existence of the sin problem does not make it go away. Redefining moral values does little to remove guilt.

If you doubt that sin still exists, look at today's newspapers. Murder, war, prejudice, rape, theft, incest, child abuse, and other crimes and world problems fill the pages. And that does not take into account the secret sins that never make headline news, such as hypocrisy, covetousness, lust, and greed. Yes, my friend, sin is as alive as it ever has been.

And sin is a universal problem. There is not a man alive who is not affected by the problem of sin. Romans 3:23 says, "For all have sinned, and come short of the glory of God."

That verse gives a very important insight into the nature of sin. Sin is not, as some people think, only a heinous act, a vile thought, or a specific infraction of God's law. Sin is missing the mark, falling short of God's standards, coming short of God's glory.

That means that even the "good things" we do can be sin in the eyes of God. A remarkable verse in Isaiah says, "But we are all as an unclean thing, and all our *righteousnesses* are as filthy rags" (Isaiah 64:6, italics added). Do you see how God sees even our righteousnesses—the "good things" that we do? He says that they are as filthy rags. They miss the mark; they fall short of His glory.

The Lord Jesus, during His earthly ministry, had more conflicts with the Pharisees, the religious leaders of Israel, than with any other group of people. One of the reasons is that He exposed their hypocrisy for what it was—sin. He taught that their tithing and constant praying were of no value in obtaining God's favor. He called them whitewashed sepulchers, "full of dead men's bones, and of all uncleanness" (Matthew 23:27).

He openly exposed their secret sins. He showed them their shortcomings. He rebuked them for their phoniness. And He said that even the best things that they did were sin—their praying, their fasting, their tithing.

Does that mean that God is cruel or unreasonable? Certainly not. The Bible reveals God as a long-suffering, kind, loving, patient God. His standards are indeed high—too high for any man to attain. But God does not expect us to conquer the problem of sin by ourselves.

The answer to man's sin is in Christ. He is "holy, harmless, undefiled, separate from sinners" (Hebrews 7:26). He "did no sin, neither was guile found in his mouth" (1 Peter 2:22). He "was in all points tempted like as we are, yet without sin" (Hebrews 4:15).

And the Bible says, "Christ died for *our* sins" (1 Corinthians 15:3, italics added). His death on the cross for us made atonement for our sins. He paid the price to free us from our sins, and God raised Him from the dead, signifying that He had won the victory over sin!

The apostle Paul, writing to the believers at Rome, said, "Knowing this, that our old man is crucified with him, that the body of sin might be destroyed, that henceforth we should not serve sin" (Romans 6:6). And it is only through faith in the blood of Christ that we can experience that power to free us from our sin.

Are there sinful attitudes or sinful habits in your life that you long to be freed from? Is there sin in your past for which you suffer guilt and shame? The Lord Jesus Christ can free you from that, if you will trust Him unconditionally and put your faith in His work for you on the cross.

That is the good news about sin! We can be freed from its evil power, its guilt, its grip on our lives. We can be redeemed from the servitude of sin.

Another unpleasant subject that is often avoided in sermons is death. Death is a fact of life. We live with death every day. But we do not like to recognize death. The fear of death pervades our entire society. Anthropologists tell us that most adults never learn to face the fact of death honestly. As a result, millions of people die each year because they are afraid to see a doctor.

Death is all around us. The moment a man is born he begins to die. Billions of cells in the body are dying each day. The process of aging brings us ever closer to the inevitable time when we will die. Statistics show that two people die every second, 99 die every minute, 5,900 die every hour. Newscasts continually report deaths from natural disasters and the holocaust of war.

In this age of uncertainty, death is a sure thing!

In his letter to Christians, James spoke of the certainty of death. "For what is your life? It is even a vapour, that appeareth for a little time, and then vanisheth away" (James 4:14).

The Bible is clear on the certainty of death. Hebrews 9:27 says, "It is appointed unto man once to die." Death may not be a happy subject, but it is certainly an unavoidable one. Like it or not, everyone must die.

But that was not God's original plan.

When God created Adam He intended for man to live forever. Life was to be an endless adventure. Death was unknown. But Adam sinned, and the Bible says that because of Adam's sin, "death passed upon all men, for that all have sinned" (Romans 5:12).

W. Somerset Maugham wrote of an Arabian merchant who sent his servant to the city of Baghdad in search of provisions. The servant hurriedly returned, saying that he had seen Death in the marketplace and that Death had made a threatening gesture at him. He pleaded for a horse and hurriedly fled to the distant town of Samara, seeking to escape Death.

That day the merchant went to the marketplace. Seeing Death, he asked, "Why did you make a threatening gesture at my servant this morning?"

"That was not a threatening gesture," answered Death. "That was a start of surprise. I was astonished to see him in Baghdad, because I have an appointment with him tonight in Samara."

Death is inescapable. Scheme as you will, you cannot avoid your appointment with death!

The Bible is clear on the certainty of death, and it is also clear on the cause of death. The cause of death is sin. "The wages of sin is death," says Romans 6:23. Ezekiel 18:4 proclaims, "The soul that sinneth, it shall die." James concluded that "sin, when it is finished, bringeth forth death" (James 1:15).

People face death differently. One may die in confidence, another in despair. One may depart from this life in beautiful peace while another is racked by pain. One may die rejoicing while another is full of remorse.

Voltaire, the French philosopher and agnostic, declared when he was healthy that Christianity was a good thing for chambermaids and tailors to believe in, but not for people of wisdom. But before dying, he called to his doctor, "I am abandoned by God and man. I will give you half of what I am worth if you will give me six months of life. Then I shall go to hell, and you will go with me. O Christ! O Jesus Christ!" What a tragic way to die!

What a contrast is seen in the passing of John Wesley. This founder of Methodism is credited with saving England from moral disintegration during a critical time of that nation's history. It is said that without the ministry of John Wesley, England would have experienced the same kind of upheaval and decline France experienced in the revolution.

During Wesley's lifetime, he rode more than a quarter million miles on horseback and preached 42,000 sermons. When he lay dying at the age of eighty-eight, he said confidently, "The best of all is, God is with us."

Abraham Kuyper wrote, "In the valley of the shadow of death, the great highway divides itself. One road leads upward into eternal life and the other downward into eternal death, and Jesus Christ makes the difference."

Yes, my friend, Jesus Christ does indeed make the difference. Just as He is the remedy for our sins, He is the remedy for the problem of death.

Jesus said, "I am the way, the truth, and the life" (John 14:6). John wrote, "He that believeth on the Son hath everlasting life" (John 3:36). Are you fearful of death? The Lord Jesus said, "I am the resurrection and the life: he that believeth in me, though he were dead, yet shall he live: and whosoever liveth and believeth in me shall never die" (John 11:25-26).

Do you understand the importance of those words? Believers in Christ have nothing to fear in death. Our Lord has been victorious over death. Eternal life is ours now. We have it as a present possession. It is not merely something to look forward to, but a blessing to enjoy here and now. Our bodies may die. But real death will never touch us. We pass from this life immediately into the presence of the Lord Himself. Paul told the Corinthian believers that "to be absent from the body [is] . . . to be present with the Lord" (2 Corinthians 5:6).

And that is the good news about death. It is a defeated foe. It holds no threat for the one who has trusted Christ and received the gift of eternal life. Probably the most familiar verse in all of Scripture is John 3:16, and it is a simple expression of that very promise: "For God so loved the world, that he gave his only begotten Son, that whosoever believeth in him *should not perish, but have everlasting life*" (italics added).

Have you trusted Him and taken advantage of that promise?

HELL

Another unpopular subject is hell. A few years ago a major denominational magazine commented on the fact that hell is "going out of style for many contemporary believers." It gave statistics to show that fewer than one in three of that denomination's members really believed in a literal place of eternal punishment.

Hell today is a joking matter with many people. It is not uncommon to hear someone dismiss the concept of hell lightly with a comment like, "I suppose I'll feel right at home there—it is where all my friends are going."

But what a distorted and unbiblical view of hell that is! What ignorance is revealed in such a view! God warns us of hell primarily not to frighten us into obedience, but because He loves us. If hell genuinely exists, we would expect God to warn us of it. And He gives us abundant warning in His Word. The Lord Jesus spoke more about hell than He did about heaven! He lovingly and tenderly, but graphically, warned men and women of the horrors of hell.

To dismiss hell as an archaic and outdated concept is as ineffective in getting rid of it as that same approach is with the idea of sin. And to ignore hell will not make it go away any more than ignoring death makes it go away. No, my friend, like the unpopular topics of sin and death, hell must be squarely confronted and honestly faced. It is real, or else the Lord Jesus is a liar. It is real, or else the Word of God is not true. It is real if any other spiritual truth is real. We must admit that at the outset.

What do we know about hell? Actually, many things. It is a place, first of all, of eternal separation from God. Paul writes in 2 Thessalonians 1:9 that those who reject Christ "shall be punished with everlasting destruction from the presence of the Lord, and from the glory of his power." Those who refuse God's love and forgiveness here and now must spend eternity cut off from Him. Hell is separation from God.

It is also a place of suffering. Jesus gave a picture of the spirits awaiting judgment in the account of Lazarus and the rich man in Luke 16:19-31. The beggar Lazarus was in a place of joy after death, but the rich man, in hell, was in torment.

Again and again, Jesus emphasized the awfulness of hell and warned that it is unchangeable and forever. He called it "outer darkness." He used terms like "torment," "weeping and gnashing of teeth," and "everlasting fire." Hell must be an awful, horrible place.

You say, Can all of this be real? My friend, God does not play games with His creation. The Bible does not mix fantasy with truth. God would not give us such vivid descriptions of hell if it were not a real place with real suffering. He does not make idle threats.

The Lord Jesus said of heaven, "In my Father's house are many mansions: if it were not so, I would have told you" (John 14:2). The same thing is true of hell—if it were not so, the Lord Jesus would have said so. But instead He repeatedly warned of the awfulness of hell. He pleaded with people to escape the consequences of sin by believing and receiving eternal life.

But there is good news about hell. God does not want to send anyone to hell. Hell was not created for man but for the devil and his demons (Matthew 25:41). God is not anxious to send men to hell, but He is anxious to redeem them from it. That is not to say that no one will go to hell. Jesus taught that the road to destruction is broad and that many will travel that way. But the way to heaven is open to all in Christ.

The Lord Jesus died on the cross to redeem us from the

threat of eternal punishment. We do not have to go to hell. But He has done all that He can. The choice now is yours. Will you trust Him and receive His gift of eternal life, or will you reject Him and by your own choice be condemned to eternal punishment and torment in hell? Every man faces the choice sometime in his lifetime. You face it now. Will you trust Him or reject Him? Your choice will determine where you spend eternity.

Sin, death, and hell. None of them are pleasant topics, but all of them are real. And the Lord Jesus in His death on the cross has conquered all three. Will you trust Him today and know the joy and freedom that comes with eternal life?

FOUR

Heaven and How to Get There

Every year, the little town of Pacific Grove, California, witnesses one of nature's spectacles. In the fall of the year, great clouds of orange and black monarch butterflies sweep down from the Canadian Rockies. They cluster on pine trees by the millions—to stay through the winter. In March, the butterflies fly off again, singly or in small groups. They drift widely, breeding wherever there is milkweed for their young.

After laying her eggs, a butterfly's work is complete. No butterfly makes the journey twice. Its life span is too short. But the next year, the offspring, who have never been to Pacific Grove, fly there to spend the winter. And each year, they arrive at exactly the same time!

How do the young butterflies know where to go? No one knows for sure. But their instincts guide them so directly that entomologists believe that the young butterflies return to exactly the same tree that their parents have come to for centuries. There is an inborn sense of direction and longing to return to the place of their ancestry in each butterfly.

In much the same way, God has planted within each man and woman a longing for a place called heaven. Romans 1 tells us that there is in every man an awareness of God. Paul writes, "That which may be known of God is manifest in them; for God hath shewed it unto them" (verse 19). And just like the butterfly that instinctively finds the right tree, so man instinctively directs his thoughts toward his Maker.

Man's inner consciousness of God has caused him to long for such a place as heaven. A study of the tombs of ancient Egypt tells us of the Egyptians' hope for the future. They believed in a future home that very much resembled what many of us conceive heaven to be like. The early American Indians also had belief in an afterlife in a place with the Great Spirit. Danish history reveals that, when a landowner died, his personal servant would also take his own life so that he could continue to serve his master beyond the grave!

In fact, virtually every civilization known to man has had an instinctive awareness of a future life. The instinct of heaven is registered in the soul. And man's soul needs such a place as heaven.

Perhaps you have unanswered questions about heaven. Most of us do. The greatest knowledge and intelligence that we can accumulate in this life is at best incomplete. We simply cannot come up with all the answers. In fact, the greater our knowledge, the more questions we have.

Isaac Newton was a brilliant English philosopher and mathematician, but he realized the limits of human wisdom. "I seem to be only a little child picking up a few pebbles on the shore," said Newton, "while a great ocean of truth stretches unexplored before me."

There really is very little that we know about our world here and now, and much less about heaven. But God's Word gives us some knowledge about this place to which every man longs to go. The truth the Scriptures give us about heaven is basic truth, but it is wonderful truth, and it answers some of the questions almost everyone wonders about.

How Can We Know There Is a Heaven?

One question the Bible answers for us is "How can we know there is a heaven?" The whole character of God demands that there be a place like heaven. God is *just*, and heaven is a place of reward for the righteous.

In a world racked by war and violence there is very little true justice. At times it seems that the wicked prosper at the expense of the righteous. And because evil continues to succeed here on earth, there must come a day when righteous judgment will be measured out.

Shall the wicked go unpunished? Shall the poor not be vindicated? Shall Jesus be crucified and not exalted? The answer from the Bible is a resounding no. Paul declared to the unbelieving people of Athens that God "hath appointed a day, in the which he will judge the world in righteousness by that man [Jesus Christ] whom he hath ordained" (Acts 17:31). And heaven is the reward of the righteous.

God is *merciful,* and His divine mercy demands that there be a heaven. God offers His forgiveness and salvation freely to those who will trust Christ. But what does that mean if there is no heaven and death ends it all?

When the Lord Jesus was dying on the cross, He told the repentant thief hanging next to Him, "Verily I say unto thee, To day shalt thou be with me in paradise" (Luke 23:43). The Lord promised that thief that, although he had spent a wasted life of sin, he could be redeemed and spend eternity in heaven. What a wonderful picture of the loving mercy of God!

God is *eternal,* and heaven is the place where we will spend eternity with Him. Paul wrote to the Corinthians, "For we know that if our earthly house of this tabernacle were dissolved, we have a building of God, an house not made with hands, eternal in the heavens" (2 Corinthians 5:1). Paul is saying that we have an eternal home where we will spend eternity with God.

God is *true,* so there must be a heaven. God would not mislead us on the subject of heaven. Our Lord said to His disciples, just prior to His crucifixion and subsequent resurrection and ascension, "In my Father's house are many mansions: if it were not so, I would have told you. I go to prepare a place for you. And if I go and prepare a place for you, I will come again, and receive you unto myself; that where I am, there ye may be also" (John 14:2-3). If heaven were not real, the Lord Jesus would have said so. But it *is* real, and He is there now, preparing a place for those who trust Him.

Yes, my friend, heaven is a real place. The Bible leaves no doubt about it. The Lord Jesus is there right now. Believers who die go to spend eternity there with Him. The reality of heaven is as sure as God Himself.

How Can We Know What Heaven Is Like?

But, you may be asking, can we possibly know what heaven is like? The Bible does give us some information about what heaven will be like.

The apostle John was given a glimpse of heaven one day in a beautiful vision. And he did his best to describe what he saw. We have it recorded in the Word of God in Revelation 21. In verses 18-19 of that chapter, John wrote, "And the building of the wall of it was of jasper: and the city was pure gold, like unto clear glass. And the foundations of the wall of the city were garnished with all manner of precious stones." The first verse of chapter 22 is part of the same account: "And he shewed me a pure river of water of life, clear as crystal, proceeding out of the throne of God and of the Lamb."

The God who painted the wings of the butterfly, who mixed the colors of the rainbow, who has painted nature with color and beauty—He is the Master Artist who has made heaven beautiful.

Yes, heaven is a beautiful place! It is a special place prepared for special people. It is a place of peace and rest and fulfillment. John tells us that in heaven "there shall be no night there; and they need no candle, neither light of the sun; for the Lord God giveth them light" (Revelation 22:5).

There is no sorrow there. "And God shall wipe away all tears from their eyes; and there shall be no more death, neither sorrow, nor crying, neither shall there be any more pain: for the former things are passed away" (Revelation 21:4). Can you imagine such a place? Surely there is no one who would not like to go to heaven.

How Can We Know How to Get to Heaven?

You may be asking, "How do I get to heaven? Can I know for sure that I will go there? Is it possible for *even me* to go to heaven?" You will be glad to know that the Bible does provide answers for those questions.

Several years ago, I thought I would like to find out exactly what the average man on the street thinks about how to get to heaven. I situated myself on one of the busiest intersections in the world—the corner of State and Madison streets in Chicago. As people passed by, I selected them at random to ask: "What are your chances of going to heaven when you die?"

Barbara, a high school senior, was the first person I questioned. "What are my chances of going to heaven?" she said. "I think my chances are very good. Not necessarily because of my own godliness, but because my father is such a good man. The Good Book says that we will meet our fathers in the next world. My father will be a saint, and I know he'll say a good word for me."

That young girl was very sincere, but very wrong. Being born in a Christian home does not make one a Christian. Basing your chances on a godly father and mother is very wrong. Godly parents may direct us in the right way, but they will not be able to "say a good word" for us to get God to accept us. Each of us is personally responsible to God.

The second person I questioned was a middle-aged businessman. "My chances of getting to heaven are pretty slim," he joked. "I can't play a harp, and I don't own any long white robes."

I meet people like that man all the time. They brush aside eternal matters with a silly remark, simply because they are not willing to confront reality.

We can speak carelessly of heaven and hell, my friend, but one day we will have to face their reality. Making light of eternal matters does no more to remove them than joking about the Grand Canyon could make it go away.

But the glib answer of that middle-aged man was only a cover-up. He was a man with a seeking mind. He promised to read the gospel of John that I gave him. Beneath his exterior of unconcern there was interest.

A young housewife was the third person I questioned. "How can I possibly tell about my chances of getting to heaven?" she asked. "You should ask my husband. He knows me better than anyone else."

I turned to her husband and asked, "What do you think of her chances of getting to heaven?"

"She has an excellent chance," he answered. "She lives a good life and is basically quite religious. I wish my own chances were as good."

As our conversation continued, it became evident that these young people were basing their hopes for heaven on their own good works, a good life, and a church relationship.

I was not surprised to find a couple that felt the way they did. As a matter of fact, I was not surprised by any of the answers I received that day. They represented a good cross section of the way people think about how to get to heaven.

But every answer I received that day was wrong, according to the Word of God.

No one gets to heaven by his own good works. If only good people went to heaven, there would not be anyone there! The Bible tells us that "all have sinned, and come short of the glory of God" (Romans 3:23). "There is none righteous, no, not one" (Romans 3:10). If we had to get to heaven on our own merits, none of us would make it! No one is righteous. No one can do enough good works to make up for his sin. It just does not work that way.

The apostle Paul wrote in Ephesians 2:8-9, "For by grace are you saved through faith; and that not of yourselves: it is the gift of God: not of works, lest any man should boast." Heaven and eternal life cannot be earned; they are gifts. They cannot be worked for or deserved. They cannot be purchased. They do not come to us because of our good works.

My friend, heaven is offered to you as a gift. It is offered freely, and the only way to get it is to receive it by faith.

Jesus said, "I am the way, the truth, and the life: no man cometh unto the Father, but by me" (John 14:6). No matter what you may have been taught, no matter what you may be doing to try to earn your way to heaven, the Lord Jesus says He is the only way to get there.

Think again for a moment of the thief on the cross next to the Lord Jesus. He did nothing to earn his way to heaven. He had lived a life of crime. He was being executed for his crimes, and by his own testimony, he deserved it. "And we indeed [suffer] justly," he told the other thief in Luke 23:41, "for we receive the due reward of our deeds."

He was repentant, but he was dying. He could not use his life to do good deeds. He had no opportunity to make restitution for what he had stolen. His life had been wasted. Completely. There was nothing left to salvage. Not even one day.

But our Lord promised the thief that that very day he would be with Him in paradise. He could be sure of it. It was the Lord's promise to him.

How did that dying thief get to heaven? The only way any man ever gets there—by faith. He trusted Christ. He put his faith in the Lord. He knew that Jesus was the promised Messiah. He knew that our Lord had done nothing worthy of death. And that thief committed himself to the Lord Jesus in his dying hours. "Lord, remember me," he asked (v. 42), and he was saved.

Will you commit yourself to the Lord Jesus in faith right now? What a tragedy to waste a life. You can reap some of the benefits of heaven right here in this life, if you will but trust Him. You can have eternal life. You can have the presence of the indwelling Spirit in your life. Have you trusted Him? If not, you need to be saved.

What must you do to be saved? Simply believe! What must you do to be lost? Nothing. Neglect is the same as rejection. Trust Christ as your Savior right now, and heaven will be yours.

FIVE

Blessed Assurance

I heard a godly man say, "I'm as sure of going to heaven as though I had already been there a thousand years."

That is quite a powerful statement! Perhaps it is shocking to you to hear of someone so certain of heaven.

Uncertainty has robbed thousands of the joy of the Christian life. It is appalling to realize how many people are made miserable by the disease of doubt. Some people who read their Bibles, pray earnestly, attend church faithfully, and live uprightly in all their dealings with others may yet have no assurance of forgiveness and salvation.

Is it really possible to know for certain that you are going to heaven? What does the Bible say? Second Peter 1:10 tells us that we are to "give diligence to make [our] calling and election sure." God wants us to *know* that we are saved. Second Corinthians 13:5 exhorts us: "Examine yourselves, whether ye be in the faith." The Lord expects us to be certain. First John 5:13 says, "These things have I written . . . that ye may know that ye have eternal life." There is no question from the Scriptures that God's plan for us includes absolute certainty of our salvation.

Let me go a step further. Assurance is not only possible

but necessary, because it is the reality of assurance that brings purpose and power to our lives. Christian assurance is a fortress of strength against the wiles of the devil. But an uncertain salvation is impotent.

My friend, don't waste years in doubt—move forward to enjoy the greater things of God. Assurance may not be necessary for salvation, but it is certainly necessary if you would experience the victorious, vibrant, overcoming life.

Many people depend on their feelings for assurance, but feelings are no basis for genuine assurance. How you feel is certainly not the best measure of whether or not you have eternal life. Feelings have their place, but they are not the best barometer of your spiritual condition.

How can you be sure you are on your way to heaven? Let me suggest four issues in the matter of assurance that must be considered in the proper order.

FACTS

The first issue is the facts of the gospel. No one can be sure of his salvation until he understands the way of salvation.

What are the facts of the gospel? In his first letter to the believers at Corinth, Paul wrote, "For I delivered unto you first of all that which I also received, how that Christ died for our sins according to the scriptures; and that he was buried, and that he rose again the third day according to the scriptures" (1 Corinthians 15:3-4). That, according to the apostle Paul, is the essence of the gospel. Those are the facts of the gospel—that Christ died for our sins, was buried, and rose again the third day. Look carefully at three facts:

First, *Christ died for our sins according to the Scriptures.* When we think of the Scriptures we think of the Old Testament and the New Testament. But when Paul wrote this letter to the Corinthians, very little of the New Testament had been written. When Paul speaks of the Scriptures, he means the Old Testament Scriptures. Christ died for our sins according to the Old Testament Scriptures!

Perhaps you did not know that the Old Testament Scriptures spoke of Christ's dying for our sins. Centuries before the birth of Christ, Isaiah prophesied the suffering and death of the Messiah. That prophecy is recorded for us in Isaiah 53.

Verse 3 is a vivid account of the sufferings of our Lord at the hands of the mockers. "He is despised and rejected of men; a man of sorrows, and acquainted with grief: and we hid as it were our faces from him; he was despised, and we esteemed him not." Why was this One suffering? Isaiah tells us that it was for our sins. "Surely he hath borne our griefs, and carried our sorrows: yet we did esteem him stricken, smitten of God, and afflicted. But he was wounded for our transgressions, he was bruised for our iniquities: the chastisement of our peace was upon him; and with his stripes we are healed" (vv. 4-5).

The consistent teaching of the Old Testament Scriptures is that there *must* be an offering for sin. Sin must be atoned for before it can be forgiven. Blood must be shed. The Bible gave the nation of Israel detailed instructions for sacrificing lambs and other animals. But those sacrifices were only temporary. They were object lessons on the doctrine of atonement, "for it is not possible that the blood of bulls and of goats should take away sins" (Hebrews 10:4).

What was needed was a perfect, sinless, spotless man—the Lord Jesus. John the Baptist called Him "the Lamb of God, which taketh away the sin of the world" (John 1:29). He was the perfect sacrificial Lamb—the only one who could make atonement for our sins.

And that is why He died—to pay for our sins. That is fact number 1 of the gospel.

Paul says also that *He was buried.* Our Lord was put in a borrowed tomb, more a cave than the kind of grave we think of today. Isaiah 53 had foretold it. "And he made his grave with the wicked, and with the rich in his death; because he had done no violence, neither was any deceit in his mouth" (v. 9). Christ's death was not trickery. He was really dead—a Roman soldier made sure of that by piercing His side with a sword.

The Lord Jesus Himself foretold that He would be dead for three days. "For as Jonas was three days and three nights in the whale's belly; so shall the Son of man be three days and three nights in the heart of the earth" (Matthew 12:40).

But that is not the end of it. Fact 3 of the gospel states that *He rose again the third day according to the Scriptures.* Without the truth of the resurrection, the rest of the gospel is meaningless. Paul writes, "If Christ be not raised, your faith is vain; ye are yet in your sins" (1 Corinthians 15:17).

The resurrection is the basis for our eternal life. In that same great chapter on the resurrection, 1 Corinthians 15, Paul writes, "For since by man came death, by man came also the resurrection of the dead. For as in Adam all die, even so in Christ shall all be made alive" (vv. 21-22).

That fact is the very basis for assurance of our eternal life. Paul wrote in Romans 6:8-9, "Now if we be dead with Christ, we believe that we shall also live with him: Knowing that Christ being raised from the dead dieth no more; death hath no more dominion over him." The resurrection is God's proof to us that we have eternal life! What a fact! And that is a good foundation on which to base your assurance.

FAITH

A second issue to consider if you would know complete assurance of your salvation is the issue of faith. Facts can do an individual no good unless he exercises faith in them. Faith is a personal appropriation of the facts. Hebrews 11:1 says, "Now faith is the substance of things hoped for, the evidence of things not seen." Faith is all the proof you need.

Faith is simply taking God at His word, believing that what He says is true, and accepting it personally for yourself.

Here's an illustration. Imagine a prisoner being offered a pardon. He is so overwhelmed after reading the document of pardon that he is in a daze.

You ask him, "Have you been pardoned?"

"Yes," he says.

"Do you feel pardoned?" you ask.

He replies, "No, I do not; it is so sudden."

"But," you ask, "if you do not feel pardoned, how can you know that you are? You are not yet released from prison. You say you do not feel anything. How can you be sure you are pardoned?"

He points to the document. "This tells me so," he says.

That is faith. He believed and accepted the truth. He felt nothing, he had experienced nothing, but he knew that the document was true!

The Word of God is God's document of pardon to you. You can accept it by faith.

And by faith is the only way you can accept it. "For by grace are ye saved through faith," wrote Paul in Ephesians 2:8-9, "and that not of yourselves: it is the gift of God: not of works, lest any man should boast." There is no way you can *earn* God's salvation. But He gives it freely to those who accept it by faith.

FRUIT

A third issue in the matter of assurance is fruit. "I am the vine," said Jesus in John 15:5, "ye are the branches: He that abideth in me, and I in him, the same bringeth forth much fruit: for without me ye can do nothing."

If you are longing for assurance of your salvation; if you understand the facts of the gospel; and if you have received God's pardon by faith, the next issue to consider is the issue of fruit. Examine your life to see if the fruits of your faith are showing up.

What did the Lord mean by "fruit"? He meant attitudes and works in the life of the believer. Again, it is vital that we understand the proper order. Faith must come before fruit. Fruit is a natural result of faith.

Fruit does not grow by effort or through labor. Fruit grows naturally, and aside from giving it the right environment in which to grow, there is absolutely nothing you can do to make it grow faster or more abundantly.

Good works in the life of a believer are like fruit. Given the right environment, enough food, light, and air, they just grow naturally. They are fertilized through exposure to the Word of God; they receive light as we walk in the light, and they get their air as we let ourselves breathe the spiritual atmosphere that comes with a constant fellowship with God in prayer.

Good works in the life of an unbeliever, however, are manufactured, artificial fruit. God tells us in Isaiah 64:6 that those works of righteousness are like filthy rags. Works without faith are not fruit, but rags.

What are some of the fruits in the life of the believer? Galatians 5:22 gives us a list of *the fruit of the Spirit:* "love, joy, peace, long suffering, gentleness, goodness, faith, meekness, temperance." Here is a test: are those qualities evident in your life?

John wrote his first epistle to help believers struggling with the problem of assurance. In 1 John 5:13 he wrote, "These things have I written . . . that ye may know that ye have eternal life." And John gave several tests—fruit to look for in our lives as evidence that we have been truly born again.

One of his tests is *the fruit of obedience.* "And hereby do we know that we know him," John wrote in 1 John 2:3, "if we keep his commandments." Do you want to know if you

631

really know God? Examine your life. Are you obedient to His Word? Do you love His Word, hunger for it, and obey it? That is evidence.

Another of John's tests is *the fruit of sound doctrine.* "Whosoever shall confess that Jesus is the Son of God, God dwelleth in him, and he in God" (1 John 4:15). Do you give to the Lord Jesus the high place that Scripture accords Him? Is your doctrine in line with the Scriptures and not just the teachings of man?

John's third test is *the fruit of love.* In 1 John 3:14 John writes, "We know that we have passed from death unto life, because we love the brethren. He that loveth not his brother abideth in death." Do you sense a bond of love with those who are believers in the Lord Jesus? Do you automatically have a feeling of kinship with those who trust Him? That, according to John, is evidence that you have passed from death unto life. That is a fruit of salvation.

FEELINGS

Have you examined the *facts* of the gospel? Do you understand and are you sure of what God's Word teaches about how to be saved—how to pass from death unto life?

And have you examined your *faith?* Do you trust Christ? Have you appropriated by faith His salvation for yourself?

Have you examined the *fruit* in your life? Is the fruit there—evidence from your attitudes, character qualities, and behavior?

Having examined those issues, we are now ready to deal with the issue of *feelings.* Feelings do have their place. When you first believed, you may or may not have felt different. Whether you did or not is not really important. But let me suggest three feelings that may be evidence of your salvation, assuming that all the other issues of assurance conform in your life.

The first is *peace.* In Philippians 4:7, the apostle Paul

writes about "the peace of God, which passeth understanding." There is a sense of peace that comes to those who do not concern themselves with personal needs but through prayer and supplication let their requests be made known to God (Philippians 4:6). It is a peace that passes understanding, a peace that keeps the heart and mind of the believer, regardless of outward circumstances, a peace that defies worries and cares. Do you know that peace? Until you experience genuine assurance you cannot know it.

A second feeling that might be helpful in the matter of assurance is *joy*. Joy is not happiness. Happiness can come and go, but real joy—the joy that is a fruit of the Holy Spirit—is not dependent upon circumstances. Paul wrote of rejoicing in the midst of tribulation. Have you experienced that kind of joy? Only true believers know it.

Confidence is a feeling that is closely related to assurance. How can we have confidence? Like peace and joy, confidence is a feeling that does not come from within. Its origin is not in us but in the Holy Spirit. Perhaps you did not know it, but it is one of the ministries of the Holy Spirit to assure our hearts that we are born of God. It is only He, ultimately, that gives assurance of our salvation. Romans 8:16 says, "The Spirit itself beareth witness with our spirit, that we are the children of God." First John 5:10 says, "He that believeth on the Son of God hath the witness in himself." That inner witness is the Holy Spirit.

God wants us to have assurance. The gospel is a "know-so" salvation. Millions have known this blessed assurance, and it is still available today.

Fanny Crosby wrote in the beautiful gospel song "Blessed assurance, Jesus is mine" (1873). Can you sing that with conviction?

It is not presumption or arrogance to be certain of eternal life; it is God's will.

What is your response? Are you sure of your salvation?

Will you examine the issues of facts, faith, fruit, and feelings, and be sure?

Perhaps you have had no assurance because you have had no basis for assurance. You have never trusted Christ, and you do not have eternal life. You need to receive Christ as your Savior today. You too can trust Him and know the assurance that the Lord makes possible in Christ and through His Holy Spirit.

SIX

All Things Are Become New

Several years ago, while waiting to board a plane, I became engaged in a conversation with a young man and his wife. After watching several jets shoot into the murky darkness, the young woman remarked, "I wish I could vanish into space just like that plane and begin my life all over again."

She was an attractive young woman, a woman of wealth and position, yet her life was filled with emptiness and regret. Why did she want to escape? Because the ugly hand of the past was spoiling the present.

Today there are millions who echo those words of despair. Perhaps you feel much like that young doctor's wife. I have good news for you. According to God's Word, everything in your life can be new and fresh and vibrant. Second Corinthians 5:17 says, "Therefore if any man be in Christ, he is a new creature: old things are passed away; behold, all things are become new."

What a wonderful truth! *All* things are become new! That is just what millions in the world are looking for. It is what that young woman was seeking. And the apostle Paul says any man can experience it in Christ.

Let me suggest three specific things that become new when a person is "in Christ"—when an individual becomes a believer.

A New Start

First, the individual that puts his faith in Christ gets a new start. "Old things are passed away," says Paul. Would you like to get rid of some of the "old things" in your life? Your old sin, your old guilt, your old cares, your old defeats, all are passed away the moment you put your faith in the Lord Jesus.

There probably is no greater challenge to any man than the challenge of overcoming the weight of his sin. Everyone is faced with guilt, and different people try to handle it in different ways.

Some people try to escape it. Many try to drink away their gloom and guilt. Some seek release through drugs and narcotics. Some try to find a way out by fulfilling the lusts of the flesh. Others create their own private fantasies. Still others give themselves over to sexual perversions and deeper sin—anything to help them forget the misery of their everyday existence. But most of those things only compound the guilt and make the sense of emptiness and misery worse.

In my counseling over the years, I have found that most people do not have to be convinced of their sin. Our conscience condemns us. We cannot even meet the artificial standards we set for ourselves, much less the standards God has set.

The apostle Paul wrote, "I am carnal, sold under sin. For that which I do I allow not: for what I would, that do I not; but what I hate, that do I" (Romans 7:19).

Isaiah lamented, "Woe is me! for I am undone; because I am a man of unclean lips, and I dwell in the midst of a people of unclean lips" (Isaiah 6:5).

Job, a moral and upright man, confessed, "I abhor myself" (Job 42:6).

And God's Word agrees, "There is none righteous, no, not one" (Romans 3:10).

What we need is indeed a new start. And the Lord Jesus said that a new start is possible, even necessary. Speaking to Nicodemus, a great teacher of the Jews, the Lord said, "Except a man be born again, he cannot see the kingdom of God" (John 3:3).

Think of it! The Lord said that it is possible to be reborn—to begin life all over again.

Martin Luther described his experience like this: "When, by the Spirit of God, I understood these words, 'the just shall live by faith,' I felt born again like a new man; I entered through the open doors into the very paradise of God."

Why is a new birth essential? No other experience can give a man a completely fresh start. A new start is not found by moving to a new place. Thousands think that if they can just run away to California, or Florida, or to someplace far away, they will be able to experience a fresh start in life.

A new start cannot be found in a new marriage partner or a new job. Those things might change our outward circumstances, but they cannot really change us on the inside.

No, my friend, a new start cannot be found in a new state, a new mate, or a new slate. Only the new birth can truly give a man a new start. Only the new birth can free us from our sins. Only the new birth can impart to us eternal life, and make us pass from death to life. Only the new birth can give us a new heart, new desires, new life.

And this new start is to be found only in Christ Jesus. If any man be *in Christ,* he is a new creature. It is through faith in Him that we are born again.

Would you like to experience this new birth and have a new start? You need to turn a new direction—turn away from your sin to the Lord Jesus. That turning is called *repentance*. Repentance is simply a change of heart, a change of mind. It is turning from self and from sin and from self-righteousness.

The other side of repentance is faith. Faith is simply looking to the Lord Jesus, trusting that what he says in His Word is true and abandoning oneself completely to Him in complete confidence that He is able to do what He says. He can give a new start. He can make all things fresh and new. Will you trust Him to do it today?

A NEW SONG

In addition to a new start, the one who trusts Christ gets a new song. For the child of God life can be filled with music. The victorious Christian life is a joyful, exuberant relationship with God. When we come to know Jesus Christ as our Savior, we have a reason to sing. He gives us a new song and puts gladness into our hearts.

God's servant David was a man who enjoyed music. As a boy he would play upon his harp while he tended his sheep. In later years, his music quieted the weary soul of King Saul as David strummed his melodies in the royal palace.

But not all of life was sweet for David. Like many of God's children, he experienced times of difficulty, opposition, and turmoil. In Psalm 40 we read of his distress. But despite David's problems, we see in that psalm the mighty hand of his God at work in his life.

Psalm 40:1-3 reads, "I waited patiently for the LORD; and he inclined unto me, and heard my cry. He brought me up also out of an horrible pit, out of the miry clay, and set my feet upon a rock, and established my goings. And he hath put a new song in my mouth, even praise unto our God: many shall see it, and fear, and shall trust in the LORD."

To know God is to possess a song in one's life. Salvation and song are inseparable. The joy of the Lord generates music in the soul. When a person is in fellowship with God, he has a new song to sing.

When Martin Luther first translated the Bible into the language of the people, a marvelous thing happened. All of Europe began to sing the praises of God. The whole concept of music was tranformed from a dull, joyless chant to harmonious melody. From the Lutheran Reformation came many great hymns of praise that are still widely used in churches today.

Music is the natural result in the heart of one fully yielded to the Lord. Colossians 3:16 says, "Let the word of Christ dwell in you richly in all wisdom; teaching and admonishing one another in psalms and hymns and spiritual songs, singing with grace in your hearts to the Lord."

You don't have to be a musician to experience that song of grace, but you do have to be Spirit-filled. Song is the result of being filled with the Holy Spirit. Ephesians 5:18-19 says, "Be filled with the Spirit; speaking to yourselves in psalms and hymns and spiritual songs, singing and making melody in your heart to the Lord."

That new song is a song of praise. In Psalm 40, David expressed his gratitude to the Lord for delivering him from a miry, horrible pit. He could sing because he had been delivered by the Lord, and his song was a song of praise.

My dear friend, do you know anything of God's deliverance? Perhaps you too find yourself in sin's horrible pit, a slave to lust or obsessed with worldly possessions. You can find forgiveness and deliverance right now—right where you are. And it will be the basis for a new song.

I want you to notice something very interesting about the nature of David's new song. It was a blessing to other people. He did not keep it to himself. Oh, I do not mean that he sang it aloud to others, although he may have. But the key is that the song made such a difference in his life that it was visible to everyone. In verse 3 David says,

641

"Many shall see it, and fear, and shall trust in the LORD."

What did they see? Didn't David use the wrong words? Did he not mean that they would *hear* it? No. He meant not the song itself but the echo of the song in his heart, which was visible in his life. He had *become* a song.

Do people see your life as a song? That is God's purpose for your life. He wants not only to *give* you a new song to sing, but also to *make* you a new song to be seen.

Perhaps you know a believer like David—someone whose life radiates music, a new song. Just being around him brings new music into your life and strengthens your faith in the Lord and His power to change a life.

The Lord wants all of us to have that kind of testimony. And if we will surrender our lives to the control of the Holy Spirit, He will fill us with song.

D. L. Moody once heard Henry Varley say, "The world has yet to see what the Lord can do through a man totally surrendered to Him."

Moody's answer was, "By God's grace I'll be that man." And he surrendered his life to the Lord as fully as he knew how.

The Lord did use D. L. Moody, and He filled his life with music. Moody, although not a musician himself, had a deep appreciation for the value of songs and hymns and spiritual songs. He was the first evangelist to use music widely in his campaigns. And from his ministry and that of his associate, Ira Sankey, came some of the finest gospel songs ever written. Moody's ministry is largely responsible for scores of the songs still in our songbooks today. The Lord gave him a new song.

A NEW STRENGTH

A third new thing available to every believer in Christ is a new strength. The apostle Paul wrote, "I can do all things through Christ which strengtheneth me" (Philippians 4:13).

Paul was not speaking there of physical strength, but of a spiritual strength, a strength of character, an inner strength that cannot be gained by natural means. It is a strength available only through Christ, but available to everyone who trusts Him.

Nehemiah told the people of Israel, "The joy of the LORD is your strength" (Nehemiah 8:10). The believer's new strength is closely related to his new song. The inner sense of joy and peace that comes from absolute surrender to the Spirit of God is a great source of strength.

But this new strength is centered in a Person—the person of Christ. Paul said, "I can do all things through *Christ*."

Do you see what that means? In Christ every believer has the power to do everything the Lord requires of him. The strength to live the Christian life comes not from within the Christian, but from Christ Himself.

Paul said, "I am crucified with Christ: nevertheless I live; yet not I, but Christ liveth in me: and the life which I now live in the flesh I live by the faith of the Son of God, who loved me, and gave himself for me" (Galatians 2:20). He wrote to the believers at Philippi, and spoke of the great desire of his heart: "That I may know him [Christ], and the power of his resurrection" (Philippians 3:10).

The real depth of the power of the Christian's strength can be comprehended in the realization that it is the resurrection power of Christ. The same power that enabled Him to rise from the dead is the power by which we can live our daily lives!

Think for a moment about the power of God that is available to the Christian. It is power that has been proved victorious over sin. It has been demonstrated to be more powerful than death. Surely the believer can do *all things* through Christ, who strengthens Him.

Paul concluded his epistle to the Christians at Ephesus with these words: "Finally, my brethren, be strong in the

Lord, and in the power of his might" (Ephesians 6:10). He went on to describe the spiritual battle that every believer knows and the weapons that are available to the soldier in the Lord's army. But the most exciting thing in that whole passage is this assurance in verse 10 that the power for the battle is the Lord's power. It is *His* strength, *His* might, *His* energy. It is the same power that already has conquered the enemy.

Trusting in that power, no Christian can be defeated. Satan cannot be victorious. The resurrection power of Christ cannot be overcome.

Are all things new in your life? Have you experienced a new start? Are you singing a new song? Are you living in new strength?

You know the needs in your life. The answer to them is found in Christ. He can make all things new. Will you trust Him today and let His resurrection power work in your life?

SEVEN

Three Kinds of Repentance

In 1927, Charles Lindberg became a national hero by flying alone across the Atlantic Ocean. During that historic flight, his plane, *The Spirit of St. Louis,* traveled at an altitude of four thousand feet and at a speed of one hundred miles per hour.

Today, supersonic jets can fly fifty thousand feet in the air and streak across the sky at more than fifteen hundred miles an hour.

In 1896, the electronic genius Marconi established the first wireless radio transmitter. With his unique invention he was able to send and receive a signal over a distance of two miles, and the age of mass communications was born.

Today, via satellites, a visual and audible signal can be transmitted live worldwide, and we have even seen live color television pictures from the moon!

This is an era of unparalleled technological achievement. You and I have seen more change in our lifetimes than all of mankind has before us!

However, in this era of change, there are some things that, unfortunately, have not changed. Mankind has not known real peace in our lifetime. Millions of people live in a constant struggle, trying to find meaning in a fast-changing world, and seeking release from the guilt of sin.

Each year in the United States, fifty million people change their places of residence. Some statistics indicate that there is now one divorce for every three marriages. Mate-swapping clubs have become quite popular in many of our nation's cities and suburbs. Narcotics arrests in one state alone have increased by two thousand times in just ten years. Clearly, people are not statisfied, and they are looking for change anywhere they can find it.

The Bible tells us that the basic need of every man is the need for a spiritual change. In Luke 13:3 Jesus said, "Except ye repent, ye shall all likewise perish." *Repent or perish;* that is the option. You may try to change your place of employment, your residence, or even your mate, but those are merely changes of surroundings. Until you repent of your sins and experience salvation, you will never know genuine peace and fulfillment.

Repentance is a wonderful thing! Suppose we could sin but were unable to repent. Suppose God let us fall but would not lift us up. Suppose we were able to wander far away but were not able to return. If that were true there would be no hope. There could be no freedom from the slavery of sin.

Yes, my friend, it is the message of repentance that makes the gospel a message of joy. Because of repentance, the sinner can be cleansed; the fallen can be lifted; the prodigal can come home; the enslaved can be freed. You can be changed!

The call to repentance is the major theme throughout the New Testament. The message that John the Baptist preached could be summed up in one word: *repent.* He challenged people to face their sin and turn from it. In Matthew 3:7-8 John told the pious, self-righteous Pharisees, "O generation of vipers, who hath warned you to flee from the wrath to come? Bring forth therefore fruits meet for repentance."

It took tremendous courage for John to preach that message. I have found that most people do not like to be told that they are sinners. Many do not want to repent. This has become the day of the placid pulpit and the comfortable pew. Very few are talking about repentance. It is not an easy message. John the Baptist was beheaded by a king's executioner for preaching the message!

Repentance itself is a widely misunderstood concept. I have found that a great many people have a false idea of what repentance is. I would like to look at three kinds of repentance and see what the Scriptures teach about this most important of subjects.

FALSE REPENTANCE

The first kind of repentance is not really repentance at all, but a kind of false repentance. In fact, there are many false substitutes that people have for repentance.

Repentance is not conviction, although conviction is necessary. It is the ministry of the Holy Spirit to convict us of our sin, true righteousness, and impending judgment. But a man may be convicted and not repent. Conviction is simply the Holy Spirit's revealing a need to the heart. It can lead to genuine repentance, but it is not repentance.

Repentance is not religion. You may be a very religious person and never repent of your sins. The Pharisees were like that, and John the Baptist told them frankly that he doubted their repentance was the real thing.

In Acts 8 we find the interesting story of a man named Simon. Simon heard Philip the evangelist preach and saw him perform miracles. He asked Peter if he, too, could have the gift of performing miracles, and he even offered him money to buy it!

Peter's answer to Simon was, "Thy money perish with thee, because thou hast thought that the gift of God may be purchased with money. Thou hast neither part nor lot in this matter: for thy heart is not right in the sight of God. Repent therefore of this thy wickedness" (vv. 20-22).

Simon was a religious man, outwardly. Simon had been a sorcerer, and according to verses 9-11, he was respected by all the people as a great man of God because of the sorcery he was able to do. Verse 13 tells us that he had believed. But he had believed without repenting. His faith was all in his head, and not in his heart.

Simon's request to Peter revealed that he had never genuinely repented. His was a false repentance. He still desired power, and the admiration of the people. He was religious, and he was personally acquainted with at least three of the apostles. But religion is not repentance, and Simon was not saved.

Repentance is not an intellectual assent to the gospel. Simon believed, but only intellectually. And it is not enough just to believe the facts of the gospel. The kind of faith Simon had did nothing to change him on the inside.

Intellectual faith is good too, but it is not enough. James wrote, "Thou believest that there is one God; thou doest well: the devils also believe, and tremble" (James 2:19). Demons have no choice but to believe the facts about God, but theirs is by no means saving faith. James taught the powerful truth that saving faith always makes a visible difference in a person's life.

Repentance is not simply being sorry for one's sins. To be sorry is not sufficient. Paul wrote to the Corinthians about two kinds of sorrow. "Now I rejoice, not that ye were made sorry, but that ye sorrowed to repentance. . . . For godly sorrow worketh repentance to salvation not to be repented of: but the sorrow of the world worketh death" (2 Corinthians 7:9-10).

650

Godly sorrow can *lead* to repentance, but it is not the same thing as repentance. And the sorrow of this world leads not to repentance but to death. Why? Because we can mistake it for repentance.

Probably the best example in the Bible of false repentance is that of Judas. Matthew 27 records his repentance for us. "Then Judas, which had betrayed him, when he saw that he was condemned, repented himself, and brought again the thirty pieces of silver to the chief priests and elders, saying, I have sinned in that I have betrayed the innocent blood. . . . And he cast down the pieces of silver in the temple, and departed, and went and hanged himself" (vv. 3-5).

Judas was *convicted*. He realized his sin and saw that he was condemned.

He was *religious*. He had been with the Lord Jesus and the other disciples for three years, and yet he had done nothing to make the other disciples suspect that he was the one that would betray the Lord. He must have even been involved in some of the healings and casting out of demons that all the disciples did.

He was *intellectually persuaded*. He realized that he had betrayed innocent blood. He had seen the Lord's miracles and heard His teaching for those three years. He surely must have believed in his head that Jesus was whom He claimed to be.

And Judas was *sorry*. But his sorrow was the worldly sorrow that leads to death. He was more sorry about his condemnation than about his sin, and so he hanged himself. His was a false repentance.

My friend, conviction, religion, intellectual faith, and sorrow for sin are all good, but even combined they do not equal true repentance. If you have looked to any or all of those things as repentance, then your repentance has been false.

What, then, *is* repentance? If it is not sorrow or conviction or religion or intellectual assent, *what is it?*

Repentance is simply a change. The word itself means "a change of mind," and that is indeed what repentance is, but it goes even deeper than that. It is a change of direction in the mind and heart and life. It is turning *from* sin and self and Satan. And it is turning *to* God.

The Lord Jesus gave an excellent picture of genuine repentance in Luke 18:10-14:

> Two men went up into the temple to pray; the one a Pharisee, and the other a publican. The Pharisee stood and prayed thus with himself, God, I thank thee, that I am not as other men are, extortioners, unjust, adulterers, or even as this publican. I fast twice in the week, I give tithes of all that I possess. And the publican, standing afar off, would not lift up so much as his eyes unto heaven, but smote upon his breast, saying, God be merciful to me a sinner. I tell you, this man went down to his house justified rather than the other: for everyone that exalteth himself shall be abased; and he that humbleth himself shall be exalted.

The outstanding thing about the prayer of the publican is its total selflessness. He wouldn't even lift up his eyes to heaven. He was turning from self and from his sin, and turning to God in absolute repentance.

It is interesting to note the words the Lord Jesus used in connection with the prayer of the Pharisee. He "prayed . . . with himself," says Jesus (v. 11). That is strikingly similar to the words Matthew used about Judas's repentance. "Repented himself" is the terminology in Matthew 27:3.

Neither Judas nor the proud Pharisee had turned from self. They were preoccupied with themselves, looking within—not looking to the Lord. They had not repented, because they had never turned from their thoughts of their own works.

Genuine repentance requires us to turn away from any works of righteousness we might think we have done. It includes a confession of deep need, a rejection of the past, and a whole new direction in life. Without that kind of repentance no one can be saved.

John Wesley taught Greek at Oxford University at the age of twenty-one. He hazarded his life for the gospel in crossing the Atlantic Ocean many times as a missionary. And yet, by his own testimony, he did not know Jesus Christ as his personal Savior until he had a life-changing encounter with the Lord at Aldersgate at the age of thirty-eight. It was then for the first time that he genuinely repented of his sin and experienced the peace and joy of God's cleansing and forgiveness.

Perhaps you have attended church for many years—perhaps, like Wesley, you have been in Christian work for years—but you realize that you never have genuinely repented. You need to turn humbly to the Lord today, my friend, and genuinely repent.

Without repentance, all your religion, all your good works, all your sorrow for your sin, all your resolves to do better—all those things you may have substituted for real repentance—are of no value whatsoever. The Lord Jesus says that unless you repent you will perish.

But, you may be thinking, I thought all that was necessary for salvation was faith. Doesn't the Bible teach that "whosoever believeth in him should not perish, but have everlasting life" (John 3:16)? Yes, that is true. But real faith is not possible without repentance. A person cannot turn to God in faith until he has turned from his sin and self.

SHALLOW REPENTANCE

Let me warn you against a third kind of repentance—shallow repentance. In Revelation 3, the apostle John records a message from the Lord Jesus to the church at

Laodicea. It was a lukewarm church. It was "neither cold nor hot" (v. 16). It had tried to stay away from extremes, and it was a church in real need but unaware of its needs. It was wretched, miserable, poor, blind, and naked.

Verse 19 records the Lord's admonition to that church: "Be zealous therefore, and repent." The Lord was warning the Laodiceans against the dangers of a shallow repentance. He was saying, "Open your eyes, be aware of your needs, repent with zeal. Repent deeply."

Perhaps you are a believer who has grown cold or lukewarm. Perhaps you repented once, but your repentance has become shallow, and you have lost sight of the poverty of your own soul. Will you open your eyes to your needs, and repent?

Repentance is not a one-time act. The attitude of the repentant publican is the attitude every believer should maintain. We are never to be proud or self-righteous. Our repentance should be a deep, constant, ongoing attitude of humble repentance before the Lord.

The Lord can fill only empty vessels. It is not until we are repentant that He can fill us with His power. It is not until we are emptied of self that we can be filled with the Spirit.

Will you repent today, and repent deeply? The Lord is speaking. His message is, "Be zealous, and repent."

EIGHT

The Conversion of Cornelius

A crisis can mean life or death! Each day we are confronted by crucial situations. Almost none of us has escaped the effects of one kind of crisis or another.

The conversion of Cornelius was one of those crisis situations. It literally revolutionized the first-century church. It brought life and power to the Great Commission.

In fact, the conversion of Cornelius was a crisis in more than one way. I would like to suggest three ways in which Cornelius's conversion was a crisis.

IT WAS A CRISIS IN GOD'S DEALINGS WITH THE WORLD

First, the conversion of Cornelius was a crisis in God's dealings with the world. Before the Lord Jesus left this earth, He marked out His strategy for carrying the gospel to the whole world. In Acts 1:8, He told His apostles, "But ye shall receive power, after that the Holy Ghost is come upon you: and ye shall be witnesses unto me both in Jerusalem, and in all Judaea, and in Samaria, and unto the uttermost part of the earth."

In Jerusalem the apostles experienced overwhelming success. Thousands were won to Jesus Christ at Pentecost alone.

People were added to the church daily. The church experienced great growth—so much that they could not provide for the physical needs of all the believers.

Things looked good from the outside. But the new Christians were failing to follow *God's* plan. They were cozy and comfortable. There was such great success in Jerusalem. Why should they move on?

Then God allowed great persecution to scatter the Christians to Judea, Samaria, and beyond. The scope of the church broadened to a wider geographic region. But the church's vision needed to be enlarged to see beyond limited ethnic boundaries as well. And the single crisis event that was mostly responsible for that was the conversion of a Gentile military officer by the name of Cornelius.

Today we tend to think of the church as a largely non-Jewish body. But in the beginning it was not that way at all. The earliest church was composed completely of Jews and some Gentiles who had converted to Judaism. The early church was distinctly Hebrew in its beginnings. The Lord Jesus had been born and lived on this earth as a Jew. The apostles were all Jewish. Christ's ministry had for the most part been among the Jewish people. The only Scriptures available to the early church were the Hebrew Old Testament writings.

It was difficult for those in the early church to conceive that God would work in any way other than through the Jews. All God's dealings in the past had been with the nation of Israel. Gentiles were considered dogs, barbarians, unclean. No one expected God to deal directly with them.

That is why the salvation of Cornelius rocked the church to its very center. It was a magnificent declaration of inclusion—a transformation of the church's vision and mission. It was a new beginning in God's dealings with the world.

Everyone was shocked by it! Those that were with Peter

were astonished, we are told in Acts 10:45. Acts 11:2-3 tells us that when Peter returned to Jerusalem, Jewish believers there "contended with him, saying, Thou wentest in to men uncircumcised, and didst eat with them." That was something no self-respecting Jew would do!

But Peter explained to them what had happened, and he concluded his explanation with these words: "What was I, that I could withstand God?" (Acts 11:17). Peter said, "It wasn't my idea, it was God's! There was nothing I could do to stop Him!" God had begun something new. From now on He would deal directly with Gentile and Jew alike. Ethnic and racial distinctions did not matter, for "God is no respecter of persons" (Acts 10:34). The gospel truly would go into all the world, to all men.

Those in the church at Jerusalem recognized that this great crisis signaled a new direction in God's dealings with the world. Their consensus was, "Then hath God also to the Gentiles granted repentance unto life" (Acts 11:18). God was now dealing with Jew and Gentile alike. What a marvelous revelation!

It Was a Crisis in God's Dealings with Peter

The conversion of Cornelius was also a crisis in God's dealings with the apostle Peter. Peter had to be dealt with concerning his prejudice before God could use him completely. In Acts 10:9-10 we are told that "Peter went up upon the housetop to pray about the sixth hour: And he became very hungry, and would have eaten: but while they made ready, he fell into a trance."

Peter saw a vision of a sheet, let down to earth, filled with animals not lawful for any Jewish person to eat. Verse 13 tells us, "There came a voice to him, Rise, Peter; kill, and eat."

Look at Peter's answer in verse 14: "Not so, Lord; for I have never eaten anything that is common or unclean."

Peter recognized the lordship of Christ with his lips, but not with his life! He called Jesus his Lord, but he did not obey Him.

The same thing happened three times, and the sheet was taken back into heaven. Peter pondered the meaning of his vision. "What God hath cleansed, that call not thou common" (v. 15). While he questioned and thought, some men came from Cornelius to call for him. They told him that Cornelius had been instructed by a messenger of God to find Peter and to hear his words.

The next day, Peter went to Cornelius's house. His first words to Cornelius show us that he was learning the lessons God was teaching him. "God hath shewed me that I should not call any man common or unclean" (v. 28).

What was God teaching Peter in this crisis experience? First, He was teaching him about the lordship of Christ. He was asking, "Why call ye me, Lord, Lord, and do not the things which I say?" (Luke 6:46). If Jesus is Lord, we must obey Him implicitly.

Second, He was teaching Peter that he was no longer under the law but under grace. Peter was to have some conflicts with Paul over this same issue later in his ministry. And this experience with Cornelius and the sheet full of animals would be a reminder to him that he was indeed no longer under law but under grace.

Third, God was teaching Peter that He is not prejudiced. Acceptance with God is not based on race, color, national origin, looks, intelligence, or ethnic background. It is not obtained by a religious ceremony, such as circumcision. God deals with each man as an individual.

It Was a Crisis in God's Dealings with Cornelius

Cornelius's conversion was, of course, a crisis in the life of Cornelius as well. Let us consider for a few minutes this man Cornelius. Who was he? What do we know about him?

First of all, he was a soldier. In Acts 10:1, Luke describes him as "a centurion of the band called the Italian band." As a centurion, he commanded a division of one hundred men. He was living in Caesarea, the civil and military capital of the Judean region. He was a part of the Roman police force, and it was his job to keep order.

That was one strike against him. The Jews resented the Roman presence in their land, and Roman soldiers symbolized everything the Jews detested.

In addition, Cornelius was a Gentile. That was another strike against him. The Jews considered him to be outside of the fold of God. It was bad enough that he was living in their land, but the fact that he exercised authority over them was a source of incomprehensible irritation to the Jews.

Cornelius did not seem to be the best candidate to become a partaker of the grace of God.

But God had been working in Cornelius's heart. Acts 10:2 states that he was "a devout man, and one that feared God." He was reverent and faithful in prayer. He was most likely what was referred to as *a Jewish proselyte of the gate.* He had forsaken the paganism of his upbringing and outgrown the superstitions of idolatry. He had perhaps had some exposure to the Greek translation of the Old Testament Scriptures.

He had probably embraced the great principles and writings of Moses and the prophets, but he had not yet actually embraced Judaism. The Jews still considered him unclean, a heathen. But God was working in his heart, and Cornelius was responding.

Acts 10:30-33 is Cornelius's account to Peter of what had happened in this great crisis in his life:

> And Cornelius said, Four days ago I was fasting until this hour; and at the ninth hour I prayed in my house, and, behold, a man stood before me in bright clothing, And said, Cornelius, thy prayer is heard, and thine alms are had

in remembrance in the sight of God. Send therefore to Joppa, and call hither Simon, whose surname is Peter; he is lodged in the house of one Simon a tanner by the sea side: who, when he cometh, shall speak unto thee. Immediately therefore I sent to thee; and thou hast well done that thou art come. Now therefore are we all here present before God, to hear all things that are commanded thee of God.

The message that Peter then gave to Cornelius was the gospel of Jesus Christ, summed up in his concluding words in verse 43, "To him [Christ] give all the prophets witness, that through his name whosoever believeth in him shall receive remission of sins."

Cornelius did believe, and God poured out His Holy Spirit on him, and on those who came with him and believed as well. God had shared His Son, His salvation, and His Spirit with the Gentiles!

Cornelius's life was transformed. Up to this point, he had been interested in spiritual things, but now he had the Spirit of God living in him! Cornelius had offered prayer, but now he knew God in a personal way! He had given his money, but now God had given him life!

Look at all Cornelius received in this great crisis experience. He received *remission of his sins.* That is what Peter had promised in the name of Christ to those who would believe. Cornelius had fasted and prayed, given alms, and sought to know God. But he had never known the peace of having his sins forgiven.

He received *the Holy Spirit.* The presence of the Spirit of God was evident in the same way as on the day of Pentecost. Cornelius and those with him spoke in unlearned foreign languages. That was proof that the Holy Spirit had come to the Gentiles in exactly the same sense as to the Jews.

He received *eternal life.* The whole impact of this account is that Cornelius, a Gentile, was saved. He was accepted into God's family, released from the power of sin and death.

What a wonderful crisis experience! All at once, God was dealing with Cornelius, with Peter, and with the whole world. He was building His church. And everyone had some wonderful truth to learn from it.

What can you learn from it?

Perhaps you, like Peter, need to be purged of prejudices. Prejudice is an ugly thing. It is a crushing sin, controlling the hearts of men and affecting their attitudes and conduct. But there is no prejudice or respect of persons with God.

The word *prejudice* means "pre-judging." It is opinion without evidence. It is determination without investigation, condemnation without trial. It is forming an opinion without due knowledge of the facts. It is giving unreasonable bent to one side of a cause or issue. Prejudice is absolutely contrary to the character of God.

If there is prejudice or class hatred in your life, you need to seek God's forgiveness and cleansing.

Or perhaps you are like Peter in that you need to learn the truth of absolute submission to the lordship of Jesus Christ in your life. Maybe you have been calling Him Lord at the same time that you have been refusing and denying Him. Submit to Him now.

Or maybe you are like Cornelius—religious, but lost. Apart from faith in Jesus Christ, Cornelius would have perished; the same is true of you.

From the story of Cornelius's conversion we learn that *salvation is available to all men.* Let us not lose sight of the accompanying truth that *all men need to be saved.* Cornelius's religion did not make him acceptable in the sight of God. He needed to repent, to trust Christ, and to be saved. That is true of every man. Each of us must experience the crisis of salvation in our lives.

And salvation *is* a crisis experience. You cannot *grow* into the Christian faith. You cannot *back* into Christianity. You cannot *slide* into salvation. Everyone who is saved passed from death unto life at a definite point in his life.

Have you experienced such a crisis? Is there a definite time in your life that you can point to and say, "That was when I passed from death unto life"? Perhaps you cannot point to the exact minute, hour, or even day, but do you know that there was a definite time and place when you were saved?

The gospel of Christ is the great leveler of society. Everyone stands equal at the foot of the cross. God's salvation belongs to all who will repent and believe. No matter who you are, no matter what your place in life, Christ will receive you if you will come to Him right now.

NINE

A Personal Revolution

For years, psychologists have been saying that it is impossible to change a person. They say that you can rearrange an individual's environment, you can adjust his ambition and goals, you can give him an education, but you can never *really* change him.

Humanly speaking that theory may be very sound, but in the spiritual realm it is absolutely false. Millions of people in this world can testify—along with me—that a man, woman, boy, or girl *can* be radically transformed in life or action through a personal relationship with the Lord Jesus Christ.

The apostle Paul wrote, "Therefore if any man be in Christ, he is a new creature: old things are passed away; behold, all things are become new" (2 Corinthians 5:17). That is a promise from the Word of God! We can be totally changed—become new creatures.

No one was more qualified to pen that verse of Scripture than the apostle Paul. His life was a classic example of a life totally transformed by the changing power of Jesus Christ. If ever a man was stopped right in his tracks and magnificently changed in every way, Paul was that man.

Let's look into Paul's life and examine three marvelous changes the Lord wrought in him.

His Purpose Was Changed

First, Paul's purpose was dramatically changed. The book of Acts relates that Saul of Tarsus was actively engaged in a deliberate program to eradicate Christianity. He hated it and everything it stood for.

The first time we are introduced to this man is in Acts 7—at the martyrdom of Stephen. Verse 58 tells us that the witnesses—probably the people who stoned him—laid their clothes at the feet of Saul, who was consenting unto Stephen's death. Saul stood by and watched the brutal stoning of Stephen and even guarded the coats of those who threw the stones.

By the next chapter, Saul became more aggressive. Acts 8:3 says that Saul "made havock of the church, entering into every house, and haling men and women committed them to prison." He became the chief persecutor of the early church.

Like many of the Jewish religious leaders of the first century, Saul was enraged by the claims of the new Christians that Jesus was Israel's Messiah. That this man Jesus could be considered divine was to Saul nothing less than blasphemy, and his anger increased his zeal and fervor in persecuting believers in this new sect.

But one day his whole being was shaken. God took hold of him and said, "It's time for a change." Out on a highway leading to Damascus, Saul was arrested by the Lord Himself. While traveling along the road, Saul was suddenly blinded by a light that surrounded him.

> And he fell to the earth, and heard a voice saying unto him, Saul, Saul, why persecutest thou me? And he said, Who art thou, Lord? And the Lord said, I am Jesus whom thou persecutest [Acts 9:4-5a].

Saul had started on the road to Damascus to find Christians there to persecute, but he was stopped short by the Lord Himself, and his whole life purpose began to undergo a total change. He undoubtedly felt he was doing the right thing in his attempt to stamp out Christianity, but he found that he was really fighting God!

This encounter represented a crisis in the life of Saul, who subsequently came to be known as Paul. For when he cried out, "Who art thou, Lord?" he was acknowledging the lordship of Jesus Christ! The same man who had been casting men and women into prison for their faith in Jesus Christ had just acknowledged Jesus' lordship. Saul called Jesus *Lord!*

Yes, Saul's conversion *was* sudden. The Scriptures contain examples of others who came to Christ after long periods of time, but Saul's conversion was a definite, dramatic experience of immediate change. Saul, the chief persecutor of the church, was about to become Paul, its chief missionary! Saul, the murderer, would become Paul, the martyr! Scarcely a man in the history of the world has undergone a more dramatic change of purpose than Saul of Tarsus. His zeal was the same as ever. His intensity had not diminished. His dedication was, if anything, more sure than before, only now it was aimed in the opposite direction. The very thing he once opposed now became his life's work. All that he had stood for in the past he now fought. What a dramatic, powerful change!

Just read through the book of Acts to see the effects of Paul's ministry. Wherever he went he started a new church. He won people to faith in Jesus Christ. He preached. He was persecuted, stoned, and even left for dead because of his testimony for Jesus Christ.

Yes, my friend, Saul had a new purpose in life. But that was not all that changed.

Saul had a new perspective. He saw things differently from that moment on. A flash of light had blinded his eyes. He could not see at all for some time, and I believe that was God's way of showing Saul that he had always been blind—spiritually blind. That flash of light may have blinded Saul's physical eyes, but it opened his spiritual eyes.

Consider for a moment the background of this man. Saul was a Jew born in Asia Minor, in the city of Tarsus. He had received the finest education possible in his day under the tutelege of the famous scholar Gamaliel. He was a Pharisee, belonging to the strictest Jewish sect, holding rigidly to the law of Moses.

He had probably been named after Saul, the first king of Israel. The name means "Big One." King Saul had been physically large—he stood head and shoulders above all other men. Saul of Tarsus was large in ambition and intellect. He had virtually every advantage of his day.

In his letter to believers at Philippi, Paul lists his credentials and heritage. He says that he was "circumcised the eighth day, of the stock of Israel, of the tribe of Benjamin, an Hebrew of the Hebrews; as touching the law, a Pharisee . . . touching the righteousness which is in the law, blameless" (Philippians 3:5-6).

Do you see Paul's perspective before he was saved? He looked at things from a human perspective. Comparing himself with other men was a source of pride to him. He was like the Pharisee the Lord Jesus spoke of in Luke 18:11-12, who stood in the Temple and prayed, "God, I thank thee, that I am not as other men are, extortioners, unjust, adulterers, or even as this publican. I fast twice in the week, I give tithes of all that I possess."

From a human perspective, Saul of Tarsus had much to be proud of. His education, his heritage, his family, his knowledge of the law and strict adherence to it, were all the kinds

670

of things other men looked up to him for.

But there was one thing that Saul, like that Pharisee in the Temple, could not see—his own sin. With all the spiritual and material benefits Saul had, he could not see his need for salvation!

But the Lord Jesus changed that. The apostle Paul gained a deep awareness of his sin and weakness.

And God gave Paul a special reminder. Paul called it "a thorn in the flesh, the messenger of Satan to buffet me, lest I should be exalted above measure" (2 Corinthians 12:7). We do not know exactly what it was, but it was some kind of infirmity that kept Paul perpetually aware of his weakness.

Paul asked the Lord three times to remove that thorn in the flesh, but the Lord's answer to him was, "My grace is sufficient for thee: for my strength is made perfect in weakness" (2 Corinthians 12:9). As a result, Paul said that he would most gladly glory in his infirmities. His perspective had been changed. Before, he had looked at himself and seen his strength, but now he saw his sin. Before, he had looked at himself and seen wisdom, but now he saw weakness.

In 1 Corinthians 15:9 Paul wrote to the church at Corinth, "For I am the least of the apostles, that am not meet to be called an apostle, because I persecuted the church of God."

Several years later, he wrote to the Ephesians, "Unto me, who am less than the least of all saints, is this grace given" (Ephesians 3:8).

Then near the end of his life, he wrote to Timothy, "Christ Jesus came into the world to save sinners; of whom I am chief" (1 Timothy 1:15).

Do you see how Paul's humility developed as his awareness of his own sin grew? He began as a proud Pharisee, denying any need. Arrested by the Lord and confronted with his own sin, he was given the office of apostle. But he saw himself as the least of the apostles. Then he saw himself as less than the least of saints. Then he saw himself as the chief of sinners. What a wonderful change of perspective!

HIS PERSONALITY WAS CHANGED

His purpose had been changed. His perspective had been changed. And there was a third change in Paul. His personality was changed.

Consider Saul's personality before his dramatic encounter with the Lord Jesus on the road to Damascus. By nature, he was obviously an intense man. He was a man of almost fanatical convictions. Those things were true of him even after his conversion. Even so, there was a noticeable difference between the personality of Saul of Tarsus and the personality of Paul the apostle.

Saul was virtually a psychopath. His intense convictions and almost fanatical zeal made him violent. He was a persecutor. He was cruel. He was vicious.

Can you imagine the scene at the stoning of Stephen? Stephen had preached his heart out. He had said some challenging things, and he obviously knew the Scriptures well. When he was being brutally stoned, he prayed for forgiveness for his persecutors. His face shone with a sense of the peace of God. As he was dying, he showed only peace, no fear. He was confident. He was fully surrendered to the Lord Jesus.

Only the coldest kind of person could stand by and watch Stephen die and not be touched by his faith and gentleness and the confident, compassionate way in which he died. But Saul stood there unmoved. In fact, if Stephen's death did anything to Saul of Tarsus, it made him more determined than ever to persecute Christians. What kind of man must he have been?

But when Saul of Tarsus encountered the Lord Jesus, all that changed. His first words to the Lord were, "Lord, what wilt thou have me to do?" (Acts 9:6). And those words characterized the rest of Paul's life.

Instead of a proud, arrogant Pharisee, ruthless and cruel in persecuting the church, Paul became a humble, submissive apostle, and he himself was persecuted.

Do you see what a transformation there was in Paul's life? He changed from hating the Lord and everything He stood for to acknowledging Him as Lord in his own life and giving his life in service. Paul went anywhere and everywhere for the Lord Jesus.

Let me suggest several truths in the account of Paul's conversion that none of us can afford to miss.

First, the more a man allows God to change him, the more useful that man is to the Lord. The secret to Paul's effectiveness as an apostle was his total surrender to the transforming power of Christ. There was no area of Paul's life that was closed to God. There was nothing in Paul's life that was off limits to the Holy Spirit.

My friend, God uses us to the degree that we commit ourselves to Him. He can best use you if you surrender to Him unconditionally.

A second truth we see from the conversion of Paul is that the Lord can save anyone. It seemed that of all the people in Judea in the first century, Saul of Tarsus was the least likely to accept Christ as Savior. But the Lord worked a miracle in his life. There is no one who cannot be reached by the saving power of the Lord Jesus. God can transform the life of anyone who will turn to him.

Finally, if Saul of Tarsus needed salvation, so do you and I. Saul was a student and teacher of the Scriptures. He was a strict follower of the law. He had dedicated his life to his religion. But he was not saved.

My friend, have you experienced a change in your life? Have you allowed the Lord Jesus to come in and revolutionize your life? Have You trusted Him and received eternal life?

In my ministry I have met many kinds of people in the same kind of situation as Saul of Tarsus—religious, but lost. I've talked with Sunday school teachers, deacons, choir members, and (believe it or not) even ministers of churches who have come to confess that in spite of many years of religious service they've never really had this personal confrontation with Jesus Christ. Unfortunately there are many who profess salvation but do not possess salvation.

How about you ? Could your life use a change? Why not surrender to the Lord Jesus right now? Trust Him for salvation. He will give you eternal life and transform you as He did Saul of Tarsus.

TEN

The Mystery of Imparted Life

It could have been your life or mine. But it happened, instead, to an asbestos worker in Pittsburgh, Pennsylvania. His name was Robert McFall.

McFall became sick and was given only months to live. The problem was his blood. Due to a deficiency in his bone marrow, doctors said, his body could not produce the red blood cells and platelets essential to his life. The only thing that could save his life was a bone marrow transplant from a related person.

After some tests, doctors determined that the only potential donor was a cousin, David Shimp, but he held back. The transplant process, a painful procedure, was forbidding. Shimp felt that the hazards were too great.

The sick man sued. Understandably, he was desperate for a transplant, and he thought he could compel his cousin to be a donor. But the court denied his plea. Said the judge, "In our law, there's no duty to save someone else's life."

The story has a sad ending. Robert McFall died, and David Shimp was left to wonder if he had made the right decision.

"I feel terrible," he said. "But he asked me for something I couldn't give."

Our hearts go out to both men—the one who died, and the one who was asked to make such a difficult decision. But their experience, by way of contrast, shows the wonder of the greatest act of compassion of all history, the death of Christ.

The wonderful truth that makes the death of the Lord Jesus so meaningful is the fact that His death was a voluntary offering of His blood for your sake and for mine.

His blood? Yes, that is what the apostle John, in Revelation 1:5, wrote about. "Unto him that loved us, and washed us from our sins in his own blood." John was saying that it is blood that saves men and women from their sins—the lifeblood of a Person who was Himself sinless. And the Bible teaches that it is blood, and only blood, that can atone for sin (see Leviticus 17:11). No wonder the Bible has so much to say about the blood of Christ.

But many today find references to the blood of Christ offensive. John Stott, a British clergyman, tells of an angry letter from a lady who had visited his church in London. She objected to a hymn sung in the service that spoke of the blood of Jesus Christ.

And she is not alone. There are many worldwide to whom any mention of the blood of Christ is offensive. Some denominations have removed from their hymnbooks hymns that mention the blood of Christ. The remedy, however, is not to set aside such hymns, but to understand them. In his reply to the woman, Dr. Stott pointed out that such references are "symbols to be understood, rather than pictures to be imagined." Wise advice. The meaning of the blood of Jesus Christ is crucial to the Christian faith. Throw it out, and you have cast away the heart of the atonement.

We must remember that it is God Himself in His Word who directs our attention to the blood of Christ. And His emphasis on the blood has a purpose. We do well to grasp it.

What is God saying when he speaks of blood? The key to

understanding lies in the Old Testament in Leviticus 17:11: "For the life of the flesh is in the blood: and I have given it to you upon the altar to make an atonement for your souls: for it is the blood that maketh an atonement for the soul."

What an amazing revelation! Fourteen hundred years before Christ, our great Creator told Moses that physical life is closely linked with blood. It took medical science some three thousand years to make that same discovery. For centuries, blood was one of four bodily fluids doctors linked with life. That view continued through the middle ages.

The discovery that blood circulates through the body was made in 1628 by the English physician William Harvey. Even after that, the practice of draining blood from sick people was continued for more than a century. It was thought that bleeding hastened healing by allowing poison to escape the system. We now know that the opposite is true.

Today our understanding of the value of blood has led to blood banks and transfusions. Most of our modern techniques for saving life with blood have originated since World War II.

Yes, the life of the flesh is in the blood, and today a junior high school student could tell you why. Our bodies are made of cells. Each one is dependent upon oxygen brought by the blood for life. Each cell is dependent upon the blood for nourishment and waste removal, and there are probably a quadrillion cells in your body.

My friend, your blood is a miracle fluid, made up of living cells, as many as five and a half million cells in a cubic centimeter of blood. And your body is constantly manufacturing cells to make up for those that die, at the rate of two million per second!

Yes, blood is life, a miracle from God. It is a gift that could have been created only by an all-wise Being.

Small wonder, then, that God commands great respect for

blood. Genesis 9:5 warns that God himself will hold both man and beast responsible for the shedding of human blood.

Think for a moment about what a wonderful thing it is that the Lord Jesus Christ would offer His own blood for sinful man. Here are three wonderful truths about the blood of Jesus Christ.

JESUS' BLOOD IS EXPENSIVE

First, the blood of Jesus Christ is costly. The price of forgiveness of sins is a price no one but the sinless Son of God could pay. Its value is beyond human understanding.

How often we try to rationalize our sins by saying, "I can make up for this by doing better next time." Not so, my friend, when we have sinned. Nothing we can say or do will wipe a single sin off God's eternal record.

Sin must be paid for, and the price is blood. And it must be the blood of One who had no sin—the blood of Jesus Christ. How can its value be calculated? He had to come as a man, suffer the shame and agony of the cross, and give His very life.

If you want to get a sense of the depth of Christ's sufferings, study Isaiah 53, Psalm 22, or Psalm 69. All of those passages were prophetic, indicating that He knew when he came exactly what He would suffer, and yet He did it anyway. What a tremendous price to pay!

Or watch as Jesus prays in agony in the garden of Gethsemane. Three times He prayed, "O my Father, if it be possible, let this cup pass from me: nevertheless not as I will, but as thou wilt" (Matthew 26:39). Luke 22:44 tells us that "his sweat was as it were great drops of blood falling down to the ground."

Read the account of His crucifixion in the four gospels. He was spat upon. He was brutally whipped with a Roman scourge, a vicious whip made of many long strands of leather with little pieces of metal and bone attached to the ends to tear the victim's flesh. He had a cruel crown of long, sharp thorns thrust onto His head. He was ridiculed, stripped, beaten, and mocked. He had nails driven through His hands and feet. A sword pierced His side. It was a slow, agonizing, painful way to die. But He was shedding His blood for you and for me; His blood was costly.

JESUS' BLOOD IS EFFECTUAL

The second great truth about Jesus' blood is that it is effectual. That means that it does what it was intended to do. The greatest power the world will ever know is the power released by the blood of Jesus Christ. That blood gave lost men a whole new standing before God. It restored relations with God. It opened a whole new way of blessing.

You see, the Lord Jesus' death had no atoning value apart from the blood, because God's way of sacrifice has always been by the shedding of blood. Hebrews 9:22 says, "Without shedding of blood is no remission."

And the purpose for which the Lord Jesus shed His blood was for the remission of sins. He said so before His death. "This is my blood of the new testament, which is shed for many" (Mark 14:24), He said, as He passed the cup at the Last Supper.

The apostle Paul taught that justification was possible only through Jesus' blood. In Romans 5:9 he said, "Much more then, being now justified by his blood, we shall be saved from wrath through him."

The blood of Christ wipes out the certainty of judgment. It assures men of God's favor and gives us access to the throne of grace. It enables us to live a whole new kind of life. It assures us of forgiveness and eternity in heaven. It purges our conscience. It cleanses our sins. It seals the new covenant with God.

In the Old Testament, blood offerings were required. Most Bible students believe that the reason Cain's sacrifice was rejected by God while Abel's was accepted is that Cain's sacrifice was a bloodless sacrifice of the fruit of the ground. Abel, on the other hand had sacrificed one of the firstlings of the flock. Hebrews 11:4 says that "Abel offered a more excellent sacrifice than Cain."

The blood was necessary to make atonement. *Atonement* means "a covering," and Hebrews 10:4 says, "It is not possible that the blood of bulls and goats should take away sins." Those sacrifices were symbolic, a covering for sins that were not taken away. And the blood of those sacrifices illustrated the blood of a perfect sacrifice, one that would be offered only once, and one that would not just be a covering for sins. The perfect sacrifice would remove sins forever.

Hebrews 10:11-12 says, "And every high priest standeth daily ministering and offering oftentimes the same sacrifices, which can never take away sins: But this man, after he had offered one sacrifice for sins for ever, sat down on the right hand of God."

Jesus' blood is effectual. It does what it was intended to do: it removes sin and the effects of sin forever, as the blood of an animal sacrifice could not. The high priest was kept so busy offering the same sacrifices over and over that he never had time to sit down on the job! The Temple had all kinds of furniture, but no chairs!

But the Lord Jesus offered His blood as the perfect sacrifice. It was offered only once, forever, and then He sat down at God's right hand. His blood is effectual.

JESUS' BLOOD IS ESSENTIAL

A third great truth about the blood of Jesus Christ is that it is absolutely essential. Do you see the fallacy of removing the great hymns that refer to the blood of Jesus from our hymnbooks? Without the shed blood of Jesus Christ, we would have no need for a hymnbook at all. Our lives would be futile. We would have no hope.

Yes, my friend, the blood of Jesus Christ is essential. Jesus taught this great truth long before that crisis week with His disciples in Jerusalem. "I am the living bread," He said in John 6:51. "If any man eat of this bread, he shall live forever: and the bread that I will give is my flesh, which I will give for the life of the world."

We know what Jesus was saying. Looking ahead to the shadows of the crucifixion, He was saying, "I am giving myself as a sacrifice. I am going to die for your sins, and you must by faith partake of Me as your sacrifice." But it was a difficult thing, understandably, for those who heard Him then to grasp.

He went on further to speak particularly of His blood.

> Verily, verily, I say unto you, Except ye eat the flesh of the Son of man, and drink his blood, ye have no life in you. Whoso eateth my flesh, and drinketh my blood, hath eternal life; and I will raise him up at the last day. For my flesh is meat indeed, and my blood is drink indeed. . . . he that eateth me, even he shall live by me [John 6:53-55, 57b].

Our Lord never spoke words more difficult to understand than those. Those words have been misapplied and misinterpreted possibly more than any other words in all the Bible.

And yet the truth that Jesus was teaching was simple. To benefit from a sacrifice, one must partake of it. The Hebrews were instructed to eat the Passover lamb that was sacrificed. The Lord was teaching that we must partake of His sacrifice—not, of course, by literally eating and drinking, but by faith.

He was saying, "I will pay the price. I will make the great sacrifice of my blood, and you can have the benefit. But you must receive it for yourself. You must partake of it by faith."

Remember God's Word through his servant Moses: "The

life of the flesh is in the blood: and I have given it to you upon the altar to make an atonement for your souls" (Leviticus 17:11). There can be no remission of your sins apart from the shedding of the blood of Jesus Christ.

Dr. James M. Gray, for many years a faithful president of Moody Bible Institute, wrote in 1900 what has become a favorite hymn:

> Nor silver nor gold hath obtained my redemption;
> Nor riches of earth could have saved my poor soul.
> The blood of the cross is my only foundation.
> The death of my Savior now maketh me whole.
> I am redeemed, but not with silver,
> I am bought, but not with gold;
> Bought with a price—the blood of Jesus,
> Precious price of love untold.

Those words are based on 1 Peter 1:18-19: "Forasmuch as ye know that ye were not redeemed with corruptible things, as silver and gold . . . but with the precious blood of Christ, as of a lamb without blemish and without spot."

Have you partaken of that great sacrifice? Are you redeemed? Do you know Him? His blood is one great thing you cannot do without.

ELEVEN

The Brazen Serpent

"You can't teach an old dog new tricks."

That's the way the saying goes. Whether it is true or not is, of course, debatable. But at least it points out a basic flaw in human nature—people do become set in their ways. And more than that, most folks are very predictable.

That was true of the children of Israel. The story of their departure from Egypt and wanderings in the wilderness is the story of rebellion. They had rebelled against Moses. They had rebelled against God. They had murmured and complained. Worst of all, they had longed to be back in Egypt.

Sin

In Numbers 21 we find the Israelites persisting in their old ways. Thirty-eight years had passed since God had led them out of Egypt. They had not been able to enter the Promised Land because of their unbelief, so God had sustained them for all of those years in the wilderness. God had fed them, led them, and delivered them from every crisis that had threatened them. They had seen His works, beheld his glory, and experienced His loving care for them.

Now a new crisis had developed. Some Canaanites, led by King Arad, had ambushed the Israelites and captured some of them.

Israel came running to the Lord with a vow. In verse 2 we read, "And Israel vowed a vow unto the LORD, and said, If thou wilt indeed deliver this people into my hand, then I will utterly destroy their cities."

The following verse tells us that God heard them. Israel was delivered, and, keeping their vow to the Lord, they destroyed the enemy.

But, as so often happened in the history of Israel, and as too often happens in our lives, the great victory was followed by a terrible defeat. The old problems of disobedience and discouragement began to plague the people. Notice verse 4: "And they journeyed from mount Hor by the way of the Red sea, to compass the land of Edom: and the soul of the people was much discouraged because of the way."

They became tired. Watch out that Satan does not take advantage of you when you are tired. They were discouraged, it says, "because of the way." I am sure that there were many in that company who remembered the miraculous deliverance from Egypt. There were a number who had been stirred by God's power in opening the Red Sea. They had seen it with their eyes. They had been there when it happened. They had marched through that sea on dry land, while God held the walls of water on either side of them. They had seen God's great hand of mercy, time and time again, as He provided water in a dry place, rained down manna from heaven, and met their every need.

They had sung a song of redemption. But now they had to go around Edom. That meant a long, hard walk, with many hills and valleys and more burning desert. Their song of redemption turned to a grumble.

Aren't we often like that? You know, it is not really an easy road that we are called to follow. There are valleys and hills and sometimes the burning deserts. It is easy to get discouraged. Amid the problems of Edom, it is easy to forget how bad Egypt was.

Complaining was nothing new to the Israelites. But here we find that their murmuring took a new twist. Before, their complaints had been directly aimed at Aaron and Moses. But now they spoke out blatantly against God. Verse 5 says, "And the people spake against God, and against Moses, Wherefore have ye brought us up out of Egypt to die in the wilderness? for there is no bread, neither is there any water; and our soul loatheth this light bread."

Can you imagine such ingratitude after forty years of miraculous care? God had provided them with manna for every day they had been in the wilderness. It was perfect to supply every need they had, yet they had the audacity to tell God that they hated it. This was the height of ingratitude and rebellion.

SERPENTS

For the people's rebellion, God sent judgment, the unavoidable consequence of sin. "And the LORD sent fiery serpents among the people, and they bit the people; and much people of Israel died" (v. 6).

The Israelites had sinned, failing to honor and obey God. "The wages of sin is death," according to Romans 6:23. So the Israelites were collecting their wages—in the form of poisonous snakes.

My friend, sin must be punished. God, merciful and kind as He is, cannot simply overlook our sin. Someone must pay the price.

It is an unchangeable rule of the universe that "whatsoever a man soweth, that shall he also reap" (Galatians 6:7). God cannot be mocked. And He simply cannot ignore sin. Sin is a direct challenge to His holiness. All sin must be dealt with, and paid for.

But why serpents? We know from the Scriptures as far back as the Garden of Eden and as far into the future as the book of Revelation that the serpent was a symbol of Satan. It seems to me that God was graphically teaching the Israelites that they would reap what they sowed. If they followed Satan and rebelled against God, their judgment would directly relate to their sin. If they followed the serpent, they would be killed by serpents.

Their judgment is a lesson for us, too. Paul refers to this account in his advice to the Christians at Corinth:

> Neither let us tempt Christ, as some of them also tempted, and were destroyed of serpents. Neither murmur ye, as some of them also murmured, and were destroyed of the destroyer. Now all these things happened unto them for ensamples: and they are written for our admonition, upon whom the ends of the world are come [1 Corinthians 10:9-11].

Why were they written for our admonition? Precisely because we are so inclined to fall into the same sins as the Israelites. The sin that they committed is exactly like what we are daily tempted to do. Their severe judgment was meant to be a lesson to us as well.

My friend, do not take sin lightly. When you see it in your life, deal with it. In 1 Corinthians 11:31, the apostle Paul informs the Corinthians, "If we would judge ourselves, we should not be judged."

SALVATION

But the real lesson of the account in Numbers 21 is a lesson of salvation, not of judgment. Look at verses 7-9:

> Therefore the people came to Moses, and said, We have sinned, for we have spoken against the Lord, and against thee; pray unto the LORD, that he take away the serpents from us. And Moses prayed for the people. And the LORD

690

said unto Moses, Make thee a fiery serpent, and set it upon a pole: and it shall come to pass, that every one that is bitten, when he looketh upon it, shall live. And Moses made a serpent of brass, and put it upon a pole, and it came to pass, that if a serpent had bitten any man, when he beheld the serpent of brass, he lived.

God's instruction to Moses was to construct a serpent of brass and put it up on a pole, so that it would be visible to all. That serpent of brass was a picture of the Lord Jesus Christ, the ultimate cure for sin. When the people who had been bitten by the deadly serpents simply turned their eyes to the uplifted serpent, they would live.

It is interesting to note that the ingredient God was looking for in His people was faith. Faith was necessary there in the wilderness, and it is necessary today for those who look to the cross of Christ for salvation.

All that was required of those people in the wilderness was enough faith to look at the brass serpent on the pole. A simple look of faith would save them.

There were a number of things that they were *not* told to do. For instance, we notice that they were not told to find or prepare a healing medicine. It doesn't take a great deal of imagination to see those afflicted people running here and there looking for some kind of medicinal plant to heal their wounds. I can picture some experimenting with various herbs, some traveling far into the wilderness, not realizing that every step took them away from the real cure for their snakebites: the uplifted serpent of brass.

We also find that they were not told to fight off the serpents. Humanly speaking, that approach might have seemed quite logical. They could have mounted a massive "Kill the Snakes" campaign. But the fact was that this kind of predicament could not be overcome by merely human means. The serpents were a judgment from God. No human plan of attack could eliminate the snakes.

691

The third thing we discover is that God did not ask the people for any kind of payment. There was nothing for them to do to atone for the sin they had committed. They were not told to offer a sacrifice. They were not told to give money. They were not told to do any good works to make up for their evil. They were simply to look, and they would live.

What a picture of grace! Grace demands nothing, asks for nothing, requires nothing. Grace does not say "do"; it says "done." The minute anything is offered in return for grace, it ceases to be grace. The people were not asked to give, but to receive.

There are several striking parallels between this brazen serpent and the Lord Jesus Christ. Both were "lifted up." The serpent was lifted up on the pole, and the Lord Jesus was lifted up on a cross. Both require only faith for salvation. The Lord Jesus said, "As Moses lifted up the serpent in the wilderness, even so must the Son of man be lifted up: that whosoever believeth in him should not perish, but have eternal life" (John 3:14-15).

The requirement is simply a look of faith! There are no works to do; there is no medicine to obtain; there are no snakes to kill. Simply turn to Him in faith, and you will be saved.

It is astounding how many people I meet who are trying to earn their way to heaven in one way or another. Some think simply attending church is enough to do it. Others try to live by the Ten Commandments or the Sermon on the Mount or the golden rule, thinking that will be enough. Others go through religious rituals. Others give money to various charities.

But do you see the folly of thinking that such acts will earn favor in God's eyes? Such thinking is really a denial and rejection of God's Grace.

Let me illustrate. Suppose an Israelite had been bitten by

one of the fiery serpents. He knew that, left to itself, the snakebite would be fatal. He had seen others deteriorate and die. And he had heard of the brazen serpent. He knew that people had simply looked at it and survived the bites of the serpents. But he thought it was a foolish idea. How could a look at a brass snake save a person?

A friend comes to him. "Why don't you go and look at Moses' brass serpent?" he suggests. "I looked at it, and I lived."

"I don't believe a snake on a pole can do anything for me," the man says. "Besides, if I stand out there and look at it, people will see. They will know I was bitten. Or worse, they might think I am foolish."

"But," says his friend, "this is your only hope! No one has survived the serpent bite except those who have looked at the snake."

The man thinks about it for a while, but he decides to go out and see if he can find some snakebite medicine.

He looks for an hour or so but finds nothing to help him. He feels his strength leaving him. He knows he is dying. He goes back to his tent and lies down.

His friend finds him there. "You must look at the brazen serpent!" he says. "Come outside now, while there is still some time."

"I just don't feel quite ready now," he says. "Wait until I feel better."

"But you will *never* feel better," pleads his friend. "You are getting sicker."

"Perhaps I am too sick for the snake to do me any good," says the man.

"No," says his friend. "Others in worse shape than you have been healed. Come now!"

But the man refuses. He offers a few more excuses—he knows a man who looked at the snake and lived, but that man is a hypocrite. He has too many other things to think about anyway.

The man dies.

What would you think of such a man? He was foolish, wasn't he? And yet there are many people right now who are just like that hypothetical Israelite. They stumble at the simplicity of the gospel. They make excuses. They put it off.

There is no hope for a person who persists like that.

Look and live! This is the call of God. It is the only requirement He makes. And the only way to be saved from our sins is to look to the Lord Jesus Christ in faith. He died on that cross to pay the price of our sins, and He rose again to demonstrate His victory over sin and death and Satan.

He is the only hope in a dying world.

Do not make excuses, my friend. Nothing else matters. What people might think does not matter. How good you are does not matter. What you have done does not matter. You must look to the Lord Jesus Christ and believe and be saved.

TWELVE

The Love of God

In 1867, D. L. Moody visited Ireland and met a young teacher-preacher by the name of Harry Moorehouse. Moorehouse was a small, clean-shaven, boyish man with a heavy Lancashire accent. He was a converted pickpocket.

"If I am ever in Chicago, I'll preach for you," offered Moorehouse.

"If you come west, call on me," offered Moody, perhaps not ever really expecting to hear from him again.

But Moorehouse did come, and Moody did let him preach, and his message revolutionized the ministry of D. L. Moody. Night after night, Harry Moorehouse preached on the same familiar and beloved text, John 3:16. Of course you know it, "For God so loved the world, that he gave his only begotten Son, that whosoever believeth in him should not perish, but have everlasting life."

At first, Mr. Moody was openly annoyed at Moorehouse's selection of such a familiar Bible text and his night-after-night exposition of the same theme. He would begin with the text, and then illustrate the love of God from other Scripture accounts. His message was different every night, but the theme and text were always the same.

But something beautiful and life-changing began to happen to Mr. Moody. The truth of God's love began to overwhelm his soul! He saw God from a new perspective. Before, all he had seen was the wrath of God and His hatred for sin. Now he saw as he had never seen before the depth of God's compassion and His love and mercy to sinners. D. L. Moody was never the same again.

In his biography of D. L. Moody, Richard Day gives Moody's own account: "I never knew up to that time that God loved me so much. This heart of mine began to thaw out; I just couldn't keep back the tears. I just drank it all in. I will tell you, there is one thing that draws above everything else, and that is the love of God."

Mr. Moody was so taken with the truth of God's love and moved by it that he had the phrase "God is love" carefully printed on the light globes in the old Moody Church that once stood where the girls' dormitory now stands at Moody Bible Institute.

"I took up that word *Love*," Moody said, "and I do not know how many weeks I spent in studying the passages in which it occurs, till at last I could not help loving people! I had been feeding on love so long that I was anxious to do good to everybody I came in contact with.

"I got full of it. It ran out my fingers. You take up the subject of love in the Bible! You will get so full of it that all you have got to do is to open your lips, and a flood of the love of God flows out."

What a marvelous experience! And yet, I find that even today, most people do not fully understand the love of God.

As a child, I had a dreadful fear of God. I thought of God as a judge sitting upon a great white throne, ready and anxious to pour out vengeance because of my sin. Then I thought that, because Jesus died for me, God *had* to love me.

That's wrong. That's false. Jesus did not die so that God

could love me. God already loved me so much "that He gave His only begotten Son." Every time I read this great verse, John 3:16, three great truths about the love of God come to mind.

THE MYSTERY OF GOD'S LOVE

The first great thing I think about in connection with John 3:16 is the mystery of God's love. Why should God love us? Well, really, I don't know. As I ponder the greatness of God, I wonder why He should love me.

David wondered at the same thing. In Psalm 8 he wrote, "When I consider thy heavens, the work of thy fingers, the moon and the stars, which thou hast ordained; What is man, that thou art mindful of him? and the son of man, that thou visitest him?" (vv. 3-4).

Yes, God is great. In the beginning, He said, "Let there be light" (Genesis 1:3), and there was light. He spoke the universe into existence. He is great in power, in wisdom, and in wealth.

I do not really understand why God loves us. But His love for us is all the more mysterious when we realize that we are sinners. Romans 3:10 says, "There is none righteous, no, not one." Romans 3:23 adds, "For all have sinned, and come short of the glory of God."

Anyone can love someone who is lovable. But it takes a special kind of love to love someone who is offensive. Our sin is more offensive to God than we could ever know, but Romans 5:8 says, "God commendeth his love toward us, in that, while we were yet sinners, Christ died for us."

The Bible teaches that our ways are not God's ways. We have all gone astray like lost sheep (Isaiah 53:6). We have rebelled against God and His ways. Our thoughts are not like God's thoughts. Our eyes have been dimmed, our ears dulled, our minds twisted, our hearts depraved. And yet the fact is that God loves us.

Some time ago I was preaching in Berlin, Germany. Many came to profess faith in Christ at the close of the service. A young man from the United States Air Force came to me. He was stationed in Germany. He poured out to me a sordid story of sin and carelessness.

He said, "I come from a good home, and I have good parents, and I grew up in a sound church. I never dreamed I could do the things I have done."

I quoted to him from Jeremiah 17:9, "The heart is deceitful above all things, and desperately wicked: who can know it?" We should not be shocked to find out the sins that we are capable of, my friend. Every time I see a man or woman caught in some horrible, wretched sin, I think, *There but for the grace of God goes George Sweeting.*

My friend, the astounding thing is not the depth of sin into which a man can fall, but the depth of God's love to those of us guilty of such sin. And all of us are guilty. There is not one of us who has not lied, or cheated, or thought vile thoughts, or been guilty of hatred. All those things are as horrible to God as the worst thing you can think of.

Sin is contrary to God's very nature. It is abhorrent to Him. He is holy. He is pure. He is righteous. Our smallest sin is monstrous in His eyes.

And yet He loves us. That is indeed a mystery.

THE MAGNITUDE OF GOD'S LOVE

A second great truth I think of in connection with John 3:16 is the magnitude of God's love for us. He gave His only begotten Son!

Only a parent can understand the full import of those words. God's love was so great that He was willing to sacrifice His only begotten Son, the Lord Jesus, to pay for our sins.

The Lord Jesus was sinless. He had no guilt. He was not worthy of death. He was as deserving of the love of God as we are of God's wrath. Hebrews 4:15 says, "[He] was in all points tempted like as we are, yet without sin." Hebrews 7:26 says that He was "holy, harmless, undefiled, separate from sinners." Peter wrote that He "did no sin, neither was guile found in his mouth" (1 Peter 2:22). John wrote, "In him is no sin" (1 John 3:5). Even a centurion at His crucifixion, seeing the way he died, "glorified God, saying, Certainly this was a righteous man" (Luke 23:47).

But 2 Corinthians 5:21 says, "For he hath made him to be sin for us, who knew no sin, that we might be made the righteousness of God in him."

"Made him to be sin for us"! It is impossible for a mortal mind fully to grasp the complete truth of that statement, I'm sure. How could the eternal, sinless Son of God be made *sin* for us?

The apostle Paul is saying in that verse that in the hours our Lord hung on that cross, He was bearing our sin and taking the punishment for it. In those awful hours, the wrath of God the Father was poured out on God the Son!

Have you ever wondered why, hanging from the cross, the Son of God cried, "My God, my God, why hast thou forsaken me?" (Matthew 27:46). It was because in that hour, as He hung there bearing our sins, God the Father had to turn His back on God the Son, because He was bearing our sin.

Galatians 3:13 says, "Christ hath redeemed us from the curse of the law, being made a curse for us: for it is written, Cursed is every one that hangeth on a tree." He was cursed for our sakes!

Do you want to see a demonstration of the love of God, my friend? Look at Christ on the cross. See His love for us. That is the profoundest picture of the love of God.

There is nothing God would not do for us. He has already given His most precious possession—His own Son. Romans 8:32 says, "He that spared not his own Son, but delivered him up for us all, how shall he not with him also freely give us all things?"

Yes, my friend, God's love is great in its depth. But it is great in its scope as well. Whom does God love? Sinners. Which sinners? All of them. "For God so loved the *world*," it says. The whole world! God's love is for you, my friend, no matter who you are.

No matter how much you have sinned, God loves you. No matter what color your skin is, God loves you. Your nationality does not matter. Your economic class does not matter. How you look does not matter. How you have acted does not matter. God loves you!

God's love is truly a marvelous thing.

THE MEANING OF GOD'S LOVE

The third great truth I think about whenever I read John 3:16 is the truth of the meaning of God's love.

In D. L. Moody's day, the love of God was not a widely known concept. Preachers preached sermons about God's wrath. God was thought of as an angry being, anxious to squash sin and wipe out sinners. The widespread view of God was much like my childhood picture of a judge sitting on a throne.

Largely because of D. L. Moody's ministry and the influence of his preaching, the message that God is love became more widely known. But many have a warped understanding of the truth.

God is love, but that does not mean that He is tolerant of sin. He hates sin. But he loves the sinner. He has paid the price to redeem us from our sins. But He will judge those who reject the Lord Jesus.

My friend, never get the idea that because God is love He will overlook our sins. Don't think that because God is love we can ignore His Word or trifle with spiritual things and have Him simply wink at it. He still hates sin. He still demands obedience. He still requires repentance. He still deserves our reverance and worship and submission.

But because God is love, we can be assured that He will forgive the repentant sinner—not because he ignores the sin, but because the sin has already been paid for.

And that is the real meaning of God's love. He has made atonement for our sins. He has paid the price. He offers forgiveness and salvation and a fresh start to those who will trust Him.

Look again at John 3:16. And notice two sets of three words, "Believeth in him," and "should not perish." What does it mean to believe in Him? It means more than simply accepting the facts about Him. It means to trust in Him, to commit one's life to Him, to cast oneself completely on Him in faith. It is a faith that results in action, according to James. It is a life-changing experience, according to Paul.

Have you had such an experience? Have you put your faith in Christ to transform your life, to save you from your sins? If you are still trying to free yourself from your sins, or if you are trying to please God by the "goodness" of your life, then you have never really trusted Him in this way.

Look at those other three words, "should not perish." We deserve to perish. The wages of sin is death. We have sinned. We should die. The Lord Jesus did not deserve to perish, and yet He died on the cross. He has paid the price. There is no need for you and me to die. He offers us everlasting life, and it is a gift that He has bought and paid for.

Perhaps you fear death. There is nothing so fearful as the thought of dying with the uncertainty of what lies beyond the grave. But God's Word says that "whosoever believeth in him should not perish." He gives eternal life. There is nothing to fear, if we have trusted Him. God is love.

John 3:18 says, "He that believeth in him is not condemned: but he that believeth not is condemned already, because he hath not believed in the name of the only begotten Son of God."

Into which category do you fall? It is all so simple; there

is no need to stumble over it. God offers eternal life as a gift. We may receive it through faith in the Lord Jesus. Or we may neglect it, do nothing, and thereby condemn ourselves.

God is love. It is not His will that any of us should perish. He has paid the price so that we need not be condemned. But by unbelief we can condemn ourselves.

My friend, what will you do with the Lord Jesus Christ? He loves you. He has already proved His love to you by bearing your sins on the cross. Will you trust Him completely right now and be freed from your sins? Will you respond to the love of God?

THIRTEEN

What Is Life?

Throughout history man has attempted to find the answer to the question "What is Life?" His search has taken him to every corner of the earth and even to the planets above. And yet, today many people are just as confused, just as uncertain as ever. To them the meaning of life remains a mystery, an unsolved and unsolvable riddle.

Let me suggest five possible answers to the meaning of life. Each of these is an answer that will, obviously, affect a person's whole philosophy and behavior. How do you view life?

LIFE IS A VEXATION

The first view, held by many people in our busy world, is that life is a vexation. It is a burden with which each of us is saddled. It is filled with problems, and little else.

Someone has called life "the predicament that precedes death." Life begins with a cry and ends with a groan, and that is about all some people see to it.

This is the view of the Hindus. They believe that life is simply a thing to endure. Did you ever wonder why there is so much suffering and starvation in the Hindu countries?

Partly it is because Hindus feel that it is of no value to help those who suffer, since each person must endure a certain amount of suffering anyway. They believe that to help a person who is suffering is to cause him to have to suffer more in the next life. They feel that, as a man is reincarnated, he moves up a step or so each time, according to how much he endured in the last lifetime.

Life, they believe, is merely a vexation, something to be endured. What a pessimistic view of life!

But there is some truth to the view that life is a vexation. Job 5:7 says, "Man is born to trouble, as the sparks fly upward." Life is not easy.

Why is life so hard? Because of man's sin. God's original intention for man was that he should have a life of peace and fullness. God created Adam and Eve and put them in a perfect environment. Everything that God had made was good. It was theirs to enjoy. Life for them was a pleasure.

But they rebelled against God. They sinned and brought a curse upon themselves and all of creation. Pain, sorrow, sweat, and toil were some of the results of that curse. Death was another result. Adam and Eve suffered the sorrow of seeing one child murdered and another become a murderer. Life was no longer a pleasure.

My friend, everything in life that is unpleasant is a result of man's sin. That is why life can sometimes seem like a vexation. Sin is the reason we all suffer heartaches and pain and disease and sorrow.

But there is more meaning to life than that. To say that life is simply a vexation and nothing more or less is a shortsighted view of things. God has a purpose for us in life.

LIFE IS A VOID

Others would say that life is simply a void—a big nothing. You might remember a popular song released several years ago by singer Peggy Lee entitled "Is That All There

708

Is?" In that song, she reached a conclusion that expressed the futility sensed by millions of people today. As she sings her plaintive tune, she recalls the memorable moments of her life—a childhood thrill at the circus, the ecstasy of falling in love—the times that stood out in her mind above all others. In her experience she sensed that something was missing, and she came to the unfortunate conclusion that life is a void.

If that's all there is to life, she concluded, "Let's break out the booze and have a ball."

What an expression of despair! And yet today millions of people give mental assent to those words, and other practice them as a life philosophy.

Matthew Arnold pictured the same kind of futility in his poem "Rugby Chapel":

> What is the course of the life
> Of mortal men on the earth?
> Most men eddy about
> Here and there—eat and drink,
> Chatter and love and hate,
> Gather and squander, are raised
> Aloft, are hurl'd in the dust,
> Striving blindly, achieving
> Nothing; and then they die—

James G. Hunker cynically said, "Life is like an onion—you peel off layer after layer and then you find that there is nothing to it."

In Shakespeare's *MacBeth,* the main character obeys his evil desires and murders the king. That leads to a succession of evil deeds. He becomes king, as he had schemed to do, but finds emptiness in the fulfillment of his desires. Shortly before his death he declares his view of life. "It is," he says, "a tale told by an idiot, full of sound and fury, signifying nothing."

What a tragic, tragic way to see life. And yet, my friend, outside of Jesus Christ, no other view is reasonably possible. There is no meaning to life apart from Him.

Suicide is on the increase in our nation. And the disturbing thing is the high rate of suicides among young people eighteen years of age and younger. The idea that life is merely a void is one of the contributing factors to this phenomenon. If life is empty, meaningless, why continue with it? Why not end it? Are we not better off dead then trapped in a meaningless existence?

But that, too, is a faulty view of life. Life is not a void. It can have real meaning. We were created for a purpose. And we can realize the fulfillment of that purpose in Jesus Christ.

LIFE IS A VACATION

A view of life that many in our world hold is that life is a vacation. Life is a time to have all the fun you can have. A popular beer commercial has for years proclaimed that since you only go around once, you should grab all the gusto you can.

It seems that our nation is caught up with this view of life. We spend more money on entertainment than on any other single item. We live in a pleasure-mad world.

This view of life is a rejection of responsibility. It is closely aligned with the attitude so prevalent in our nation that the world owes us everything.

The tragic thing about thinking of life as merely a vacation is that, while it sounds so good and promises so much, it proves to be a very empty way of life. Pleasure becomes drudgery. Things that once were thrilling and exciting become empty and boring.

I do not say that there is no pleasure in sin. On the contrary, sin can be enjoyable, but that enjoyment is short-lived. The thrill of sin becomes a crushing burden. Poet Robert Burns expresses quite well the brevity of pleasure.

> Pleasures are like poppies spread,
> You seize the flower,
> Its bloom is shed.
> Or like a snowfall on a river,
> A moment white, then gone forever.

And that is the problem with looking at life as merely a vacation. Pleasures do not satisfy. Sin does not fulfill—it only makes the desire greater and more difficult to satiate. Sin arouses the appetite for more sin. And the fleeting pleasures of sin are quickly forgotten.

There is no hope in such a life-style. What looks and sounds like so much fun and excitement is in reality empty. Instead of a vacation, it becomes enslavement.

LIFE IS A VAPOR

A fourth view of life is that it is a vapor. That is a scriptural way of looking at life. James asks, "What is your life? It is even a vapour, that appeareth for a little time, and then vanisheth away" (James 4:14).

Amidst all the uncertainty about life, one thing is certain, and that is that life is short. An interesting Bible study is to make a survey of the metaphors the Bible uses about life. There are eighteen of them, and they all refer to the fact that life is short.

Job says, "My days are swifter than a weaver's shuttle" (Job 7:6). And again, "My life is wind" (Job 7:7).

The psalmist compares our life to a fading flower or falling leaf. "As for man, his days are as grass: as a flower of the field, so he flourisheth. For the wind passeth over it, and it is gone; and the place thereof shall know it no more" (Psalm 103:15-16).

The writer of Chronicles records for us the words of

David: "Our days on earth are as a shadow, and there is none abiding" (1 Chronicles 29:15).

Psalm 90:9 says, "We spend our years as a tale that is told."

Life is short. Someone has said that the wood of the cradle rubs against the marble of the tomb. There is no question about it—the days of our lives pass very swiftly.

That does not mean that life is unimportant. When the Bible acknowledges the brevity of life, it is not saying that all is futility. Life is indeed short, but that is not a reason for despair.

LIFE IS A VICTORY

The ultimate view of life given to us in the Bible is that life is a victory. Romans 5:17 says that it is God's intention that "they which receive abundance of grace and of the gift of righteousness shall reign in life by one, Jesus Christ."

God wants us to reign in life! We are to live like kings. We are to be victorious. We are to see life as a victory, not a defeat.

How can we live life as a victory? I think Romans 5:17 suggests answers to that question.

First, it is "by one, Jesus Christ." God does not ask us to be victorious in our own power! He does not say, "Do the best you can; break all your bad habits; free yourself from your sin; clean up your life; and you will know victory." If we had the ability to do those things, victory would not be a problem.

No, my friend, victory does not come through our personal effort and striving. The way of victory in life may surprise you. God's way of victory in life for us is the way of death!

Death? Yes, not physical death, but death to self. Jesus said, "Except a corn of wheat fall into the ground and die, it abideth alone: but if it die it bringeth forth much fruit. He that loveth his life shall lose it; and he that hateth his life in this world shall keep it unto life eternal" (John 12:24-25). He urged His followers to take up a cross—an instrument of death!

Paul understood what the Lord Jesus meant. He wrote, "I am crucified with Christ: nevertheless I live; yet not I, but Christ liveth in me" (Galatians 2:20).

The answer to victory is found in simply dying to self and letting the Lord Jesus Christ take over our lives and live in and through us. He is always victorious.

A second secret of victory in Romans 5:17 is in those words "abundance of grace." God's grace is sufficient, but it goes even beyond that. His grace to us is abundant!

God, in His abundant grace, can enable us to be victorious in any circumstance in life. One of the most precious promises in all of the Word of God is 1 Corinthians 10:13, "There hath no temptation taken you but such as is common to man: but God is faithful, who will not suffer you to be tempted above that ye are able; but will with the temptation also make a way to escape, that ye may be able to bear it."

God, in His grace, promises to protect us from any insurmountable temptations. He will give us the power to say *no* to every temptation that Satan can hurl at us. He will not test us above our ability to endure. He wants us to be victorious!

Yes, my friend, His grace is abundant. But the key to experiencing victory in life is to understand that victory is available only to those who have received God's gift of eternal life. God's abundant grace and the power of the indwelling Christ are, according to Romans 5:17, companion gifts with the gift of life.

Have you been born again? Have you received God's gift of eternal life? If not, you can never see life as a victory. The means of victory in life are available only in Jesus Christ, and we must come to Him in faith.

Will you trust Christ today and know the freedom of living life as a victory? The apostle Paul said, "For to me to live is Christ" (Philippians 1:21). The victorious life begins when we allow the Lord Jesus Christ to come in and take over. Will you trust Him today and begin to enjoy that victory?

FOURTEEN

God's Favorite Word: *Come*

Jesus said, "Heaven and earth shall pass away: but my words shall not pass away" (Mark 13:31). Every word spoken by God is important and worthy of our most careful attention. They are all significant, but none is more significant than the one I've chosen to call "God's favorite word."

The word of which I'm thinking is a special word, a personal word, a word of invitation. It is the word *come*.

No one, of course, fully knows the mind of God. But it is my feeling that this word *come* is special to God because of the way it is used in the Scriptures.

A Word Spoken with Frequency

First, *come* is a word spoken with frequency. It is the word that God spoke to man before He judged the earth with the Flood. It is the same word that changed Simon from a rugged and coarse fisherman into Peter, a devoted disciple of the Lord Jesus Christ. It is the word that Jesus spoke to the little children that gathered about Him. He spoke it to the sick and burdened multitudes.

The hands of the Lord Jesus are always outstretched, open. To the weary He offers rest and comfort. "Come to me, all ye that labor and are heavy laden," said our Lord in Matthew 11:28, "and I will give you rest."

The hands of Christ are outstretched and open to lift the fallen, to bless the children, to touch the sick, and to save the lost.

Consider the account of Noah found in Genesis 6-8. The earth was corrupt, much as it is today. The Lord saw that every imagination of man's heart was only evil continually. The world was in bad shape. So the Lord decided to destroy it.

It was under those circumstances that God spoke the first recorded use of the word *come*. It was an invitation to salvation to Noah and his whole family (see Genesis 7:1).

In the midst of evil and judgment and destruction, God spoke in compassion and grace, and the word He used was *come*.

Throughout the Bible we find God's invitation to come for forgiveness and salvation. In fact, the word *come* is found more than six hundred times throughout the Bible.

A WORD SPOKEN WITH CLEMENCY

And *come* is almost always a word spoken with clemency. From the first time God said "come" to Noah and his family, through the last occurrence of the word in the final chapter of the book of Revelation, God spoke the word *come* in mercy and grace and forgiveness.

Think with me for a moment about Christ's confrontation with the blind beggar Bartimaeus. In Luke 18 we are told of this interesting encounter.

It was probably a beautiful morning in Jericho, and blind Bartimaeus found a warm, sunny spot against a wall where he would be sure to meet many people. But soon he began to hear the hum of many voices and the shuffling of feet. His trained ears told him that this was not the usual crowd of passers by.

Luke 18:36 tells us that, "hearing the multitude pass by, he asked what it meant." He was told that it was Jesus of Nazareth passing by. Bartimaeus had heard of Him! And he knew the Lord's reputation for doing miracles.

"Jesus, thou Son of David," he cried, "have mercy on me" (v. 38).

And although those who stood by him began to rebuke him and push him out of the way, he pushed forward. Something within him must have told him that it was now or never. He knew that this might be his only opportunity to meet Jesus. He began to cry more loudly.

Verse 40 tells us Jesus' response. "Jesus stood, and commanded him to be brought unto him." Can you hear the compassion in the Savior's voice as He says to Bartimaeus, "Come"? Can you see the love in this One who reaches beyond the shouts of the crowd to call a poor, blind beggar?

The Lord Jesus stopped. He paused where He was and called for Bartimaeus. This was the Omnipotent One, reaching out to meet the need of a beggar. The Lord asked, "What wilt thou that I shall do unto thee?" (v. 41).

Notice how Bartimaeus replied. He did not ask for money. He did not request new clothing. He did not ask for power or for wealth. He simply said, "Lord, that I may receive my sight" (v. 41).

And the Lord Jesus gave him what he asked for.

My friend, the Lord Jesus says, "Come." He is not calling us for judgment but for mercy. He calls us with love and compassion. He calls us to trust Him. He calls us to take His yoke upon us, but His yoke is easy and His burden is light (see Matthew 11:29-30). He promises us rest.

A WORD SPOKEN WITH URGENCY

More than anything else, I want you to notice that *come* is a word spoken with urgency. Bartimaeus understood that. He wanted to meet the Lord Jesus right away. And it was a good thing he did, too. The Lord Jesus never returned to Jericho. That turned out to be the only opportunity Bartimaeus would ever have had to meet the Savior.

Luke 19 tells about another encounter the Lord Jesus had in Jericho. While He was there, great crowds of people thronged around Him. Because of the masses of people, a little man named Zacchaeus decided to climb up into a tree to get a better view of the Savior. In verse 5 we read that "when Jesus came to the place, he looked up, and saw him, and said unto him, Zacchaeus, make haste, and come down; for today I must abide at thy house."

"Come," said Jesus. "Make haste . . . to day." Can you hear the urgency in His voice? There is not much time.

The Lord speaks with tender, loving compassion, but He speaks with urgency. Do you remember the account of the destruction of Sodom and Gomorrah? Lot was warned that God would destroy the city. He was told to take his family and flee. But he delayed. He waited.

Genesis 19:16 says, "And while he lingered, the men [who were angelic messengers] laid hold upon his hand . . . the LORD being merciful unto him: and they brought him forth, and set him without the city." The Lord was merciful to Lot. The angels took Lot and his family by the hand, and led them out of the city.

But Lot still delayed. Verse 22 tells us that God told him, "Haste thee, escape thither; for I can not do any thing till thou be come thither." "Come," said God, and He said it with urgency. But He was waiting.

God cannot be mocked. He does not wait forever. You know what happened. As they were leaving, Lot's wife turned back to look. It was a fatal mistake. The Bible tells us that "she became a pillar of salt" (Genesis 19:26).

My friend, God is patient. Second Peter 3:9 says, "The Lord is not slack concerning his promise, as some men count slackness; but is longsuffering to us-ward, not willing that any should perish, but that all should come to repentance." There is that word again, *"come."*

When David Brainerd, the great missionary statesman, was seventeen years old, he was confused about God's plan of salvation. He knew that the Bible told him to come to Christ, but he didn't know how to come. He said, "I thought I would gladly come to Jesus, but I had no directions as to getting through."

As he prayed, Brainerd thought, *When a mother tells her child to come to her, she does not tell him how to come. He may come with a run, a skip, a jump, or a bound. He may come crying or singing or shouting. It doesn't matter how he comes, so long as he comes.*

My friend, it doesn't matter how you come to Christ. The important thing is that you do come. We sing a song in the church:

> Just as I am, without one plea,
> But that Thy blood was shed for me—
> And that thou bid'st me come to Thee.
> O Lamb of God, I come, I come.*

People of all kinds came to the Lord Jesus. Bartimaeus was a poor, blind beggar. Nicodemus was a ruler of the Jews. The woman at the well was a Samaritan. Zacchaeus was a tax collector. Jesus accepted all people who came to Him in repentance and faith. He accepted publicans and prostitutes, Pharisees and lepers. He ministered to Jews and Gentiles, men and women, slaves and free men.

My friend, no matter who you are, no matter what your circumstances are, the Lord Jesus invites you to come.

How should we come? Come with a repentant heart. The Lord Jesus said, "They that be whole need not a physician, but they that are sick. . . . I am not come to call the righteous, but sinners to repentance" (Matthew 9:12-13).

---

*Charlotte Elliott, 1834.

Read the New Testament. Many people came to the Lord Jesus; the only ones who turned away from Him were those who came to Him without a sense of their own need.

Matthew 19:16-24 tells of a wealthy young man who came to Jesus and asked what he could do to get eternal life. The account tells us that he went away from Jesus sad. Why? The beggars and sinners that came to Him never went away sad. He taught that He could give life to those who would come to Him. What was wrong?

Look closely at the passage, and you will see. The young man had no genuine sense of his own need. He felt that he had everything that he needed. When the Lord Jesus told him that he should keep the commandments, the young man's response was, "All these things have I kept from my youth up: what lack I yet?" (v. 20).

"What do I need?" he asked. "I have kept all the law. I am not a sinner."

There was nothing the Lord Jesus could do for him. My friend, we must come to the Lord Jesus with a deep sense of need. He came not to call the righteous, but sinners unto repentance. And all of us have sinned.

How should we come? Come believing. Faith is the ingredient He is looking for. A Gentile woman came to Jesus looking for deliverance for her daughter. Unlike the rich man, she was filled with a sense of her own need. And she would not be put off. The Lord Jesus said several things to her that would have discouraged most people, but she was insistent. Finally He said to her, "O woman, great is thy faith: be it unto thee even as thou wilt" (Matthew 15:28). She was rewarded for her faith.

My friend, Your good works mean nothing to God; it is your faith that He wants to see. Isaiah 64:6 says, "All our righteousnesses are as filthy rags."

On the other hand, Hebrews 11:6 says, "He that cometh

to God must believe." Salvation is by grace through *faith*. God is looking for your faith.

The very last chapter in the Bible is a wonderful appeal to each of us. God is saying, "Come." Revelation 22:17 says, "And the Spirit and the bride say, Come. And let him that heareth say, Come. And let him that is athirst come. And whosoever will, let him take the water of life freely."

The invitation is open. It is an invitation to life. It is an invitation for you. God is saying, "Come," to whosoever will. Someone has taken the word *come* and made an acrostic. *C* is for children; *O* is for the old; *M* is for middle-aged; *E* is for everyone. God is calling you to come.

My friend, won't you come today and drink freely of the water of life that He has promised?

Moody Press, a ministry of the Moody Bible Institute, is designed for education, evangelization, and edification. If we may assist you in knowing more about Christ and the Christian life, please write us without obligation: Moody Press, c/o MLM, Chicago, Illinois 60610.